W9-CAX-426

Million Dollar Nickels
MYSTERIES OF THE ILLICIT
1913 LIBERTY NICKELS REVEALED

by

Paul Montgomery, Mark Borckardt, and Ray Knight

Million Dollar Nickels

MYSTERIES OF THE ILLICIT
1913 LIBERTY HEAD NICKELS REVEALED

by

Paul Montgomery, Mark Borckardt, and Ray Knight

Copyright © 2005
BOWERS AND MERENA GALLERIES, INC.
18022 Cowan #107, Irvine, CA 92614

Published under license from
Bowers and Merena Galleries, Inc. by
Zyrus Press Inc.
PO Box 17810, Irvine, CA 92623
Tel: (888) 622-7823 / Fax: (800) 215-9694
w w w . z y r u s p r e s s . c o m
ISBN # 0-9742371-8-3 (hardcover)

Copyrighted material found in this book reprinted with permission.

All rights reserved, including duplication of any kind or storage in electronic or visual retrieval systems. Written permission is required for reproduction, in whole or part, of this book.

The Parable of the Lost Coin

Or suppose a woman has ten coins and loses one. Does she not light a lamp, sweep the house, and search carefully until she finds it? And when she finds it, she calls her friends and neighbors together and says, "Rejoice with me; I have found my lost coin."

— Luke 15: 8,9 NIV

ABOUT THE AUTHORS

Paul Montgomery became interested in coin collecting as a child because of his father, a NASA aerospace engineer in Houston. The elder Montgomery had an eclectic collection of coins he had picked out of pocket change, none of them in particularly good collectible condition. Paul shared the collection with his father, upgrading it gradually as he learned more about the coins. Sports and other attractions sidetracked him as a teenager, but his interest in coins was re-ignited in 1979 when gold bullion topped $800 and he discovered he could make a career of it. After graduating from Baylor University in 1983, he set his sights on becoming a professional numismatist, developing his skills as a wholesale trader. He progressed into management, serving as president and CEO of Jefferson Coin & Bullion and later as president of Bowers and Merena Galleries. In 2005, Paul semi-retired to part time work as a numismatic consultant and is working toward a post graduate degree in theological studies. He is a life member of the American Numismatic Association, a member of the board of directors of the Professional Numismatists Guild, board member and past chairman of the Industry Council for Tangible Assets, and a regular contributing editor to *The Official Guide Book of United States Coins*. While numismatics is his career, Paul's life is centered on his love for Christ and his family — wife Amy, and their three children Myra, Katy, and David.

Mark Borckardt caught the coin collecting bug very early in life, becoming a serious collector by the time he was 12. He and his father, a speech professor at Findlay College, became regular exhibitors on the midwestern and national coin show circuit, a partnership that evolved to The Collectors Cabinet, a coin shop in his hometown of Findlay, Ohio. Mark began his career as a professional numismatist in 1980 and is a life member of the American Numismatic Association, a 30-year member of the  Early American Coppers club, and a member of numerous other numismatic organizations. He joined Bowers and Merena Galleries in 1989 as senior numismatist, and served as the firm's vice-president under Paul Montgomery. In 2004, he became Senior Cataloger at Heritage Numismatic Auctions, Inc. in Dallas, Texas. He has published extensively, winning the Early American Coppers Literary Award and Numismatic Literary Guild's Book of the Year Award for *Encyclopedia of Early United States Cents, 1793-1814*. He has been a major contributor to several books by Q. David Bowers and the award-winning *Rare Coin Review*. He is a long-time contributor to *A Guide Book of United States Coins* and has served as an instructor for the American Numismatic Association summer seminar program. When away from the office, Mark is an avid bowler who carries a 200+ average and has officially recorded several perfect 300 games. Mark and his wife, Mary, have three children, Mathew, Michelle, and Melissa.

Ray Knight began his career as a radio and TV broadcaster, migrating in the mid-60s to the advertising agency business as a creative writer and broadcast producer, growing eventually into upper management. In the early 90s, he directed his organizational and writing skills to business communication and corporate strategic planning. In the late 90s, he set out on his own as a freelance writer, specializing in corporate communication and business journalism. Though not a coin collector, he became keenly interested in the historical and  economic aspects of numismatics as a result of working with Paul Montgomery on projects for Jefferson Coin & Bullion and later Bowers and Merena Galleries, leading to his involvement with telling the 1913 Liberty Head nickels story.

ACKNOWLEDGEMENTS

Our special thanks go to the many people whose help was invaluable in creating this book.

First and foremost, we are grateful to Michael Haynes and David Hall of Collectors Universe and Greg Roberts at Spectrum Numismatics for their support of the project.

We especially appreciate the contributions of those individuals who went out of their way to provide extraordinarily useful assistance:

John Dannreuther	R.W. Julian	John Snyder
Beth Deisher	Cheryl Myers	Cindy Tucker
Ryan Givens	Eric Newman	Fred Weinberg
	Donn Pearlman	

We are indebted also to the many other people who took the time to share their knowledge, experience, suggestions, and perspectives on the 1913 Liberty Head nickels with us:

Mason Adams	John Hamrick	Pam Roberts
Stephen Bobbitt	Art Kagin	Daniel Shaver
Q. David Bowers	Edward Lee	Laura Sperber
Chris Cipoletti	Lawrence Lee	Alvin Stern
William D. Coe	Debbie McDonald	David Tirell-Wysocki
Jeff Garrett	Dwight Manley	Carol Travers
Paul Gilkes	Sue Mitchell	Lucille Walton
Nancy Green	Douglas Mudd	Greg Weinman
David Hall	Tom Mulvaney	Judith Wyman
	Noah Reynolds	

"Superman's Girlfriend, Lois Lane" #54 ©1965 DC Comics.
All Rights Reserved. Used with Permission.

TABLE OF CONTENTS

CHAPTER 1
Dark of Night and Unknown Secrets 13

CHAPTER 2
America's Early Nickels 21

CHAPTER 3
Covert Origins 33

CHAPTER 4
A Question of Legitimacy 65

CHAPTER 5
The Mysterious Mr. Brown 91

CHAPTER 6
The "Set" Period: Beginning of an Enigmatic Pedigree 115

CHAPTER 7
The "Single" Period: Separate Paths to Glory 143

CHAPTER 8
Disappearing Act 183

CHAPTER 9
The Clockwork Miracle 225

CHAPTER 10
Secret Midnight Meeting 259

CHAPTER 11
Found! Numismatic Shock of the Century .293

CHAPTER 12
An Unfinished Tale 315

APPENDIX A
The Liberty Nickel Timeline 319

APPENDIX B
Pedigree Notes 327

APPENDIX C
Additional Owner Biography Notes 335

Bibliography 355
Index 364

- Chapter One -

DARK OF NIGHT AND UNKNOWN SECRETS

In the witching hour of July 30, 2003, a small band of coin experts huddled in a secret meeting behind closed doors under the sharp scrutiny of armed guards. On a cloth-covered table before them lay the most famous coins in American history. There were five of the coins, the only five ever made, collectively worth more than $12,000,000. Tense but muted excitement electrified the room as they examined the coins with minute care, one by one. They were searching for telltale clues that would solve a mystery which had baffled and obsessed coin collectors for more than four decades. What they discovered stunned and thrilled the numismatic world with the most monumental coin news in a century.

The six noted experts, including two of the authors, confirmed the identity of The Missing Nickel. It was there in the room. They held it in their hands.

In that historic moment, a coin that had vanished from public view more than 40 years before emerged from the shadows of time to regain its place in coindom's most celebrated quintet. In that historic moment, all five known 1913 Liberty Head nickels were reunited for the first time in more than 60 years.

When it was announced to the public a few hours later, the shocking revelation in one

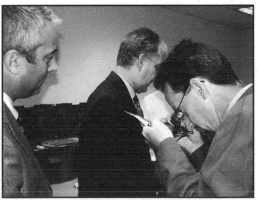

Paul Montgomery and Mark Borckardt (with loupe), search for clues to identify the mystery nickel as coin expert John Dannreuther (background) studies photographic comparisons. Courtesy of Coin World. © Coin World

sweeping stroke rewrote numismatic history, because it wasn't what anybody — including the team of experts — had expected. Numismatic lore had for decades been telling and re-telling what proved to be a totally misguided story of the missing coin's fate.

In one respect, the announcement no doubt came as a disappointment to the millions of people who had for months been picking through their pocket change hoping to claim the million dollar reward posted a few months earlier by coin auctioneer Bowers and Merena Galleries to anyone who came forward with the missing nickel.

A Bizarre Adventure in Coin History

The dramatic discovery marked the latest bizarre twist in a mystery maze that would likely stump even Sherlock Holmes with its unexpected turns, false leads, and blurry dead-ends. The epic saga of the 1913 Liberty nickels traces a serpentine path that slithers from darkness to light, from obscurity to clarity. You don't even have to be a "coin weenie" (as avid numismatists sometimes call themselves) to get caught up in the adventure of this tale.

From their very beginning, the five famous nickels have more than once been shrouded in the dark of night to shield dealings with them from the public eye — secret and possibly illegal late night activities in the Mint, death on a lonely stretch of highway, a secret midnight gathering in Baltimore under armed guard, to tease you with just a few of the tantalizing mysteries. The tale tickles the imagination, at once mystifying and illuminating. It's a tale enlivened by a twisting plot, quirky sub-plots, even quirkier characters, and hints of occasional skullduggery. It's a whodunit with a more generous line-up of suspects than an Agatha Christie dinner party murder yarn.

Who created the nickels? No official record of them was ever found at the U.S. Mint in Philadelphia where they were believed to have been struck. The Mint director had specifically given orders that no 1913 Liberty nickels were to be produced.

How did Samuel W. Brown come to possess the nickels? Brown was the first person to hint at the existence of the nickels publicly in 1919.

Who was "Reynolds," the Mister X whom the numismatic folklore for 40 years said was believed to have been the probable owner of the missing nickel? Did anybody named Reynolds ever own one of the nickels? No one has produced any evidence to prove it.

Why did Mint Director Stella Hackel Sims destroy records for the time when the nickels were believed to have been made? The Mint has been unable to produce a credible explanation.

Are there more than five 1913 Liberty Head nickels? Rumors that six or even eight of the nickels exist continue to surface on the edges of numismatic folklore, largely ignored but never completely disproved.

These are but a few of the tangled threads that weave a riveting detective story, which numismatists[1] have been trying to unravel for the better part of a century. The perennial fascination with the mystery gets rejuvenated each time a new development in the course of the nickels hits the headlines.

The nickels continually set price record after price record as the clamor to be one of the elite owners escalates to stratospheric heights. The roster of past owners reads like a mini-Who's Who of the coin world — Eric Newman, Abe Kosoff, Louis Eliasberg, King Farouk, Colonel Green, and other bright lights of numismatics. Competition to own the fabled nickels grew even sharper when two of the nickels were effectively denied to collectors when they were donated to museums, removing them from the market. Now there are only three in private ownership, and they come dear. In 2003, a buyer paid a reported $3 million for the best of the lot. In early 2004, reports indicated that the sale of another of the coins set a new price record for the nickels, making it the third most expensive coin in history.

Glorified in Mythology and Legend

No doubt the uninitiated must marvel that a handful of humble nickels, among the least pretentious of American coin denominations, can command such powerful awe. After all, they aren't made of gold. They aren't even made of silver. They're made of relatively cheap base metals (nickel and copper), and compared to most U.S. coins struck during that period, they are plain and boring in design. Their face value totals just 25 cents — two bits.

Such is its power that the 1913 Liberty Head nickel is credited with popularizing coin collecting in America, according to award-winning *Coin World* editor Beth Deisher. Writing for *Numismatist* magazine (July 2003), Deisher awarded the crown to the nickels "because for more than seven decades, more people have searched for a 1913 Liberty Head nickel than any other single U.S. coin. Mystery, rarity, publicity, and record prices have elevated it to a legendary status, the likes of which few coins in the world can claim."

---

[1] *Coin World* defines a numismatist as "A person knowledgeable in numismatics, with greater knowledge than a collector." Considerable study of and experience with coins is involved. Relatively few people involved in collecting or trading rare coins are actually numismatists.

Coin World's first 2004 edition (January 5) carried a front page retrospective headlined "Remembering 2003" with the subhead, "Looking back at 'the year of the nickel.'" The lowly nickel figured in three of the editorial staff's top 12 stories for the year. William T. Gibbs wrote that "The resurfacing of the missing 1913 Liberty Head five-cent coin at the American Numismatic Association convention was easily the year's top story."

Even people who have little or no knowledge of coin collecting have heard of the 1913 Liberty nickel. Two generations of everyday Americans in the early to mid-20th century eagerly searched in vain to find one, spurred by the standing offer by a savvy Texas coin marketer to pay a princely sum for an authentic specimen. Through the years, handsome rewards have been offered several times to lure the elusive nickels from hiding, each time re-igniting the popular fever to discover a fortune hidden in a pocketful of change.

This is indeed the stuff of legends. In fact, "legend" and "legendary" are among the words most frequently appearing in news articles about the 1913 Liberty Head nickels. Their fame spread beyond numismatic borders to catch on in the popular imagination.

An entire episode of a popular TV series, Hawaii Five-O, was scripted around and starred one of the nickels, and one was featured in the Hardy Boys/Nancy Drew television series. Superman and Lois Lane spoke of them in a special edition comic book in 1965. The national student magazine Weekly Reader featured an item on "A Million-Dollar Nickel" in September 2003 detailing the re-discovery of the missing nickel. Disney's Scrooge McDuck, an expert on coins if ever there was one, got in on the act, too, starring in a poster accompanying the nickels for a gala display of the 1913 Liberty nickels.

When veteran coin experts Jeff Garrett and Ron Guth polled numismatic masters of the Professional Numismatists Guild to select the entries for their award-winning book "*100 Greatest U.S. Coins,*" the 1913 Liberty Head nickel ranked at the top of the list, save for the 1804 silver dollar. The latter coin sold at auction for $4,140,000…little wonder it got top billing from the coin pros, even though the 1913 Liberty nickels are more famous.

Mythology confers upon the 1913 Liberty Head nickel its grand stature and whets the lust to possess one. Well-known numismatic author Q. David Bowers described the 1913 Liberty Head nickel as "the most famous American coin rarity," declaring it to be "the rarest of the rare."

Two 1913 Liberty Head nickels enrich a charity drive headed by Superman's favorite girl, Lois Lane.
"Superman's Girlfriend, Lois Lane" #54 ©1965 DC Comics. All Rights Reserved. Used with Permission.

Tracing a Twisted Trail

Owning one of these treasures automatically elevates the holder upon a pedestal of honor in the numismatic community. "The ownership of a 1913 Liberty head nickel has been a sure way to register its possessor in the 'numismatic hall of fame,'" said Bowers.

The problem is, it hasn't always been easy to figure who the owners really are. Constructing a reliable pedigree for the 1913 Liberty Head nickels becomes an article of faith for certain periods in the provenance records.

The historic re-discovery of the missing nickel in the summer of 2003 cleared up at least part of one of the largest mysteries of ownership, but left many questions unanswered and shed no light at all on other fuzzy links in the ownership chain. Even the identity of the very first owner of the coins remains hidden.

Probing the story of 1913 Liberty Head nickels tests the resolve of the most determined researcher. The absence of written documentation leaves large parts of the story reliant on anecdotal references which, even if they were accurate to begin with (too often not a valid assumption), have been muddled by the passage of time, the deaths of people involved, and the distortion of hearsay and folkloric embellishment.

With rare coins, there's a natural desire to enhance the romance. The neater the story, the greater the glory. Rarity and condition most certainly figure into the attractiveness of a specimen, but there can be no denying that a coin with a fetching story fetches a higher price than one with a boring life history.

In the business of numismatics, price is important. Coin collecting may be a hobby to many, but make no mistake about it: when you can hold in the palm of one hand five coins worth more than $12 million, this is serious business.

To a very large extent, accuracy in the record of the 1913 Liberty nickels — or most coins, for that matter — falls victim to the human nature of coin collectors themselves. Collectors not uncommonly tend to be secretive and guarded — even intentionally deceptive — about their dealings as a strategy of security, privacy protection, and, unhappily, sometimes to defraud others. While understandable, this kind of behavior leads to sketchy or no information being revealed about the trail of the coins or, perhaps worse, the spread of disinformation deliberately intended as a red herring distraction from the real facts.

Factual accuracy is often further sacrificed by the culture of the numismatic community, which readily warms to a juicy tale whether supported by fact or not. The nature of numismatic literature and bourse[2] floor gossip at coin shows transforms opinion and speculation into accepted assumptions. "Once a rumor is repeated and put into print, it becomes fact," Memphis coin dealer John ("J.D.") Dannreuther observed. "When one person repeats it and the next guy repeats it and the next guy repeats it, it becomes absolute fact. Then it becomes part of numismatic lore."

Thus, the journalistic rule of thumb that more than one source tends to corroborate a piece of information as credible doesn't always hold up in numismatic research. Because of this phenomenon, it's entirely possible to find three, four, five or more sources to back up a "fact" that is entirely wrong because it's simply an error that got repeated many times over. As a case in point, virtually the entire body of numismatic literature written about the 1913 Liberty Head nickels has been completely wrong about the whereabouts of the missing coin because of a mistake made over 40 years ago that was accepted as fact. The assumption was never challenged until the summer of 2003.

---

[2] Originally a stock exchange in continental Europe, especially Paris, bourse has come to mean any open marketplace such as those always found at coin shows.

In the case of the 1913 Liberty nickels, tracing the pedigrees of the individual coins gets complicated after the coins were split up because of the lack of uniformity in nomenclature. That is, how do you designate each coin?...What do you call each one? There's no rhyme or reason to the nomenclature of famous coins, so it's often difficult to know exactly which coin is being discussed.

These circumstances are not likely to change greatly or soon, and maybe not at all. In some cases, it may never be possible to clear up the record entirely because the evidence simply does not exist, and the events cannot be reconstructed forensically. However, as numismatic chroniclers embrace a stricter standard of evidence, which appears to be an encouraging trend in recent times, the body of knowledge about not just the 1913 Liberty Head nickels but all rare coins will become more reliable.

The story in the pages ahead attempts to sort fact from fiction about the 1913 Liberty nickels and clearly label which is which. Given the gaps in the historical record, no one can warrant with 100 percent certainty the accuracy of every detail.

Still, having sifted the evidence thoroughly, we will know more at the end than we do at the beginning. So don your cloak and deerstalker cap and let's join the chase. "Quick, Watson. The game is afoot!"

Chapter 1 References

Bowers, Q. David. 1975. "The Legendary 1913 Liberty Head Nickel," *Bowers and Ruddy Galleries Rare Coin Review* 22 (Spring), p. 32-37.

DC Superman National Comics. 1965. *"Superman's Girl Friend Lois Lane"* JAN No. 54.

Dannreuther, John. 2003. Interview (October 4).

Deisher, Beth. 2003. "Liberty Head Legends," *Numismatist* (July), p. 37.

Garrett, Jeff, and Ron Guth. 2003. *100 Greatest U.S. Coins* (Atlanta: Whitman Publishing), p. 10-11.

Snyder, John K. 2003. *"90 Years of Liberty"* poster. Baltimore: American Numismatic Association, Diamond International Galleries.

Superior Stamp & Coin Co., Inc. 1978. Press release: *"1913 Liberty Nickel Sold by Superior for $200,000.00 to Anonymous Collector."*

Weekly Reader. 2003. "A Million-Dollar Nickel" (Vol. 82 No. 4, September 19), p. 6

- Chapter Two -

AMERICA'S
EARLY NICKELS

To understand fully the rambunctious history of the 1913 Liberty nickels, it is instructive to examine the tumultuous ancestry of the American nickel itself. The stage for the 1913 Liberty Head nickel drama was set by a series of developments in American coinage dating back to the beginning of the country. A brief review of this chain of events will help set the scene for the debut of the stars of our mystery story.[3]

America's Coins of Independence

The first American five-cent coin was not a nickel. The first American nickel coin was not a five-cent coin…and it was only barely nickel.

The original five-cent denomination in U.S. currency was the silver half disme (pronounced DEEM in the Gallic accent or DIZ-me in the Americanized version) from the French word "dixième" for tenths, issued in 1792. It survived 81 years as a silver coin. In later years, the term was informally Anglicized to half "dime," the form of the term that survives to today.

On April 2, 1792, George Washington signed a bill authorizing a national coinage for the young nation with the requirement that they should bear "a device emblematic of liberty" rather than a presidential portrait on the coins as was originally proposed. Washington considered that to be too monarchial. He also reportedly supplied an estimated $100 worth of his own personal silver[4] to hasten production of a native specie[5] and sever dependence on English coins.

The same act established a decimal system of currency for the United States, with a dollar divided into tenths, cents, and mills. It was a radical new idea at the time and pointedly, defiantly different from the British system of

---

[3] For in-depth studies on the subject, see Don Taxay's *The U.S. Mint and Coinage*, and *The Complete Guide to Shield and Liberty Head Nickels* by Gloria Peters and Cynthia Mohon.

[4] Several myths about Washington's donation of "silver plate" have been circulated, variously claiming, among other things, that it was his household silverware or Martha Washington's dinner service. However, it's unlikely that guests of the Washington's at formal dinners suffered the indignity of being served on common tableware. In the 1790s, "silver plate" referred to bullion silver, so Washington's contribution could have been in the form of foreign silver coins or bars.

[5] Specie is coined money.

pounds, shillings, and pence. The feisty Americans wanted to establish and declare their independent national identity via their coinage.

The bill authorized gold coins in denominations of $10, $5, and $2.50 (eagle, half eagle, quarter eagle), five silver coins — dollar, half dollar, quarter dollar, dime, and half dime — and copper cents and half cents. The half dime was the only coin produced in any quantity. The other denominations of 1792 that were produced — various cents, dismes, and quarter dollars — are considered patterns, making the half dime the first regular issue coin of the United States.

The first U.S. coin containing nickel was the one-cent coin introduced in 1857. It contained mostly copper, being only 1/8 nickel. It was enough nickel, though, to make the coins lighter than older copper coins. So people started calling them "white cents." They also got the nickname "nicks," because of their nickel content.

Civil War Wipes Out Coin Supply

The nickel as we have come to know it was born of war…the Civil War, to be precise. Numismatic researcher and historian R.W. Julian wrote, "The half dime would have remained a staple of commerce had it not been for the Civil War (1861-65)." He explained, "The public became increasingly nervous and hoarded gold coins as early as December 1861. Silver's turn came the following June, and by autumn even the lowly cent was stowed away."

To pay the enormous costs of the dreadful, protracted conflict, both the Union and the Confederacy printed reams of paper money IOUs backed with nothing more than a promise. The ebb and flow of victories and defeats for both sides left the citizenry in doubt as to the eventual winner of the struggle, so they didn't trust the promises of either side when it came to money. It didn't help matters that both governments were cranking out paper notes at a prodigious rate, with the inevitable result of runaway inflation making the paper bills worth less (and for the Confederacy, eventually worthless).

Rebel and Yankee citizens alike began hoarding wealth they could trust — coins made of gold and silver, precious metals that had real value they could count on. Until 1964, the guiding philosophy had always been for American coins to have an intrinsic "melt" value approximately equal to the face value. So, a gold coin stamped "5 dollars" theoretically would bring approximately five dollars worth of goods if it was melted down and traded as metal on the open market.

Coins started rapidly disappearing from circulation. Soon it became difficult to conduct everyday business, because there simply were not many coins to make change for ordinary transactions. A simple exchange like buying a plug of chewing tobacco, paying for a shot of whiskey at the saloon, stocking up with a sack of flour, a tin of coffee, and a few pounds of beans, or taking home a new gingham bonnet became a complicated chore.

When the guns fell silent, one of the most urgent tasks facing the reconstituted Union was to redress the shortage of small denomination coins. Several schemes were introduced, all with miserable lack of success. The government tried postage stamps, which quickly turned into a sticky mess in people's hands and pockets, and there weren't enough of them to do any good anyway. "Shinplasters," private scrip, postage currency, and fractional currency met with no better success than did the stamps.

Fractional currency paper notes continued to circulate after the war's end, but the citizenry was restive and in a sullen mood about it. The three-cent and five-cent notes were especially irksome. Congress knew it had to do something quickly to keep a lid on things in the still-shaky postwar economy. The lawmakers couldn't authorize redemption of the federal fractional notes at face value for the simple reason that there wasn't enough gold and silver available to do it even if they were so inclined (which they weren't).

The Act of March 3, 1865, authorized the issue of three-cent coins made of nickel to retire the three-cent paper notes. This cleared the way for doing the same thing with the five-cent notes.

The demise of the five-cent note was hastened when Congress discovered that the face on the third issue five-cent note was not explorer William Clark (of the Lewis and Clark expedition) as they had intended but Spencer M. Clark of the Currency Bureau!

Congress exploded in a fury at such utter bureaucratic gall and quickly harrumphed through a bill retiring the denomination and making it illegal to use the likeness of any living person on U.S. coins or currency (of course, the rule has routinely been ignored over the years since).

The Nickel Debate

Having duly displayed their indignity at the outrage, it dawned on the lawmakers that the country would be without a five-cent denomination of any kind if they didn't act fast. So they moved to adopt a five-cent coin made of nickel.

The use of nickel in U.S. coins churned in controversy from the time it was first proposed to Congress in 1837 by Dr. Lewis Feuchtwanger, who suggested small coins made of German silver.[6] Mint Director Robert M.

---

[6] Also known as argental or nickel silver; an alloy of nickel, copper, and zinc.

Patterson objected. He made plain his opinion of German silver in a note to Senator Thomas Hart Benton:

> Nickel, which is a characteristic constituent of German silver, is chiefly obtained from a mineral called copper nickel, and from the refuse of smalt-works. It is never found, and cannot be practically obtained, wholly free of cobalt; and it likewise contains arsenic and iron; and as these metals are in variable proportions, the compound into which they enter cannot be uniform.

Patterson's assessment of problems with using nickel apparently got a nod of approval from Professor James Booth of the Franklin Institute. In fact, Patterson even quoted from Booth in making his argument against using German silver.

Booth was either playing games or had an epiphany of some sort, because he changed his tune later. He became melter and refiner at the Mint under Mint Director A. Loudon Snowden by the early 1850s. Booth advised Snowden to go ahead and use German silver to make coins. He "launched a project for the local manufacture of nickel" (Taxay).

He reported to Director Snowden: "Since no single metal, possessing qualities requisite for coinage, can be found for an intermediate value between silver and copper…a proper substitute for such metal may be found among alloys." The alloy Booth recommended was German silver.

The recommendation was rejected because German silver looked too much like real silver. The Mint started experimenting with other alloys, so Booth dumped his nickel interests. With the professor no longer involved, the nickel project crumbled and was abandoned.

The idea of nickel in coins hadn't been abandoned, though. After a good bit of wrangling in Congress, the "nick" cent coin, made of 88 percent copper and 12 percent nickel debuted in May 25, 1857. It was a big hit with the public, as described in the *Philadelphia Bulletin*[7]:

> Every man and boy in the crowd had his package of coin with him. Some had their rouleaux[8] of Spanish Coin done up in bits of newspaper or wrapped in handkerchiefs, while others had carpet bags, baskets and other carrying contrivances, filled with coppers — "very cheap and filling," like boardinghouse fare.

---

[7] Per Don Taxay: reprinted in *Bankers Magazine*, August 1857; also, Eric P. Newman, "An Excited Mob Besieges the Philadelphia Mint Money Changers," *Numismatic Scrapbook Magazine*, October 1962.

[8] A small roll, especially of coins wrapped in paper.

The popularity of the "nicks" opened the door to use nickel for a three-cent coin made of 25 percent nickel and 75 percent copper to redeem the paper three-cent notes. It must have seemed a logical next step to make a five-cent coin along the same lines.

However, things got very political as the debate frothed about how much nickel the "nickel" should hold. Originally, it was proposed to weigh 50 grains, which would be proportional to the 30 grains in the three-cent coin. But Joseph Wharton had other ideas.

The Wharton Factor — A Force to be Reckoned With

Mining tycoon Joseph Wharton founded the famed Wharton School of Business at the University of Pennsylvania. He also wielded a lot of clout in federal government circles.

When Booth's nickel venture collapsed, the local source of nickel for the Mint dried up. In 1863, Wharton, a local metallurgist, took notice and got involved in nickel, sinking $200,000 in the Gap Nickel Mine in Lancaster, Pennsylvania. Mint Director James Pollock apparently egged him on at first, but later had a change of heart and decided he liked bronze better than nickel for coins.

Pollock's defection didn't deter Wharton, though. He basically held a monopoly on the nickel supply in the country. He naturally had a vested interest in massaging government agents to buy as much of his nickel as he could coax them to. Joe Wharton was very good at "coaxing" politicians to get what he wanted. He was one of the most effective lobbyists of his time. Wharton was a master of the crony circuit, plying the craft of backroom political persuasion with the arm-twisting skill of a professional wrestler.

The chief coiner at the Philadelphia Mint in the 1870s called Wharton the best "nickel man" around. Mint Director James Pollock never really liked nickel for coins, but Wharton must somehow have persuaded him to change his mind because he proposed increasing the weight of the nickel to 60 grains. A House committee took it further, upping the weight to 77.16 grains, supposedly to make it an even 5 grams to satisfy the request of scientists who wanted the country to adopt the metric system. It is more likely the higher nickel content was to boost the size of shipments from Wharton's nickel mine.

Wharton got what he wanted, in the form of the Act of May 16, 1866, authorizing America's first real "nickel," the five-cent piece we know today.

Shield With Rays — The First True American "Nickel"

The first true American "nickels" appeared in circulation soon after. Then, as today, nickels were composed of 25 percent nickel and the rest copper. Nickel is a very hard metal. It needs to be alloyed with some other metal like copper to soften it enough so it won't shatter the dies striking the planchets.[9]

The task of designing the new nickel fell on the troubled shoulders of James Barton Longacre. With the help of the fiery and powerful orator John C. Calhoun, then Secretary of State, Longacre secured appointment as chief engraver of the U.S. Mint when the position was vacated by the death of Christian Gobrecht in 1844.

Longacre holds the distinction of designing the first U.S. coin with the motto "In God We Trust."

America's first real "nickel," James Longacre's Shield With Rays nickel, issued beginning in 1866. It was comprised of 25% nickel, 75% copper. The same alloy is still being used to produce U.S. nickels. © DLRC Press, Reprinted with Permission.

Because he was an ethical man, Longacre often faced conflicts with the Mint hierarchy over what may charitably be called "irregular" practices that were then common at the Mint. These questionable practices included using employees illegally for work outside the establishment and minting medals for private sale. The environment of loose governance at the Mint would later be a probable factor in the mysterious origin of the 1913 Liberty Head nickels.

Despite constant harassment and unsuccessful efforts to boot him out, Longacre persevered, probably more because he needed the job (his own business had gone bankrupt) than from love for the job.

He produced three proposed designs for the new nickel, including a shield design adapted from the two-cent coin, several ideas using the bust of

---

[9] Blank metal disks used to stamp coins. Also called flans.

Washington, and a design with a bust of Lincoln. The Lincoln concept was eliminated because of concerns it would not be acceptable in the South. Treasury Secretary Hugh McCulloch approved what has come to be known as the "Shield with Rays" design.

The design didn't exactly inspire critical hurrahs for its aesthetic appeal. Joseph Wharton would say of it:

> The diameter of this coin being too small for its weight, it has an awkward and humpy appearance, and is entirely devoid of resonance. The design of its face strongly suggests the old fashioned pictures of a tombstone surmounted by a cross and overhung by weeping willows, which suggestion is corroborated by the religious motto. It is a curiously ugly device.

The shield motif was modified several times but endured until 1883, outlasting Longacre, who died on New Year's Day in 1869.

Liberty Head "V" Nickel Debuts

In 1881, Philadelphia mint superintendent A. Loudon Snowden asked chief engraver Charles Edward Barber to design a series of small denomination coins (1, 3, and 5 cents) with a common Liberty design on the obverse.[10] On the reverse, he wanted a wreath of wheat, corn, and cotton framing Roman numerals designating the denomination - I, III, V. The one-cent and three-cent coins were dropped because it was decided they would be too small to be practical in everyday usage (easy to lose, for example) and too difficult to mint. The Liberty Head nickel was released for circulation on January 8, 1883.

There was a problem with the "V" nickel, though…a big problem. Josh Tatum spotted it right away. Nowhere on the coin did it say what the value was, and it resembled the $5 gold coin.

Bill Dickerson, writing on the Professional Coin Grading Service web site (www.pcgs.com), cites a popular tale that credits young Josh Tatum with single-handedly shutting down production of the first Liberty nickel. As the story goes, Tatum hooked up with a jeweler friend who was skilled in electroplating. Using 24-carat gold electroplate, they whipped up 6,000 new

---

[10] The obverse is considered to be the side of a coin, medal, or badge that bears the principal stamp or design. The reverse is the opposite side, usually specifying the denomination in U.S. coins. The "third side" is the edge of the coin, which can be smooth, lettered with a simple inscription, or "reeded" with a series of vertical grooves to discourage counterfeiting.

SERIES FACTS

Series
Liberty Head Nickels

Series Run
1883-1912

Designer
Charles E. Barber

Weight
5 grams

Composition
.750 copper
.250 nickel

Diameter
21.2 millimeters

Edge
Plain

Mints
Philadelphia, Denver (1912 only),
San Francisco (1912 only)

"gold" coins. Tatum happily traipsed from town to town, purchasing items valued at five cents with his gold-plated nickels and getting $4.95 in change. Peters and Mohon described how he did it:

> Then Tatum, a rather distinguished looking gentleman, ventured from one tobacco shop to another. At each store, after inspecting the displayed merchandise, he pointed to a particular box of nickel cigars. The store clerk took the box out of the glass display case and placed it on the counter. Tatum would place his gilded nickel on the counter and select one of these nickel cigars from the box. He would roll it gently in his fingers and slowly sniffed the aroma. This ritual gave the clerk time to look the coin over. Many merchants would give Tatum $4.95 in change. This process was repeated in one tobacco shop after another.

Tatum's scheme was uncovered, and he was arrested and tried. He was acquitted, however, when no witness could be produced who could say Tatum ever actually said the coin he tendered was a five-dollar piece. He was a deaf-mute. All he did was put the nickel on the counter to pay for an item worth five cents or less; so it could not be shown that he intended to defraud anyone. He accepted the $4.95 in change as a donation or gift.[11]

Whether or not the Tatum adventure happened exactly as the tale describes, there's no denying that enterprising counterfeiters quickly seized the opportunity, gold-plating the five-cent coins and passing them off at 100 times their actual value. They became known as "Racketeer Nickels."

Liberty NO CENTS nickel (Variety I), issued in 1883 with no specified denomination. Counterfeiters gold-plated it and passed it off as a $5 gold piece. More than 5 million of the NO CENTS nickels were issued before production was halted. © DLRC Press, Reprinted with Permission.

When the impact of the gaffe became clear, production was quickly shut down, and Snowden juggled the hot potato into Barber's hands. Barber shuffled some design elements around to make room for the word CENTS added below the Roman numeral V. When the modified nickels came out on June 26, 1883, (the same day production of the Shield nickel was officially halted) the public started hoarding the NO CENTS (or WITHOUT CENTS) nickels, and they remain popular collector coins even today.

Liberty CENTS nickel issued beginning June 26, 1883, with the denomination "CENTS" clearly spelled out on the reverse beneath the "V." © DLRC Press, Reprinted with Permission.

---

[11] The American slang term "joshing," meaning to joke with or trick someone, is often mistakenly said to have originated from the name of Josh Tatum. However, the term was in use at least 30 years earlier, appearing as early as 1852 and more frequently after humorist Josh Billings (pen name for Henry Wheeler Shaw) began his career in 1860, possibly influencing the popularization of the word.

The Liberty Head nickel, which Easterners preferred to call the "V" nickel, continued to be coined until late 1912, when it was discontinued to make way for the Buffalo design introduced early in 1913.

In the two months between the cessation of Liberty Head nickel production and the startup of Buffalo nickel production, it was forbidden to make any U.S. nickels. Somebody didn't obey the order. It would be seven years before anybody found out about it. The plot thickens…

Chapter 2 References

American Numismatic Association web site. Accessed November 2003 at www.money.org/h_tml/edu_nick.html.

Breen, Walter. 1988. *Complete Encyclopedia of US and Colonial Coins* (New York: Doubleday), pp. 246-252.

CoinPeople.com's Virtual Coin Museum web site. Accessed November 2003 at www.coinpeople.com/forums/viewtopic.php?t=74.

Coin World. 2003. "Five-cent coins remain staple of circulating coinage in U.S.," (November 24), p. 16.

Dickerson, Bill. 1999. "The Man Who Could Stop the Mint," PCGS, Professional Coin Grading Service web site. Dated June 1999. Accessed November 2003.

Etymology Online web site. Accessed December 2003 at www.etymonline.com/j2etym.htm.

Hight, Mitch. 2003. Coin-Gallery Online web site. Accessed November 2003 at www.coin-gallery.com/cguscoinage.htm.

Jordan, Louis. University of Notre Dame web site. Accessed November 2003 at www.coins.nd.edu/ColCoin/ColCoinIntros/HalfDisme.intro.html.

Morris, Evan. 2003. The Word Detective web site. Accessed December 2003 at www.word-detective.com/070698.html.

Numismedia. 2003. Series Spotlight: Liberty Head Nickels. Web site accessed August 19 at www.numismedia.com/series/liberty5.shtml.

Peters, Gloria, and Cynthia Mohon. 1995. *The Complete Guide to Shield & Liberty Head Nickels* (Virginia Beach, Virginia: DLRC Press), pp. 2-7; 46-47.

Taxay, Don. 1966-69. *The U.S. Mint and Coinage* (New York: Arco Publishing Company, Inc.), pp. 232-248.

- Chapter Three -

COVERT ORIGINS

W hodunit?

The answer to that question has eluded numismatists for more than 90 years. The mystery of who actually turned the crank on the presses to stamp out the five 1913 Liberty Head nickels bedevils collectors to this day. It's like a phantom feather tickling the mind, teasing and tormenting, just brushing near but not quite there. It is among the most fabled of all numismatic conundrums in history.

What we know from the documented facts is that the 1913 Liberty nickels first appeared publicly in 1920 in the possession of one Samuel W. Brown, a former employee of the Philadelphia Mint. Prior to that, the chronicles remain maddeningly silent, refusing to surrender the secrets of how the coins came to be.

"Under what circumstances were the 1913 Liberty nickels struck? Who made them? How many persons were involved?" asked Q. David Bowers in a 1975 issue of *Rare Coin Review* for Bowers and Ruddy Galleries. "Numismatists, writers, and editors have sparred for years as they attempted to sift fact from legend."

They're still sparring. At the beginning of the 21st century, we are no closer to unraveling the mystery. Unless some lucky stroke of research turns up heretofore unknown evidence, it appears we will never know the real truth of how the coins came to be. In the eight decades since the existence of the 1913 Liberty nickels has been known, a steady parade of diligent and talented numismatic researchers have snooped and poked and sniffed at the trail trying to track down the perpetrators without success.

"The history of the 1913 nickel has long been shrouded in mystery," Bowers wrote. "The actual facts probably remain buried with those persons who might have been able to account for them during their lifetime. Perhaps the true account would increase or decrease the value of the coins; as long as the mystery does continue, they will probably be the cherished coins of our age."

Indeed, a sizeable part of the numismatic community would probably just as soon the answer never be found. Like learning how a magician's illusion is done, it would destroy the mystique, the vibrant aura of magic these coins hold for collectors.

In the void of fact, we're left with abundant speculation — a specialty of numismatic literature. Certain points of the speculation have been told and re-told for so long and with such frequency that they have taken on the conviction of reality.

It should be useful to set forth here what is known and what is presumed, and to distinguish between fact and hypothesis.

What is known and documented is that production of the Liberty Head nickel officially ceased on December 13, 1912. On that day, Mint Director George E. Roberts told his staff, "Do nothing about the five-cent coinage for 1913 until the new designs are ready for use." The last official United States Liberty Head nickel was struck on that same day.

The whole affair of the 1913 Liberty nickels would possibly never have come up — and the coins may never have been created — had it not been for The Hobbs Episode.

Buffalo/Indian Head Design Replaces Liberty

The "new designs" Mint Director Roberts was waiting for were the approved obverse and reverse dies for the Buffalo/Indian Head nickel (commonly known simply as the Buffalo nickel) scheduled to commence production at the beginning of 1913. The dramatic new nickel was to feature a standing buffalo (to be accurate, it should be called a bison) on the reverse and a striking Indian chief's profile on the obverse.[12] The designs were the work of James Earle Fraser, a world-renowned sculptor and student of sculptor Augustus Saint-Gaudens. Saint-Gaudens was the revered creator of what is considered by most to be America's most beautiful coin, the Saint-Gaudens gold double eagle.

The change in nickel design at this time may well have been spurred by a letter to Secretary of the Treasury Franklin MacVeagh from his son Eames. The younger MacVeagh pointed out to his dad that he only had one shot at making a lasting impression on U.S. coinage, and he'd better get cracking. On May 4, 1911, Eames MacVeagh wrote:

---

[12] A coin is usually known by the design on its obverse, but in this case, the buffalo image captured the public imagination, so the coin became widely identified by it.

> A little matter that seems to have been overlooked by all of you is the opportunity to beautify the design of the nickel or five-cent piece during your administration, and it seems to me it would be a permanent souvenir of the most attractive sort. As possibly you are aware, it is the only coin the design of which you can change during your administration, as I believe there is a law to the effect that the designs must not be changed oftener than every twenty-five years. I should think also it might be the coin of which the greatest numbers are in circulation...

Nobody had to use a two-by-four to get Secretary MacVeagh's attention on this issue. It was a chance to make his lasting imprimatur on U.S. coin history in a tangible way the American public could hold in its collective hand. Not long after receiving his son's letter, MacVeagh had assistant Secretary Andrew spread the word that the Treasury was in the market for a new coin design.

James Earle Fraser got wind of it and pursued the assignment. Mint Director George E. Roberts prodded Fraser toward a Lincoln head theme. Fraser played the game and seemingly went along with the director's desires. "I think your idea of the Lincoln head is a splendid one and I shall be very glad to make you some sketches as soon as possible and let you see them." But Fraser was nobody's toady, and he had some definite ideas of his own for the nickel.

He whipped up some wax models of Indian head and buffalo devices. He thought they were distinctive symbols of America. Assistant Secretary Andrew and Director Roberts liked Fraser's ideas so much that they recommended them straight away to Secretary MacVeagh, suggesting that they be adopted without waiting for the customary design competition.

MacVeagh took a real shine to the Buffalo nickel design, too, but hesitated to forego the requisite competition. He relented, but it took awhile for word to get to Fraser that his designs were to be adopted.

On January 13, 1912, MacVeagh sent a letter to Fraser apologizing for the delay. He also instructed Director Roberts to inform Fraser he had won the commission.

In his annual report for fiscal 1912, Roberts stated:

> During the year, Mr. J.E. Fraser of New York was invited to submit designs for a new 5-cent piece and he has prepared designs that have been accepted. The features of the piece, in addition to the inscriptions required by law, are an Indian head for the obverse and a buffalo for the reverse. The coin is distinctively characteristic of America, and in its execution

promises to take high artistic rank among the coinages of the world. It seems peculiarly appropriate that the Indian and buffalo should be associated permanently in a national memorial, and there can be no better form for such memorial than a popular coin.

Secretary MacVeagh approved the completed designs in July 1912 and presented them to the Commission of Fine Arts, which heaped high praise on his work.

Things seemed to be going along quite smoothly with the new design. But nobody had figured on the Hobbs complication.

It seems the Hobbs Manufacturing Company had some concerns about the new coin design. Hobbs produced coin detecting machines designed to discriminate against counterfeit coins. They raised the question whether the new design nickel might muck up the works of their machinery. Apparently they held strings connected somewhere important in the bureaucracy, because the mint director asked Fraser to meet with the Hobbs people and work out any problems if there were any. There were.

Evidently, the tolerances on their coin-detecting device were fine enough that a thousandth of an inch here and a thousandth of an inch there in the dimensions of a coin could make a big difference on whether the machine worked right or gagged on the coin. The Hobbs people asked for a number of changes to Fraser's designs, which vexed him greatly. "What I was expected to do," he grumbled, "was to make a large model so perfect that when it was reduced five times it would open a combination lock on being run through it."

The wrangling with Hobbs over design changes dragged on, resulting in delays in getting the final production dies prepared. When the Mint shut down production of the Liberty nickels on December 13, the dies for the Buffalo nickel still weren't ready.

Finally, Fraser managed to get a pair of models approved, with Hobbs' reserved blessing, and immediately sent them to the Mint. Chief engraver Charles Barber received them the day after Christmas, December 26. The first experimental pieces were struck on January 7, 1913. The test was a big success. Press people said it took even less pressure to raise the new design on the metal than it did with the Liberty design.

But it wasn't champagne time for Fraser yet. Those Hobbs people were back in his face again like a recurring bad dream. After checking the test strikes with a micrometer, they demanded more changes. Much to Fraser's chagrin and bewilderment, Director Roberts folded to Hobbs' demands. Back to the drawing board for Fraser.

Sculptor James Earle Fraser's classic Buffalo nickel, finally issued beginning February 21, 1913, after numerous delays for changes to accommodate a vending machine manufacturer. ©Bowers and Merena Galleries.

In the meantime, on January 18, 1913, the mint director again warned the Philadelphia Mint superintendent to "Do nothing about any coinage at Philadelphia until you receive formal instructions to that effect."

Fraser might have thought he was living a preview of coin designer's hell. He would fix one thing the Hobbs representatives demanded and submit it, only to learn they wanted something else fixed. More changes. More delays. Fraser was at his wits' end.

It all came to a final showdown on February 15 at a meeting involving Secretary MacVeagh, Director Roberts, Fraser, Hobbs, and various assistants and attorneys. A few hours after the meeting, Secretary MacVeagh wrote to Director Roberts that "it would be injudicious to make any further changes in the coin." He put an end to the wrangling and delays, concluding the letter: "You will please, therefore, proceed with the coinage of the new nickel."

The Mint superintendent received formal authority to begin production of the Buffalo nickel on February 19, 1913, and actual production commenced at last on February 21. A gap of two months had elapsed since the last official nickel had been produced at the Mint. It was a window of opportunity someone couldn't resist.

"Stories, Theories, Rumors"

Mystery enshrouds the identity of the person who slipped into the press room and secretly stamped out five shiny new Liberty Head nickels with the date 1913. Mentally revisiting the scene of the "incident" — or was it, in fact, a crime? — the history detective faces an impenetrable fog of baffling questions.

When did it happen? Was it day or night? How did the person gain access to the building, to the press room? Why did he do it? Why did he keep it secret? Why were the coins hidden for seven years? Was more than one person involved? How long did it take? How was it accomplished unobserved? Did the higher-ups at the Mint know about it? Did they just look the other way, or were they in on it?

With no written records of the event and the party or parties involved long dead, no definitive answers exist. We can speculate, we can suppose, we can guess, but we can never know for certain.

In lieu of documented knowledge about the creation of the 1913 Liberty nickels, speculation abounds. In December 1971, *Numismatic Scrapbook Magazine*, in a 13-page illustrated feature, "Liberty 1913 Nickel Offers Mystic Aura," cited several possible scenarios earlier proposed in the numismatic literature:

● Lee Hewitt, editor of *Numismatic Scrapbook Magazine*, March 1958:

> Various stories have circulated concerning the issuance of the 1913 nickels, but actual proof of the circumstances surrounding their leaving the Mint has never been documented. As coinage of the buffalo type did not commence until February 21, 1913, the Mint had almost two months to strike the Liberty head type and supply all the demand from collectors, had the Mint been so inclined.

Hewitt went on to suggest:

> Stories, theories, rumors, or what have you concerning these coins boil down to these main versions:
>
> (1) They were struck to exchange for coins needed for the Mint collection.
> (2) The coiner and engraver were amusing themselves and struck the pieces which years later found their way into the numismatic market.
> (3) They were struck exclusively for a wealthy collector.

Hewitt added:

> Regardless of the "why" of issue, under standard Mint practices of the period all that was necessary for those who were responsible for their striking was to pay the proof and medal fund eight cents for each coin and walk out of the Mint building with them.

In a later issue — September 1963 — Hewitt commented:

Unless the order for the buffalo nickel design was received in mid-summer of 1912, the engraving department probably changed the 1912 hub[13] to 1913 as a matter of routine and the five specimens of the 1913 Liberty head nickels are die trials.

- Don Taxay, noted numismatic researcher and historian, in 1963 disclosed that Samuel W. Brown, the first person to expose the existence of the 1913 Liberty nickels, had been an employee at the Mint. Taxay wrote that in his view, these were not trial pieces or set-up pieces for die testing at all, but were made up expressly for Brown as a caprice.[14] Taxay and Hewitt became locked in a testy debate on the topic that spread to include Eric Newman and others.

- Clyde D. Mervis, *Numismatic Scrapbook Magazine*, July 1968:

Fraser's new designs were slow in coming, and since the Mint had a schedule to maintain with the new year 1913 breathing down its neck, the diemaker presumably went about his business of preparing advance dies, making up sets for the now-famous 1913 Liberty head nickel.

Satisfied the dies were satisfactory, he later showed the nickels to his superior for approval. The superior acknowledged the trial pieces, but told the worker the dies would not be used — to destroy them since the new buffalo design had been approved and should be made ready in time for the year 1913. The worker is then reputed to have carelessly tossed the five trial coins into a desk drawer where they lay for some time.

In the 1996 Bowers and Merena catalog for the sale of the Louis Eliasberg, Sr., coin collection (which included the finest known 1913 Liberty Head nickel), Bowers hints that Samuel Brown had a confederate.

---

[13] A hub is a specialized master die positive image of the coin design, used not for creating coins but for creating the dies that will be used for stamping the coins. The production dies become worn or broken by the repeated stamping pressures and have to be replaced at intervals.

[14] Short for "piece de caprice." Also called a "fantasy piece." Defined by Don Taxay in *Counterfeit, Mis-Struck, and Unofficial U.S. Coins*: "The piece de caprice is a coin struck from official hubs or dies, or from simulated official dies, illegally or unofficially, in or out of the Mint, by either Mint personnel or laymen - and solely for the purpose of providing a numismatic curiosity or rarity."

The presumption is that he [Brown] acquired them at the Mint when he worked there, quite possibly via engraver George T. Morgan[15], who produced rarities upon occasion for sale to dealers (in particular, Henry Chapman) and collectors (Cleveland industrialist Ambrose Swasey is an example), and who is believed to have been involved in making the famous MCMVII Extremely High Relief double eagles.

Walter Breen also proposed that Brown was in collusion with someone else, arguing that Brown had probably faked the purchase of the coins by advertising in journals, (such as the Numismatist), once he knew 'certain' Mint employees who might uncover the plot were no longer alive, or were otherwise unavailable. In effect, Breen states quite plainly his opinion that dishonest employees working in the Coiner's Department most likely secretly struck the coins for Brown.

Another version of the coins' origin appeared around the same general time in several North Carolina newspapers with almost identical wording, suggesting the information came from a common source. The source was very likely George O. Walton, one of the pivotal — and most mysterious — characters in the plot. This account from an article about Walton appeared in the *Greensboro Daily News* October 10, 1959.

When the Philadelphia Mint closed December 23, 1912, a strip of the alloy of which the nickels are made was left in the six-ton die that turned them to prevent swaging, or damage to the die. After Christmas, when the Mint reopened, it was to turn out buffalo nickels dated 1913.

A workman asked the mint superintendent what he should do with the strip of metal left in the die. The superintendent told the workman to go ahead and make 1913 nickels out of it and to turn them over to him. The strip produced five coins.

What the superintendent did with the coins is not known, but in 1915 they turned up in the possession of Col. Thomas H. Green, son of Hetty Green, the famous financier.

Several notable points cast doubts on this version, suggesting it is an entertaining but very likely fanciful invention. Since the articles were based on interviews with Walton, it is likely that he provided the information and may have been misinterpreted or misquoted by newspapermen unfamiliar with Mint terms and procedures. It is also possible that Walton provided

[15] British-born engraver George T. Morgan created the famous (and much-loved by collectors) Morgan silver dollar. He was considered a first class diesinker.

incorrect information to the reporters (or "reporter" in the singular; it could have been a case of Walton having an interview with only one reporter and the other newspapers picking up the story). In any event, these are the factual errors in the account:

- All production of nickels ceased on December 13, ten days before the Mint closed for the Christmas holiday, and the Mint director specifically instructed that no action should be taken on producing nickels until further notice. There should have been no activity on the presses regarding the Liberty Head nickel.
- There is no six-ton die. The presses are heavy, but the dies can be held in your hand.
- Strips of alloy are never placed in the coin press. The strips are put into a punch, which stamps out disks to be inserted into the coin press.
- It is unlikely that a lowly workman would be speaking to the mint superintendent at all, let alone to bother him with an insignificant operational detail like "Boss, what should I do with this hunk of metal in the press?" It's absurd. Mint superintendents didn't normally attend to such minutiae and were unlikely to engage in shop talk with a workman in the press room.
- Col. Green's name was Edward Howland Robinson (E.H.R.), not Thomas H.
- The coins could not have turned up in Col. Green's hands in 1915 because their existence wasn't even known to the public until 1919, four years later.

The scenarios suggested by Hewitt and Mervis suffer from weaknesses as well. They are possible but improbable, according to Fred Weinberg, a foremost expert on mint processes (and a member of the team that authenticated the missing nickel).

The Mervis version uses the terms "presumably" and "reputed," indicating that the story is hearsay and not necessarily presented as factual evidence.

Weinberg further questions the Mervis account because it is predicated on the resulting coin samples being made with "normal" dies. The ones used to make the 1913 Liberty nickels weren't normal.

Weinberg recalled something unusual about the 1913 Liberty nickels the night in July 2003 when he and the five other members of an expert team examined all of the known specimens in the same room. "The thing that

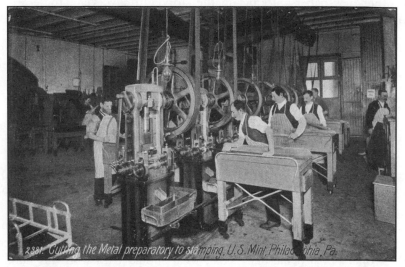

Machinery in the Mint used to cut the metal strips from which the blank coin disks (planchets) will be cut out. The postcard caption reads "2381. Cutting the Metal preparatory to stamping, U.S. Mint, Philadelphia, Pa."

Coin press room in the Mint where the actual coins are produced. The caption on the card reads, "2382. Where the Metal is converted into coin, U.S. Mint, Philadelphia, Pa."

Machinery used to imprint "reeding" on coin edges to discourage counterfeiting or shaving metal flakes from coins. The caption says, "2389. Putting the Rough Edge on Coins, U.S. Mint, Philadelphia, Pa."

Cutting planchets out of the alloy strips.

Steam-powered coining press which stamped the designs onto the planchets.

A viewing of the Coining Room at the Philadelphia Mint, circa 1885.

struck me in looking at all those coins that night is that those are hand-made dies. I disagree with [Mervis]. The mint employee who normally makes dies did not make up 1913 dies because those are not 1913 U.S. mint '3's. The dies are U.S. Mint, but the '3' is hand punched. There's no '3' that looks like that on any U.S. coin made in 1903, 1913, 1923, 1933...it was obviously hand-made," Weinberg said. "It doesn't make sense. Because those are hand-cut '3's, there's no die person in the U.S. Mint who would have prepared official dies in December 1912 that looked like these coins."

So, either the Mervis version "is very, very wrong — because maybe in 1968 nobody realized it was hand-cut '3' instead of a normal punch," according to Weinberg, or the story is true but the evidence was destroyed.

"The only way that that [the Mervis] letter makes sense? and this goes on to further speculation off the top of my head ? is that everything he says is true except that the dies were totally destroyed and then somebody went back and took some old 1912 dies and re-engraved them. So, what he's saying may be true, but all evidence of that is totally wiped out and does not exist."

But Weinberg isn't convinced. "I can tell you...I want to say 'categorically' because I feel rather strongly about it ...those 1913 Liberty nickel dies with the hand-cut '3' were not done by a normal mint die-cutter in the normal course of preparing dies for the next year. It's impossible. There's never been another hand-cut '3' like that, especially in the 20th century," he said.

Maybe the story was a cover invented by the perpetrator, Weinberg suggests. "We can speculate six different angles. Maybe that story was made up — by Samuel Brown or the guy who worked with him at the Mint — to partially legitimize the coins. If you think about it, if that letter [Mervis'] is true, then those coins were struck 'legally' as test pieces or pattern pieces, something to show the supervisor of the Philadelphia Mint: 'Hey, look, this is what they're going to look like next year.' So that story helps make production of the coins much more legitimate. However, based on the '3's on the coins, I don't buy that story."

R.W. Julian minimized the significance of the oddball "3." In response to an email query on the subject, Julian replied, "The fact that it was different means very little as the engraver's department might have prepared in-house a new figure 3 in the summer of 1912. No records exist on this point, however. If the figure was, in fact, hand-engraved, then one must still account for the fact that the perpetrators had access to an unhardened die missing only the last figure. The most likely explanation is still that the single set of proof dies was used for the clandestine coinage, but I have no way of proving this."

If Weinberg's theory is correct, that they engraved a "3" in place of the "2" in a 1912 die, then it would not have been necessary to have a die missing the last digit of the date. The absence of markings on the nickels indicating that a "2" had been there does not in itself prove that a die with a blank last digit was used and the "3" hand engraved into it. The die would have been effaced to remove the "2" completely (ground off, in other words) before adding the "3."

Queried by email about the issue, John Dannreuther, also considered an expert on Mint processes, laid to rest the notion that a die with a blank final digit could have been available:

> Nearly every U.S. coin from 1840 until about 1907-1916 era had four-digit logotypes (date dies). Thus, each 4-digit date was punched into each working die by the process of lining up the date die and hitting [it] with a small hammer. If the date did not "come up" properly, it was repunched. Only in the early years of the Mint was the practice of having 3 digits in the die used.....if at all. Another myth.

Hewitt's suggestion that the coiner and engraver made them on a whim or that they were produced for a wealthy collector could have been true; however, there is no clear evidence to corroborate these scenarios. They make interesting hypotheses but are purely theoretical.

The Hewitt speculation that there was nothing amiss in creating the 1913 Liberty nickels as long as someone paid eight cents for each of them into the medal fund doesn't seem to hold water. If it was that easy and there was no illegal act involved, why were the coins kept secret for seven years? Why was no record of the transaction entered into the Mint journals?

Weinberg's answer was that it was "because they weren't official coins. Because they were hand-engraved dies. He could have paid the eight cents and walked out with them — which I don't believe happened, but because the dies were not official — well, the dies were official but the '3' was not — that tells me they were made on purpose, made up surreptitiously. Out of the three scenarios listed [by Hewitt], I don't buy the first one. Although there was precedent in the 1870s where they struck patterns and traded them for coins the national mint museum needed, I don't think they were doing that in 1913. The second and third scenarios would make sense."

WHY DID STELLA HACKEL SIMS DESTROY VALUABLE MINT RECORDS?

Eva Adams Guilty, Too?

Sorting out the puzzle of where the dies came from to make the 1913 Liberty Head nickels would have been helped by examining the Mint records of the period. The problem is, they were destroyed.

At a minimum, the records would have shown what hubs and dies were on hand, how many, and when and how they were disposed of. The information could have shed some light on the source of the dies used to make the illicit nickels. Unfortunately, the information is lost forever, thanks to Stella Hackel Sims and Eva Adams.

Stella Hackel Sims was confirmed as the 29th Director of the United States Mint on November 4, 1977 and served until April 1981. She had been state treasurer of Vermont prior to this appointment.

Not long after she took office, Stella Hackel Sims ordered the destruction of large numbers of Mint records, including the period covering 1912-1913.

The circumstances surrounding the order remain suspicious to this day, though no connection has been made between Sims and the conspiracy to create the 1913 Liberty Head nickels.

The wanton act of destroying irreplaceable historical records continues to outrage numismatists, some of whom are still trying to find answers to the big question: Why? An item posted on the Numismatic Bibliomania Society's E-Sylum web site illustrates:

> In response to our discussion of library deaccession (and sometime destruction) of runs of periodicals, Henry Borgos writes: "Let's not forget what Hackel did!!! Who said the Vandals died out? She destroyed Mint records!!! We, the numismatic community, went berserk — there were a few groups who wanted to take them if the government couldn't store them, but NO!!!!!! — She ordered them destroyed — and so they were."

(Henry is referring to Mint Director Stella Hackel (November 1977 — April 1988 [sic]), who ordered the destruction of a large group of U.S. Mint records. Can anyone give us more information on what was destroyed, or the circumstances of the action? — Editor)

Numismatic historian R.W. Julian, who had an opportunity to examine some Mint records before Sims had them destroyed, responded to the E-Sylum editor's query with the following description of the frustrations he encountered in trying to get to the bottom of the mysterious order:

(1) In 1984 I was planning a trip to Washington to do research in the Archives but thought a visit to the GSA record center in Philadelphia might be of value. I asked Eleonora Hayden, then Mint Historian, to obtain for me the necessary written permission from the Bureau.

(2) There was some delay in obtaining permission (for technical reasons) but while I was in Washington permission was received.

(3) I then went up to Philadelphia where I planned to read Philadelphia Mint letters and ledgers for various years through about 1935.

(4) When I arrived at the Records Center I was informed that Stella Hackel had destroyed the records in 1978 and I was shown a thick sheaf of destruct orders that had been kept on file. Hackel used one of her office staff to sign off on the destruction and then went to an Archives employee to get the necessary authorization from that quarter. No effort was made by Hackel to consult with Miss Hayden or the people in the Archives who actually dealt with such records. It was done in secret and those who should have been informed were deliberately kept in the dark.

(5) I then returned to Washington on other matters. I informed Miss Hayden of the destruction; it was all news to her. I found out later that Donna Pope had reversed the policy but Hackel seems to have destroyed most of the working mint records from 1900 through at least 1960 and perhaps as late as 1970. I also informed the proper people in the Archives, who were equally in the dark; they had been expecting this material to be sent down in due course.

(6) About two years ago a friend asked Hackel why she had destroyed the records. She claimed that she could not remember the matter at all.

(7) Eva Adams also destroyed records but not to as great an extent. One record that she trashed, for example, was a die record book which listed every die made from 1844 to 1925. Her assistant, speaking for her, said that collectors had no legitimate interest in such matters and that I must be a front for a counterfeiting gang. I filed an Freedom of Information Act request but Adams replied, a year later, that it was an internal memo and thus off-limits. When Mary Brooks became director she had, at my request, a search made for this book but it could not be found; she did find many other records of value which were made available to me.

The authors queried the U.S. Mint about the destruction of Mint records by Sims. Greg M. Weinman, attorney with the Office of Chief Counsel for the U.S. Mint, replied:

On November 4, 1977, Stella Hackel Sims was confirmed as the 29th Director of the United States Mint. She served until 1981. We have no way of determining which documents Ms. Hackel Sims may or may not have disposed of during her tenure. Record management is governed by the Federal Record Act of 1950, as amended, which establishes the framework for records management programs in Federal Agencies. Federal records may not be destroyed except in accordance with the procedures described in Chapter 33 of Title 44, United States Code. These regulations include a General Records Schedule (GRS) that gives record descriptions of records that are common to most Federal agencies and authorizes record disposals for temporary records.

Title 44, Chapter 33, Section 3303 of the United States Code mandates that the head of each agency in the United States government must submit to the national Archivist lists of any records it considers unnecessary to keep and wants to destroy. The archivist is appointed by the President and presides over the National Archives and Records Administration (NARA).

Section 3303a directs that the Archivist must examine the lists of records to be destroyed and decide if they do not have value that warrants continued preservation. If no such value is determined, the archivist must publish a notice in the Federal Register of the intent to destroy the records and allow "interested parties to submit comment thereon." If no reason to save the files is forthcoming, the Archivist then must notify the head of the agency that he or she is empowered to destroy the records.

No record apparently exists, as required by federal law, to show that the procedure mandated in Title 44, Chapter 33, was followed in the case of destroying Mint records during Sims' tenure as director.

At best, Stella Hackel Sims' destruct order would appear to be a case of high-handed bureaucratic stupidity. At worst, it could very well be an act of malfeasance in violation of federal law, for which prosecution may have been warranted. The fact that it was not and was apparently never even officially investigated is, in itself, curious. Was this a cover-up of some wrongdoing or just the misguided bungling of a political appointee?

The actions of Eva Adams (Mint Director from October 1961 to August 1969) are also suspect. Her implication, through a flunky, that a respected numismatic scholar was "a front for a counterfeiting gang" is as idiotic as it is arrogant and offensive to numismatists in general. It rings of protesting too much to deflect suspicion from a serious misdeed. Adams' refusal to explain what happened to valuable die records from 1844 to 1925 raises questions about her stake in having them destroyed. Was she hiding something? Why was the matter never investigated? The questions still await answers.

Not Necessarily a Man?

Could the perpetrator have been a woman instead of a man? Or was there a female accomplice? The possibility has not been explored in the numismatic lore. Since this discussion is about theoretical speculations, the scenario of a female being involved has a legitimate place.

It's not so far-fetched as it might at first seem. It's certain that there were women on the premises working at the Mint, according to Weinberg (he does not propose that a woman was involved with the 1913 Liberty nickels, but was asked if it were possible). "Women are shown in pictures of the period checking the planchets before they went into the presses, checking the coins for errors afterwards, and doing some of the packaging and bagging. Women were definitely at the Mint because we have pictures of them there. But I don't know what their glass ceiling was. In other words, were they prevented from being press operators? I don't recall ever seeing or reading anything that woman was a press operator. I don't believe women were press operators."

Illustration from an 1885 book on Mint processes indicates that it was feasible to have women as coining press operators.

Two woman operate presses in the Coining Room at the Philadelphia Mint, circa 1900.

Woman at work in the Mint milling the planchets.

As a matter of fact, an 1885 book by George G. Evans, *Illustrated History of the United States Mint*, carried a woodcut illustration by F.B. Schell showing a woman operating the coining press! It is not clear from the illustration, though, that the woman is an actual Mint operator. The crowd of well-dressed onlookers in the background suggests that perhaps the picture was of an exhibition or public tour of some sort. The woman at the press could have been pleasant decoration, as attractive models are employed today at trade shows to call attention to product demonstrations. The accompanying text makes no mention of the operator's gender. In fact, it doesn't mention the operator at all. However, the illustration indicates that it was acceptable and not impossible to have a female operator.

More conclusive evidence can be seen in a photo from the New York Public Library Collection showing the Coining Room at the Philadelphia Mint, circa 1900. Two women can be seen operating the coin presses. The photo is unquestionably of a working environment in this case, not a demonstration for the public.

Even if a woman did not actually stamp out the coins, it is theoretically possible that a female accomplice could have aided in access to the facility and the equipment. Of course, there is no more hard evidence to prove or disprove this theory than any of the other speculative scenarios.

Are There More Than Five?

The Sixth Nickel Theory hovers on the edges of numismatic lore, never quite accepted and welcomed by mainstream coin collectors. Still, there's just enough plausibility to the theory to keep it alive and give collectors pause sometimes to wonder "What if?" After all, there is no concrete evidence that there are not six, or even more.

Two people can be credited with giving the sixth nickel myth a purchase on life: B. Max Mehl and George O. Walton.

Fort Worth, Texas, coin dealer B. Max Mehl spent a lot of money advertising to buy a 1913 Liberty Head nickel, even though he knew perfectly well where all five of the known ones were. Mehl never actually said that there were more of them, but his intense advertising for one certainly fed the assumption there must be more of them.

North Carolina collector/dealer George Walton is the most likely candidate for giving form to the assumption. *Numismatic Scrapbook Magazine* interviewed Walton for a December 1953 item that declared "Looks Like There Are Six 1913 Liberty Head Nickels":

When the late B.G. Johnson offered the 1913 Liberty head nickels from the Col. E.H.R. Green estate to various dealers, the coins were in a leather plush case and the set consisted of five pieces of the Liberty nickels and one 1913 buffalo type in bronze (the buffalo has since been reported to be a cast piece).

It has been presumed that five specimens were all of the 1913 Liberties although the number six has frequently been mentioned.

According to George Walton, who still owns the piece he obtained direct from Johnson, the coin which James Kelly sold to Dr. Bolt is in the collection of a wealthy North Carolina business man. Mr. Walton states that he helped arrange the trade between Dr. Bolt and the business man. Mr. Walton expresses the opinion that the Buffalo piece in bronze was substituted for one of the Liberties so there wouldn't be a vacant spot in the case, the substitution being made before Johnson obtained them or possibly before Green had them.

Samuel W. Brown, North Tonawanda, N.Y., came to the 1920 Chicago convention and exhibited one specimen. He left that specimen with the late Alden Scott Boyer, who kept it about four months. In any event, if there is a specimen in the Farouk collection, that makes six accounted for.

The item went on to list the assumed pedigrees for six 1913 Liberty Head nickels. The only problem is that the story is pure fabrication.

The story said that George Walton "still owns the piece he obtained direct from Johnson" and that another of the nickels "is in the collection of a wealthy North Carolina business man." The verb tenses give the impression that Walton owned a 1913 Liberty Head nickel at the same time as did the mysterious North Carolina business man — two different coins, in other words. Since the whereabouts of four others was well documented, that would mean there had to be six.

However, Walton himself contradicted this premise in other published interviews in which he is quoted as saying he had an opportunity once to buy "all five" of the 1913 Liberty nickels but passed up the deal. He is also quoted as saying he obtained his 1913 nickel in a trade with that same North Carolina business man, rather than getting it directly from Johnson as stated in the *NSM* story. In other words, they were one and the same nickel, not two different ones.

The fatal flaw in the *NSM* item is the apparent assumption that there were six coin slots in the leather case. The reference to a buffalo nickel being substituted to cover up the fact that a 1913 Liberty was missing makes no sense. The leather case had eight slots, not six, and held *eight* coins, not six, when B.G. Johnson and Eric Newman had it. Besides the five 1913 Liberty Head nickels, the leather case displayed three Buffalo/Indian Head nickels, one in copper (not bronze).

In fairness to the myth, since there were no records kept of the 1913 Liberty Head nickels' origin, no one can legitimately say with absolute certainty that only five were made. There are only five that we know of. There could conceivably have been six…or more.

It is profoundly unlikely, however, that any more than five exist. The high-powered prices commanded by these nickels would have long since drawn any others into the marketplace.

The most convincing argument that there are only five comes from the December 1923 ad by August Wagner in *The Numismatist* offering the coins for sale to the public for the first time. He had either obtained the coins from Samuel Brown, believed by many to be the creator of the coins, or was acting as his agent. In his ad, Wagner referred to "The only Five-Cent Liberty Head Coins of this design and year in existence."

The Sixth Coin myth will very probably live on. Hope springs eternal, and there are always those willing to believe there really is a pot of gold at the foot of a rainbow. The sixth coin theory lets them hold onto the dream of one day finding the mythical nickel in their pocket change.

A Matter of Time

The question of when the coins were actually struck remains as much a mystery as the identity of the hand that struck them. In theory, they could have been struck anytime from 1912 to 1920!

Numismatic writer Brent H. Hughes of Falls Church, Virginia, explored various theories of the nickels' origin in a slide presentation prepared in 1971, including some on the edge of credulity:

> Another theory that has been mentioned is that a friend of Brown could have gotten to the dies as late as 1919 and used Mint presses to make the coins. This is hard to accept. First of all, the risk of detection would have been great. It is hard to believe that it could have been done this way without more than one employee in on the deal.[16]

Curiously enough, an article about Masonic coin collectors posted on The Masonic Forum on America Online (Samuel Brown belonged to the

---

[16] Source provided by Eric P. Newman.

Shrine in North Tonawanda) mentioned a possible connection with a security guard at the Mint:

> It can be argued that someone else produced the coins and brought them to him as he was known to be an avid collector associated with the Mint. Nothing in his job descriptions would permit access to the secured dies and there is much concern about the activities of a security guard at the Mint who was later dismissed in 1918 under unclear circumstances.

The possibly wayward security guard is not identified, and no mention of him could be found by the authors in any other published research on the topic. Neither can the story be discounted, however.

Unfortunately, because the coins were made under a clandestine cloak, no official record of their existence was entered into the Mint journals.

The likely reality, though, presents a much smaller time window to examine. On the early end of the time bracket, the coins could have been struck on or after December 13, 1912, when regular production of Liberty nickels ceased and the dies were no longer in use. It's improbable that anyone would have bothered making Liberty nickels after production started on the Buffalo nickels in February 1913. That leaves us with a two-month window of probable opportunity for the coins to be struck.

James F. Kelly, a Dayton, Ohio, coin dealer who was involved in distributing the 1913 Liberty nickels when the set was broken up, said of the coins in a 1967 catalog:

> There has always been, and always will be, considerable mystery surrounding the origin of the 1913 Liberty head nickel. For what it may be worth, it is my opinion that these coins were struck at the Mint during the period when the dies for the buffalo nickel were being prepared. I base this opinion on extensive conversations with the late James Macallister, B.G. Johnson, and Ira Reed during that period when I handled three of these nickels. The reason for the person or persons involved in striking these coins and obtaining them from the Mint, along with withholding knowledge of their existence, can only be speculation and never a known fact...

David Bowers suggested in the Eliasberg auction catalog that they could have been made at anytime during the latter part of 1912:

> Alternatively, the 1913 Liberty Head nickels could have been struck as test pieces in autumn 1912 when dies for the next year's coinage were being made, and before it was decided not to use the design.

Information uncovered by R.W. Julian lends some credence to Bowers' premise. The most detailed and perhaps most plausible account of the origin of the 1913 Liberty nickels appeared in a piece by Julian in the April 1987 *Coin World*. Julian spent a considerable amount of time poring over available mint records while tracking the elusive trail of the coins' origins. Julian wrote:

> In the fall of 1912 the engraver's department made the usual preparations for the 1913 coinage by beginning the process by which the dies of 1913 were made and distributed to the mints. A set of proof dies for the 1913 nickel was made first (probably in mid-November) and stored in the engraver's department for use during the coming January.
>
> Chief Engraver Charles E. Barber supervised his workmen as they executed an order for ten sets of 1913 Liberty Head dies for the Mint at San Francisco. The date of the order is not presently known, but the dies were duly shipped from Philadelphia on November 25, 1912, and received in California early in December, long before they would need to be used for actual striking of 1913 nickels. Denver dies were mailed to that institution in December, but the shipment did not contain any dies for five-cent pieces. It may be that Denver officials had some advance warnings that the Liberty Head design would not be coined in 1913.

Even though James Fraser was working feverishly behind the scenes to get his new Buffalo/Indian Head design approved, apparently there had been no official announcement to the Mint staff that a change was in the works. With delays in producing the new nickel dies and the year rapidly running out, the mint superintendent wondered about future use of the Liberty Head design:

> As early as the first week of December, the rumors about a new coinage of five-cent pieces was becoming so persistent that Superintendent Landis of the Philadelphia Mint wrote Director Roberts inquiring on the matter with a particular request to know if the Liberty Head design would be used in 1913. The Director's answer was received in Philadelphia on Monday, December 16, and as of that date, those officials at the parent Mint needing to know would have been told of the plans for the change in design.
>
> Once the news had reached the proper ears, steps were taken to recall the Liberty Head dies from San Francisco. The ten pairs sent to the western Mint arrived back at Philadelphia as early as December 23, which may mean that Landis had telegraphed instructions. The 10 pairs of 1913-S five-cent dies were almost certainly defaced immediately upon their

return, though this might just barely have waited for the annual die destruction in the first week of January. The precise date of defacement is of moot interest since, so far as is known at present, no strivings were made from these dies.

According to Julian, in proof[17] coinage the coins were struck on a hydraulic press in the coiner's department. Although authority for striking proofs and medals had been returned to the engraver's department in 1901 for the first time since 1873 and remained so in 1912, it was the accepted practice that responsibility for proof coinage was shared by the engraving and coining departments.

In normal operations, mint employees followed a prescribed procedure for producing proof specimens:

> Proof coins were supposed to be struck on carefully selected blanks and then inspected by several different persons to make certain that they were of the highest quality possible. An ordering clerk in the medal department actually oversaw the selling and shipping of proof coins and medals to collectors.

> Because nickel was still a difficult metal to work with, it was necessary to use several proof dies for even a small coinage of such pieces. Normally, proofs were struck twice to bring out all the detail but it seems possible that the five-cent piece was struck three times in some years in order to achieve as fine as possible a result…

> Until actually used for coinage, all proof dies were kept in the custody of the engraver. It can be safely assumed that the engraver delegated the authority to handle the proof dies to just one person, who was then responsible for seeing to it that needed proof coins for sale to collectors were struck in plenty of time and in sufficient quantities.

If this procedure was followed in the case of the 1913 Liberty nickel dies, then the list of suspects who might have produced the nickels that left the Mint narrows dramatically. Charles Edward Barber was chief engraver. George T. Morgan assisted him. Both were reputed to be accommodating to coin collectors wanting special favors. However, Barber and Morgan weren't necessarily the only ones with access to the 1913 Liberty nickel dies. It must be remembered that custody of the dies was shared with the coining department:

---

17 Proof coins are "specially-struck coins generally with a mirror-like surface sold to collectors at the United States Mint." (James F. Ruddy, Photograde)

Whatever the exact course of events in connection with the San Francisco dies, the engraving department and coining department still held a form of joint custody over the 1913 proof nickel dies. It is not quite clear just how dies would have been kept under such circumstances but one would think that the engraving department would have had physical possession of the dies, since they would not normally be issued for use until the new year.

An item in the April 1928 issue of *The Numismatist* said mint officials made up the 1913 Liberty dies just in case there was an extended delay in getting the new Buffalo nickels into production:

> As there was some doubt as to when the new design would be used first, the mint officials had dies prepared of the old Liberty-head type and dated 1913. This was a precautionary measure in case they were ordered to coin nickels early in 1913 before it was decided to use the Indian-head-buffalo type.

Curiously, the item also states that the coins were shown later in 1913 by an unidentified person, a "gentleman" who reportedly obtained the nickels from the Mint:

> From a source believed reliable it is said that five pieces, in proof, of the Liberty-head type, dated 1913, were struck early in that year. These are all the genuine Liberty-head type dated 1913 that are known. None passed into circulation. The five pieces were obtained from the mint by a gentleman who showed them at the Detroit Convention of the A.N.A. in August, 1913. Nothing more was heard of them until in December, 1923, when a gentleman living in Philadelphia advertised in *THE NUMISMATIST* as follows: "For Sale — Five Five-Cent Liberty-head 1913 coins, proof, the only five-cent Liberty-head coins of this design and year in existence." These were undoubtedly the five referred to. There is no record of the whereabouts or the present owner of these coins.

This is the only reference to such an appearance found by the authors and no corroborating evidence could be located to support it. The item, "Two Extreme Rarities in Recent U.S. Coinage — The Liberty Head 1913 Nickel" (the other coin referenced in the item was the 1894 San Francisco Mint Dime), carried no byline, and the source for the information is not identified. Frank G. Duffield was editor at the time. The October 1913 issue of *The Numismatist* carried a detailed report on the Detroit convention activities, describing sixteen exhibits. The 1913 Liberty Head nickels were not mentioned in any of the exhibit reviews. Samuel W. Brown did not attend, according to the published roster of ANA members who registered for the convention.

Numismatic writers Gloria Peters and Cynthia Mohon, whose book *The Complete Guide to Shield & Liberty Head Nickels* is considered one of the most authoritative references on the topic, point the finger directly at Samuel Brown as the originator of the nickels:

> Since the annual destruction of the dies was scheduled to occur in the first week of January and the highest probability was that any dies remaining would be defaced at the latest by that date, the most likely hypothesis is that Samuel W. Brown, possibly with the assistance of one person from engraving or coining departments, perhaps both, would have had to mint the coins sometime between mid-November and the first week in January.

The Elusive Line-up

Who was the accomplice? Take your pick of suspects. Peters and Mohon noted:

> Although many theories have been proposed as to Brown's accomplices, including engraver Charles Barber, nothing definite has been proven about their identities or their roles in this numismatic scandal.

Julian claimed that Brown could not have done the actual striking, though he may in some fashion have been an accessory to the act:

> When word filtered down about the new design for 1913, at least one individual working at the Mint was determined to have specimens of the 1913 Liberty Head coinage. The dies were liable to destruction at any time and would certainly have been destroyed by the first week of January 1913 regardless of circumstances. Time was of the essence.
>
> It has generally been claimed that a storeroom employee at the Mint, Samuel W. Brown, was solely responsible for the 1913 Liberty Head nickels, but this is not possible. It may just be possible that, as a storeroom employee, he had access to the 1913 Liberty Head nickel dies, but this did not give him access to the coining department where the actual striking must have been done. Someone in the engraving or coining departments — or both — must have been involved with the special clandestine striking.

With speed being essential, there is a fair chance that the 1913 Liberty Head nickels were struck as early as December 17 or 18 and certainly not too much later than that. The striking was done hurriedly, because being caught in such a move would have cost the perpetrators their Mint jobs. The striking of any kind of coins, proof or otherwise, was under very strict scrutiny in 1912 and Mint officials would not have tolerated any kind of action such as this.

If Brown didn't actually press the coins, then somebody else had to be in on it. Why would someone take such a risk and surrender the fruits of illicit labor to Brown? It's highly improbable anybody would have done it out of the goodness of his heart, even if it was Christmas time. Some possible answers are: a) Brown paid for the service. b) Brown blackmailed someone to do it. c) Someone owed Brown a huge favor and was paying it back.

A different angle must consider that Brown was not the mastermind of the deed, that someone else put it in motion and he was only a cog in the plan. He may only have assisted in the plot. He may not have even been present when the coins were struck but received them at a later time, perhaps much later.

No evidence has been uncovered so far that would support or disprove any of these possible scenarios.

In any event, Julian maintained that whoever the perpetrators were, they did not use the 1913 Liberty dies returned from San Francisco to make the famous nickels:

> It was my opinion that the single set of proof dies was the source for the nickels so struck, not the San Francisco dies, which probably had not yet been prepared (basined and polished) for coinage. At any rate, the perpetrators did not use the S mint reverse. I suppose one could argue that a SF obverse was used along with a 1912 regular reverse, but I would doubt this very much.

According to one account, the coins were struck on December 24 or December 26, 1912 — Christmas Eve or the day after Christmas. That being a holiday period, it seems logical that there would have been more time when the presses were unattended and staff attention was diverted by festive distractions. Christmas Eve might be considered the more likely prospect.

Fred Weinberg describes how it might have happened: "So my assumption is that it was a scenario like it's Christmas Eve, a short day, so you send everybody home. But you have one or more key employees, who know how to use the mint press — 'We're going to stand around here and sweep up.' — and then there's only one or two people in that particular area where the presses are. And then you strike them, and it's about 5:00 o'clock or even 4:30, let's say, when everybody else has gone home."

The day after Christmas might have been more problematic, as far as presenting a convenient opportunity to make illicit coins. It has been stated that Charles Barber received a set of Buffalo/Indian Head models from James Earle Fraser on December 26. This implies that Barber was on the Mint premises the day after Christmas and suggests that the Mint was open for business, making it more difficult to pull off any private coin pressings unnoticed. That is, unless Charles Barber himself was party to it, a prospect that cannot be reliably discounted.

Unless and until some new shred of evidence surfaces that can definitely link a particular Mint employee to the five nickels in question, with no eyewitness and no smoking gun, this unsolved whodunit will have to remain an open cold case file.

Along with the questions of who, when, how, and why, a central issue is this: Was the creation of the five 1913 Liberty Head nickels illegal or just sneaky?

Chapter 3 References

Bowers, Q. David. 1975. "The Legendary 1913 Liberty Head Nickel," *Bowers and Ruddy Galleries Rare Coin Review* 22 (Spring), p. 32-37.
— Bowers. 1980. *Adventures with Rare Coins* (Los Angeles: Bowers and Ruddy Galleries, Inc.), pp. 6-15.
— Bowers. 1983. *United States Gold Coins, An Illustrated History* (Wolfeboro, New Hampshire: Bowers and Merena Galleries), p. 84.
— Bowers. 1996. *"The Louis E. Eliasberg, Sr., Collection,"* Bowers and Merena Galleries auction catalog (May 20-22), pp. 221-228.

Breen, Walter. 1988. *Complete Encyclopedia of U.S. and Colonial Coins* (New York: Doubleday), pp. 254.

Cassel, David. 2003. "Glossary of Numismatic Terms." Accessed November 2003 at www.uspatterns.com/uspatterns/glossary1.html.

Dannreuther, John. 2004. Email message (January 12).

Evans, George G. 1885. "Coining Press" illustration by F.B. Schell, *Illustrated History of the United States Mint* (Philadelphia: Dunlap & Clark), p. 38.

Evans, Torence. 2003. "Freemasonry - The 1913 Liberty Head Nickel & Its

Masonic Link", The Masonic Forum on AOL web site. Accessed December 2003 at members.aol.com/forumlead/History/Freemasonry-1913.htm

Greensboro (N.C.) Daily News. 1959. "1913 Liberty Head Nickel Is Rare; Only Five Minted" (October 10).

Hughes, Brent H. 1971. "The 1913 Liberty Head Nickel," Slide presentation. Manuscript courtesy of Eric P. Newman.

Julian, R.W. 1987. Coin World (April).
— Julian. 2001. "Hackel's Mint Record Destruction." Numismatic Bibliomania Society E-Sylum web site (Vol. 4, No. 22, May 27), accessed November 10, 2003 at www.coinbooks.org/club_nbs_esylum_v04n22.html.
— Julian. 2003. Email (December 2).

Legal Information Institute. 2004. United States Code. Web site accessed February 11, 2004, at www4.law.cornell.edu/uscode/.

National Archives and Records Administration. 2004. Web site accessed February 11, 2004, at www.archives.gov/welcome.

Numismatic Scrapbook Magazine. 1953. "Looks Like There Are Six 1913 Liberty Head Nickels" (December 1953). p. 1169.

The Numismatist. 1913. "Proceedings of the Annual Convention" (Vol. XXVI, No. 10, October), pp. 487-503.
— The Numismatist. 1928. "Two Extreme Rarities in Recent U.S. Coinage" (Vol. XLI, No. 4, April), p. 236

Peters, Gloria, and Cynthia Mohon. 1995. The Complete Guide to Shield & Liberty Head Nickels (Virginia Beach, Virginia: DLRC Press), pp. 164-172.

Ratzman, Leonard J. 1964. "The Buffalo Nickel, A 50-Year-Old Mystery," Whitman Numismatic Journal (Vol. 1, No. 5, May), p. 21

Ruddy, James F. 2005. Photograde (Irvine: Zyrus Press, Inc. by license from Bowers and Merena Galleries, Irvine, California), p. 14

Taxay, Don. 1963. Counterfeit, Mis-Struck, and Unofficial U.S. Coins (New York: Arco Publishing Company, Inc.), p. 15.
— Taxay. 1966-69. The U.S. Mint and Coinage (New York: Arco Publishing Company, Inc.), pp. 340-346.

Weinberg, Fred. 2003. Interview (November 26).

Weinman, Greg M. 2004. Email (February 6)

- Chapter Four -

A QUESTION OF LEGITIMACY

"Our official coinage register reflects no production of Liberty Head nickels in 1913 and it is obvious…that none was authorized." The letter from the Director of the Mint makes clear that the five 1913 Liberty Head nickels hold no official standing as legitimate coins. Therefore, by law they are still the property of the U.S. Mint.

The letter, dated July 3, 1962, was from Eva Adams, Director of the Mint, to Eric P. Newman, president of the Eric P. Newman Education Society. Newman was the last person to own all five of the 1913 Liberty Head nickels. An almost identical letter was sent to Don Taxay on June 5, 1962.

Adams' letter, which refers to information gleaned from the National Archives in Washington, confirms several points enumerated in R.W. Julian's account with these statements:

— On December 13, 1912, the then Director of the Mint, George E. Roberts, instructed the Superintendent of the United States Mint at Philadelphia: "Do nothing about five cent coinage for 1913 until the new designs are ready for use." Again, on January 18, 1913, the Director instructed the Superintendent at Philadelphia, in reference to the five cent piece: "Do nothing about any coinage at Philadelphia until you receive formal instructions to that effect."
— Formal authority for commencement of nickel coinage in calendar year 1913 was sent to the Superintendent of the Philadelphia Mint on February 19, 1913.
— The official coinage register of the Bureau of the Mint shows that no nickel coinage was produced from January 1 until February, 1913. Coinage of the new nickel design commenced that year at Philadelphia on February 21st, at Denver on February 24th, and at San Francisco on March 3rd.

1913 Liberty Head Nickels Are Not Coins

The letter proves that the 1913 Liberty Head nickels, in the strictest sense, are not really coins, at least not recognized as legal tender coins by the U.S. government. Since they were never registered in Mint records as having been produced, they could not have been "monetized" as official U.S. legal tender coins. The product of the U.S. Mint does not officially become money until it is "circulated" by being accepted by the Federal Reserve Bank and a receipt issued.

Greg M. Weinman, legal counsel for the Mint, stated in an email to the authors the government's definition of when a stamped disk becomes an actual coin:

> Issuance is the act of making a coin available for use as legal tender. It occurs at the point in time at which the Government no longer holds title to the coin, and after which title to the coin lawfully can be held by whomever possesses it. It requires monetization (i.e., receipt of its full face value) and, if applicable (such as with a numismatic issuance), the receipt of any additional charge imposed by the Government.

In his 1971 slide presentation, Brent Hughes declared:

> Actually, if we wish to be technical about it, the 1913 Liberty Head nickel does not exist at all. If you were to write to the Mint tomorrow about this coin, you would probably receive the same answer that has been given out for years — "no Liberty Head nickels dated 1913 were officially issued by the United States Government." As numismatists we know that a coin is a piece of metal marked and issued by governmental authority to be used as money; therefore by definition the 1913 Liberty Head nickel is not a coin, it never was and it never can be. Technically it is nothing but a token. It is a tragedy of numismatics that collectors are still willing to pay huge prices for these so-called coins. Many of us have seen the coin, attended the ANA convention where one was sold, or at least been part of a whole generation of Americans which actually believed that many of these coins were in circulation just waiting to be discovered.[18]

"Technically, they are not coins," John Dannreuther agreed. "They are not even money." Dannreuther is considered a top authority on coins and was one of the six experts on the team that examined all five 1913 Liberty Head nickels for the first time in more than 60 years in Baltimore at the 2003 ANA convention. "They are round stamped disks of metal. The 1913 Liberty nickels are not coins but objects of art. They are historical objects, and that's why we collect them." In other words, to collectors it doesn't matter whether the nickels are legitimate coins or not.[19] But it matters to the Mint.

---

18 Source: Eric P. Newman.

19 The semantics of whether or not the nickels are coins puts too fine a point on it for the purpose of this narrative; so for the sake of readability, the widely accepted term "coins" will be used from time to time to refer to the nickels.

The nickels were produced on the Mint premises with Mint equipment and Mint supplies. They were never emitted into circulation as real coins. That would seem to make them Mint property. And that poses the big question: Are they stolen property? Dannreuther said yes. "They were stolen from the Mint and the Mint wouldn't go after anyone because at that time it [the total value of the stolen goods] was 25 cents." Dannreuther also pointed out that it was seven years before the existence of the coins was even known publicly, just long enough that the perpetrators could not be prosecuted for the crime.

An undated handwritten note by Eric P. Newman read:

> As to the 1913 Nickel,
> In 1910 the Director of the Mint said about patterns:
> Since 1873 there was no authority
> for experimental or pattern pieces
> and those removed are without authority
> No title has passed & the pieces belong
> to the United States. (not exact quote)[20]

Some numismatic writers have soft-pedaled the legality issue attached to the 1913 Liberty Head nickels, suggesting that there was nothing wrong with some boys in the back room popping out a few souvenirs for themselves or their friends. The rationale is that it was common practice in those days, and in the context of the times, no wrongdoing occurred.

As noted earlier, Lee Hewitt said it was standard Mint practice to allow anyone in the Mint to pay eight cents (for nickels) to the proof and medal fund for each coin "and walk out of the Mint building with them." If that were the case in this instance, why was no record of the transaction made? Why was the existence of the nickels kept secret for seven years? Why did Samuel Brown refuse to reveal how he got the coins?

What Did Sam Brown Know and When Did He Know It?

Although acknowledging the suspicions cast upon Samuel Brown, Q. David Bowers tried to give Brown the benefit of the doubt, suggesting that he was an upstanding citizen unlikely to be guilty of a crime:

> It should be noted that Brown was well regarded in his time, was elected to the post of mayor of North Tonawanda, New York, and was

---

20 From Eric P. Newman's 1913 Liberty Head nickel files.

Samuel W. Brown, storekeeper at the U.S. Mint in Philadelphia when the 1913 Liberty Head nickels are believed to have been struck. Courtesy Coin World.

invited to serve on the Assay Commission[21] at the Philadelphia Mint in 1924 and 1925. No evidence has come to light that Brown was viewed with disfavor by his contemporaries or did anything of a disreputable nature at the Mint, and he seems to have been an active participant in the numismatic community.

...Mr. Brown's record of service in North Tonawanda was certainly outstanding. This, coupled with the fact that he openly advertised for 1913 Liberty head nickels, would lead one to think that Mr. Brown was secure in his position regarding the coins and risked no scandal or unfavorable investigation. It is certainly possible that he obtained the pieces legally, although perhaps not openly.

Bowers also explained away the minting of the nickels as unremarkable under practices of the day:

> For someone in the Medal Department of the Mint to have struck a few 1913 Liberty Head nickels for cabinet purposes early in January 1913 would have been neither unusual nor illegal.

No record exists at the Mint of any 1913 Liberty nickels being struck for cabinet purposes nor were any ever noted as being found in the Mint's possession. Furthermore, there should have been no reason to strike such coins in January when new designs for the year were expected at any

---

21 The U.S. Assay Commission was a committee of American citizens who met once each year to weigh and assay random samples of United States coinage for conformity to standards. The commission was disbanded in 1977 as a cost-cutting measure.

moment and the director of the Mint had twice instructed that no 1913 Liberty nickels were to be produced.

Experience has taught us that even at the highest levels of private and public trust (including the presidency of the United States), the appearance of propriety is no guarantee of innocence. Mr. Brown was no choirboy. He felt safe from the law because the seven-year statute of limitations had run out, and he could not be prosecuted for misusing or being party to misusing Mint facilities for his private purposes. There is no mistaking that he was aware of his guilt.

"I'm sure he knew at the time that what he did was illegal," said Fred Weinberg. "And it was a matter of having the intestinal fortitude to keep your mouth shut for seven years, which couldn't have been easy. At least it wouldn't be easy with our mentality today. Maybe it was easier then."

Weinberg thinks Brown and his accomplice(s) obviously knew something was wrong about it or they wouldn't have kept quiet. "They knew something was wrong, because they hand-engraved the '3' into the die. Don't forget. These were not 1913 Liberty nickel dies that were already prepared to be used and some order came down [not to produce 1913 Liberty nickels] and then they said, 'Well, gee, we've got these dies; let's strike some anyway.' They *purposely* took a 1912 die, we have to assume, and engraved a '3' into it. So that gives you premeditation right from the beginning."

Ed Reiter noted in a 1994 *COINage* item:

> It is intriguing — and possibly instructive — to note that 1920, the year when Brown announced his "discovery," marked the expiration of the seven-year statute of limitations for prosecuting anyone who might have removed the coins from the Mint in 1913.

"Mint-Made Frauds"

Eric Newman was blunt about the coins — calling them "mint-made frauds" in a 2003 interview — and even more blunt about Brown's guilt. Writing October 25, 1963, to *Coin World*, Newman said:

> The 1913 Liberty Head Nickel opinions recently published in *Coin World* on October 15, 1963 indicate that the opinions of Don Taxay and Lee Hewitt differ substantially.
>
> I believe that I am entitled to get into the melee because I still have the special leather case made for these nickels and formerly had the opportunity to study all five coins at one time.

The important fact which I think should be further emphasized is that Samuel W. Brown, original owner of all five nickels, was guilty of deceptive practices from which one could conclude that the coins were improperly or unlawfully acquired by him. He worked for the Philadelphia Mint in various capacities from December 18, 1903, until his resignation on November 14, 1913. Although a coin collector and a member of the ANA since 1906, he kept the nickels he obtained secreted for seven years and told no one about them. He obviously feared disclosure of them. He then advertised in *The Numismatist*, beginning in December 1919, to buy for $500 (later $600), 1913 Liberty nickels which were then unknown and which he knew no one else could have. Why should he want to buy such a coin when he already had five of them? ...The reason was to build up the price of the pieces he possessed.

In the summer of 1920, he showed the pieces, privately, in the special case at the Chicago ANA convention and said that the disclosure was off the record...When asked, he did not disclose how he had obtained them.

One of the nickels was exhibited at the convention, according the to the October, 1920 *Numismatist*. One man is still living who saw all of them, in 1920, and heard Brown's comment about keeping quiet about them.[22]

The foregoing actions of Brown are sufficiently deceitful to permit one to conclude that the coins were not acquired properly by him and that he knew it.

Eric Newman's notes of phone conversation with Samuel Brown's daughter,
Mrs. George Brillinger of Cleveland, Ohio. Courtesy of Eric Newman.

[22] An apparent reference to a Mr. Mike Carey, mentioned by ANA historian Jack W. Ogilvie in a letter to Don Taxay, October 14, 1963.

There is no published account of Brown ever revealing his source for the coins. Newman spoke to Brown's daughter, Mrs. George Brillinger of 21960 Lorain Rd., Fairview Park, Cleveland, on July 30, 1962. Newman's handwritten note from the call reads:

> daughter of Samuel Brown - spoke to her & she knew nothing of source of 1913 Lib Hd Nickels. She has 20 [other] coins. Her stepmother took balance.

The Debate Gets Hot

Newman and Don Taxay, joined by John J. Ford, Jr., engaged in a sharp running public debate with *Numismatic Scrapbook Magazine* editor and owner Lee Hewitt over the legitimacy of the 1913 Liberty Head nickels themselves, a controversy that remains open to question even today.

Taxay rebutted Hewitt's attempt to put a favorable light on the legitimacy of the coins and their makers. In a 1963 letter to *Coin World*, he wrote:

> I cannot accept the claim the 1913 Liberty Head nickels are trial pieces because die trials are not struck from every new pair of dies, and in modern times they are only taken when a new design is introduced. Such was not the case with the 1913 Liberty Head nickel.
>
> What Hewitt possibly had in mind were set-up pieces, though these are something quite different. Set-up pieces are the same as regular issue coins except that their relief is not fully brought up. They are simply impressions taken when setting up a press, to test the alignment of and pressure on the dies. They are only seen by the die setter and not held for examination. These set-up pieces are supposed to be immediately remelted, although they do escape from time to time, and make their way into circulation.
>
> All of the 1913 Liberty Head nickels are perfectly struck up, and show no evidence whatsoever of being set-up pieces.[23]
>
> Even if these pieces were die trials, their emission from the Mint would be no more legal than it is in their present status as pieces de caprice, and they would still be subject to confiscation upon complaint. We should not forget that the precedent for such an action was set by the government's seizure of a 1933 double eagle from Stack's auction room, March 25, 1944. The government alleged that the coin, though lawfully minted, was either stolen or, through a fraudulent breach of trust, removed from the Mint, and this decision was upheld by the court.

---

[23] Actually, the five coins are not perfectly struck up as they show variance, but Taxay's point that they are not set-up pieces is correct.

I know that nothing dies quite so hard as old ideas, and that there will always be a few apologists for the 1913 Liberty Head nickel, just as some persons still insist that the 1804 dollars were struck in the year of the date.

In Taxay's letter published October 22, 1963, Taxay he further disputed Hewitt's claim that the nickels were die trials:

There would have been no great difficulty in "getting up" a 1913 Liberty Head nickel die, as there would undoubtedly have been some Liberty Head nickel dies without the date punched in left over from the previous year. The date was not included on the nickel hub until the Indian Head-Buffalo design. As for the person or persons involved talking or reporting the affair as Hewitt suggests, this is the sheerest conjecture, and hardly logical as it would have meant their dismissal.

Since there is no record of any Liberty Head nickel dies for 1913, I would like to see Hewitt or anyone else prove that these coins were even struck before 1919!

It is hardly possible that any such trial pieces could have been taken and not destroyed, since their existence would have been known to the chief coiner and the engraver. There are records in the archives of trial pieces being taken for the Buffalo nickel, and in each case there is a notation that the pieces were destroyed in accordance with the regulation.

Set-up pieces could conceivably have been taken without the knowledge of the coiner and the engraver, but all of the 1913 Liberty Head nickels are perfectly struck up and show no evidence of having been produced this way.

Even if the 1913 Liberty Head nickels had been legally struck (as Hewitt claims, die trials) their illegal emission from the Mint would subject them, like the 1933 double eagles, to "recall" by the government.

The December 27, 1963, issue of *Coin World* compiled the array of arguments opposing Hewitt under the heading "Three Numismatic Scholars Share Comments on Controversial Nickel."

Taxay sought to clarify what he considered were the issues that had become obscured in the exchange of rhetoric in the Letters to the Editor of *Coin World*.

It was said that the source who advised me that the Mint did not set dies into the presses and strike trials or set-up pieces before the first of the year was biased. My source was, in fact, the Philadelphia Mint. Several inquiries including my own have been answered by the Mint with an emphatic assurance on this point. If, therefore, any exceptions have been lately made by the coiner, they do not represent common Mint practice.

That a comparison should have been drawn between such pieces and the 1913 Liberty Head nickels was, however, erroneous to begin with. It was publicized in *The Numismatic Scrapbook* article that if it could be shown that the Indian Head and Buffalo designs were approved before the fall of 1912, when new dies would have been made, then the die trial theory advanced would not hold.

I have gone through all the national archives relating to the adoption of the Buffalo nickel, and find, indeed, that in early July, 1912, Secretary of the Treasury MacVeagh specifically approved Fraser's designs, requesting only that the medalist lower his relief slightly, and if practicable, increase the size of the lettering which showed the denomination.

The archives also indicate that at no time after this was there any question that the new nickel would be used from the outset of 1913. The delay, until February, in actually striking the coins resulted only from the Mint's trying to please a certain vending machine company which kept asking for slight adjustments in the relief of Fraser's designs. The Mint finally gave up its efforts to satisfy the company's apparatus, and belatedly proceeded to strike the new coins.

Taxay, never one to suffer fools gladly, minced no words as he warmed to the topic, rebutting arguments attempting to legitimize the 1913 Liberty Head nickels:

> The statement printed in the letters-to-the-Editor column by a Mr. Brian Cohen to the effect that the Indian did not model for Fraser until some time between Nov. 1912 and April 1913, is an absurdity which hardly requires further comment. Fraser has already made electrotypes of his Indian Head and Buffalo design by September 1911, and his original sketches were executed at a much earlier date.
>
> In an attempt to vitiate my earlier arguments it was said that they were all given "long ago" in a talk by Mr. Ogilvie[24]. I find that this "long ago" means November 1962 [the previous year], long after my book had gone to press. Also, the facts presented were only partial.
>
> It was said that in the twentieth century, it would be too difficult for employees at the Mint to get up an artificial issue. The truth of this

---

[24] Jack W. Ogilvie, American Numismatic Association historian. Ogilvie published information about Samuel Brown in *The Numismatist*, November 1962.

statement would depend on when in the twentieth century he means. It would not apply to the 1913 Liberty Head nickel for the reason that the date was still punched into the working dies for the five cent denomination until the commencement of the Buffalo type. All that would have been required then, was for someone in the Coiner's or Engraver's department during late 1912, to take an unused, dateless die left over from the previous year and punch in the new date.[25]

Taxay raised the specter of confiscation by the government, a prospect that continues to be a worrisome risk for the current owners of the coins, a risk magnified to nail-biting proportions by the record prices being paid to own one as their reputation grows.

My reference to the Bernard trial[26] and the confiscation of the 1933 double eagle has been completely misunderstood. I was attempting to point out that even if the 1913 Liberty Head nickels should be considered as die trials (though there is no reason to do so) their emission from the Mint would still be illegal and they would be subject to confiscation.

Lastly, I should mention that I have in my possession a letter from the present Director of the Mint which states that no 1913 Liberty Head nickels were authorized to be struck. This is good enough for me!

If any of the owners of these coins, however, still have doubts on the subject, I would humbly suggest that they submit their coin, together with the accumulative data presented in this issue of *Coin World*, to the Treasury Department, and solicit its opinion on the matter.

John J. Ford, Jr., a noted collector, numismatist for New Netherlands Coin Co., and a colleague of Taxay's, weighed in with these comments:

From the year 1920, when the existence of the 1913 Liberty Head nickels was first disclosed, these coins were considered to be an artificial issue. Even more than the dubious behaviour of Samuel W. Brown, the fact that the Mint repeatedly denied responsibility for the emission, was responsible for this opinion. The coin was born bad, and its upbringing was no better.

The late B. Max Mehl, for many years, advertised to purchase 1913 Liberty Head nickels for $50 each, knowing full well that, in addition to the

---

[25] This premise conflicts with Fred Weinberg's insistence that a 1912 die was used and a "3" was hand-engraved into it. John Dannreuther also disagrees with this premise, but disagrees with Weinberg as well, suggesting that a four-digit date punch was used.

[26] Bernard vs. United States regarding seizure of a $20 double eagle coin. The government won.

original five, no more were to be had at any price. His promotional ads were actually intended to sell his $1 premium booklets, but a side effect of them was to produce numerous altered coins purporting to be 1913 Liberty Head nickels.

During the last few years it has been dinned into our ears, on the strength of "undisclosed bids," "attempts to purchase" etc. that these pieces are now individually worth in excess of $50,000. The fact of the matter is, however, that no 1913 Liberty Head nickel was ever actually sold for more than a small fraction of this amount at public sale.

To my knowledge, no dealer who ever sold this piece has even hinted at its status, and the only persons who ever undertook a defense of it either had some direct or indirect financial interest in the issue, or an emotionally based bias, predicated upon an affinity for sensationalism.

Thus, while Don Taxay's view regarding the pieces was not original, the proofs he dug up in support of it certainly are. To use a metaphor, Taxay didn't bake the cake, but he added the icing.

The controversy embroiled Hewitt, Taxay, Newman, Ford, and Margo Russell (then editor of *Coin World*) in a spirited and sometimes bitter debate on the topic. The intensity of the exchange was reflected in these excerpts from letters by Taxay to Newman:[27]

October 22, 1963: Margo Russell is so mad at me over the Coppola deal she printed the Lib. five-cent controversy without waiting for my answer to Hewitt...I think numismatics is going to hell — or in the words of the auctioneer — going — going GONE!

November 17, 1963: When I saw that Margo Russell, after refusing to publish my reply, was, on top of it, publishing provocative letters in the letter-to-the-editor column, I called her up and gave a mellifluous blast. She has agreed to publish our letters now, but is going to add one from Jim Kelly!! She promised to send me proofs first, but whether or not she will keep her promise I do not know. I don't know why she has aligned herself with these characters except, as you said and I agree, that they just don't care what garbage they print.

November 27, 1963: Yes, I certainly sent your comments re the 1913 nickel to *Coin World*. JJF[28] has also submitted some of his own. Margo's procrastination is inexcusable. She says she is going to try her best to publish them all before Xmas.

---

[27] Correspondence from Don Taxay courtesy of Eric P. Newman
[28] John J. Ford, Jr.

A few weeks ago Coin World run an exchange of ideas by Mr. Hewitt and myself regarding the legitimacy of the 1913 Liberty Head nickel. These were followed by certain comments in the letters-to-the-Editor column, with the result that the issue has again become obscured. I would therefore like to take the opportunity to clarify it.

It was said that the source who advised me that the Mint did not set dies into the presses and strike trials or set-up pieces before the first of the year was biased. My source was, in fact, the Philadelphia Mint. Several inquiries including my own (a copy of which is in the possession of Mrs. Margo Russell) have been answered by the Mint with an emphatic assurance on this point. If, therefore, any exceptions have been made lately by the coiner, they do not represent common Mint practice.

That a comparison should have been drawn between such pieces and the 1913 Liberty Head nickels was, however, erroneous to begin with. Even Mr. Hewitt admitted in his Scrapbook article that if it could be shown that the Indian Head and Buffalo designs were approved before the fall of 1912, when new dies would have been made, that his die trial theory would not hold. To please Mr. Hewitt I have gone through all the national archives relating to the adoption of the Buffalo nickel, and find, indeed, that in early July, 1912, Secretary of the Treasury MacVeigh specifically approved Fraser's designs, requesting only that the medallist lower his relief slightly, and if practicable, increase the size of the lettering which showed the denomination.

The archives also indicate that at no time after this was there any question that the new nickel would be used from the outset of 1913. The delay, until February, in actually striking the coins resulted only from the Mint's trying to please a certain vending machine company which kept asking for slight adjustments in the relief of Fraser's designs. The Mint finally gave up its efforts to satisfy the Com-

The text of Taxay's letter as published differs from a rough draft in Eric Newman's archives, in which Taxay directed his comments pointedly to Hewitt by name. The changes were made by Coin World editor Margo Russell. Courtesy of Eric Newman.

1913 Liberty Head nickel -- 2

pany's apparatus, and belatedly proceeded to strike the new coins.

The xxx statement printed in the letters-to-the-Editor column by a Mr. ~~Roger~~ Bryan Cohen to the effect that the Indian did not model for Fraser until some time between Nov. 1912 and April 1913, is an absurdity which hardly requires further comment. Fraser had already made electrotypes of his Indian Head and Buffalo design by September 1911, and his original scetches were executed at a much earlier xxxxx date.

Mr. Hewitt attempts to vitiate my earlier arguments by saying that they were all given "long ago" in a talk by Mr. Ogilvie. I find that this "long ago" means November 1962, long after my book had gone to .ress. Also, the facts presented were only partial.

Mr. Hewitt says that in the twentieth century it would be too difficult for employees at the Mint to get up an artificial issue. The xxxxixx truth of this statement would depend on when in the twentieth century he means. It would not apply to the 1913 Liberty Head nickel for the reason that the date was still punched into the wor.ing dies for the five cent denomination until the commencement of the Buffalo type. All that would have been required then, was for someone in the Coiner's ~~departmentxxxxxxx~~ or Engraver's department during XXXX late 1912, to take an unused, dateless die and punch in 1913.

Mr. Hewitt completely misunderstood my reference to the Barnard trial and the confiscation of the 1933 double eagle. I was attempting to make him rea..ize that even if the 1913 Liberty Head nickels should be considered as die trials (though there is no reason to do so) their emission from the Mint would still be illegal and subject ~~them~~ they would be to confiscation.

Lastly, I should mention that I have in my possession a letter from the present Director of the Mint which states that no 1913 Liberty Head nickels were authorized to be struck. If this isn't good enough for Mr. Hewitt, it is at least good enough for me.

~~Should any doubts remain, however, I would examine among the owners of these coins, I would humbly suggest that~~

If any of the owners of these coins, however, still have doubts on the subject, I would humbly suggest that they submit their coin, together with the accumulative data presented in this issue of Coin World, to the Treasury Department, and solicit their opinion on the matter.

December 18, 1963: I received a copy of your letter to Hewitt with interest. Hewitt is not interested in fair play and it would not be wise to give him information which he may try to use against you at a later time. I think I wrote to you that he had originally prevailed on Margo Russell not to print my replies to his nonsense. She has finally agreed to do so with some editing, and you will see them in the Monday issue, I believe. But Hewitt on receiving copies of my, your, and JJF's reply to his remarks, told her that he didn't want his name mentioned and Margo has agreed to the extent that while printing my replies she is deleting reference to Hewitt. I am really too disgusted with the whole thing to care at this point.

The feud with Hewitt didn't end there. In "Letters to the editor" in *Coin World*, August 23, 1978, Newman fired off a sly jibe at Hewitt in a note headed "A few corrections":

The 1913 Liberty nickel feature in the July 26 issue of *Coin World* aroused my curiosity. I probably should be disturbed by the description of my unique 1913 copper colored Indian Head nickel.

In column one on page 25 is a quote from Lee Hewitt in the March, 1958, *Numismatic Scrapbook Magazine*, that the coin was an "electrotype impression and not a trial striking." I wonder who checked my coin which I've had for over 35 years. What is an electrotype impression?

Then, the fifth column (no pun intended) on page 25 refers to the coin as a bronze electro-type; I've never heard of a bronze (copper and tin mixture) electrotype. No one who has seen the piece has ever called it an electrotype.

Long ago the coin was tested and its content was found to be 95 percent copper, 2½ percent zinc and 2½ percent nickel. Can someone suggest a reliable modern way to test it nondestructively? It might throw some light on the mystery in general, then my problem can be cured.

Eric P. Newman — St. Louis

Stolen Goods

The preponderance of circumstantial evidence leaves virtually no doubt that the 1913 Liberty Head nickels were created illegally and were removed from the Mint illegally. Therefore, they are, in effect, stolen property - stolen from the United States Mint. The logical conclusion must be that anyone who comes into possession of them is party to receiving stolen goods, whether or not the person has knowledge that they're "hot."

The proposition that the most celebrated coins in numismatic history could, at any time the Treasury Department chooses to enforce the law, be confiscated and legal action taken against the owners stirs instant outrage in the coin community. Still, there it is, warts and all. And it isn't going away.

At the time the nickels were made, the Mint was subject to a regulation issued July 1, 1887 by the Bureau of the Mint:

The emission of impressions of experimental dies, whether in soft metal or in metal of the same weight and fineness proper to coins of the same denomination, is unlawful except in the case of pattern pieces of such denominations of coins as are coined for general circulation during the calendar year of its date.

All impressions taken in copper, bronze, or other soft metal from an experimental die, are required to be destroyed as soon as the purpose for which it has been struck has been subserved.

The above provisions, prescribed by the "General Instructions and Regulations in Relation to the Transaction of Business at the Mints and Assay Offices of the United States," approved by the secretary of the Treasury, have been in force since May 14, 1874.

The striking of a piece in the semblance of a United States coin in a metal or alloy, or of a weight or fineness, other than prescribed by law, is a violation of section 5460 of the Revised Statutes.

The emission or offer for sale or exchange of an impression from any die of a coin of the United States, or of a proposed coin of the United States, but with a device or devices not authorized by law, whether such die has been prepared at the Mint of the United States or elsewhere, is contrary to the provisions of sections 3517 and 5461, Revised Statutes.

No impression from any coinage die of the United States struck in other metal than that authorized by law or of a weight and fineness other than prescribed by law (Revised Statutes 3513, 3514, 3515), or pattern piece bearing a legend of a coin of the United States, and bearing a device or devices not authorized by law (Revised Statutes 1516, 3517, vide Mint regulations) should be in existence longer than required for the lawful purpose for which it was authorized to be struck.

Any emission, for private or personal use or possession, from the Mints of the United States of pieces of the character above specified has been in violation of the coinage laws of the United States.

Approved:

C.S. Fairchild

Secretary of the Treasury

James P. Kimball

Director of the Mint

If the coins were struck in December 1912, as many speculate, they are illegal because they were produced in a year other than their date of issue. The 1913 Liberty nickels, because they were never authorized and, in fact, were expressly forbidden, thus carry a "device...not authorized by law" and are illegal. Because the coins were not official, they had to have been removed from the Mint "for private or personal use or possession," and thus are "in violation of the coinage laws of the United States."

It seems laughable to envision Secret Service agents swarming into the Smithsonian in Washington and the American Numismatic Association (ANA) Money Museum in Colorado Springs to seize a nickel. These venerable institutions number among the current owners of 1913 Liberty Head nickel specimens (a third specimen was on loan to the ANA in 2004). The ensuing uproar would cause a ruckus that would almost certainly enflame not only the numismatic world but the general public as well.

Nevertheless, it could happen. On more than one occasion, federal government officials have unsheathed their legal claws to let everyone know they can. Though the "G-men" haven't actually smashed down any doors, the threat is always there beneath the surface. It awaits only the trigger to set it off.

A Controversy in Kind: 1933 $20 Double Eagle

Consider the case of the 1933 $20 gold piece. The case has been a perennial headliner, rivaling the 1913 Liberty Head nickels for notoriety. Certain aspects of the case may hold precedent for the legality of owning the 1913 Liberty nickels.

The saga of the 1933 Saint-Gaudens double eagle $20 coins was launched by Executive Order 6102 signed by President Franklin Roosevelt. That infamous order declared:

> UNDER EXECUTIVE ORDER OF THE PRESIDENT
> Issued April 5, 1933
> all persons are required to deliver
> ON OR BEFORE MAY 1, 1933
> all GOLD COIN, GOLD BULLION, AND
> CERTIFICATES now owned by them to
> a Federal Reserve Bank, branch or agency, or to
> any member bank of the Federal Reserve System.

The notice issued by Postmaster General James A. Farley over the signature of Secretary of the Treasury William H. Woodin specified

"Criminal penalties for violation of Executive Order" to be a "$10,000 fine or 10 years imprisonment, or both, as provided in Section 9 of the order."

With the stroke of a pen, Roosevelt criminalized ownership of gold by Americans with few exceptions.[29] As it happened, the Mint had already struck some 445,500 $20 gold pieces dated 1933 that they then could not issue. Production was halted, and the coins were ordered melted down into gold bars. None of them were officially circulated.

Somehow, though, a few of them "escaped" the crucible and slipped away from the Mint, with the help of human hands, into the black market of coindom. When the government got wind of it, the Treasury let it be known loud and clear that owning any of the coins was illegal because they were removed without authorization from the Mint. Secret Service agents pursued the trail of the coins with relentless zeal, seizing them whenever they came on the open market. Nine of the specimens have been seized from collectors by the Secret Service since 1944.

One successful "escapee" was recently legitimized in a formal ceremony. The coin left the country with an export license issued apparently in error by the U.S. Treasury Department. The recipient of the coin was none other than King Farouk of Egypt, an avid coin collector who also numbers among the owners of 1913 Liberty Head nickels.

Legal eagles argued that the fact that a legitimate export license was granted for the coin amounted to tacit admission by the federal government that it was okay for someone to receive the coin outside the country. That it was an apparent bureaucratic slip-up, they argued, was not King Farouk's fault.

After Farouk was deposed by a military junta in 1952, the coin vanished from public view until it reappeared in 1996. Secret Service agents arrested a British coin dealer trying to sell the coin at the Waldorf-Astoria hotel in New York.

A court battle eagerly watched by coin collectors resulted in a U.S. Federal Court settlement paving the way for private ownership of the Farouk specimen of the 1933 Saint-Gaudens $20 double eagle.

The coin was auctioned by Sotheby's auction galleries New York on July 30, 2002, for a stunning $7.59 million. It is the only one of the three known specimens that is legal for private ownership (the other two are in the Smithsonian collection; four or five more have been rumored to exist, held illicitly in private hands). As the final act of legitimizing the coin and removing any question of a clear legal title, David Redden, vice chairman of

---

[29] Rare and unusual gold coins with special value to collectors were excepted, but the 1933 Saint-Gaudens $20 double eagle did not qualify as a rare coin since it was then in production.

Sotheby's, handed a $20 Federal Reserve note to U.S. Mint Director Henrietta Holsman to pay for the coin and officially monetize it. Until that moment — 6:35 p.m. New York time — the coin had been "a piece of gold struck with coin designs," said Paul Gilkes, *Coin World* staff writer.

The absurdity of that last act - paying for a $7 million coin with an essentially worthless piece of paper with $20 printed on it — underscores how capricious and idiotic the entire issue is. Most experts in the numismatic world brush aside any suggestion that the Treasury Department would seriously consider trying to confiscate the 1913 Liberty Head nickels on the same grounds as they pursued the 1933 Saint-Gaudens double eagles. They assume that the government would not risk the political backlash that would likely result. That's a naïve and risky assumption. It's a Russian roulette game.

Unpredictable Government Vigilance

A *Coin World* reader (August 25, 2003) wondered about the apparent willingness of the numismatic community and press, as well as the Treasury Department, to look the other way and ignore blatant misconduct. Dan Murdock wrote in a letter to the editor:

> [I have] one observation about the rare coin market and the public's perception about "rarities," such as the 1933 double eagle and the five 1913 Liberty Head nickels, which aren't even real coins in that they were produced illegally, by people with questionable integrity. The lack of reaction by the press regarding these matters is disturbing, but even more so is the public's acceptance of unethical behavior and the Treasury Department's inaction regarding these pieces.
>
> Am I alone in my observation here? Or am I missing some obvious reason that excuses crooks when they succeed in ripping off the American people (Mint employees, directors, etc. getting away with unethical behavior)?

The editor's response to the letter begged the question and failed to address the principle of the issue, with the somewhat lame argument that "Many rare coins trading on the market today, particularly dating to the 19th century, were produced or entered the collector market under questionable circumstances." The statement is true, but it's a non-answer. Worse, it implicitly condones winking at the law by failing to condemn the questionable practices.

The U.S. government has shown it is fully willing to enforce the letter of the law when it so chooses. The potential for confiscation hangs over the 1913 Liberty nickels like a sword of Damocles. Until that is put to rest for good, the danger lurks, maybe not in full view but always in the shadows.

"Mint Would Confiscate '64 Dollars" blared a headline in the February 27, 1973, issue of *Numismatic News*. The circumstances of the '64 Peace dollars creation bore some common characteristics with the 1913 Liberty nickels:

> U.S. Mint officials feel that 1964 Peace dollars were never lawfully issued — and they'll confiscate any that fall into their hands.

According to the item, the coins were made, then later melted. But a report surfaced in the February 6 (1973) issue of *Numismatic News*[30] that seven of the dollars somehow escaped the furnace and were offered to a West Coast dealer "some time ago." The article quoted unidentified Mint sources as issuing a clear warning to anyone who might traffic in the forbidden dollars:

> The sources said the Mint would regard these coins — "if there are" any — the same as it does the Liberty Head nickels. It wouldn't actively track them down and try to seize them, they said, but would confiscate them under Title 31 of the U.S. Code if they ever came into the government's possession — if, for example, they were submitted for authentication.

That wasn't the last word on the controversy. By June, aggressive saber-rattling by the government and angry reaction from numismatists escalated to a bitter rumble. The front page of the June 19, 1973, *Numismatic News*[31] declared "Mint Ready to Seize 1964 Dollars, Maybe 1913 'V' Nickels, Too."

> The United States Mint says it is "entitled to recover" any 1964 Peace dollars in the hands of the public since the pieces "were never issued."
>
> A spokesman would not say whether the Mint would actively seek out such coins, or whether only those sent in — for authentication, for example — would be subject to seizure.

The Mint maintained that, like the 1913 Liberty Head nickels, the '64 Peace dollars are the property of the American people.

[30] Reference material courtesy of Eric P. Newman.
[31] Source: Eric P. Newman.

Because the coins were never legally issued, it is the opinion of the general counsel of the Treasury that they continue to be the legal property of the United States.

Although the seven-year statute of limitations has expired for prosecuting anyone who may have taken the coins from the Denver Mint, Assistant General Counsel Hugo Ranta believes there is no similar statute covering the coins themselves. "The coins could still be seized," Ranta told *Numismatic News.*

The article acknowledged that the threat of seizure posed a significant worry reaching beyond the '64 Peace dollar issue:

The possibility of such seizure, on grounds that the '64 dollars were never legally issued by the Mint, has serious ramifications throughout the hobby.

The 1913 Liberty Head nickel, clandestinely manufactured and surreptitiously removed from the Philadelphia Mint, presumably would also be classified as a coin never legally issued. Ranta agrees, saying that "generally, the same principle applies."

This, conceivably, could lead to the seizure of the five 1913 "V" nickels, each of which is now valued at more than $100,000.

The reaction from at least one of the owners of a 1913 Liberty nickel was predictable:

Aubrey Bebee, the owner of one 1913 Liberty nickel,[32] thought this preposterous. "They'd have a good fight in court if they tried to take the nickel," he said.

Bebee also pointed out that the 1804 silver dollar, an existing 1933 double eagle, and numerous patterns struck but never issued by the Mint, also fall within the definition set forth by the Mint.

The Mint brushed aside any concerns about a court battle over a potential seizure and held firm to its mandate:

Nonetheless, a Mint spokesman said that "any piece not officially struck and issued" would be subject to seizure, and that this would apply equally to 1964 dollars, 1913 Liberty nickels, pattern coins, and trial strikes.

---

[32] The specimen later donated by Aubrey and Adeline Bebee to the American Numismatic Association.

"They were never officially issued, and the statutes say they remain the property of the government," the spokesman said. "The burden of proof," he continued, "would be on the holder of the coin."

That was in 1973. No seizures of '64 Peace dollars or 1913 Liberty Head nickels have occurred as of 2003, thirty years later. So, was the Mint just bluffing and blustering to prove a point? Don't count on it. Owners of coins with questionable origins would be well advised to keep looking over their shoulders.

Twenty years after the Peace dollar flap, the issue of coin seizure still nagged at the edges of the numismatic consciousness, like an itch you can't reach to scratch. David L. Ganz, then president of the ANA, revisited the nettlesome issue in his column "Law and Collectibles" in an October 4, 1993, piece headlined, "Officials claim some famous rarities illegal...Counterfeits illegal to own."[33] Ganz pointed out that there's no time limit on when the government can seize coins it considers its property:

> The government's view on coins with a mysterious pedigree when it comes to issuance by the U.S. Mint is precise: They can seize them at any time. They did so in the mid-1940s, when a Tennessee collector's 1933 $20 coin was confiscated. The collector sued.
>
> A U.S. District Court judge, in 1947 in *Barnard vs. the United States*, ruled in favor of the government. The rationale: The coin was never legally issued, gold was illegal to own, the coin was illegal to own, and hence, the government was entitled to it.
>
> The same rationale was used to persuade Sotheby's not to sell the King Farouk specimen of the same coin in Egypt. And in the mid-1970s, Hugo Ranta, then assistant general counsel of the Treasury Department, cited this to me as a reason why the J.V. McDermott 1913 Liberty Head "nickel" would be subject to seizure. "Just let them try," was what Aubrey Bebee told me at the time in an interview.

The coin cops were still baring their teeth about confiscation in 2003. A front-page headline in the August 25 *Coin World* announced "Secret Service assumes control of investigation." That was just a few weeks after the discovery of the long-missing 1913 Liberty Head nickel in Baltimore that generated worldwide publicity. The report by Paul Gilkes said the U.S. Secret Service in Philadelphia had taken over jurisdiction of an investigation into

---

[33] Source material courtesy of Eric P. Newman.

whether the government could be justified in seizing the ten known double-denomination Sacagawea dollar mule[34] error coins.

The facts of the case didn't bear directly on the 1913 Liberty nickels, but Gilkes cited a statement from the Mint's chief counsel, Daniel P. Shaver, earlier in the year that cast a shadow over ownership of the nickels:

> "Only the Secretary of the Treasury has the authority to issue coins. Unissued coins, including coins not properly issued pursuant to the secretary's authority, remain the public property of the government of the United States. Accordingly, the United States Mint's title and right to possession of such public property survives, notwithstanding larceny or other acts amounting to unlawful conversion."

The 1913 Liberty Head nickels were "not properly issued pursuant to the secretary's authority," so according to the letter of Shaver's statement, the nickels "remain the public property of the United States." Does the U.S. government have any intentions of taking action to retrieve what appears within the law to belong to the Mint?

In an email dated February 6, 2004, Greg M. Weinman[35], legal counsel for the U.S. Mint, responded to the authors' question, "What is the official position of the Treasury Department/U.S. Mint regarding the possibility of confiscating the 1913 'V' nickels?":

> Because the United States Mint has no record tending to prove that these pieces were produced in the United States Mint at Philadelphia as alleged, the United States Mint currently has no position concerning private ownership of them. By contrast, the United States Mint had records establishing that 1933 double eagles were produced in the Philadelphia facility but never issued. Thus, that coin could not be privately owned until it was officially issued in 2002.

On the face of it, this statement from the Mint would seem to resolve the issue of confiscation in this case. It says that since no record that can be found that the coins were produced by the Mint, they don't exist officially. They aren't real coins, so the Mint has no jurisdiction over them.

---

[34] A mule is a coin struck using two different dies for the opposites sides that were not intended to be used together.

[35] Greg Weinman was involved in the monetization of the lone 1933 Saint-Gaudens double eagle and received on behalf of the Mint a 20-dollar bill in payment, thus legitimizing private ownership of the coin.

The question is, though, is this interpretation the final word? This position differs from the statements made by Hugo Ranta of the Mint legal staff in 1973. So it would appear that the safety of owning these nickels depends on who occupies the Mint's legal office at the time.

Then there's the Secret Service, which can have its own ideas independent of the Mint about what steps if any it might take about the Liberty Head nickels. Keep in mind the headline on Paul Gilkes *Coin World* story about the Sacagawea dollar mule error coins — "Secret Service assumes control of investigation." That suggests that the Secret Service can seize control of a matter regarding U.S. money whenever it chooses, regardless of what the Mint says. The Mint produces; the Secret Service enforces.

Would the solution to the dilemma be as simple as the owners of the 1913 Liberty Head nickels paying five cents to the U.S. Mint Director? The precedent of the 1933 Saint-Gaudens double eagle would seem to make it possible. It's an interesting prospect.

Perhaps there could be another grand ceremony, with all of the nickel owners meeting with the Director on the steps of the Philadelphia Mint to exchange nickels and put the issue to final rest. However, this may not be considered by the Mint to be appropriate, given its interpretation (in 2004) that the government has no official ties to the 1913 Liberty Head nickels.

The Bare Facts

Filtering out the hearsay, myth, misinformation, and speculation, what remains are the reliable facts:

1) No 1913 Liberty Head nickels were authorized by the U.S. Mint.
2) Five 1913 Liberty Head nickels were struck in direct violation of an order given twice by Mint Director George E. Roberts that none were to be produced.
3) Since the nickels were not authorized and were expressly prohibited, they were struck illegally.
4) The nickels were never monetized, are not legal tender coins, and remain the property of the U.S. Mint.
5) The nickels were removed from the Mint illegally. They were, and are, stolen property.
6) Samuel W. Brown was in possession of the five 1913 Liberty Head nickels; therefore, he received stolen goods.
7) Neither Brown nor any co-conspirators were ever charged with violating the law. Brown got away scot-free.

The bare facts don't resolve whether or not Brown was a clever mastermind who schemed an elaborate plan that took years to execute, or was merely an opportunistic Mint employee who took advantage of a tempting moment and had the infinite patience to play it out to a profitable conclusion.

An examination of what is known about Brown's life reveals no hint of his being a master criminal, nor even guilty of so much as jaywalking. Yet, he was always secretive and evasive about how he came to own the 1913 Liberty Head nickels.

Chapter 4 References

Adams, Eva. 1962. Letter to Eric P. Newman (July 3).

Bowers, Q. David. 1975. "The Legendary 1913 Liberty Head Nickel," *Bowers and Ruddy Galleries Rare Coin Review* 22 (Spring), p. 32-37.
— Bowers. 2002. *More Adventures with Rare Coins* (Bowers and Merena Galleries), p. 316-317.

Coin World. 1963. "Three Numismatic Scholars Share Comments On Controversial Nickel" (December 27), p. 26.

Dannreuther, John. 2003. Interview (October 2).

Ganz, David L. 1993. "Officials claim some famous rarities illegal," *Coin World* (October 4).

Gilkes, Paul. 2002. "1933 double eagle brings $7.59 million!" (posted July 30, 2002), CoinWorld.com web site. Accessed December 5, 2003, at www.coinworld.com/news/081202/News_bulletin1.asp.
— Gilkes. 2003. "Secret Service assumes control of investigation," *Coin World* (August 25), pp. 1, 18.

Murdock, Dan. 2003. "Unethical behavior," Letters to the editor, *Coin World* (August 25), p. 11.

Newman, Eric P. 1962. Handwritten note of phone conversation with Samuel Brown's daughter, Mrs. George Brillinger (Cleveland)
— Newman. 1978. Letter to the editor "A few corrections." *Coin World* (August 13), p. 4.

Numismatic News. 1973. "Mint Would Confiscate '64 Dollars," (Vol. XXI, No. 9, February 27), p. 1, 8.
— *Numismatic News*. 1973. "Mint Ready to Seize 1964 Dollars, Maybe 1913 'V' Nickels, Too," (Vol. XXI, No. 25, June 19), p. 1, 48

Numismatic Scrapbook Magazine. 1971. "Liberty 1913 Nickel Offers Mystic Aura" (Vol. 37, No. 430, December 24), pp. 1158-1178.

Numismaticworld. 2003. "1933 Saint-Gaudens Auction Ignites Red Hot Coin Market at New York ANA," (Blanchard and Company , Inc. web site Numismaticworld, Vol. 4, No. 1), accessed December 5, 2003, at http://numismaticworld.net/vol4-1/article1.html.

Peters, Gloria, and Cynthia Mohon. 1995. The Complete Guide to Shield & Liberty Head Nickels (Virginia Beach, Virginia: DLRC Press), pp. 164-172.

Reiter, Ed. 1994. "Flirting with a Million," *COINage* (Vol. 9), p. 109

Taxay, Don. 1963. Personal correspondence to Eric P. Newman (October 22, November 17, December 18).

United States Department of the Treasury. 2003. "Important Events in Treasury History in November." Web site, accessed November 10, 2003, at www.ustreas.gov/education/history/events/11-nov.html.

Weinman, Greg M. 2004. Email (February 6).

Woodin, William H., Secretary of the Treasury. 1933. "Under Executive Order of the President," Publication 2-16064, U.S. Government Printing Office.

- Chapter Five -
THE MYSTERIOUS
MR. BROWN

WANTED
1913 LIBERTY HEAD NICKEL
In Proof condition, if possible.
Will pay $500 cash for one.
Samuel W. Brown,
North Tonawanda, N.Y.

T hat one-column box of text measuring less than two inches catapulted Samuel W. Brown into everlasting numismatic notoriety. The classified ad appeared in the December 1919 issue of *The Numismatist*, the official publication of the American Numismatic Association and unofficially the community forum and bulletin board for the coin world. It gave coin collectors the first clue that a 1913 Liberty Head nickel existed. There had been no hint of such a coin prior to that time.

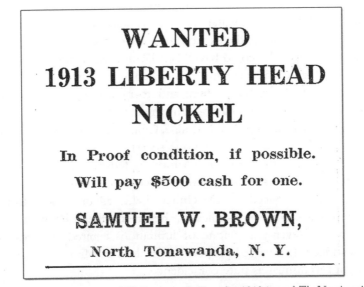

Classified ad posted by Samuel W. Brown in the December 1919 issue of The Numismatist.
The same issue also carried ads by Wayte Raymond and B. Max Mehl, who would later play a
role in the history of the 1913 Liberty Head nickels. Courtesy of the ANA.

The notice stirred a buzz of instant curiosity in the numismatic world. Was it possible such a thing existed? Where did it come from? Could there be more than one? Who was Samuel Brown? How did he know about it?

Brown's offer of $500 amounted to a princely sum at the time. According to a survey of retail prices advertised in the Morris County, New Jersey, Daily Record in 1912,[36] $500 would buy a used 1-year-old Ford Model T ($450), with change left over to buy an 8-piece dining room set ($39.50) and still have money to get decked out in a spiffy new outfit. The remaining $10 would have bought a new suit ($1.98), hat ($1.95), shirt ($.95), and a pair of custom made shoes ($5.00).

Yet, why would Brown advertise to buy something he undoubtedly had reason to believe he owned exclusively? And why did he choose 1919 to make the offer?

Brown was careful not to suggest there was more than one 1913 Liberty nickel, leaving the impression that it was a one-of-a-kind rarity. In the hindsight of history, it's obvious he was creating a market for his goods with the intention of stirring up a bidding frenzy that would drive the price as high as possible. He rightly deduced that coin collectors would leap at the chance to acquire such a rare discovery if it could be found. It was a brilliant marketing ploy.

Peters and Mohon suggested he may have had another motive with a darker side. They observed that Brown "could have had several motives, not the least would be to test the waters for the Treasury Department's reactions while he could still conceal the existence of the coins."

If that were true, he could have been laying a deniability smokescreen to cover his tracks when he eventually revealed he had the nickels. He could be evasive about where, how, when, and from whom he got the coins, leaving people to assume he had bought them from someone who wished to be anonymous. It was a plausible dodge. Coin collectors not uncommonly want to keep private treaty transactions secret — for reasons of privacy, security, and avoiding the scrutiny of snooping federal agents.

The timing of the surprise announcement is of major significance. If the coins were produced in December 1912, as deduction from the circumstantial record strongly indicates, then December 1919 would be the precise time the seven-year statute of limitations expired for prosecuting anyone who illegally removed property from the U.S. Mint. The correlation is too blatant to dismiss as pure coincidence.

---

[36] Survey conducted by Morris County Library (New Jersey) of retail prices advertised in the *Daily Record*, May 1-15, 1912.

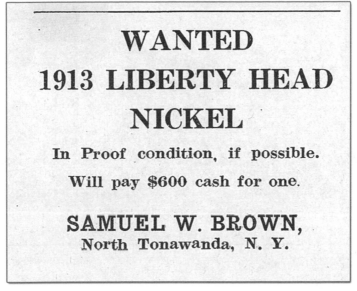

Second ad posted by Brown, in the January 1920 issue of The Numismatist, raising the offer to $600. The ad was repeated in February and March.

Apparently, Brown didn't sense any threatening reaction from the Treasury agents, because he followed up the next month with another ad in *The Numismatist*, this time upping the ante another $100. The wording of the ad was the same, with the amount offered changed to $600. The second ad, with a 20 percent richer price, most likely was intended to give the impression that desire to own the coin was intensifying, making it an even more compelling story. He persisted, re-running the second ad in February and March.

In any event, Brown was at no risk of having to pay out the price, whatever it may be, because he owned all the existing 1913 Liberty nickels.

Brown's Coin Career

Samuel W. Brown wasn't a household name when the ads appeared. He wasn't known as a coin dealer or even as an exceptional collector. However, he had established connections with people influential in numismatics. He was proposed for membership in the ANA in April 1906, while he was employed at the Mint, and was accepted as member number 808. His bid for membership was sponsored by Dr. George F. Heath, who had founded the ANA 15 years earlier in 1891, and Stephen K. Nagy. Heath's endorsement may have been perfunctory, as Peters and Mohon said it is probable that Heath and Brown never met. Brown's association with Nagy was a different situation, they said:

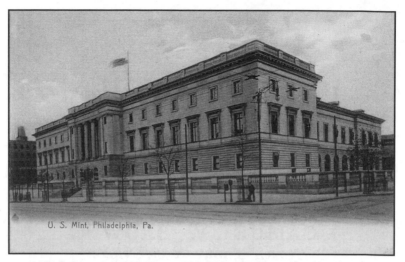

Third edition of the U.S. Mint in Philadelphia, located on Spring Garden Street between Sixteenth and Seventeenth Streets.

Mr. Stephen Nagy…is another matter altogether; and his name pops up fairly frequently, if mysteriously, in the saga of the 1913 nickels. Mr. Nagy lived in Philadelphia. He was believed to have close connections at the Mint and was involved in private purchases of restrikes from those connections. Mr. Nagy joined the ANA only six months earlier than Mr. Brown.

The connection hints that perhaps Nagy could have been party in some unknown respect to the plot to produce and market the illicit coins. Given his proximity to and affinity for the Philadelphia Mint, it's conceivable, said Peters and Mohon, that Nagy could have become acquainted with Brown during the latter's employment there:

> Where and how Mr. Brown acquired the coins, whether he had a hand in their manufacture is not proven to date. The "coincidence" of his mint employment, his sponsorship by a Stephen Nagy, who had a reputation of cultivating mint employees and officers for his own gain, and the amazing ease that he managed to "locate" these five extraordinarily improbable coins would speak to his unethical involvement at the very least in the brokerage of the coins — and implies a great deal more collaboration in the removal and sale of illegally produced mint products.

Brown had signed on at the Philadelphia Mint, then located between Sixteenth and Seventeenth Streets in Philadelphia fronting on Spring

GENERAL SERVICES ADMINISTRATION

Federal Records Center
111 Winnebago Street
St. Louis 18, Missouri

Date: July 6, 1962

In Reply Refer To: 6NRS-1

Mr. Eric P. Newman
400 Washington Avenue
St. Louis 2, Missouri

Re: Brown, Samuel W.
       DOB: 1879
       Ref: Phone call

[XX] An official transcript of Civilian Federal Employment prepared from records
maintained in the Federal Records Center is shown on the reverse side.

[ ] The enclosed correspondence is forwarded for your disposition.

OFFICIAL TRANSCRIPT OF EMPLOYMENT

Action	Effective Date	Position, Grade and Salary	Agency and Location
Appointment	12-18-03	Helper, $2.90 p/d	Treasury Department U. S. Mint Philadelphia, Pa.
Promotion	9-26-04	Asst. Curator $1000 p/a	Same
Promotion	2- 1-07	Storekeeper $1200 p/a	Same
Promotion	3- 2-08	Same, $1400 p/a	Same
Change in Designation	7- 1-10	Clerk (Storekeeper) $1400 p/a	Same
Resignation Reason: To enter business for self.	11-14-13	Same	Same

No record of Federal employment for Samuel W. Brown can be found after 11-14-13.

*Official transcript of Samuel W. Brown's record of employment at the U.S.
Mint in Philadelphia. Courtesy of Eric P. Newman.*

Garden Street, on December 18, 1903, as a "Helper" earning $2.90 per day, according to the official transcript of his employment provided by the General Services Administration to Eric Newman (July 6, 1962.)

Brown earned regular promotions and raises:

- September 25, 1904 - promoted to "Asst. Curator" at a salary of $1,000 per year.
- February 1, 1907 - promoted to "Storekeeper," with an increase to $1,200 per year.
- March 2, 1908 - salary raised to $1,400 (listed as a "Promotion" but his position was noted as "Same").

- July 1, 1910 - designation changed from "Storekeeper" to "Clerk"; his salary stayed at $1,400 per year.

The record shows Brown resigned from the Mint on November 14, 1913. The reason listed on his official employment transcript was "To enter business for self." A notation at the bottom of the record says, "No record of Federal employment for Samuel W. Brown can be found after 11-14-13."

Rumors have circulated from time to time in various sources that Brown was asked to resign or was fired. In an October 14, 1963, letter to Don Taxay, ANA historian Jack W. Ogilvie said of Brown: "There are NO RECORDS in the ANA publications as to WHY he left the mint, but again rumor persists that he was fired. You will note in my article that I stuck to published facts." Ogilvie further explained:

> I do have one record...He was a registered ANA member at the October 1919 Philadelphia Conv. Just a little over two months later the first of the five nickels appeared at the Chicago Coin Club meeting. I consulted Mr. Mike Carey who was present that night, but he is too senile at present to recall this incident. So — the question arises — were the five struck in 1913 and held for Mr. Brown until he attended the convention or struck at a later date and passed on to him during this period? In my estimation, the 1913 nickel was struck in the mint by someone having access to the coin machines and KNEW WHAT HE WAS DOING. But when?

The Respectable Mr. Brown

After leaving the Mint, Brown moved the same year to North Tonawanda, New York, some 12 miles downriver to the east-southeast of Niagara Falls, to enter "into association with Wayne Fahnestock in Frontier Chocolate Company," according to his obituary notice in the North Tonawanda *Evening News*, June 19, 1944. His function with Frontier isn't clear, but the phrasing of the reference seems to imply that he had some equity interest in the business.

It was a temporary association, in any case, because the obituary notice continued, "Later Brown was employed by Pierce-Brown, Co., retiring in 1924." It does not give details of the nature of business conducted by Pierce-Brown nor of Brown's function with the company. From the name, it would appear probable that he was a partner in the firm.

Eight years after "retiring" from the business world, Brown campaigned as a Republican candidate for mayor of North Tonawanda and won. He served as mayor of the city from 1932-33.

Brown's death on June 17, 1944, at the age of 64 was duly noted in the numismatic press. *The Numismatist* posted this notice in August 1944:

> Samuel W. Brown, 64, of North Tonawanda, New York, died on June 17 after a year's illness. A native of Pennsylvania, he had resided in North Tonawanda for many years, taking an active part in civic affairs, serving as mayor for several terms, and for ten years was a member of the Board of Education. Before leaving his native state he was employed for a time as storekeeper in the Mint at Philadelphia, and afterwards located himself in New York State. He at one time was appointed a member of the Assay Commission. His former membership in the American Numismatic Association was acquired many years ago, his number being 808.

Numismatic Scrapbook Magazine had this to say of Brown in "Liberty 1913 Nickel Story Footnotes" (June 1961)[37] :

> Born in Brownstown, Pennsylvania, Mr. Brown moved to North Tonawanda in 1913 and became associated with Wayne Fahnestock in the Frontier Chocolate Co., Payne avenue. Later he was associated with the Pierce-Brown Co. on River road, a building occupied in 1944 by the Crane Co. He retired in 1924.
>
> He was a member of Sutherland Lodge No. 826, F. & A.M. of which he was past master. He served as district deputy grandmaster of the Niagara Orleans district and was a member of the Buffalo consistory, the Ismailia temple and the Shrine club of the Tonawanda.
>
> His widow, Carry B. Brown, and a daughter, Mrs. George Brillinger, Cleveland, Ohio, survived. Funeral services were conducted by the Rev. G. Howard Mickelsen of the North Presbyterian Church. Burial took place in Brownstown.

Thief or Model Citizen?

The mysterious Mr. Brown confounds understanding. Just when you think you have him pegged as a crafty, scheming thief, he conducts the rest of his life in what appears to be a completely exemplary manner. Was his adventure into crime merely a one-time fling of youth? Or did he learn valuable lessons of how later to avoid not only being detected of questionable dealings but to conceal even the deeds themselves so not even a question of suspicion would ever be raised?

---

[37] Excerpt courtesy of Eric P. Newman.

This much we know: while he was busy establishing himself as a model citizen of North Tonawanda, Mr. Brown was playing out the scheme he had put into play years earlier in Philadelphia. After stirring up a buzz of curiosity among coin collectors with his two ads in *The Numismatist* offering to pay a handsome price for a 1913 Liberty Head nickel, Brown kept silent on the coins for several months.

Then he registered to attend the August 1920 ANA convention in Chicago. It was time to play the next gambit in his clever game.

Public Sees Mystery Nickel for the First Time

The public got its first ever view of an actual 1913 Liberty Head nickel at the August 1920 Chicago show.[38] Brown displayed one of the nickels, perhaps to prove they existed. He apparently did not intend to sell the coin.

The October 1920 issue of *The Numismatist* described Brown's and his coin's appearance in its "Notes of the Convention":

> Samuel W. Brown of North Tonawanda, N.Y., was present for a short time on Monday. He had with him a specimen of the latest great rarity in U.S. coinage — the nickel of 1913 of the Liberty Head type. It was among the exhibits the remainder of the Convention, with a label announcing that it was valued at $600, which amount Mr. Brown announced he is ready to pay for all proof specimens offered to him. An explanation of its rarity is that at the close of 1912, the mint authorities not having received orders to use the dies of the buffalo type nickel at the beginning of 1913, prepared a master die of the Liberty Head type dated 1913, and from this master die a few pieces — believed to be five — in proof were struck. None of these are believed to have been placed in circulation.

The notice reveals several crucial points.

The first is that it very obviously describes the display of a single 1913 Liberty Head nickel. One of the most pervasive bits of misinformation that continues to circulate in the numismatic press is that the public first saw all five of the nickels at the 1920 Chicago convention. The myth has been told and retold by even the most venerable of numismatic writers until it has become accepted as fact.

---

[38] As noted in Chapter 3, a 1928 item in *The Numismatist* mentioned a display of the nickels "by a gentleman who showed them at the Detroit Convention of the A.N.A. in August, 1913." However, no other references could be found to corroborate this appearance of the coins.

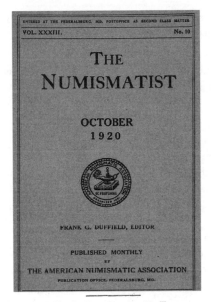

ENTERED AT THE FEDERALSBURG, MD, POSTOFFICE AS SECOND CLASS MATTER
VOL. XXXIII.   No. 10

THE
NUMISMATIST

OCTOBER
1920

FRANK G. DUFFIELD, EDITOR

PUBLISHED MONTHLY
BY
THE AMERICAN NUMISMATIC ASSOCIATION
PUBLICATION OFFICE, FEDERALSBURG, MD.

Samuel W. Brown of North Tonawanda, N. Y., was present for a short time on Monday. He had with him a specimen of the latest great rarity in U. S. coinage—the nickel of 1913 of the Liberty Head type. It was among the exhibits the remainder of the Convention, with a label announcing that it was valued at $600, which amount Mr. Brown announced he is ready to pay for all proof specimens offered to him. An explanation of its rarity is that at the close of 1912, the mint authorities not having received orders to use the dies of the buffalo type nickel at the beginning of 1913, prepared a master die of the Liberty Head type dated 1913, and from this master die a few pieces—believed to be five—in proof were struck. None of these are believed to have been placed in circulation.

The Numismatist, October 1920, notes the appearance of a 1913 Liberty Head nickel for the first time, displayed by Samuel Brown at the Chicago convention.

The item refers to "the nickel," in the singular case, saying "It" (again singular) was among the exhibits with a label announcing "it" was valued at $600. The item further states that Mr. Brown said he would pay that amount "for all proof specimens offered to him." That would imply that he intended the public to believe he had only one of them and sought the others, "believed to be five." The most obvious source for the number of coins existing would have to have been Brown himself. If there were "believed" to be only five of them, and he was still offering to buy some, then logically he could not have been displaying all five of them at the convention.

Second, the notice introduces the potential cover story, most probably proposed by Brown, that the coins were the result of advanced preparations as part of a normal mint procedure. It appears to be an effort to legitimize the coins.

Third, this is the first time the number of 1913 Liberty nickels — five — was publicly specified.

The source of the misconception about how many 1913 Liberty nickels Brown revealed in Chicago might have been an erroneous description of the event published 15 years later, according to Peters and Mohon:

> It is probable that an account in the Numismatic Scrapbook of a Chicago Coin Club meeting in 1935 is the source of reports, apparently inaccurate, that more than one coin was displayed:
>
> "The 1913 Liberty Head Nicked [sic] was the sensation of the American Numismatic Association Convention held in Chicago in 1920. Some gentlemen [sic] from New York State exhibited either six or eight specimens of this famous rarity. He left one with Mr. Alden Boyer for several months; in requesting its return the owner asked that it be expressed and insured at $600.00" (Numismatic Scrapbook, May 1935)
>
> The above report contributed greatly to the mass of misinformation that has mislead researchers for years.

Notwithstanding careless spelling, the accuracy of the *Scrapbook* account is called into question by the ambiguity of the number of coins reported to have been displayed — "six or eight" — and the amount of insurance requested ? $600 rather than $750 as requested in a letter to Boyer by Brown (quoted in *The Numismatist*, January 1921):

> Dear Mr. Boyer,
>
> I would appreciate it very much if you would return the 1913 Liberty head nickel you have with your coins in the Masonic Temple vault in your city. I have a deal pending for the sale of this coin, and it is necessary that I have it within the next ten days. If you will, kindly send it to me express, charges collect, and estimate the value at $750. Thanking you for your courtesy in this matter."
>
> [Signed Samuel Brown]

It is not known what the relationship of Samuel Brown and Alden Boyer was (except that it may have been a fraternal Masonic connection), why Brown entrusted the specimen to someone else for that period, and what transpired with the "pending" deal to sell the coin at that time.

A possible cause of confusion about how many coins were displayed publicly at the 1920 convention might be a possible leaked account of a private luncheon meeting, supposedly "off the record," in which Brown discussed the coins with a handful of confidants and may have showed the coins to the group, as described in an undated handwritten notation by Eric Newman:

Vernon Sheldon — says 8/16/61 Atlanta ANA Convention
    Sheldon saw case with 1913 Liberty Head nickels
in 1920 at ANA Convention in Chicago.
    Says Samuel Brown was not ANA member
and was a mint employee — a janitor, this Vernon
learned from Zerbe.
    Says Ira Reed knew about 1913 Lib Head
Nickels.
    Boyer left 1913 nickels in his safe deposit for over a year
after the Chicago ANA convention & the ads were to find out
if there were any more outstanding.
    At a luncheon in Chicago at which Alden Boyer, Ed Wilson
[Farran] Zerbe, Vern Sheldon & others 1913 nickels were discussed
    Ira Reed was close to mint employees & was
            investigated by govt
Vern heard Brown say that showing of 1913 nickels in Chicago was
off the record. Brown teased Boyer about buying
them but would never offer them for sale.
    Ira Reed was investigated again after the nurled [sic] edge 1¢ and 5¢
of 1937 showed up & he quit the coin business. Secret Service has big file
on Reed

In a July 10, 1962, letter to Newman, Vernon Sheldon wrote:

I have not been able to get any secret service data on Ira Reed except that I know he was investigated with respect to the 1933 double eagle and the 1937 milled edge cents and nickels.

Peters and Mohon referred to this meeting, but with a date several months earlier:

Just for the record, there is mention of a coin club meeting — possibly in December 1919 — at which Vernon Sheldon, Ira S. Reed, and Boyer were present where Brown displayed all five of the 1913 nickels.

Even if it was a club meeting, it could hardly be called a public display, since it was a closed gathering and supposed to be "off the record."

Notes by Eric P. Newman of conversation with Vernon Sheldon describing a 1920 Chicago meeting with Samuel Brown at which the five 1913 Liberty nickels were probably shown. Coustesy of Eric Newman.

Numismatic News Managing Editor Robert R. Van Ryzin examined what is known and not known about the 1913 Liberty Head nickels in an October 15, 1993, article and observed:

> Unfortunately, no written record apparently exists proving that Brown had all five coins at the convention. Word has been passed from generation to generation that this was indeed the case, but there is no primary evidence, only hearsay.

The distinction of being first to display all five nickels openly in public probably should go to the Rochester (NY) Numismatic Association, which bills itself as "the oldest, continuously active coin club in the United States," founded January 4, 1912.

William D. Coe, past president of the Rochester group, wrote in a letter to *Numismatist* in October 2003:

Unless additional references surface, I claim that the Rochester Numismatic Association has the distinction of being perhaps the only local coin club to have had all five nickels displayed at a regular meeting.

Coe's source for the claim was a program booklet from the May 1965 Empire State Numismatic Association 30th Anniversary Convention hosted by the Rochester Numismatic Association. The occasion attracted a display of one of the 1913 Liberty nickels, identified as the McDermott specimen. The program also said:

> In 1920, Samuel Brown of North Tonawanda, N.Y., attended a meeting of the Rochester Numismatic Association held in the old Rochester Museum in Edgerton Park and there laid out 5 of these rare coins to the amazement of the members.

That was the last recorded instance of a public display of all five 1913 Liberty Head nickels until July 2003, more than 80 years later.

After taking great pains to make a big splash publicizing the nickels in 1920, Samuel W. Brown fell strangely silent on the coins. Except for a notation in *The Numismatist* in January 1921 about his letter to Alden Boyer, nothing more was heard of them publicly for the next three years. August Wagner broke the silence at the end of 1923.

Chapter 5 References

Coe, William D. 2003. Letters: "Rochester Club Viewed American Legends in 1920" (Vol. 116, No. 10, October), p. 14

Davis, M.D., Chief of Reference Service Branch, General Services Administration. 1962. Official transcript of employment of Samuel W. Brown (July 6, 1962).

Empire State Numismatic Association. 1965. Convention program: "A Distinguished Visitor" (May).

Provided via email by William D. Coe.

Evans, Torence. 2003. "Freemasonry - The 1913 Liberty Head Nickel & Its Masonic Link", The Masonic Forum on AOL web site. Accessed December 2003 at members.aol.com/forumlead/History/Freemasonry-1913.htm

Morris County Library . 2003. "How much did it cost in Morris County, New Jersey?" Web site, accessed September 2003 at www.gti.net/mocolib1/prices/1912.html.

Newman, Eric P. Handwritten note re: ownership title to 1913 Liberty nickels (undated).

— Newman. Handwritten note (on Edison Brothers Stores, Inc. letterhead) re: 1920 convention (undated).

The Numismatist. 1919. Samuel W. Brown classified ad (Vol. XXXII, No. 12, December), p.513.

— *The Numismatist.* 1920. Samuel W. Brown classified (Vol. XXXIII, No. 1, January), p. 44

— *The Numismatist.* 1920. Samuel W. Brown classified (Vol. XXXIII, No. 2, February), p. 90

— *The Numismatist.* 1920. Samuel W. Brown classified (Vol. XXXIII, No. 3, March), p. 131

— *The Numismatist.* 1920. "Notes of the Convention," (October), p.466.

— *The Numismatist.* 1921. "The Rare 1913 Nickel" (January), p. 17.

— *The Numismatist.* 1944. Samuel W. Brown obituary notice (August), p. 707.

Numismatic Scrapbook Magazine. 1973. "Liberty 1913 Nickel Story Footnotes" (April), pp. 368-372.

Ogilvie, Jack W. 1963. Letter to Don Taxay (October 14). Letter provided by Eric P. Newman.

Peters, Gloria, and Cynthia Mohon. 1995. *The Complete Guide to Shield & Liberty Head Nickels* (Virginia Beach, Virginia: DLRC Press), pp. 164-172.

Smith, Pete. 1992. *American Numismatic Biographies* (Minneapolis, Minnesota: Remy Bourne-Ramm Communications, Inc.), p. 37.

Van Ryzin, Robert R. 1993. "Tale of 1913 Liberty Head nickel fit for Hollywood." *Numismatic News* (October 15), p. 16.

#1 Smithsonian Specimen

Courtesy of The Smithsonian Institute and Tom Mulvaney.

#2 Hawn Specimen

Courtesy of The American Numismatic Association and Legend Numismatics.

Courtesy of The American Numismatic Association and Dwight Manley.

#3 Eliasberg Specimen

#4 Walton Specimen

Courtesy of The American Numismatic Association and Cheryl Myers.

#5 ANA Specimen

Courtesy of The American Numismatic Association.

1913 LIBERTY HEAD NICKEL
OWNER REGISTRY

The "Set" Period

Samuel W. Brown
1913-1924
|
August Wagner
1924-1926
|
Stephen K. Nagy
1926
|
Wayte Raymond
1926
|
Col. E.H.R. Green
1926-1941
|
Eric P. Newman &
B.G. Johnson
1941-1943
|

The "Single" Period

#1 Smithsonian Specimen	#2 Hawn Specimen	#3 Eliasberg Specimen	#4 Walton Specimen	#5 ANA Specimen
F.C.C. Boyd 1943-1944	James Kelly 1943	Eric P. Newman 1943-1949	James Kelly 1943	James Kelly 1943
Abe Kosoff/Abner Kreisberg 1944	Fred Olsen 1943-1944	Abe Kosoff/Abner Kreisberg 1949	Dr. Conway A . Bolt, Sr. 1943-1945	J.V. McDermott 1942-1967
King Farouk 1944-1952	B. Max Mehl 1944	Louis Eliasberg, Sr. 1949-1976	Winston-Salem Businessman 1945	Aubrey/Adeline Bebee 1967-1989
Government of Egypt 1952-1954	King Farouk 1944-1946	Eliasberg Estate 1976-1996	George O. Walton 1945[39] -1962	American Numismatic Association 1989...
Sotheby's 1954, Lot 1695	Numismatic Fine Arts 1946, Lot 1058	Bowers and Merena 1996, Lot 807	Walton Estate 1962-1965	
Sol Kaplan/Abe Kosoff 1954-1955	King Farouk 1946-1947	Jay Parrino 1996-2002	Melva W. Givens 1965-1992	
Norweb Family 1955-1978	B. Max Mehl/Will W. Neil Auction 1947, Lot 2798	Superior Galleries 2002, Lot 728	Givens Estate 1992...	
Smithsonian Institution 1978...	Edwin H. Hydeman 1947-1961	Dwight Manley/ California Gold Marketing Group 2002-2003		
	Abe Kosoff/Abner Kreisberg 1961-1972	Edward C. Lee 2003-2005		
	World Wide Coin Investments (And Bowers & Ruddy) 1972-1978	Legend Numismatics 2005...		
	A-Mark/Robert L. Hughes Enterprises 1978			
	Superior Stamp & Coin 1978			
	Dr. Jerry Buss 1978-1985			
	Superior Galleries 1985, Lot 366			
	Reed Hawn 1985-1993			
	Stack's 1993, Lot 245			
	Dwight Manley/ Spectrum Numismatics 1993-2002			
	Legend Numismatics 2002-2004			
	Anonymous 2004...			

Table of owner registry for 1913 Liberty Head nickels. The Walton Specimen (#4) holds the record for being held the longest in a family succession — 59 years to date. The Eliasbergs held their nickel (#3) for 47 years.

---

[39] Date variously reported as 1945 and 1946. No written record has been found to establish the true date.

- Chapter Six -

THE "SET" PERIOD:
BEGINNING OF AN ENIGMATIC PEDIGREE

The pedigree of the 1913 Liberty Head nickels can be divided into two distinct period classifications: The "Set" Period when the coins changed ownership together as a set, and The "Single" Period after the set was split up and sold to separate owners. Although certain individuals have owned more than one of them at different times, no one person has owned all five of them at the same time since the set was broken up in 1943.

The "Set" Period lasted just twenty years, from 1923 to 1943.

Samuel W. Brown
(b. ca. 1880, d. 6-17-1944)

After stirring up a tempest in 1920 by revealing the existence of the 1913 Liberty Head nickels, Samuel W. Brown inexplicably clammed up about the coins. Except for his cryptic note to Alden Boyer mentioning "a deal pending for the sale" of one of the coins, the record is silent on his involvement with the nickels from that point forward.

Did he get wind that federal agents were on his tail and decide to lay low? Was he being coy to let the collector buzz build up the price he could get for his distinctive nickels? Or did he simply get busy in other pursuits and put the coins aside for awhile? Only Mr. Brown knew his motives, and he can no longer reveal them even if he were so inclined.

August Wagner

The public was kept in the dark about the whereabouts and status of the nickels until they were exposed by the following ad placed inconspicuously by August Wagner in *The Numismatist* in December 1923:

FOR SALE
Five (5) Five-Cent Liberty
Head 1913 Coins. Proof.
The only Five-Cent Liberty Head
Coins of this design and year in existence.
AUGUST WAGNER
31st and York Sts.,
Philadelphia, Pa.

115

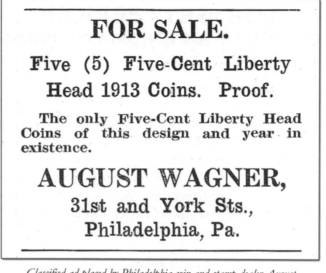

Classified ad placed by Philadelphia coin and stamp dealer August Wagner in The Numismatist. The same ad appeared in three consecutive issues from December 1923 to February 1924.

The same ad appeared two more times, in January and February 1924. It was tucked in quietly among other small-space, all-text classified notices touting coins, war medals, numismatic books, paper money, and postage stamps.

The ad does not mention the asking price, but it is reported to have been $2,000. That's two-thirds of the value Samuel Brown had been stumping for in his 1920 promotional campaign.

Peters and Mohon suggest that there was more to the offer than appeared in the ad:

> There were five Liberty Head nickels offered for sale — and possibly three 1913 Buffalo nickels: one a 1913 copper pattern, later listed as Judd 1790. The other two were a Type I and Type II. The five Liberty head coins were displayed in an eight coin holder made of soft leather and hard paper board with flaps lined with high quality fabric, all in black. The price was $2000 for the set — and whether the Buffalo pieces were in the holder at the time of this sale is unknown; however, it is considered likely. It is not known how Wagner got the coins; in fact, there is remarkably little known about Mr. Wagner.

The coins were in that same holder nearly 20 years later when the set was acquired by Eric Newman and B.G. Johnson, and it included the three Buffalo nickels.

Photo of the original black leather case retouched digitally by Brent Hughes to show what it would have looked like with the coins in the slots as they appeared when Newman and Johnson acquired them. Courtesy of Eric Newman.

Eric P. Newman in a St. Louis bank vault displays the 8-coin leather holder that contained the five Liberty Head nickels and three Buffalo nickels when he and B.G. Johnson acquired them from the estate of Col. E.H.R. Green. Courtesy of Eric Newman.

117

The ad, simple and unassuming as it may appear, carries huge numismatic significance for two reasons:

1) It offers the 1913 Liberty Head nickels for sale to the public for the first time.
2) It states publicly for the first time that there are five and only five of the 1913 Liberty Head nickels.

The only way Wagner could have been so cocksure that just five 1913 Liberty nickels existed would be to have learned it from the party or parties who actually made the coins...or to have been one of those parties himself.

Who was August Wagner, and how did he get into the plot? He was a coin and stamp dealer in Philadelphia, that much is known. Beyond that, Wagner is an enigma.

He may have been a rascal adept at avoiding detection and notice of his misdeeds. Or he could have been just an ordinary fellow with an ordinary job living an ordinary life doing nothing noteworthy enough to write about. Little if anything was printed about him.

Wagner's name appears several times in correspondence among Don Taxay, Eric Newman, and Jack Ogilvie. They got curious about him and sought to determine if he had any connection with the clandestine nickel plot. They were apparently unsuccessful in making the link.

Ogilvie wrote to Taxay (October 14, 1963):[40]

> Just had an idea. About August Wagner of Phil. He may have been the missing man in the whole deal. You mention that he was a dealer. This, I do not know — BUT — he was NEVER an ANA member that is — unless after 1932 or 33. Would like to know more about him...if he was ever in the mint employ.

Newman investigated in 1962 and was advised by the General Services Administration: "We find no record of employment for August Wagner with the United States Mint."

If there were skeletons in August Wagner's closet, apparently no one discovered them. The fact that he was in Philadelphia means he could have had some prior association with Brown when the latter worked at the Mint, but there's no evidence making that connection or that Brown and Wagner even knew each other previously.

---

[40] Courtesy of Eric P. Newman.

GENERAL SERVICES ADMINISTRATION

Federal Records Center
111 Winnebago Street
St. Louis 18, Missouri

Date: July 6, 1962

In Reply Refer To: 6NRS-1

Mr. Eric P. Newman
400 Washington Avenue
St. Louis 2, Missouri

Re: Wagner, August
DOB: Not shown
Ref: Phone call

☐ An official transcript of Civilian Federal Employment prepared from records maintained in the Federal Records Center is shown on the reverse side.

☐ The enclosed correspondence is forwarded for your disposition.

☐ We have no record of having received the official personnel folder for this employee. If your records show that the folder was sent here, please tell us when it was sent and whether the name as shown above is entirely correct.

☐ Records show folder was sent to your office on:

☒ We find no record of employment for August Wagner with the United States Mint.

M. D. DAVIS
Chief,
Reference Service Branch

rao/hc

RS-108
MARCH 1961

Form reply from the General Services Administration to Eric Newman's inquiry about whether August Wagner was ever employed at the U.S. Mint. He wasn't. Courtesy of Eric Newman.

Wagner may have only been acting as an agent for Brown, according to Peters and Mohon:

> The most logical hypothesis is that Brown either sold or consigned the coins to Wagner. It is not known why Brown did not sell the coins himself even though he had obviously been manipulating the market.

This hypothesis would certainly square with the proposition that Brown was keeping a low profile to avoid attracting the attention of the law.

However, it is also possible that Wagner bought the coins or received them on consignment from an unknown owner who had acquired them from Brown. Peters and Mohon mention the possibility of an interim owner between Brown and Wagner who is not included in most pedigrees for the nickels, citing a letter from Edwin Marshall quoted in *Numismatic Scrapbook Magazine* (1972) under the title "Liberty 1913 Nickel Story Footnotes":

> In the early 1930s...I went to Henry Chapman's shop in Philadelphia. Chapman told me of purchasing these nickels [1913 Liberty Heads] from a former Mint employee and as I recall, he sold them to, or they ended up, in Colonel Green's possession.

Evidently the Chapman claim was considered questionable, because the article went on to state:

> A genealogy owners' chart in the December 1971 *Scrapbook* showed the nickel passing from Samuel Brown to August Wagner to Colonel Green, without mention of Chapman. Henry Chapman died on January 4, 1935.

The coins did, in fact, wind up in the hands of Col. E.H.R. Green, but not directly from the hand of August Wagner. According to Peters and Mohon, coin dealer James Kelly claimed in a 1967 auction catalog:

> The entire set was subsequently obtained by the late Colonel Green through dealers B.G. Johnson and J.B. [sic] Macallister.[41]

Clyde D. Mervis also mentioned that B.G. Johnson was involved in brokering the nickel set to Col. Green in a July 1968 *Numismatic Scrapbook* article, "World's Most Valuable Coin."

Eric P. Newman, who had a close, long-running association with B.G. Johnson, disputes the claim that Johnson sold the nickels to Col. Green. Asked about it in December 2003, Newman said, "To my knowledge, B.G. Johnson had no relationship or business dealings with Green and had no part in selling the set of nickels to Green. I believe Johnson would not have concealed this matter from me. I was under the impression that Green bought primarily through Wayte Raymond. Macallister did do business separately with Raymond and Johnson on many items, but Macallister, I believe, was not held in great respect, according to gossip I heard. I have no

---

[41] Apparent reference to James G. Macallister, Philadelphia coin dealer.

information whatever as to Green's source of the nickels. Fred [F.C.C.] Boyd would have known."

James G. Macallister was at one time a colleague of Wayte Raymond at the famed auction house of J.C. Morgenthau.

Walter Breen, Q. David Bowers and others name August Wagner, Stephen K. Nagy and Wayte Raymond as the chain of custody between Samuel Brown and Col. Green. Since Breen is said to have been a protégé of Raymond and could have had personal knowledge of some of the transactions, the credibility of his version of the lineage might be given extra weight. However, the issue remains open to debate.

Stephen K. Nagy

Exactly when Nagy acquired the 1913 Liberty Head nickels from August Wagner and sold them to Wayte Raymond is not certain, though it had to have occurred between 1924 and 1926, when Col. Green took possession of them.

Wayte Raymond
(b. 11-9-1886, d. 9-23-1956)

Wayte Raymond's stint as owner of the 1913 Liberty nickels was brief. He acquired them from Stephen K. Nagy apparently only for the purpose of placing them (along with three buffalo nickels in the same coin case) with Colonel Green in 1926. The page facing Samuel Brown's want ad for a 1913 Liberty Head nickel in the December 1919 issue of *The Numismatist* displayed a half-page ad for New York coin dealer Wayte Raymond, doing business under the auspices of Anderson Galleries at 489 Park Avenue. Raymond described himself as a "Dealer in rare coins of all countries."

Colonel E.H.R. Green
(b. 8-22-1868, d. 6-8-1936)

In numismatic circles, Colonel Edward Howland Robinson Green was a big man — quite literally. He stood six feet four inches and weighed in at 300 pounds.

Colonel Green acquired the 1913 Liberty nickels from Wayte Raymond in 1926 and still had them when he died on June 8, 1938, at Lake Placid, New York. Philadelphia stamp dealer Willard Snyder helped with the appraisal of the estate, which was considerable. Snyder said Green was known as a man who never let go of anything he acquired:

What also bothered collectors was that he hung on to almost everything even when he had a complete monopoly. Take the 1913 Liberty head nickels. If you were a coin collector when you were a kid you must have seen the ads in magazines which read: 'Will pay up to $10,000 for a 1913 Liberty head nickel.'

Naturally, kids went nuts examining five-cent pieces wherever they saw them. The ad was probably placed by Col. Green as a practical joke. The truth is that 1913 was the year the buffalo nickel was minted, and there weren't supposed to be any more Liberty heads. But five and only five were minted and these were illegal. The colonel owned them all. I don't think he meant to be cruel and I don't believe he was when he placed that ad. He was simply having fun, providing excitement, and creating lots of new collectors.

Snyder may have been mistaken in attributing the ads for a reward for the nickels to Colonel Green. Such rewards have been offered through the years, not least by B. Max Mehl, who spent more than a million dollars advertising to buy a 1913 Liberty Head nickel. It's questionable whether Green ever ran such an ad. The authors found no record of an ad posted by Green offering $10,000 for a 1913 Liberty nickel. He would have little motive to do so, unlike others who had their own agendas in posting the rewards. He had the nickels, was not interested in marketing them, and may not have really paid that much attention to them since they were but a few trinkets in his vast hoard of treasures.

After Green died, his collection was transferred to the First National Bank of Boston. It took eight armored cars, guarded by sixteen private guards and seven state policemen, to move the collection. His coin collection was valued at $5 million at the time, and his stamp collection at $3.5 million. F.C.C. Boyd appraised the collection in 1937. For tax purposes, the courts valued it at $1,240,299. The total estate was valued at $40 million.

B. Max Mehl, Fort Worth, Texas, coin dealer who spent over $1,000,000 seeking to own a 1913 Liberty Head nickel. Courtesy of ANA

B. MAX MEHL:
"P.T. Barnum of Numismatics"

"I plead guilty to being responsible for making this coin so famous, having used it in all of my national advertising for a period of about a quarter of a century, during which time it appeared in advertising totaling an expenditure of well over a Million Dollars!...Certainly, this great coin will prove a most gratifying source of possession to the fortunate owner and also a profitable investment as well." — B. Max Mehl, 1944

B. Max Mehl would never stand accused of excessive modesty. The Fort Worth, Texas, coin dealer became famous for his showmanship and promotional marketing brilliance, earning him the appellation as the "P.T. Barnum of Numismatics." Abe Kosoff said of Mehl, "Whatever he did, he did with a flair and a touch of class. It was always the biggest and the best or some other superlative."

Many credit Mehl with single-handedly building the coin collecting hobby into a popular culture by virtue of his standing offer to pay $50 for a nickel — a 1913 Liberty Head nickel. "Mehl's advertising campaigns planted visions of wealth in the minds of millions," wrote Beth Deisher, editor of *Coin World*, in the July 2003 *Numismatist*. "Searching pocket change in hopes of finding a 1913 Liberty Head nickel popularized coin collecting and was a major factor in establishing it as a hobby for mainstream America."

Because of the mystery surrounding the origins of the 1913 Liberty Head nickels, rumors and speculation persisted that a sixth one existed besides the five that Samuel Brown had introduced. Mehl had an uncanny nose for a good story. He seized the public imagination by

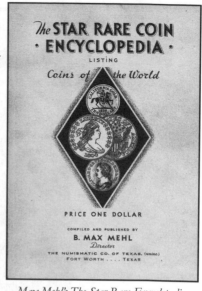

Max Mehl's The Star Rare Encyclopedia and Premium Catalog, unabashedly dubbed "An elaborate encyclopedia of the Coins of the World."

holding out the carrot of a princely reward for anyone who brought him the missing nickel:

OLD MONEY WANTED. WILL PAY FIFTY DOLLARS FOR NICKEL OF 1913 LIBERTY HEAD (NO BUFFALO)
I pay cash premiums for all rare coins. Send five-cent for Large Coin Folder. May mean much profit to you.
B. MAX MEHL
150 Mehl Bldg.
Fort Worth, Texas

In the Depression 30s, fifty dollars was a good down payment on a Ford V-8 sedan, advertised at $495, or would buy fifty pairs of men's work shoes.

Of course, Mehl knew where the five known 1913 Liberty Head nickels were all along — in Colonel Green's collection. He almost certainly had no expectations that anyone would come forward with another one. That was never his real intent.

He did buy quite a number of coins from responses to his ads, but what Mehl really intended to sell was his *Star Rare Coin*

Encyclopedia and Premium Catalog — offered at $1 a copy. "AN ELABORATE ENCYCLOPEDIA OF THE COINS OF THE WORLD" stated the cover. The publication, considered by experts to be of limited numismatic reference value, basically amount to a bid list, showing prices Mehl offered to pay for rare coins. It stirred the prospect in readers' minds of finding valuable coins in their pocket change and getting paid handsomely for them. The generous use of illustrations helped to excite public interest in coins as artistic treasures as well. It is said that Mehl made his profit more from selling books than from dealing in coins.

Though Mehl's scheme was self-serving, it did no harm to anyone and, indeed, probably introduced large numbers of people to the rewarding, wholesome, satisfying hobby of coin collecting. In 1931, *The Numismatist* Editor Frank G. Duffield wrote: "We congratulate Mr. Mehl on the tenacity with which he clings to the belief that there are many rare coins still in hiding throughout the country and that extensive advertising will bring them to light. He has been one of the largest, consistent and persistent advertisers among the coin dealers of the United States, and much of it has been along the same lines as his latest venture, though not on so large a scale. While the results are known only to him, it is assumed that he finds it a good business getter."

For all his flamboyance and hyperbole, Mehl has always been highly regarded in the coin world as a gentleman of honor. He is invariably treated kindly in the numismatic literature, described in endearing terms.

Though he spent, by his own estimate, over a million dollars looking for one, Mehl never owned a 1913 Liberty Head nickel. It wasn't for lack of opportunity; he was instrumental in handling the Hawn specimen in transactions involving King Farouk and could have owned the coin himself had he had been so inclined.

Eric Newman and Burdette Johnson

(Newman b. 3-11-1911; Johnson b. 1-2-1885, d. 2-24-1944)

Eric Pfeiffer Newman and Burdette G. Johnson were the last to own the entire set of 1913 Liberty Head nickels, acquiring them from the estate of Colonel Green. In fact, for more than 60 years — until the summer of 2003 — they were the last even to see all five nickels in one place at the same time.

When Green died in 1936, Newman, who had once met Colonel Green, wrote to the estate inquiring to buy an item from Green's collection. "I had known, since being a coin collector, that he had a wonderful collection and had been buying like crazy. I asked whether I could buy a piece of Missouri money, a United States demand note from St. Louis. But they hadn't gotten around to doing anything about the collection."

ERIC NEWMAN, COLONEL GREEN, & APPENDICITIS IN THE ANTARCTIC

Eric Newman met Colonel E.H.R. Green ("I knew him through a handshake") while a student at MIT. Green owned one of the only two radio stations in the country, in Roundtree, Massachusetts. Newman and his classmates built crystal radios to listen to it.

During this time, the Byrd Antarctic expedition communicated with contacts in America via shortwave broadcasts, answered via Green's radio station. Static was so bad that only about 20-25% of a transmission got through. MIT volunteers, including Newman, volunteered to man the station 24 hours to monitor all transmissions.

A member of the Byrd expedition got appendicitis. They were underground with oil flame heat in the 40-below-zero climate of the Antarctic, so they couldn't use ether for an operation for fear it would blow the place up. Newman and his classmates were assigned to contact doctors all over the world, including some in Norway and Sweden with experience dealing with medical emergencies in brutal cold, to find out how to do the operation at 40 below zero.

"The determination was made by the doctors that if you put two inches of felt around the body and just had a slit for the appendicitis operation, you could keep the body warm enough if you did the operation fast enough," Newman said. The MIT group relayed the information to the Byrd expedition through Green's radio transmitter. "They heated the place up, shut off the oil heaters, and it was 0 degrees when the operation was completed...but the guy lived. Colonel Green was kind of our hero for having provided the means to keep radio contact."

Newman received a response from none other than Farran Zerbe, the legendary numismatist who was Curator of the Chase National Bank (New York) Collection of Moneys of the World and publisher and editor *The Numismatist* at one time:

> So far as I know the late Colonel Green or his mother, whose collection he is said to have inherited, never endeavored to acquire any repudiated or non-negotiable notes, such as state scrip and issues of private banks and individuals. I doubt if at this time there are any Missouri items in the Green collection unless probably Missouri National Bank Notes. The popular sale items in the Green material have not been destroyed. It is probable the remainder will eventually come on the market. Just in what way I do not know, but I doubt if it will be in the near future.

Newman persisted. "I wrote again after awhile to the attorneys of the estate, and they said 'No, we will not sell you the demand note,' and said that 'You would have to buy the whole set.' They forced me to buy the Missouri money, which was separately priced. So I sent them a check and told my friend Johnson about it."

Johnson was astounded (and probably not a little pleased and proud of his protégé's coup). "He said, 'My goodness! Everyone in the U.S. has been trying to buy the Green collection or some part of it. Can you get more?'"

Newman couldn't afford to buy much, he said, but Johnson had an idea. "He said, 'I tell you what you do. If you can buy some more, we will go 50/50. You get them and put up what you can to buy it. I will put up the rest. You can take your choice of what you want, and I will take out equal value. There should be some left over for me to sell. That should give you enough money to pay for the coins you have bought.'"

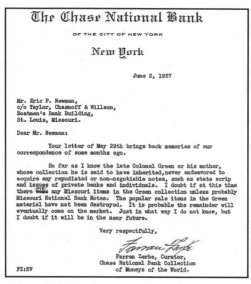

Letter from Farran Zerbe, June 2, 1937, responding to Eric Newman's inquiry about Missouri money pieces in Colonel Green's collection. Courtesy of Eric Newman.

So the informal partnership was formed. Newman was the liaison. "I marched myself to New York and started buying sections of the collection. Over a year or so, I would make five or six trips to New York. The stuff would be sent back here [St. Louis] when we purchased them. And I was wallowing in coins like nobody has ever seen the like."

Eventually Newman worked his way through the estate to Green's huge collection of nickels, consisting of some six hundred coins, along with the five 1913 Liberty nickels and three buffalo nickels in a leather case. Johnson had reservations about the 1913 Liberty nickels. "When we go to the nickel collection," Newman said, "I went to see it and arranged to buy it. But Johnson told me they knew the 1913 nickels were important. They wanted $500 for each of the five Liberty Head nickels. Johnson says, 'Don't buy them. Those are fantasy pieces. Being unauthorized, it would be risky to buy them.'

"A fantasy coin is a piece de caprice. That's the best way to describe it. In other words, something made without authority, improperly made. And that's regardless of whether it is made by an official mint or outside the mint."

After some discussion, Johnson relented partially. "He decided it was too risky to pay $500 apiece for the items and that we should offer to buy two of them at that price, and then offer $333 apiece for the other three. So I made that offer, and they accepted it," Newman said.

In correspondence to Alexander A. McKenna, Second Vice President of The Chase Manhattan Bank, Newman offered this proposal first:

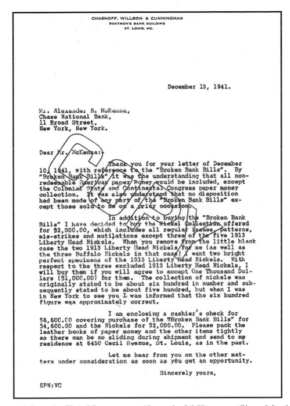

CHASNOFF, WILLSON & CUNNINGHAM
BOATMEN'S BANK BUILDING
ST. LOUIS, MO.

December 13, 1941.

Mr. Alexander A. McKenna,
Chase National Bank,
11 Broad Street,
New York, New York.

Dear Mr. McKenna:

Thank you for your letter of December 10, 1941, with reference to the "Broken Bank Bills". By "Broken Bank Bills" it was the understanding that all non-redeemable American paper money would be included, except the Colonial State and Continental Congress paper money collection. It was also understood that no disposition had been made of any part of the "Broken Bank Bills" except those sold to me on a prior occasion.

In addition to buying the "Broken Bank Bills" I have decided to buy the Nickel Collection offered for $2,000.00, which includes all regular issues, patterns, mis-strikes and mutilations except three of the five 1913 Liberty Head Nickels. When you remove from the little black case the two 1913 Liberty Head Nickels for me (as well as the three Buffalo Nickels in that case) I want two bright perfect specimens of the 1913 Liberty Head Nickels. With respect to the three excluded 1913 Liberty Head Nickels, I will buy them if you will agree to accept One Thousand Dollars ($1,000.00) for them. The collection of nickels was originally stated to be about six hundred in number and subsequently stated to be about five hundred, but when I was in New York to see you I was informed that the six hundred figure was approximately correct.

I am enclosing a cashier's check for $6,600.00 covering purchase of the "Broken Bank Bills" for $4,600.00 and the Nickels for $2,000.00. Please pack the leather books of paper money and the other items tightly so there can be no sliding during shipment and send to my residence at 6450 Cecil Avenue, St. Louis, as in the past.

Let me hear from you on the other matters under consideration as soon as you get an opportunity.

Sincerely yours,

EPN:VC

Carbon copy of letter by Eric Newman to Alexander McKenna at Chase Manhattan Bank proposing to buy the "Broken Bank Bills" and the Nickel Collection from Colonel Green's estate, minus three of the 1913 Liberty Head nickels. Courtesy of Eric Newman.

In addition to buying the "Broken Bank Bills," I have decided to buy the Nickel Collection offered for $2,000.00, which includes all regular issues, patterns, mis-strikes and mutilations except three of the five 1913 Liberty Head Nickels. When you remove from the little black case the two 1913 Liberty Head Nickels for me (as well as the three Buffalo Nickels in that case) I want two bright perfect specimens of the 1913 Liberty Head Nickels. With respect to the three excluded 1913 Liberty Head Nickels, I will buy them if you will accept One Thousand Dollars ($1,000.00) for them. The collection of nickels was originally stated to be about six hundred in number and subsequently stated to be about five hundred, but when I was in New York to see you I was informed that the six hundred figure was approximately correct.

I am enclosing a cashier's check for $6,600.00 covering purchase of the "Broken Bank Bills" for $4,600.00 and the Nickels for $2,000.00. Please pack the leather books of paper money and the other items tightly so there can be no sliding during shipment...

The Chase National Bank

OF THE CITY OF NEW YORK

TRUST DEPARTMENT
II BROAD STREET

New York   December 16, 1941.

IN REPLYING PLEASE REFER TO
1-29-168

Mr. Eric P. Newman,
    Boatmen's Bank Building,
    St. Louis, Missouri.

Dear Mr. Newman: Re: Estate of E. H. R. Green

        Your letter of December 13th, in which you enclosed
check for $6600. in payment for the collection of broken
bank bills and the nickel collection, including the two
1913 Liberty heads, has been received. These will be shipped
to you as instructed within the next day or two.

        Your offer of $1,000. for the remaining three
Liberty heads will be referred to the Co-administrators for
consideration.

                Yours very truly,

                    Alexander A. McKenna,
wf   Second Vice President.

*Letter from Alexander McKenna acknowledging receipt of Eric
Newman's check for $6,600 and an offer to buy the remaining three
1913 Liberty nickels. Courtesy of Eric Newman.*

McKenna responded by letter on December 16, 1941:, acknowledging receipt
of the $6,600 check and the offer to buy the other three 1913 Liberty nickels:

> Your offer of $1,000.00 for the remaining three Liberty heads will be
> referred to the Co-administrators for consideration.

Two days later, on December 18, 1941, a second letter followed from
McKenna advising Newman that his purchase was on the way and that his
offer for the remaining 1913 Liberty nickels was acceptable:

> We have shipped via Railway Express Agency three trunks containing
> the Broken Bank Bills and nickels which you purchased. Enclosed are keys
> to the locks of the trunks. These are being forwarded in this manner, as we
> felt this method of packing was no more expensive than having the crates
> made. Therefore, we will be glad to make a present of the trunks to you.
>   Our Co-administrators have agreed to accept your offer of $1,000.
> for the remaining three 1913 Liberty Head nickels. Upon receipt of your
> check, the coins will be forwarded to you.

Newman acknowledged on December 27, 1941, that he had received
the shipment and enclosed payment for the other 1913 Liberty nickels:

The Chase National Bank

OF THE CITY OF NEW YORK

TRUST DEPARTMENT
11 BROAD STREET

New York   December 18, 1941.

IN REPLYING PLEASE REFER TO

1-29-168

Mr. Eric P. Newman,
     Boatmen's Bank Building,
     St. Louis, Missouri.

Dear Mr. Newman: Re: Estate of E. H. R. Green

We have shipped via Railway Express Agency three
trunks containing the Broken Bank Bills and nickels which
you purchased. Enclosed are keys to the locks of the
trunks. These are being forwarded in this manner, as we
felt this method of packing was no more expensive than
having the crates made. Therefore, we will be glad to
make a present of the trunks to you.

Our Co-administrators have agreed to accept your
offer of $1,000. for the remaining three 1913 Liberty
Head nickels. Upon receipt of your check, the coins will
be forwarded to you.

Yours very truly,

Alexander A. McKenna,
Second Vice President.

Enclosure
wf

*Notice from Alexander McKenna to Eric Newman that the Broken Bank Bills
and nickels had been shipped and advising that his counter-offer for the remaining
1913 Liberty nickels was acceptable. Courtesy of Eric Newman.*

CHASNOFF, WILLSON & CUNNINGHAM
BOATMEN'S BANK BUILDING
ST. LOUIS, MO.

December 27, 1941.

Mr. Alexander A. McKenna,
Chase National Bank,
11 Broad Street,
New York City, New York.

Dear Mr. McKenna:-

The three trunks containing
the broken bank bills and nickels arrived safely
during the Christmas rush and the contents were
delivered in good condition. The new keys which
you had made for the trunks did not fit too well
and I had to pry open two of the trunks.

Thank you for having them
packed so well.

I am enclosing a cashier's
check in the sum of $1,000.00 in purchase of the
three remaining 1913 Liberty Head Nickels.

I look forward to hearing from
you in the near future on the other items in which
I am interested.

With kindest personal greetings
for the Holiday Season to yourself and your associates, I am,

Very truly yours,

EPN:VC

*Eric Newman's acknowledgement to Alexander McKenna that the
merchandise arrived safely, with payment enclosed for the other three 1913
Liberty Head nickels.. Courtesy of Eric Newman.*

The three trunks containing the broken bank bills and nickels arrived safely during the Christmas rush and the contents were delivered in good condition. The new keys which you had made for the trunks did not fit too well and I had to pry open two of the trunks.

Thank you for having them packed so well.

I am enclosing a cashier's check in the sum of $1,000.00 in purchase of the three remaining 1913 Liberty Head Nickels.

McKenna consummated the transaction with this letter on December 29, 1941:

Your letter of December 27, 1941, in which you enclosed a cashiers check for $1,000. in payment for the three 1913 Liberty Head nickels, has been received. We are pleased to enclose the nickels herewith.

For the completion of our records, would you mind acknowledging receipt of the coins by signing and returning the accompanying copy of this letter.

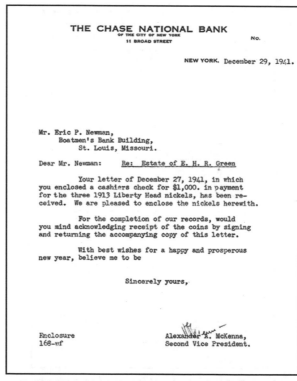

Alexander McKenna's acknowledgement of Eric Newman's check for three of the 1913 Liberty nickels. Courtesy of Eric Newman.

B.G. Johnson's inventory record detailed the coins in the leather case:

Coins in leather case -
1913 Liberty head. Proof
"   "   "   "
"   "   "   "
"   "   "   "
"   "   "   Unc.
"   Indian"   Pattern. The principal
                difference from the accepted type being
                that the rim around the coin on the obv.
                is very broad. The short feathers of the
                head dress is also slightly different
                from the regular type being broader and
                touching the rim of the coin. Proof and
                probably unique. $75.00
        "   Indian Head. Second type. In copper
                Unc., probably unique   100.00
        "   Indian Head. Regular type of the 2nd
                design. Unc.   1.00

B.G. Johnson's inventory record of the five 1913 Liberty Head nickels and three buffalo nickels included in the leather case with them. Courtesy of Eric Newman.

Beth Deisher reported in *Coin World* (June 11, 2001) that Newman recalled that he and Johnson thought the coins could be fakes. "He also noted the five 1913 Liberty Head five-cent coins appeared to have been struck on different qualities of planchets, possibly whatever was available to the person who struck them, and that they were of different conditions."

Eric Newman (left) shares his extensive knowledge and files about the 1913 Liberty Head nickels with author Mark Borckardt (November 2003). Courtesy of Ray Knight

In a handwritten note on a legal pad, Eric Newman set down what is probably the first and, until 2003, the only description of all the coins compared side by side (Mark Borckardt's notations identifying the coins by their nicknames as used in this narrative appear in brackets):

> 1913 Nickels
> #1 Brilliant proof Dent on obv edge next to second 1 in 1913. Dent on edge next to first T of STATES on reverse   [Eliasberg Specimen]
> #2 Proof - Several slight lines in field opposite 12th star - High wire edge on reverse [Smithsonian Specimen]
> #3 Dull Proof - Two slight lines in field opposite 13th star   Dot on neck opposite end of hanging curl [Walton Specimen]
> #4 Dull Proof - rev brighter than obverse   Dot on neck above chin level next to hair [Hawn Specimen]
> #5 Unc   Dot in left center of neck at chin level [ANA Specimen]

For his part of the bargain, Newman got his pick of the litter. He selected the finest of the 1913 Liberty nickels, the "Brilliant proof" specimen (which has become known as the Eliasberg specimen) and the Indian Head regular issue die trial in copper, which is considered to be "the rarest of the bunch" and which he still owns. He also kept the leather case.

Eric Newman's handwritten notes on his opinion of the grading for the individual 1913 Liberty Head nickels. Courtesy of Eric Newman.

Octogenarian coin dealer Art Kagin said he briefly handled one of the coins Johnson and Newman owned. "I had one of the five on approval in 1941 at $900." Kagin, age 83 when interviewed in 2003 and still actively trading coins, said he got the coin from Johnson and Newman to try to sell it. "I figured it would sell for $1,000," Kagin said. "I had to return it. Had it for three weeks and couldn't sell it for $1,000. I didn't have the money to buy it, so I had to return it in 1941."

In the August 20, 1953, issue of *Numismatic Scrapbook Magazine*, James P. Randall wrote (commenting on an NSM article on the 1913 Liberty Head nickels in the July 20, 1953, issue):

> I believe the late Mr. Johnson's price was $1,000 less 10% to dealers. He retained the best specimen, which had proof surface, until last and I am sure he obtained a much higher price for it.[42]

---

[42] An apparent reference to the finest known nickel (Eliasberg Specimen) that Eric Newman kept, not B.G. Johnson.

March 11th   / 43

r. James Kelly
3rd & Bdwy. Dayton, Ohio

RED

1913 U.S. 5¢ Nickel. Liberty head
                    Proof   750 00

U.S. DOLLARS
1838 U.S. Flying Eagle. Bril. proof.
                           @cexn   265 00 —
1839 "   "   "   "   proof
                           bfexe   95 00 —
      "   "   "   "   " proof
                           bfexe   95 00 —
1851 Proof   buexe   100 00 —
      "   buexe   100 00 —
U.S. 1/2 DOLLARS
1876 CC Mint. Abt. unc.   bnxn   20 00 —
     "   "   "   Fine   bnex   11 00 —
     "   "   "   Unc., dark bfex   95 00

                    $1,461.00

March 11th   / 43

r. James Kelly
S.E. Cor. 3rd & Bdwy. Dayton, Ohio

RED

1913 U.S. 5¢ NICKEL. Liberty
      Head. Proof $750 00

```
                                        March 17th      / 43
                        r. James Kelly
                            3rd & Broadway, Dayton, Ohio




                        RED
      1913  U.S. Nickel. Liberty head
            Uncirculated with proof
            surface              $750  00   OXCHM.
```

```
                                        April 22nd      / 43
                        r. F. C. C. Boyd
                            121 V  ick St., New York, N.Y.




      1913  U.S. 5¢ Nickel. Liberty head
                     Proof     $1000  00
```

B.G. Johnson's invoices show four 1913 Liberty Head nickels sold in March and April 1943, three to James Kelly for $750 each and one to F.C.C. Boyd for $1,000. This is the first time these documents have been published. Courtesy of Eric Newman.

A letter from Abe Kosoff appeared in the same issue:

> An interesting note on the 1913 nickels comes to me from a source close to B.G. Johnson. This party [Eric Newman] selected the best of the 5 coins for his own collection, and this specimen is now in the Eliasberg Collection. The comment, which we cannot corroborate, indicated that only two of the 1913 nickels were in proof condition, the others uncirculated.[43]

Johnson sold the other Liberty nickels, three of them to Ohio coin dealer James Kelly and one to F.C.C. Boyd (who had appraised the Green estate). It is commonly and incorrectly reported in the numismatic lore that the 1913 Liberty Head nickel set was broken up and distributed in 1942, but Johnson's inventory record shows transactions in March 1943. "The written notations on the inventory sheets next to the 1913 nickels are in Johnson's handwriting and indicate the date of the sale of the adjacent item," said Eric Newman.

The sale dates indicated on Johnson's inventory notations differ slightly from the actual invoices that were issued. Newman searched through his extensive archives to locate for the authors the four invoices in B.G. Johnson's records for these transactions. They have not been published previously.

The invoices show that two "1913 U.S. 5¢ Nickel. Liberty head Proof" coins were sold to "James Kelly 3rd & Bdwy, Dayton, Ohio" on March 11, 1943, for $750 each. The first of these two invoices indicate that the transaction also included five U.S. dollars and three U.S. half dollars. The total transaction on that invoice was for $1,461.00.

Johnson sold a third coin, "1913 U.S. Nickel. Liberty head Uncirculated with proof surface," to Kelly a week later on March 17.

The following month, April 22, 1943, Johnson sold a "1913 U.S. 5¢ Nickel. Liberty head Proof" to "F. C. C. Boyd 131 Varick St., New York, N.Y." for $1,000.

Thus ended The "Set" Period as the collection of five 1913 Liberty Head nickels was broken up and the nickels dispersed to follow their separate paths of glory. They would not be seen again together in the same place or even the same state for more than six decades, and then only for four days. It was a reunion that would make headlines around the world.

---

[43] An uncirculated coin is a new coin showing no evidence of circulation, although not necessarily brilliant. (James Ruddy, Photograde). The 1913 Liberty nickels might best be called "Special Strikes," not Proofs as we know them but also not circulation strikes. They were certainly not intended for use in circulation.

(See appendix for additional information on pedigree and owner biographies.)

Chapter 6 References

Bowers, Q. David. 1975. "The Legendary 1913 Liberty Head Nickel," *Bowers and Ruddy Galleries Rare Coin Review* 22 (Spring), p. 32-38.
— Bowers. 1991. *American Numismatic Association Centennial History Volume II* (Wolfeboro, New Hampshire: Bowers and Merena Galleries for American Numismatic Association), p. 460.
— Bowers. 1997. *American Coin Treasures and Hoards.*

Coin World Almanac, Millennium Edition. 2000. (Sidney, Ohio: Amos Press) p. 560.

Davis, M.D., Chief of Reference Service Branch, General Services Administration. 1962. Reply to Eric Newman regarding employment of August Wagner (July 6, 1962).

Deisher, Beth. 2001. "How'd you like to sell a 1913 five-cent for $2,000?" *Coin World* (June 11), p. 1.
— Deisher. 2003. "Liberty Head Legends," *Numismatist* (July), p. 37.

Hughes, C.W. & Co., Inc., Mechanicville, New York. Hetty Green residence picture postcard (1916).

Kagin, Art. 2003. Interview (October 17).

Kelly, James. 1967. Auction catalog, Annual ANA Convention, Miami, Florida (August 11).

Lewis, Arthur H. 1963. *The Day They Shook the Plum Tree* (New York: Bantam Books/Harcourt, Brace & World), pp. 126-127.

McKenna, Alexander A. 1941. Letters to Eric Newman (December 16, 18, and 29).

Mervis, Clyde D. 1968. "World's Most Valuable Coin," *Numismatic Scrapbook Magazine.*

Newman, Eric P. "1913 Nickels," handwritten coin descriptions (undated).
— Newman, 1941. Letters to Alexander McKenna, (December 13 and 27).
— Newman, 1941. B.G. Johnson's inventory of 1913 Liberty nickels.
— Newman, 1943. B.G. Johnson's invoices for sales of 1913 Liberty Head nickels.
— Newman. 1976. *The Early Paper Money of America* (Iola, Wisconsin: Krause Publications, Inc.), jacket notes.
— Newman. 2003. Interview (November 17).
— Newman. 2003. Email response to query about B.G. Johnson selling nickels to Col. E.H.R. Green (December 17).

— Newman. 2003. Email response to query about date notations on B.G. Johnson's inventory sheet (December 20).

— Newman. 2004. Email response to query about date and price of sale to Abe Kosoff (January 17).

New York State Historical Association web site. "The 1930s." Accessed December 21, 2003, at http://www.yorkers.org/leaflets/pdfs/1930s.S.pdf.

Numismatic Scrapbook Magazine. 1968. "World's Most Valuable Coin" (Vol. 34, No. 389, July), pp. 1064-1073.

— *Numismatic Scrapbook Magazine.* 1971. "Liberty 1913 Nickel Offers Mystic Aura" (Vol. 37, No. 430, December 24), p. 1158.

— *Numismatic Scrapbook Magazine.* 1973. "Liberty 1913 Nickel Story Footnotes" (April), p. 368-372.

The Numismatist. 1919. Wayte Raymond classified ad (Vol. XXXII, No. 12, December), p.512-513.

— *The Numismatist.* 1921. "The Rare 1913 Nickel" (January).

— *The Numismatist.* 1923. August Wagner classified ad (Vol. XXXVI, No. 12, December), p. 612.

— *The Numismatist.* 1924. August Wagner classified ad (Vol. XXXVII, No. 1, January), p. 51.

— *The Numismatist.* 1924. August Wagner classified ad (Vol. XXXVII, No. 2, February), p. 208

Ogilvie, Jack W. 1963. Letter to Don Taxay (October 14). Letter provided by Eric P. Newman.

Peters, Gloria, and Cynthia Mohon. 1995. *The Complete Guide to Shield & Liberty Head Nickels* (Virginia Beach, Virginia: DLRC Press), pp. 164-172.

Smith, Pete. *American Numismatic Biographies,* (Minneapolis, Minnesota: Remy Bourne-Ramm Communications, Inc.), pp. 43, 105, 129, 190-191.

Zerbe, Farran. 1937. Letter to Eric Newman responding to his inquiry about Missouri money in Colonel Green's collection (June 2).

- Chapter Seven -

THE "SINGLE" PERIOD:
SEPARATE PATHS TO GLORY

In the strictest sense, the executors of Colonel E.H.R. Green's estate were the first to break up the set of five Liberty Head nickels. They agreed to sell two of them to Eric Newman and B.G. Johnson, then later also sold the other three to them. All the coins wound up in the same hands, though, so as a practical matter, Newman and Johnson were the ones who dispersed the nickels singly.

The trail gets much more complicated with the onset of The "Single" Period, when the coins were split off individually to follow their separate bloodlines of ownership. Some of them have had relatively few owners, but others — the Hawn Specimen most notably — have a long list of handlers. To be as accurate as the available information will allow, the pedigrees listed here include all parties who are known to have had custody of the coins, even dealers who may have held them only briefly for the purpose of resale.

#1 SMITHSONIAN SPECIMEN

"Proof — Several slight lines in field opposite 12th star - High wire edge on reverse" (Eric Newman notes)

Pedigree: F.C.C. Boyd, Abe Kosoff/Abner Kreisberg, King Farouk, Government of Egypt, Sotheby's, SolKaplan/Abe Kosoff, Norweb Family, Smithsonian Institution.

Owned by a Middle Eastern potentate, a rebellious North African government, an American ambassador's wife, and the prestigious Smithsonian Institution, this specimen can easily lay claim to having the most stately masters.

F.C.C. Boyd
(b. 1-29-1887 d. 6-16-1953)

Collector and part-time coin dealer Frederick Cogswell C. Boyd appraised the coin collection of Colonel E.H.R. Green, so he was familiar with the 1913 Liberty Head nickels Newman and Johnson had bought from the estate. When they offered them for sale, Boyd purchased one of them in March 1943. He kept it only briefly, though, selling it in 1944 to Abe Kosoff, partners with Abner Kriesberg in Numismatic Gallery.

Abe Kosoff / Abner Kriesberg (Numismatic Gallery)
(Kosoff b.12-31-1912, d. 3-19-1983)

Abe Kosoff, ANA life member #81.
Courtesy of Coin World. © Coin World

Abe Kosoff figured prominently in the history of three of the 1913 Liberty Head nickels — the Smithsonian, Eliasberg, and Hawn specimens. After acquiring the Smithsonian Specimen from F.C.C. Boyd, he lost no time in selling it (acting for Numismatic Gallery, which he co-owned with partner Abner Kriesberg) to King Farouk of Egypt in 1944, reportedly for $2,750 (circumstances would bring him into contact with it again later).

King Farouk
(b. 2-11-1920, d. 3-18-1965)

King Farouk, deposed monarch of Egypt and prolific collector. Courtesy of Coin World..

King Farouk of Egypt, one of the more colorful characters to own a 1913 Liberty Head nickel, was a compulsive collector. His coin collection alone, one of the largest in the world, is reputed to have included more than 8,500 gold coins and medals and 164 platinum pieces along with numerous silver and copper coins. He was known as an "accumulator" rather than as a student of coins.

Farouk was a better collector than he was a ruler. He was ousted by a military junta led by Gamel Abdel Nasser in 1952. He was exiled to Italy, but his coin collection stayed in Egypt in the hands of the new government.

Government of Egypt

Military officers are better suited to tasks other than auctioning rare coins, as the new Egyptian government was to prove. The sale of the Farouk coin collection suffered from confusion and poor handling. Abe Kosoff devoted a chapter in his book *Abe Kosoff Remembers* to the pre-sale uncertainty and complicated negotiations.

Eventually, the Egyptian government enlisted the London firm of Baldwin & Co. to do the cataloging and Sotheby's to publish it as *The Palace Collections of Egypt*. It reportedly took over three months for Sotheby's experts to sort out the hoard of varied collections Farouk had accumulated.

145

The auction was held at Koubbeh Palace, Cairo, in February and March 1954. It wasn't exactly a rousing success from the Egyptian government's standpoint. However, dealers and collectors must have enjoyed the opportunity to scoop up astonishing bargains.

Sol Kaplan / Abe Kosoff
(Kaplan - b. 12-24-1899)

Sol Kaplan, born 1899 in Odessa, Russia.
Courtesy of Coin World. © Coin World

Ambassador and Mrs. Henry Norweb wanted to buy the 1913 Liberty Head nickel included in the collection, but noted Cincinnati coin dealer and numismatic writer Sol Kaplan bought the coin for $3,750 in partnership with Abe Kosoff (co-owner with Abner Kriesberg of Numismatic Gallery). Kaplan, in turn, sold the nickel to Emery May Norweb in 1955 for a reported $3,900.

Norweb Family
*(Henry - b. 5-31-1895, d. 10-1-1983;
Emery May - b. 11-30-1895, d. 3-27-1984)*

*Hon. R. Henry Norweb, Sr.
Courtesy of Coin World.*

If you believe, as many numismatists do, that R. Henry Norweb owned a 1913 Liberty Head nickel, you're in for a big surprise!

Raymond Henry Norweb, Sr. was stationed with the diplomatic corps in Paris during World War I. There he met Emery May Holden, who drove an ambulance and worked in French hospitals during the war. Norweb eventually became an ambassador.

What few people realize, including many expert numismatists, is that it was Mrs. Norweb who owned the coin, rather than Ambassador Norweb, as *Numismatic News* News Editor Bob Lemke explained:

> Many numismatists will be surprised to learn that it was Mrs. Norweb, not her husband, who has owned the coin for the past two decades. It will come as a surprise to most numismatists to learn that Mrs. Norweb was the actual owner of coin. Most histories of this famous American coin list R. Henry Norweb as the owner. Queried about this, Mrs. Norweb said, "No, I owned the coin."

The Norwebs donated their 1913 Liberty Head nickel to the Smithsonian Institution in 1978 to commemorate their 60th wedding anniversary.

Smithsonian Institution

A press release from the Smithsonian Insitution dated August 31, 1978 (cited by Peters and Mohon), announced the donation of the Norweb nickel under the heading "SMITHSONIAN RECEIVES RARE 1913 NICKEL":

> A 1913 Liberty head nickel, one of the best known of rare American coins, has been added to the numismatic collection at the Smithsonian's National Museum of History and Technology.

The press release gave brief notes about how the 1913 Liberty Head nickels came into being, then concluded:

> One of these coins has now been added to the Smithsonian's priceless collection. Vladimir and Elvira Clain-Steffaneli, curators of the Smithsonian's Division of Numismatics, said that without the piece, the Smithsonian's 20th-century collection of United States coins would not be complete.
>
> The coin was donated by the Honorable and Mrs. R. Henry Norweb who presented it to the Smithsonian in commemoration of their 60th wedding anniversary.
>
> The coin will go on exhibit in conjunction with a ceremony scheduled for October 6, 1978, at which the Norwebs will be among those awarded the James Smithson Society's Gold Medal for the effective ways they helped the Smithsonian Institution in fulfilling its mandate.

#2 HAWN SPECIMEN

"Dull Proof - rev brighter than obverse   Dot on neck above chin level next to hair" (Eric Newman notes)

Pedigree: James Kelly, Fred Olsen, B. Max Mehl, King Farouk, Numismatic Fine Arts, King Farouk, B. Max Mehl(Will W. Neill auction), Edwin Hydeman, Abe Kosoff/Abner Kriesberg, World Wide Coin Investments with Bowers and Ruddy Galleries, A-Mark/Robert L.Hughes, Superior Galleries, Dr. Jerry Buss, Superior Stamp & Coin, Reed Hawn, Stack's, Dwight Manley/Spectrum Numismatics, Legend Numismatics, Anonymous.

The Hawn Specimen (also variously known in the numismatic lore as the Olsen Specimen, Hydeman Specimen, Legend Specimen, and combinations of these) is arguably the most viewed by the public of all the 1913 Liberty Head nickels. It has been frequently displayed at major conventions and was seen by millions of viewers in episodes of two popular television series — "Hawaii Five-O" and the Hardy Boys/Nancy Drew anthology. It also earned an entry into the Guinness Book of World Records for a record-setting coin price.

James Kelly
(b. 4-20-1907, d. 12-27-1968)

James F. Kelly, Dayton, Ohio, coin dealer who bought three of the 1913 Liberty Head nickels from B.G. Johnson. Courtesy of Coin World. © Coin World

James F. Kelly became a coin dealer in 1936, working with B.G. Johnson in St. Louis until 1946. When his former colleague B.G. Johnson offered the 1913 Liberty Head nickels for sale in March 1943, Kelly snapped up three of them — the Hawn, Walton, and ANA specimens. Kelly didn't keep the coins long, though, as Clyde D. Mervis writes in the *Numismatic Scrapbook Magazine* (July 1968):

> Kelly resold the three specimens he'd purchased—one to Dr. Conway Bolt, Marshville, N.C., for $1,000; one to Fred E. Olsen, Alton, Illinois, for $900; and the last to J.V. McDermott, South Milwaukee, Wis., for $900.

Fred Olsen

Fred E. Olsen, Alton, Illinois. Courtesy of Numismatic Scrapbook Magazine. ©Amos Press, Inc.

Collector Fred E. Olsen acquired a 1913 Liberty Head nickel from James Kelly in 1943 for $900. According to Peters and Mohon, this is the first of the nickels that changed hands publicly rather than in private treaty[44] transactions:

> Mr. Olsen's coin was the first of the set to be put in public auction. [B. Max] Mehl offered the coin in November 1944, The Fred E. Olsen Collection.

King Farouk of Egypt placed the winning bid of $3,750.

---

[44] A private treaty transaction is one between two individuals (or groups) that is not public, as is an auction.

King Farouk

True to his reputation for trying to take advantage of coin dealers, King Farouk allegedly pulled a double-shuffle maneuver to better his position with the 1913 Liberty Head nickels, as reported by Peters and Mohon:

> Later, King Farouk apparently obtained the F.C.C. Boyd 1913 nickel [the current Smithsonian Specimen] through a private sale brokered by Abe Kosoff. He then wished to sell the Olsen coin and commissioned Mehl to resell it for him. Mehl offered the coin in a second public auction in his Will N. Neill Collection June 17, 1947. It sold to Edwin C. [sic] Hydeman for approximately $3,750, the same amount that King Farouk had paid for it in 1944.

Peters and Mohon said that Farouk paid $2,750 for the coin he bought from Abe Kosoff, $1,000 less than the price he had paid for the Olsen coin.

Coin World staff writer William T. Gibbs reported in 1993 that Farouk first tried to auction the coin off through Numismatic Fine Arts, the New York firm co-owned by Edward Gans and Henry Grunthal through a mail-bid sale on May 21 (originally scheduled for May 7), 1946:

> Farouk attempted to get the Olsen coin sold. Grunthal told *Coin World* June 11 [1993] that Farouk sent the Olsen coin to him and asked him to attempt to sell it. Grunthal noted that Farouk owed him money at this time.
>
> Grunthal said the coin did not sell in the May 1946 sale. Laughing, he said he wishes now that he had bought it himself, since he could have gotten it for $500.
>
> Grunthal returned the coin to Farouk, who sent it back to Mehl. Mehl finally sold the coin for Farouk during the first six months of 1947, apparently to the next owner, Edwin Hydeman.

Grunthal's reference to his having been able to buy the coin for $500 is cryptic, since the List of Prices Realized[45] from the sale shows Lot #1058 to have brought "$2450.00" even though it didn't actually sell. It's not uncommon for auction listings to post the reserve value as a realized price when a coin does not bring high enough bids to suit the consignor. Though there are no records of the debt, it could be hypothesized that the amount Farouk owed Grunthal was $1,950, so the $500 would have made up the difference.

---

[45] Source: Numismatic Fine Arts Mail Bid Sale Catalog and List of Prices Realized, from the American Numismatic Association Library via Alvin Stern.

Edwin M. Hydeman

Edwin M. Hydeman. Courtesy of Numismatic Scrapbook Magazine. ©Amos Press, Inc.

Collector Edwin M. Hydeman, ANA life member # 137, acquired the first 1913 Liberty Head nickel owned by King Farouk in 1947. The coin was auctioned March 1961 in Abe Kosoff's offering of the Edwin M. Hydeman Collection of United States Coins in Los Angeles (Peters and Mohon). The description of the coin in the catalog read:

> This is a superb coin, sharply struck, as choice a specimen as could possibly be attained. It has been handled with the utmost care, a statement which, unfortunately, cannot be made of two of the pieces. This may be called the Olsen-Hydeman Nickel.

Kosoff retained the nickel until 1972, when he offered it in *The Numismatist* for $100,000.

World Wide Coin Investments
(And Bowers and Ruddy Galleries)

World Wide Coin Investments, owned by John B. Hamrick, Jr., and Warren Tucker, jumped at the offer, plunking down a cool hundred grand for the coin on October 3, 1972. It was the first time an American coin had ever commanded as much as $100,000. The sale drew wide publicity also for the fact that the Idler Class III 1804 dollar was paired up with the 1913 Liberty Head nickel and sold for $180,000. *Coin World* ran a full page article on the deal, according to Hamrick, and printed a picture of the $180,000 check. The deal earned the coins entry into the *Guinness Book of World Records*.

Hamrick, head of John B. Hamrick & Co. in Atlanta, recalled that acquiring these coins didn't happen by accident. It was part of a broader strategy of accumulating "celebrity" coins. "Basically, I was trying to buy every major rarity there was so I could say that I owned them."

It wasn't an ego trip, however. "I always thought I could market them," he added.

Hamrick's nickel became a TV star. The coin was featured in Episode #134 in the sixth season of the hit CBS series "Hawaii Five-O," a cop series featuring Jack Lord as the head of the Hawaii state police bureau. The title of the episode was "The $100,000 Nickel" and featured noted character actor Victor Buono. The program aired originally on December 11, 1973. Hamrick's nickel is seen in four close-ups in Buono's hand.

The plot involves an engraver taking a 1903 nickel and re-engraving the "0" to make it look like a rare and extremely valuable 1913 Liberty Head nickel. A magician takes the fake "altered date" coin to a coin show and, using sleight of hand, swaps it for a real 1913 Liberty Head nickel. The switch is detected and the building sealed before the thief (Victor Buono) can exit. He drops the coin into a newspaper vending machine! He manages to exit the building without raising suspicion and returns later to retrieve the coin, but the paperboy has already made his collection. A struggle for the coin ensues, with the paperboy being killed. The nickels are scattered all over the ground, and a young boy passing by with his grandfather picks up a "lucky nickel," which just happens to be the rare 1913 Liberty Head. Not knowing its value, the boy spends the coin, but the thief has no idea where. Eventually, after the coin passes through many hands, the coin is returned to its rightful owner.

Record-breaking check for 1913 "V-Nickel" and Idler 1804 Silver Dollar. The transaction was reported to have occurred on October 3, 1972, but the check is dated October 2. Courtesy of Warren Tucker

Photo from Coin World report on purchase of a 1913 Liberty Head nickel and 1804 silver dollar by World Wide Coin Investments from Abe Kosoff. (Left to right: John Hamrick, Abe Kosoff, Warren Tucker.) Courtesy of Coin World. © Coin World

The music theme for "The $100,000 Nickel" episode, written by Bruce Broughton, was nominated for an Emmy for Best Music Composition - Series. It didn't win, though. The Emmy was won by another "Hawaii Five-O" episode theme, "Hookman," by Morton Stevens, who also wrote the popular series theme song.

Hamrick was not himself involved in the filming, being tied up with business at home. Instead, he sent his Vice President of Public Relations, Robert Cornely, to accompany the coin on the shoot, which took four days. "They paid all his expenses, and I think they paid us a couple of thousand dollars as a fee," Hamrick recalled.

There were no special security arrangements for transporting the coin to the film set. "Cornely carried it in his pocket on the airplane," Hamrick said. It was not unusual in those days for coin dealers to have expensive coins on their person. "We carried coins in our pockets. I remember one night after the coin show, we put the nickel behind the green door," Hamrick said.

He explained that there used to be a coin show in downtown Los Angeles that closed on Sunday night. "Back then, you would stay at the coin show until 6:00 Sunday night and didn't have a flight home until midnight, so we went to the movies…took all the coins with us." On one occasion, with the 1913 Liberty Head nickel in their possession, Hamrick and some friends went to see "Behind the Green Door," the first widely popular porn movie. "It [the nickel] was in somebody's pocket who went to see the movie," Hamrick said. (Hamrick's partner at the time, Warren Tucker, said in 2005 he believed the film playing that night was another porn classic, "Deep Throat," rather than "Behind the Green Door.")

Less than three months after World Wide bought the nickel, Hamrick got a call from someone interested in the coin. "Jim Ruddy from Bowers and Ruddy called me...actually, I am not sure if it was him or Dave Bowers." In any case, they were interested in buying into the nickel. "So what happened, I sold them a half interest in the coin for $105,000," Hamrick said.

An item in the November 23, 1974, *Numismatic News* proclaimed: "2½ Cents Worth of Famous Nickel Costs Bowers & Ruddy $100,000." The article said:

> Two and a half cents worth (50 per cent) of a 1913 Liberty nickel has been purchased by Bowers and Ruddy Galleries for an undisclosed sum in excess of $100,000.

The item also mentioned that "World-Wide refused an offer of $225,000.00 for the ownership of the piece in September, 1974." They were holding out for a bigger price.

"We kept the coin together for a little over a year-and-a-half. We were trying to market the coin for $300,000 at that point, and we were never able to do it." As part of the deal for the partnership, at any time one of them could request a "Chinese auction" of the coin.

A Chinese auction, also known as a Dutch auction, is the opposite of a regular auction, in which the bids increase incrementally until there are no higher bids. In a Chinese auction, one party says, "I'll take X dollars for my interest." The other party may reply, "No, I won't pay you that much, but I'll take X dollars for my interest," naming an amount lower than the first offer. The bidding continues incrementally lower until someone says, "Okay, I'll pay your price."

In this particular case, they had agreed in advance on $5,000 increments for the bidding. Bidding began at $105,000. "It's like a chicken game," Hamrick said. "It's a good way to keep people honest."

Hamrick wound up buying out Bowers and Ruddy's half interest in the coin for $65,000, netting $40,000 profit on the round trip. He eventually sold it for $145,000 to Bob Hughes at Robert L. Hughes Enterprises, a subsidiary of A-Mark Precious Metals. Hughes offered the coin for $225,000 in the June 1977 issue of *The Numismatist* (Peters and Mohon). There were no takers.

Dr. Jerry Buss

Superior Stamp & Coin issued a press release written by Mel Wacks and postmarked July 22, 1978,[46] announcing:

1913 LIBERTY NICKEL SOLD BY SUPERIOR
FOR $200,000.00 TO ANONYMOUS COLLECTOR

The release touted the sale as a record-breaker:

> Now, 75 years after their rather unassuming beginnings, one of the 1913 Liberty Nickels is again making news. It has just changed hands at a record-breaking $200,000.00, making it one of the most expensive coins in the world! Only two other coins have higher recorded prices — an Athenian Decadrachm from 470 B.C. ($272,240.00) and an 1804 Silver Dollar ($225,000.00)…but the five lone examples of the 1913 Liberty Nickel make it the rarest of the rare!
>
> The sale was made by … Superior Stamp & Coin Company, Beverly Hills, California.

The release called Superior "Coin Dealer to the Stars" and claimed to have sold the coin collections of celebrities Harold Lloyd, Buddy de Silva, "and other prominent hobbiests" [sic].

Superior would not identify the new owner of the 1913 Liberty nickel, referring to him only as "Mister X":

> The new owner prefers to remain anonymous, but [Superior Galleries] indicates that he is a "big name" in the entertainment industry, who is a true collector.

The deal was offered on a grocery list at a dinner party, according to Superior's press release:

> While in the past, 1913 Liberty Nickels often changed hands under the spotlight of public auctions, the sale of the Hughes-Superior specimen took place under rather different circumstances. [Superior Galleries] had discussed the possible acquisition of the 1913 Liberty Nickel with his client on several occasions. In the meantime, [Superior] had guided the collector who quietly acquired a comprehensive collection that includes some of the most outstanding rarities in the field of numismatics.

---

[46] Provided courtesy of Eric P. Newman.

One evening, when the Goldbergs were having dinner out with the collector and his wife, the client asked for a piece of paper. The only thing handy was a grocery list written on an envelope reminding Goldberg to pick up "foil, tissues, and mustard." On the back, the client wrote down his offer for the fabled 1913 Liberty Nickel — $200,000.00, and dated it June 7, 1978. Goldberg thereupon negotiated with [Robert] Hughes until the price was agreed upon...and history was made! © Superior Galleries. Permission by Silvano DiGenova

Numismatic News picked up the story in the July 22, 1978, issue with a front-page banner headline that read "Rare Liberty Nickel Fetches Record Price In Private Sale to Unnamed Show Biz Star":

A "star" of the entertainment world has purchased a "star" of numismatics — at a record price, according to Ira Goldberg of Superior Stamp & Coin Co. of Beverly Hills, Calif.

The numismatic "star," in this instance, is the Hydeman specimen of the 1913 Liberty Head nickel, which was sold in early July for $200,000 to an unnamed "big star" in the entertainment industry, who is a true collector and prefers to remain anonymous, Goldberg said.

The "big star" identified only as "Mister X," the world eventually came to know, turned out to be Dr. Jerry Buss, owner of the Los Angeles Lakers NBA pro basketball team. Buss got his Ph.D. in chemistry but made his fortune in real estate. He bought the Lakers in 1979. Buss is known to love high-stakes dealings. He appeared in the Travel Channel's World Poker Tournament on television, competing in the championship series for No Limit Texas Hold 'Em Poker (he was eliminated from the tournament).

Dr. Buss put the coin up for auction by Superior Galleries in January 1985. The hammer bid was $380,000, $80,000 more than the 1804 dollar in the same auction, according to Peters and Mohon. Texas collector Reed Hawn was the winning bidder.

೦ఌ

Reed Hawn

Reed Hawn, well-known Texas collector. Courtesy of Coin World. © Coin World

Renowned Austin, Texas, collector Reed Hawn had a taste for top of the line coins.

Among his most notable coin acquisitions, two stand out in particular - the 1913 Liberty Head nickel and the Mickley specimen of the Class I 1804 Draped Bust Dollar. Both coins were put on public display at the American Numismatic Association's 1987 anniversary convention in Atlanta, and in March 1993 were displayed at the ANA's Money Museum in Colorado Springs, Colorado.

Hawn decided in 1993 to part with his two prize treasures "hopefully to make some money" and to give other collectors "the joy of ownership" of the legendary coins. "Since I never thought I'd own them in the first place, they've been very important to me to own," he told Paul Gilkes. "I really didn't have an idea of what it meant to own them until I did. You own something knowing it will go on, knowing someone else is going to have it. They're wonderful coins to own. It's been a privilege, especially the nickel."

Hawn consigned the coins to the New York auction firm Stack's. The auction was held October 13-14, 1993. A full-page ad by Stack's in the November 8, 1993, *Coin World* declared "Records Are Made To Be Broken":

> Mr. Reed Hawn of Austin, Texas, purchased his 1913 Liberty Head Nickel at auction in 1985 at the Jerry Buss Sale in California for $385,000[47] and it just sold for $962,500.

[47] The purchase price for the nickel given by Stack's is $5,000 more than reported by Peters and Mohon.

The 1804 Silver Dollar, the Massachusetts Historical Society Specimen, sold in 1970 at a Stack's auction for $77,500 and later in 1973 Mr. Hawn acquired the coin through private treaty for $150,000. The 1804 Silver Dollar sold on the evening of October 14th at auction for $522,500.

The ad does not specify which price records were broken, but such lofty valuations seem almost certain to have raised the bar to new heights. Setting new price records has been a hallmark of the 1913 Liberty Head nickels

Dwight Manley, collector-dealer-sports agent. Courtesy of Minkus & Pearlman Public Relations, Inc.©

Dwight Manley/Spectrum Numismatics

Entrepreneur and promoter Dwight Manley, famed for marketing the "Ship of Gold" treasure of gold coins from the *S.S. Central America* shipwreck, owned two of the 1913 Liberty Head nickels. The Hawn Specimen was the first one he bought, bidding it to what was then a world record price of $875,000 ($962,500 with commissions added) on behalf of Spectrum Numismatics of Irvine, California. He would later break more records, coming and going, with the Eliasberg Specimen.

Legend Numismatics

"Legend Numismatics buys legend — 1913 Liberty Head 5¢ sells for undisclosed 'record' sum" read the headline of an item posted January 20, 2003, on the CoinWorld.com web site.

Legend Numismatics of Lincroft, New Jersey, bought the Hawn Specimen for a sum reported to be greater than the record price of $1.84

million paid by Dwight Manley for the Eliasberg Specimen. "It was more than that. We paid close to two million dollars[48]," said Laura Sperber, one of the three partners who comprise Legend Numismatics. The other partners are George Huang and Bruce Morelan. Sperber said the terms of the purchase agreement prevented her from revealing publicly the exact amount of the deal.

Sperber is the spokesperson for the group. It was her long-time dream to own the 1913 Liberty Head nickel. She saw it in 1976 when she attended her first American Numismatic Association convention and was awe-struck. She never conceived then that she would one day own one of the legendary nickels.

"Superior had it in their case. They let me hold it. I got goose bumps just holding it," Sperber said. "It's what made me want to become a coin dealer. Ever since I've wanted to own a 1913 nickel."

Sperber maintained at the time that Legend Numismatics intended to hold onto the coin. "It's not for sale. It's part of a collection we're building," she said then. The tune would change by summer 2003, when Legend was in active negotiations to sell the coin.

Anonymous

Details remain hush-hush but it is known that Legend Numismatics sold the Hawn specimen in early 2004 for an estimated $3 million, making it the third most expensive coin in history (behind the 1933 Saint-Gaudens double eagle sold for $7.59 million by Sotheby's in 2002 and the 1804 Draped Bust silver dollar sold for $4.14 million in a 1999 auction). The buyer's identity and exact selling price was not disclosed publicly for privacy and security reasons.

---

[48] Sperber disputed the $1.84 million transaction price published by *Numismatist* in a July 2003 article by Beth Deisher, pointing out that the reference probably was meant for the Eliasberg transaction by Dwight Manley in 2002. Deisher noted in a 2005 interview that the chart that accompanied the Numismatist article incorrectly gave the Legend purchase price as $1.84 million but that the text correctly said it was more than that.

#3 ELIASBERG SPECIMEN

"Brilliant proof Dent on obv edge next to second 1 in 1913. Dent on edge next to first T of STATES on reverse" (Eric Newman notes)

Pedigree: Eric P. Newman, Abe Kosoff/Abner Kriesberg, Louis Eliasberg, Sr., Eliasberg Estate, Bowers and Merena, Jay Parrino, Superior Galleries, Dwight Manley/California Gold Marketing Group, Edward C. Lee.

The Eliasberg Specimen, finest known of the five, is the darling of news reporters because it continues to post new record highs for coin sale prices each time it changes hands.

Eric P. Newman

Eric Newman officially took sole possession of the finest of the 1913 Liberty nickels in 1943. A handwritten notation by B.G. Johnson on his inventory record indicates ownership of the Liberty nickel was transferred to "EPN" on March 11.

Newman held onto the nickel, having no intent to sell it. However, "smooth talker" Abe Kosoff coaxed him into parting with it in 1949.

In a 1996 letter to Q. David Bowers (Bowers and Merena were preparing to auction the Louis Eliasberg, Sr., collection), Newman described how he came to part with the nickel, despite of his reservations about selling what he believed were fake coins:

> As to the 1913 Liberty Head nickel matter, I was telephoned by Abe Kosoff in the late 1940s and he said he would be in St. Louis on the way east and wanted to see me. He arrived and wished to see my 1913 nickel holdings. I believe my mentor, B.G. Johnson, had died by then. I showed Kosoff the special black leather case with 8 circular slots of nickel size and opened it up to show him my 1913 Indian head nickel in copper, my 1913 normal uncirculated Indian head nickel, and the 1913 Liberty Head nickel I had retained. He was a smooth talker and told me he thought he could get me a big price for the Liberty Head. I told him that even though I thought it was a fake, I really didn't want to sell anything. He used his customary convincing charm and knew Johnson had sold other 1913 Liberty Head nickels for $500 each and he would give me $2500. I felt at

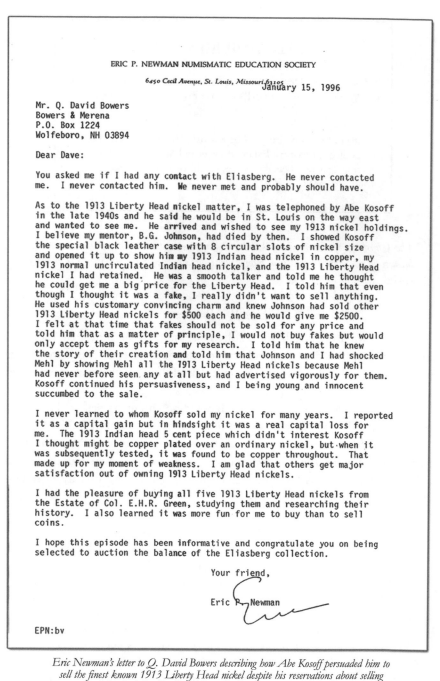

ERIC P. NEWMAN NUMISMATIC EDUCATION SOCIETY

6450 Cecil Avenue, St. Louis, Missouri 63105
January 15, 1996

Mr. Q. David Bowers
Bowers & Merena
P.O. Box 1224
Wolfeboro, NH 03894

Dear Dave:

You asked me if I had any contact with Eliasberg. He never contacted
me. I never contacted him. We never met and probably should have.

As to the 1913 Liberty Head nickel matter, I was telephoned by Abe Kosoff
in the late 1940s and he said he would be in St. Louis on the way east
and wanted to see me. He arrived and wished to see my 1913 nickel holdings.
I believe my mentor, B.G. Johnson, had died by then. I showed Kosoff
the special black leather case with 8 circular slots of nickel size
and opened it up to show him my 1913 Indian head nickel in copper, my
1913 normal uncirculated Indian head nickel, and the 1913 Liberty Head
nickel I had retained. He was a smooth talker and told me he thought
he could get me a big price for the Liberty Head. I told him that even
though I thought it was a fake, I really didn't want to sell anything.
He used his customary convincing charm and knew Johnson had sold other
1913 Liberty Head nickels for $500 each and he would give me $2500.
I felt at that time that fakes should not be sold for any price and
told him that as a matter of principle, I would not buy fakes but would
only accept them as gifts for my research. I told him that he knew
the story of their creation and told him that Johnson and I had shocked
Mehl by showing Mehl all the 1913 Liberty Head nickels because Mehl
had never before seen any at all but had advertised vigorously for them.
Kosoff continued his persuasiveness, and I being young and innocent
succumbed to the sale.

I never learned to whom Kosoff sold my nickel for many years. I reported
it as a capital gain but in hindsight it was a real capital loss for
me. The 1913 Indian head 5 cent piece which didn't interest Kosoff
I thought might be copper plated over an ordinary nickel, but when it
was subsequently tested, it was found to be copper throughout. That
made up for my moment of weakness. I am glad that others get major
satisfaction out of owning 1913 Liberty Head nickels.

I had the pleasure of buying all five 1913 Liberty Head nickels from
the Estate of Col. E.H.R. Green, studying them and researching their
history. I also learned it was more fun for me to buy than to sell
coins.

I hope this episode has been informative and congratulate you on being
selected to auction the balance of the Eliasberg collection.

Your friend,

Eric P. Newman

EPN:bv

*Eric Newman's letter to Q. David Bowers describing how Abe Kosoff persuaded him to
sell the finest known 1913 Liberty Head nickel despite his reservations about selling
what he believed to be a fake coin. Courtesy of Eric Newman.*

that time that fakes should not be sold for any price and told him that as a matter of principle, I would not buy fakes but would only accept them as gifts for my research. I told him that he knew the story of their creation and told him that Johnson and I had shocked [B. Max] Mehl by showing Mehl all the 1913 Liberty Head nickels because Mehl had never before seen any at all but had advertised vigorously for them. Kosoff continued his persuasiveness, and I being young and innocent succumbed to the sale.

I never learned to whom Kosoff sold my nickel for many years. I reported it as a capital gain but in hindsight it was a real capital loss for me. The 1913 Indian head 5 cent piece which didn't interest Kosoff I thought might be copper plated over an ordinary nickel, but when it was subsequently tested, it was found to be copper throughout. That made up for my moment of weakness. I am glad that others get major satisfaction out of owning 1913 Liberty Head nickels.

I had the pleasure of buying all five 1913 Liberty Head nickels from the Estate of Col. E.H.R. Green, studying them and researching their history. I also learned it was more fun for me to buy than to sell coins.[49]

Beth Deisher reported the sale price to be $2,000 in a 2001 *Coin World* article, rather than $2,500 as stated by Newman in his letter to Bowers. Asked by the authors for a clarification of the discrepancy, Newman responded: "I found the information you asked for in my 1949 income tax file, believe it or not. I sold my beautiful 1913 nickel to Abe Kosoff on 11/2/49 for $2,000."

Deisher asked Newman how he felt about selling a coin "for $2,000" that had sold for $2 million (a record at that time), Newman replied, "I never look backwards," adding that a coin's historical importance has always been of greater importance to him than its monetary value.

Abe Kosoff/Abner Kriesberg

Abe Kosoff was not only a "smooth talker," as Eric Newman described him, but he surely knew how to reinforce a sale. Kosoff sold the 1913 Liberty Head nickel he acquired from Newman to one of America's premier coin collectors, the man whose name would become permanently affixed to the coin — Louis E. Eliasberg, Sr. Eliasberg paid $2,350 for the nickel, according to the Western Union telegram he sent to Kosoff on December 16, 1948, confirming the purchase:

---

[49] Letter and content courtesy of Eric Newman

> Will buy Nineteen Thirteen Nickel for Two Thousand Three Hundred and Fifty Dollars if condition is satisfactory Stop Advise
>
> Louis Eliasberg

Kosoff replied on December 22:

> SHIPPING NICKLE [sic] AIR MAIL TODAY=
>
> A KOSOFF=

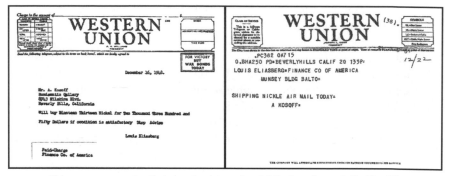

Telegrams consummating the transaction between Louis Eliasberg, Sr., and Abe Kosoff for a 1913 Liberty Head nickel. Courtesy of Eric Newman.

A couple of weeks later, on January 8, 1949, Kosoff followed up with a letter intended to boost Eliasberg's satisfaction with his purchase. Kosoff skillfully applied a generous coating of after-the-sale reinforcement:

> Relative to the 1913 nickel which you just purchased from us, it would undoubtedly be of interest to you to learn that this particular specimen is the finest of the 5 pieces minted.
>
> You will recall that all 5 were acquired by Colonel Green and remained in his collection until his estate was liquidated.
>
> Mr. B.G. Johnson, proprietor of the St. Louis Stamp and Coin Company then acquired all 5 specimens and Mr. Johnson's attorney, a Mr. E. P. Newman, a collector of rare coins, selected the finest of the 5 for his own collection.
>
> It is precisely this specimen which we have sold to you, having acquired it directly from Mr. Newman.
>
> Another point of interest is that only 2 of the 5 coins were in proof condition, the other 3 being uncirculated. It happens, also, that our firm sold the other proof specimen a few years ago and I believe I can accurately state (and I have verified this with the previous owner of the other proof) that your coin is the finer of the two.

I know that if the acquisition of the coin was at all a happy incident, then this information will make it doubly so.

Whether or not Eliasberg was affected by this ego massage isn't known, but he still owned the coin when he died in 1976.

The Home of America's Finest Coin Sales

A. KOSOFF
ABNER KREISBERG

NUMISMATIC GALLERY

8943 WILSHIRE BLVD., Beverly Hills, CALIFORNIA

Crestview 14281   Cable: NUMGALLERY BeverlyHillsCalifornia

January 8, 1949.

Mr. Louis Eliasberg,
Box 508,
Baltimore 3, Maryland.

My dear Mr. Eliasberg:

Relative to the 1913 nickel which you just purchased from us, it would undoubtedly be of interest to you to learn that this particular specimen is the finest of the 5 pieces minted.

You will recall that all 5 were acquired by Colonel Green and remained in his collection until his estate was liquidated.

Mr. B. G. Johnson, proprietor of the St. Louis Stamp and Coin Company then acquired all 5 specimens and Mr. Johnson's attorney, a Mr. E. P. Newman, a collector of rare coins, selected the finest of the 5 for his own collection.

It is precisely this specimen which we have sold to you, having acquired it directly from Mr. Newman.

Another point of interest is that only 2 of the 5 coins were in proof condition, the other 3 being uncirculated. It happens, also, that our firm sold the other proof specimen a few years ago and I believe I can accurately state (and I have verified this with the previous owner of the other proof) that your coin is the finer of the two.

I know that if the acquisition of the coin was at all a happy incident, then this information will make it doubly so.

Very sincerely yours,

NUMISMATIC GALLERY

A. Kosoff

ec

Abe Kosoff strokes the ego of Louis Eliasberg as owner of the finest known 1913 Liberty Head nickels. Courtesy of Eric Newman.

Louis E. Eliasberg, Sr.
(b. 2-12-1896, d. 2-20-1976)

Louis E. Eliasberg, Sr. Courtesy of Coin World.

Louis Eliasberg's ambition as a coin collector was grandly simple and simply grand. He wanted nothing less than to own one of every single regular issue United States coin ever issued! He very nearly made it.

At the time of his death on February 20, 1976, Eliasberg was only a few pieces short of his goal to assemble a complete collection of regular issue U.S. coins. He was missing only four half eagles — the 1841-O, 1797 Capped Bust, 16 Star, and Large Eagle pieces.

Eliasberg Estate

Eliasberg was survived by his wife, Lucille, and two sons, Louis, Jr., and Richard. The family sold off the fabled collection in a series of auctions from 1982 to 1997.

It was at an auction conducted by Bowers and Merena May 20-22, 1996, that Eliasberg's 1913 Liberty Head nickel brought a record $1,485,000. The sale of the nickel shattered the million dollar barrier in numismatics for the first time and set a new world record for an individual U.S. coin sold at auction. Jay Parrino was the buyer.

Jay Parrino

Jay Parrino, owner of The Mint in Kansas City, Missouri, claims to have "personally bought, sold and placed more six and seven figure rarities than any other individual in numismatic history." He became the first person in history to pay more than a million dollars for a single coin at a public auction when he bought the Eliasberg 1913 Liberty Head nickel for $1.485 million.

Parrino offered the Eliasberg Specimen for $3 million in a full-page ad in the December 1, 1998, *Numismatic News*. The ad also announced that the coin would be on display at the F.U.N. Show[50] on January 7-10.

The $3 million tab proved to be too rich for the time, so Parrino put the nickel up for auction in 2001 through Superior Galleries. Dwight Manley, acting for the California Gold Marketing Group, picked it up for $1.84 million, another world record.

Dwight Manley/California Gold Marketing Group

Dwight Manley and the California Gold Marketing Group kept the Eliasberg Specimen for a couple of years, shopping it around for the best price. The buyer turned out to be New Hampshire coin dealer Edward Lee. The transaction was announced in Baltimore the night before the American Numismatic Association's 112th Anniversary World of Money Convention opened July 30, 2003.

Edward C. Lee hands over check for "about $3 million" to Dwight Manley for purchase of the Eliasberg 1913 Liberty Head nickel. Courtesy of Coin World. © Coin World

---

[50] Annual coin show presented by Florida United Numismatists, Inc., the first major coin show of the year.

Both Manley and Lee kept mum about the transaction price, but said that it was "about $3 million," setting another new world record.

The surprise announcement of the sale came at a pre-opening gala at Diamond International Galleries in Timonium, Maryland, on Tuesday evening, July 29, 2003. The gala — which had been organized by Laura Sperber, another 1913 Liberty Head nickel owner — featured a display of the four known 1913 Liberty specimens, the first time they had been seen together publicly in 83 years.

The startling announcement would be overshadowed by even more stunning news the following morning at the ANA show opening ceremonies — the rediscovery of the 1913 Liberty Head nickel missing for more than 40 years.

Edward C. Lee

Edward C. Lee, president of Lee's Certified Coins, Ltd., in Merrimack, New Hampshire, has been involved professionally with coins since 1958. He gained his experience as a dealer in New York City and ran his first national ads in *Numismatic Scrapbook Magazine* in 1963.

Lee told *Coin World*'s Beth Deisher in an interview following the announcement (*Coin World*, August 18, 2003) of his purchase of the Eliasberg Specimen from Dwight Manley that he had no immediate plans to sell the coin. Deisher wrote:

> He purchased it for his personal collection and said he intends to hold it for several years. During his ownership, he said he will make it available for public exhibit, just as Manley did during his ownership.
>
> "I plan to be known as the only person in history who ever retired on a nickel," Lee said. He predicted that within one to three years he will be able to sell Specimen No. 1 [Eliasberg Specimen] for "at least $5 million."

Legend Numismatics

Edward Lee certainly earned the right to retire on a nickel. On June 2, 2005, Mr. Lee sold his nickel to Legend Numismatics for $4.15 million. If the sale price was "at least" $850,000 short of a solid retirement plan, no one seemed to notice. The sale shattered yet another record, once again propelling the 1913 Liberty nickel and its owners into the news and public spotlight.

#4 WALTON SPECIMEN

"Dull Proof - Two slight lines in field opposite 13th star   Dot on neck opposite end of hanging curl" (Eric Newman notes)

Pedigree: James Kelly, Dr. Conway A. Bolt, Sr., Winston-Salem businessman (?), George O. Walton, Walton Family.

Unquestionably the most mystifying of the 1913 Liberty Head nickels, the Walton Specimen's whereabouts baffled numismatists for more than four decades. Even after it was rediscovered in 2003, its early pedigree has remained shrouded in mystery.

James Kelly

Clyde D. Mervis reported in *Numismatic Scrapbook Magazine* (July 1968) that James Kelly sold one of the three 1913 Liberty Head nickels he acquired from B.G. Johnson to Dr. Conway A. Bolt of North Carolina. Peters and Mohon also listed the sale price to Dr. Bolt as $1,000 in *The Complete Guide to Shield and Liberty Head Nickels.*

Beth Deisher reported the sale price as $2,450 in "Liberty Head Legends" (*Numismatist*, July 2003). This figure is improbable, given that it is almost three times the price Kelly received for the other two nickels sold at around the same time — $900. Perhaps it was mistakenly transposed from the reported $2,450 listed by Gans and Grunthal of Numismatic Fine Arts as the price realized for the Olsen specimen (which did not sell) in a 1946 mail-in bid sale.

The confusion over the reported price contributed to at least one theory that a sixth 1913 Liberty Head nickel exists.

Dr. Conway A. Bolt, Sr.

Noted as a prominent pattern specialist, Dr. Conway A. Bolt, Sr. of Marshville, North Carolina, began collecting coins in 1913 with a few specimens from his grandfather's estate, according to Pete Smith in *American Numismatic Biographies*. Little personal information was given about him, except that he died in 1974. Bolt was reportedly a Union County, North Carolina, health officer.

Dr. Conway A. Bolt, Sr., Marshville, N.C. Courtesy of Coin World.

According to Smith, Stacks auctioned Bolt's collection, which included "many series of complete sets of proof coins," on April 21, 1966. In 1975, Pine Tree auctioned the remainder of the collection. Smith reported that Bolt's collection once included the same 1913 Liberty nickel that was often spotted with George Walton prior to his fatal car accident in 1962.

The path of the 1913 Liberty Head nickel owned by Dr. Bolt after it left his hands gets lost in a murky mystery. According to Peters and Mohon, the nickel was not included in any of the lots auctioned by Stack's and Pine Tree. They described two theories about what happened to the nickel.

One is that either Dr. Bolt or George Walton, also of North Carolina, sold the coin to the wealthy North Carolina tobacco magnate, R. J. Reynolds. Writing in *Coin World*, Abe Kosoff quoted a letter he said was from Dr. Bolt to Aubrey Bebee that claimed: "My specimen was traded to Reynolds." *Which* Reynolds is the question. The quote does not specify whether Bolt meant he himself traded the coin to Reynolds or if he is reporting that someone else (i.e., Walton) made the trade. Apparently the letter gave no other details about the identity of the buyer. No record has been found that R.J. Reynolds ever owned this coin, although the numismatic literature for years referred to it as the "Reynolds specimen."

Another theory posed by Peters and Mohon is that Walton traded a batch of double eagles for Bolt's 1913 Liberty nickel, reportedly in 1948, according to a report in *Numismatic Scrapbook Magazine* (March 1958).

Peters and Mohon framed the puzzle in this way:

> So, is the missing 1913 nickel sailing the eternal seas as cargo in a finely crafted model ship? It would be a fitting chapter in a progression of enigmas.

What is known for certain is that the nickel wound up in George Walton's possession, and it went missing for more than 40 years until being rediscovered in 2003. The decades-long gap in this story demands more than a few paragraphs to tell. The chapters ahead will explore in detail this long-silent blank in the record.

Winston-Salem Businessman

Though there is no clear record of who the mysterious "wealthy Winston-Salem businessman" was, analysis of the published comments by Dr. Bolt, George Walton, and others seems to confirm that an unknown party owned the nickel between Bolt and Walton.

George O. Walton
(b. 5-15-1907, d. March 9, 1962)

However he came to own it, North Carolina coin collector and dealer George O. Walton had a 1913 Liberty Head nickel with him when he died in 1962. Though Walton's name has been frequently mentioned in the numismatic lore, little was written about the man and his life. Stories speaking of him tended sometimes to be dismissive, in a sense brushing him aside. The mainstream press, especially in his home area, was kinder to Walton, as a family scrapbook of clippings reveals. The upcoming chapter will flesh out a picture of George Walton not generally known to the numismatic community.

Walton Estate

George Walton never married. Upon his death, his considerable estate, which included a spectacular coin collection along with notable collections of stamps and guns, was sold at auction and the proceeds divided among his five brothers and sisters. The Walton heirs included Melva W. Givens, Vesta W. Roberts, Billie Mae Walton, Charles B. Walton, and Frank Walton.

Melva W. Givens
b. 8-19-1913, d. 3-25-1992

The 1913 Liberty Head nickel was among the coins that went to George Walton's sister Melva Givens. Because of a mistaken appraisal that identified the nickel as an altered date fake instead of a genuine specimen, its value was listed as "NONE." The coin was put away as a family keepsake.

Melva Givens died March 25, 1992, leaving her estate, including the supposed altered date nickel, to her heirs — Ryan Givens, Richard Givens, Bette Givens, and Cheryl Myers.

Givens Estate

The family was unaware that the coin sequestered in a plain manila envelope in Melva Givens' closet was actually one of America's foremost numismatic treasures, so it lay forgotten in the dark for more than 40 years. They would discover the truth in the summer of 2003.

#5 ANA SPECIMEN

"Unc   Dot in left center of neck at chin level"   (Eric Newman notes)

Pedigree: James Kelly (Paramount International Coin Corp.), J.V. McDermott, Aubrey and Adeline Bebee, American Numismatic Association.

Sometimes called the most popular of the 1913 Liberty Head nickels, this specimen was probably seen up-close and personal, even actually touched, by more people than all the others combined…all because of a hard-drinking man known far and wide simply as "Mac."

James Kelly

Of the three 1913 Liberty Head nickels James Kelly bought from B.G. Johnson, he sold one for $900 in March 1943 to J.V. McDermott, a "one-time steeple-jack and professional coin dealer" (Peters and Mohon).

J.V. McDermott
(b. ca. 1898, d. 9-29-1966)

J.V. ("Mac") McDermott, one of several colorful characters who have owned a 1913 Liberty Head nickel. Courtesy of Numismatic Scrapbook Magazine. © Amos Press, Inc.

By all accounts, J.V. McDermott was probably the most colorful, rip-roaring, larger-than-life character in a 1913 Liberty Head nickel saga populated with a cast of many extraordinary characters. "Mac," as he was affectionately known even to people he had just met (and by many more he never met), was partial to "a taste of the creature" (he admitted to having a problem with liquor) and loved to frequent bars to show off his "Miss Liberty" nickel — which also was dubbed the "MacNickel" — to any patrons who were interested. He carried it in his pocket and would not hesitate to pass the coin casually down the bar for all to see and touch.

Carl H. Allenbaugh, in a *Coin Prices* perspective titled "A Pair of Brash Pretender Coins Challenge for the $100,000 Pinnacle,"[51] described McDermott's free spirit:

> The man was as memorable as his nickel, as different from his fellow coin dealers as they from chimney sweeps. No one ever saw "Mac" wearing a tie, or a suit that didn't appear to have been slept in. On more than one occasion, his entrance to a convention hall was blocked by the sergeant-at-arms who thought "Mac" had wandered in from a freight yard. At such times, he would emit the call of a melancholy moose, and await rescue by a flying wedge of his friends.
>
> Having gained entrance to the hall, "Mac" would wander down the rows of bourse tables, greeting old friends, making new ones, and chiding all about their neckties. Then across the street to the nearest bistro where he would spread his merchandise upon a table, and amid the blare of the juke box and the merry chatter of happy glasses conduct his business in an atmosphere he found more congenial than the decorum of the convention hall.
>
> Under his ownership, "MacNickel," as his specimen was quickly dubbed, became the carefree vagabond of numismatics. Any coin show wishing to cash in on the publicity value of "MacNickel" had but to ask for it. If "Mac" could attend, he brought the coin in his pocket. If not, he simply mailed it.

Numismatic Scrapbook Magazine (April 1973) carried an item about the experience of one observer at a McDermott bar appearance with "Miss Liberty":

> From Tucson, Arizona, Charles N. Cooley reminisces, "I knew McDermott and his nickel very well. I was in Chicago when he bought the

---

[51] Source provided by Cherly Myers.

nickel but didn't see it at that time. Later, I saw it when the American Numismatic Association convention was held in Chicago in 1956 at the Congress hotel. We were at the bar with Mac, Sam Carlson, Ernest Jonas and Mike A. Powills. The nickel was passed up and down the bar, then housed in plastic.

"Powills took the nickel into the next room and it was gone for about 15 minutes. We asked Mac if he wasn't worried and his answer was, 'No, it will be OK,' and it was returned in good time.

"This was the same time we took Mac to his room and persuaded him to dress up with tie and coat. He hadn't been dressing up at any of the ANA banquets. When he appeared at the banquet his wife, Betts, nearly fainted. As for Mac, we all gave him a nice hand and we thoroughly enjoyed his dress, as this was an event," Cooley concludes.

"Mac" apparently never met a stranger. He was a trusting soul and considered everyone a friend. An anecdote published in *Numismatic Scrapbook Magazine* (same issue as the preceding story) illustrates how McDermott could instantly put people at ease:

"During the late 1950's I was living in a small town in Oklahoma," writes S.A. Cullum, Dallas, Texas. "One evening my doorbell rang, and I found a stranger at my door. Without saying a word he handed me a small plastic case.

"I saw that it contained a Liberty Head nickel, and without needing to see the date I shouted, 'McDermott.' Then I hastened to invite Mac and Betts into the house. Mac and I had corresponded in the past, and he had decided to stop over and look me up enroute to Arizona.

"He had checked into a nearby motel, and I hastened to call other coin 'nuts' I knew who would want to see the nickel and whatever other merchandise he might have available. Soon he had a room full of people, and the famous 1913 nickel was circulating freely among them.

"I was somewhat security minded, and so tried to keep up with the nickel which was then worth around $10,000. But Mac was completely at ease; he was selling coins and knew nothing would happen to the nickel among coin collectors. And he was right; after everyone left the nickel was still there, safe and sound.

"I heard Mac's version of the history of the 1913 nickel, and spent an evening with the most famous of them all. That was indeed the high point of a small collector's coin career," Cullum concludes.

McDermott liked to speak in his ads about big offers he received for the nickel, offers that he refused as inadequate. The offers ranged as high as $50,000. Among the offers he turned down was one from "J.B. Trotter" (actually Powell B. Trotter of Memphis, Tennessee) for $19,000, according to *Numismatic Scrapbook Magazine* (December 1971):

> In his advertisement in *Scrapbook*, September 1957, he [McDermott] refers to the ANA convention in Philadelphia, Pennsylvania: "Wow, it really was the biggest convention yet. I sure was happy to see so many old friends, also to meet folks I've been writing and sending coins for years. Why, I even met folks I never sold coins to, Ouch! That man, J.B. Trotter, was there and trying to steal that thar 1913 nickel from me but the best he'd do was $19,000, so I still have it."

The outgoing McDermott was always generous in loaning his nickel to be exhibited as a drawing card for club functions and coin shows. He showed it so much and so often that stories began to circulate about it being suspiciously in more than one place at the same time. Pete Smith reported in *American Numismatic Biographies*:

> Although there is no doubt that McDermott owned a legitimate coin, he may also have occasionally exhibited an altered coin.

Smith also related that McDermott's wife, "Betts," was driving alone in her car in 1957 when it stalled on a railroad track. She bailed out of the car just before it was struck by a train. Some $25,000 in coins she carried with her were strewn around the wreck site. Most were recovered, Smith said. It was not reported that the "Miss Liberty" nickel was involved in the accident.

McDermott was born around 1898 in Iowa. He worked as a steeple-jack and later had some experience in the vending machine business. He became a coin dealer in Milwaukee, Wisconsin. He died in a South Milwaukee hospital September 29, 1966.

Gloria Peters and Cynthia Mohon described what happened to the coin after McDermott's death:

> His widow, Betts McDermott, auctioned the coin at the ANA Convention on August 11, 1967. The auctioneer was the same man who had sold the coin to McDermott for $900 in 1942 [sic], James Kelly. He described the coin as follows: "This coin is in Uncirculated condition but does have a slight rough surface which existed at the time it was purchased and no doubt occurred in the striking."[52]

---

[52] The carefree and probably sometimes careless handling of the coin in many a bar could not have helped the condition of the coin any.

James Kelly started the bidding on Lot number 2214 by stating to the excited crowd, "Ladies and Gentlemen: We are now going to start bidding on the 1931 nickel..." At the crowd's startled response, he corrected himself, "You know that would be more rare than the 1913 because they didn't make a '31. We're starting the bidding tonight on the 1913 nickel... I have $38,000...can I hear 40,000?" After a bid for $40,000 from Aubrey Bebee, James Kelly continued, "I have $40,000; can I get $42,000?" A bid of $45,000 was forthcoming from Abe Kosoff and Sol Kaplan, but the final bid went to Bebee who purchased the coin for $46,000. An excited crowd took photos and had their catalogs autographed by Mr. and Mrs. Bebee, James Kelly and Betts McDermott. Mrs. McDermott died in Lubbock, Texas on December 18, 1967, at the age of 64 [just four months after the auction].

Numismatic Scrapbook Magazine said of the auction:

The McDermott nickel unquestionably "stole the show" at the 76th annual ANA convention as the auction room was jammed to capacity, with little standing room for latecomers as the historic event approached.

Personable James Kelly of Paramount International Coin Corp., Englewood, Ohio, was the auctioneer and had cataloged the sale. He announced lot number 2214 to the tense crowd as cameras clicked and tape recorders began to whir.

Aubrey Bebee

Aubrey Bebee's world record check for the winning bid of $46,000 and his new coin were put on display for the benefit of those who could not find room in the jammed auction room. Collectors clamored to get near enough to take pictures and get autographs.

Aubrey Bebee's record-setting check for his winning bid of $46,000 for the McDermott nickel at a 1967 auction. Courtesy of ANA.

Aubrey Bebee, Omaha, Nebraska, collector who outbid Abe Kosoff and others to buy J.V. McDermott's 1913 Liberty Head nickel (the ANA Specimen). Courtesy of ANA.

Bebee told reporters he had made up his mind when he left Omaha to come to the show that he intended to have that nickel. He had transferred money into a special bank account specifically for that purpose. It was all a complete surprise to his wife, Adeline.

Numismatic Scrapbook Magazine reported in December 1971 that Bebee turned down offers of $56,000, $60,000, and $75,000, as well as a trade for an 1804 silver dollar.

The Bebees eventually decided to retire from the coin business and, in 1989, donated their 1913 Liberty Head nickel to the American Numismatic Association's Money Museum in Colorado Springs, Colorado.

American Numismatic Association

In 2003, the ANA's 1913 Liberty Head nickel was joined by one of its siblings, the Walton Specimen, on loan from the Walton heirs after it had been authenticated at the end of July.

Chapter 7 References

Allenbaugh, Carl H. 1972. "A Pair of Brash Contender Coins Challenge for the $100,000 Pinnacle - A History of Intrigue Surrounds The King of American Coins and Its Heir Presumptive." *Coin Prices* (May) pp. 1-5.

Bowers, Q. David. 1996. "*The Louis E. Eliasberg, Sr., Collection*," Bowers and Merena Galleries auction catalog (May 20-22), pp. 221-228.

Certified Coins web site. 2003. Accessed October 21, 2003, at certifiedcoins.com/credentials.asp.

CoinWorld.com. 2003. "Legend Numismatics buys legend." Posted January 20, 2003. Web site accessed September 25, 2003, at http://www.coinworld.com/news/012703/news-5.asp.

Deisher, Beth. 2001. "How'd you like to sell a 1913 five-cent for $2,000?" *Coin World* (June 11), p. 1.
— Deisher. 2003. "Liberty Head Legends," *Numismatist* (July), pp. 36-43.
— Deisher. 2003. "Finest known 1913 5¢ sets new price record." *Coin World* (August 18), pp. 2, 30.

Eliasberg, Richard A. 1996. "The Collector, My Father - A Biographical Sketch." From *Louis E. Eliasberg, Sr. King of Coins* by Q. David Bowers (Wolfeboro, New Hampshire: Bowers and Merena Galleries), pp. 1-7.

Gans, Edward, and Henry Grunthal. 1946. Mail Bid Sale and List of Prices Realized.

Gelbert, Doug. 2003. "Who Was Hetty Green?" Web site, accessed January 15, 2003, at http://coco.essortment.com/whowashettygr_ricf.htm.

Gibbs, William T. 1993. "Mystery surrounds pedigree of coin." *Coin World* (June 28), p. 1.

Gilkes, Paul. 1993. "Reed Hawn says time has come to pass along 'joy of ownership.'" *Coin World* (June 21), p. 1.

Hamrick, John B., Jr. 2003. Interview (December 10).

Lemke, Bob. 1978. "Smithsonian Institution Receives American Rarity." *Numismatic News* (August 26), p. 3.

Lester, Carl N. 2003. Gold Rush Gallery web site - "Writers Corner - Numismatic Gumshoe: On the Trail of King Farouk." Accessed September 18, 2003, at www.goldrushgallery.com/gumshoe.html.

Nationmaster.com Encyclopedia. 2003. "Gamel Abdel Nasser." Web site accessed January 7, 2004, at www.nationmaster.com/encyclopedia/Gamel-Abdel-Nasser.

Mervis, Clyde D. 1968. "World's Most Valuable Coin." *Numismatic Scrapbook Magazine* (July), p. 1070.

Myers, Cheryl. 2003. Email (December 20).

Newman, Eric P. 1996. Letter to Q. David Bowers (January 15).

Numismatic News. 1974. "2½ Cents Worth of Famous Nickel Costs Bowers & Ruddy $100,000" (November 23), p. 51.
— *Numismatic News*. 1978. "Rare Liberty Nickel Fetches Record Price In Private Sale to Unnamed Show Biz Star" (July 22), p. 1.

Numismatic Scrapbook Magazine. 1958. "Proof That Advertising Pays - The Story of the 1913 Liberty Head Nickel" (Vol. XXIV, No. 3, March), p. 457-459.
— *Numismatic Scrapbook Magazine*. 1971. "Liberty 1913 Nickel Offers Mystic Aura" (December), p. 1176.
— *Numismatic Scrapbook Magazine*. 1973. "Liberty 1913 Nickel Story Footnotes" (April), p. 368, 370.

Parrino, Jay. 2003. The Mint (Kansas City, Missouri) web site, accessed January 11, 2003 at http://www.jp-themint.com/about.cfm.

Peters, Gloria, and Cynthia Mohon. 1995. *The Complete Guide to Shield & Liberty Head Nickels* (Virginia Beach, Virginia: DLRC Press), p. 166-172.

Smith, Pete. *American Numismatic Biographies*, (Minneapolis, Minnesota: Remy Bourne-Ramm Communications, Inc.), pp. 32, 37, 81, 84, 176, 133, 138, 158.

Smithsonian Institution. 2004. "The National Numismatic Collection." Smithsonian National Museum of American History web site, accessed January 8, 2004, at americanhistory.si.edu/csr/cadnnc.htm.

Sperber, Laura. 2003. Interview (October 10).

Stack's. 1993. "Records Are Made To Be Broken!" Post-sale full-page ad in *Coin World* (November 8), p. 29.

Wacks, Mel. 1978. "1913 Liberty Nickel Sold by Superior for $200,000.00 to Anonymous Collector." Superior Stamp & Coin Co., Inc., press release issued July 22.

- Chapter Eight -

DISAPPEARING ACT

What happened to the 1913 Liberty Head nickel owned by Dr. Conway Bolt?

Second only to the mystery of the five nickels' origin, the puzzle of where this particular nickel went after Dr. Bolt owned it has baffled numismatists for three generations. Who did he sell or trade it to and when? Where did it go from there?

Controversial Pedigree Gap

The Marshville, North Carolina, collector bought the nickel from James Kelly in 1943. From that point forward until July 2003, the path of this enigmatic 1913 Liberty Head nickel eluded numismatic historians. Shrouded in myth, speculation, rumor, and controversy, the pedigree of this famous nickel remains blurred even today for the period after it was owned by Dr. Bolt.

Until 2003, the numismatic community assumed that it was in the possession of the Reynolds clan of North Carolina. R.J. Reynolds, the tobacco magnate, acquired rare coins and was known to have associations with Dr. Bolt and with George O. Walton. The coin even came to be named the Reynolds specimen in most published pedigrees.

Ironically, according to *Coin World* Editor Beth Deisher, it was Mrs. Reynolds who was the coin collector, not her husband. However, it was uncommon in that age for a woman to be involved in coin collecting on that exotic level of rarity, so apparently her husband bought and sold coins on her behalf. Thus he became identified in the numismatic lore as a famous collector.

There was no public announcement in the numismatic press about the transfer of the nickel from Bolt to whomever came next. So the assumption was drawn from sparse cryptic hints.

Abe Kosoff cited a line from a letter he said was from Dr. Bolt to Aubrey Bebee in which he said he traded the coin to someone named Reynolds. The line quoted — "My specimen was traded to Reynolds." — did not specify any other name, so it could have been *any* Reynolds. The quote does not even say that Dr. Bolt himself made the trade. He might have been referring to a transaction that occurred after it left his possession.

Coin World staff writer William T. Gibbs said in a June 28, 1993, write-up on the missing nickel:

> Bolt also wrote Bebee (according to Kosoff) that "Reynolds" traded the coin to "either Mr. X or [Alex] Shuford." Kosoff disputes that, since he sold the Shuford collection later; it did not contain the coin.
>
> Kosoff again blames Walton for the misinformation, saying Bolt could have only gotten the information from Walton.

If Kosoff was right about Shuford not being involved, then who was "Mr. X"? Could Bolt have been referring to George Walton?

Walton, described as "a freelance estate appraiser" who divided his time among Charlotte, North Carolina; Jacksonville, Florida; and Roanoke, Virginia, was known to have a connection to R.J. Reynolds. He was rumored to have supplied coins to Reynolds and handled sales transactions for the tobacco tycoon. A MANA (Middle Atlantic Numismatic Association) tribute to him said:

> As a "side line" he acted as buyer-agent for several millionaires in the Carolinas, who did not wish to reveal their numismatic interests or identities.

At one point, he also was in charge of setting up an exhibit of Alex Shuford's collections at the Hickory (North Carolina) Museum of Art. A newspaper clipping from the Walton family archives, date and publication unknown (probably the Hickory, North Carolina, *Daily Record*), said that at the time of Walton's death he "had been working at the Hickory Museum of Art over a period of approximately a year."

The brief item explained that his work schedule was erratic and punctuated by two or three days of work followed by a time of absence. Walton worked on the second floor of the Hickory Art Museum where he was charged with displaying the coins and firearms from a collection owned by A. Alex Shuford.

Walton told *Numismatic Scrapbook Magazine* in the December 1953 issue[53] that he brokered the transaction between Bolt and the mystery buyer. NSM

---

[53] Source material provided by Cheryl Myers, George Walton's niece, and family attorney Hugh B. Wellons. Myers collected numerous press clippings and photos about Walton from various family members and old estate documents and compiled them into a digital archive. Many of the references in this account of George Walton's life are based on this invaluable resource. Because the clippings were cut from pages, the dates and publications are not known in some cases.

indicated that Walton also claimed he "obtained" a 1913 Liberty Head nickel from St. Louis coin dealer B.G. Johnson:

> According to George Walton, who still owns the piece he obtained direct from Johnson, the coin which James Kelly sold to Dr. Bolt is in the collection of a wealthy North Carolina business man. Mr. Walton states that he helped arrange the trade between Dr. Bolt and the business man.

Assuming this item is an accurate report of what Walton told *NSM*, it appears to eliminate him as Bolt's "Mr. X," since he claims to have been the go-between, not the end buyer. Walton's contention that he obtained a 1913 Liberty Head nickel from B.G. Johnson, by definition, has to be either an error (possibly a misquote by the publication) or startling evidence that there were actually six of the 1913 "V" nickels! Rumors of a sixth coin have bubbled on the edges on numismatic lore for decades.

Johnson showed five entries for 1913 Liberty Head nickels in his inventory listing. Eric Newman kept one of these for himself, and invoices retrieved from B.G. Johnson's archives by Newman show three sales by Johnson to James Kelly and one to F.C.C. Boyd. That adds up to five.

If Walton still owned the nickel he said he bought from Johnson at the same time the nickel that had been owned by Dr. Bolt was "in the collection of a wealthy North Carolina business man," then there would have to be a sixth coin, because four others are accounted for.

However, Walton himself seems to contradict his own claim that he bought his nickel directly from B.G. Johnson in two different newspaper articles.

Interviewed by the *Greensboro* (N.C.) *Daily News*[54] when he was in town for the annual convention of the North Carolina Coin Clubs Association, Walton claimed he had turned down a chance to buy all five nickels from Johnson. The article, which appeared in the Saturday, October 10, 1959, edition, reported:

> ...the five nickels were bought by B.G. Johnson of St. Louis, a coin dealer. Walton made a trip to St. Louis to see them and could have bought the lot for $4,500. About three weeks later, Walton decided to buy them and went back to St. Louis, but the coins had been sold separately.
>
> One was bought by Dr. C.A. Bolt of Marshville, who later decided to sell it. He called Walton and the latter arranged for its sale to a Winston-Salem man, collecting a commission of $1,000. Walton will not reveal the name of the Winston-Salem man.

---

[54] Courtesy of Cheryl Myers. ©*News & Record*.

In 1946, Walter [sic] decided he'd like to have the nickel owned by the Winston-Salem man. Walton owned an 1855 $50 gold piece known to collectors as a "Kellogg" $50 gold piece. The Winston-Salem man gave Walton the nickel and $500 "boot" for the Kellogg coin.

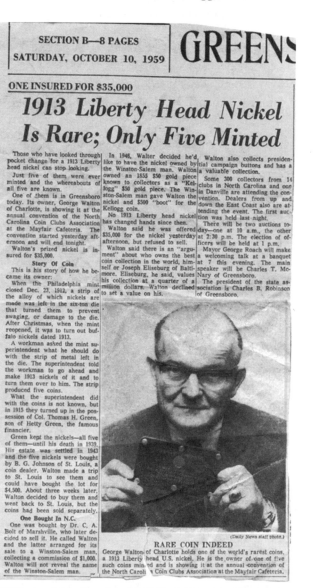

SECTION B—8 PAGES
SATURDAY, OCTOBER 10, 1959 | **GREENS**

ONE INSURED FOR $35,000

1913 Liberty Head Nickel Is Rare; Only Five Minted

Those who have looked through pocket change for a 1913 Liberty head nickel can stop looking.

Just five of them were ever minted and the whereabouts of all five are known.

One of them is in Greensboro today. Its owner, George Walton of Charlotte, is showing it at the annual convention of the North Carolina Coin Clubs Association at the Mayfair Cafeteria. The convention started yesterday afternoon and will end tonight. Walton's prized nickel is insured for $35,000.

Story Of Coin

This is his story of how he became its owner:

When the Philadelphia mint closed Dec. 23, 1912, a strip of the alloy of which nickels are made was left in the six-ton die that turned them to prevent swaging, or damage to the die. After Christmas, when the mint reopened, it was to turn out buffalo nickels dated 1913.

A workman asked the mint superintendent what he should do with the strip of metal left in the die. The superintendent told the workman to go ahead and make 1913 nickels of it and turn them over to him. The strip produced five coins.

What the superintendent did with the coins is not known, but in 1915 they turned up in the possession of Col. Thomas H. Green, son of Hetty Green, the famous financier.

Green kept the nickels—all five of them—until his death in 1939. His estate was settled in 1943 and the five nickels were bought by B. G. Johnson of St. Louis, a coin dealer. Walton made a trip to St. Louis to see them and could have bought the lot for $4,500. About three weeks later, Walton decided to buy them and went back to St. Louis, but the coins had been sold separately.

One Bought In N.C.

One was bought by Dr. C. A. Bolt of Marshville, who later decided to sell it. He called Walton and the latter arranged for its sale to a Winston-Salem man, collecting a commission of $1,000. Walton will not reveal the name of the Winston-Salem man.

In 1946, Walter decided he'd like to have the nickel owned by the Winston-Salem man. Walton owned an 1855 $50 gold piece known to collectors as a "Kellogg" $50 gold piece. The Winston-Salem man gave Walton the nickel and $500 "boot" for the Kellogg coin.

No 1913 Liberty head nickel has changed hands since then.

Walton said he was offered $35,000 for the nickel yesterday afternoon, but refused to sell.

Walton said there is an "argument" about who owns the best coin collection in the world, himself or Joseph Eliseburg of Baltimore. Eliseburg, he said, values his collection at a quarter of a million dollars. Walton declined to set a value on his.

Walton also collects presidential campaign buttons and has a valuable collection.

Some 300 collectors from 14 clubs in North Carolina and one in Danville are attending the convention. Dealers from up and down the East Coast also are attending the event. The first auction was held last night.

There will be two auctions today—one at 10 a.m., the other at 2:30 p.m. The election of officers will be held at 1 p.m.

Mayor George Roach will make a welcoming talk at a banquet at 7 this evening. The main speaker will be Charles T. McNary of Greensboro.

The president of the state association is Charles B. Robinson of Greensboro.

(Daily News staff photo.)

RARE COIN INDEED
George Walton of Charlotte holds one of the world's rarest coins, a 1913 Liberty head U.S. nickel. He is the owner of one of five such coins minted and is showing it at the annual convention of the North Carolina Coin Clubs Association at the Mayfair Cafeteria.

October 10, 1959, report in the Greensboro (N.C.) Daily News citing Walton's claim that he had an opportunity to buy the lot of 1913 Liberty Head nickels from B.G. Johnson. Reprinted with permission of the News & Record. ©

A memorial write-up about Walton in *The MANA Journal* repeated the story, but the offered purchase price reported was less than half that mentioned in the *Greensboro Daily News* report ($2,000 instead of $4,500):

> He once told an acquaintance that he had the opportunity to purchase all 5 of the 1913 Liberty head nickels, which later became so valuable, for about $2,000, a modest price — but declined! MANA's President, Dr. Conway Bolt, earlier owned Walton's nickel, but traded it to a Winston-Salem millionaire. Walton obtained it in 1945 in a trade for about $3750. At MANA's 1956 Richmond Convention his nickel was exhibited along with one belonging to J.V. McDermott and one of E.M. Hydeman, which is probably the last time the 3 were together. (Efforts to "borrow" the other two for exhibit did not materialize.)

Asked in a 2003 interview by the authors about Walton's visit to St. Louis, Eric Newman, Johnson's partner in the 1913 nickel venture, said he did not know Walton personally and was unaware of any visit by Walton to St. Louis or of his being offered the opportunity to buy the coins for $4,500, let alone $2,000. However, he does not necessarily discount the claim. "He would have come to Johnson, not me," Newman said.

Walton's comments to Laurens Walker, a staff writer for the Charlotte, North Carolina, *Observer*[55] gave the year he acquired the coin as 1945, rather than 1946,[56] and reinforced the notion that Reynolds had owned the coin at some point, though he did not identify Reynolds by name.

Walton did indicate that the seller was "a wealthy Winston-Salem Collector," who had originally acquired the coin in a purchase from Dr. C. A. Bolt. The article further suggested that Walton was unsure of the exact price he paid, (though he guessed it was around $3,750), on account of having received the coin in trade for other coins. "I am a pretty tough trader," Walton told the *Observer*.

Another interview with Walton in October 1959 by the *Charlotte Observer*[57] again names 1946 instead of 1945 as the year when he acquired the nickel and also mentions the mystery man from Winston-Salem:

---

[55] Source provided by Cheryl Myers

[56] The two dates, 1945 and 1946, appear with about equal frequency in press accounts of when Walton acquired the nickel. The authors were unable to find any clues that would favor one year over the other as the reliable date of the transaction. Walton may have had reason to be intentionally ambiguous about the exact date; however, the reason has never been discovered.

[57] Courtesy of Cheryl Myers.

Walton swapped for the coin in 1946. He gave a Winston-Salem man $500 plus a gold piece that had cost him $3,750.

The same man offered him $35,000 Friday to get the nickel back, he said. He won't sell it but his reason's not sentimental.

"I'd have to give the government too much money," he laughs.

If Walton got a nickel directly from Johnson, as was reported by *NSM*, and he acquired a different nickel from "a wealthy Winston-Salem collector," as he told the *Charlotte Observer*, then he had to have owned two nickels out of what had to be six total. Only two other explanations could account for these conditions: 1) Walton was misquoted in one or more of the published accounts, or 2) Walton either forgot or mixed up the actual facts, or was being a bit creative with the truth (as some coin dealers occasionally are known to be).

A letter from Lee Hewitt, editor of *Numismatic Scrapbook Magazine*, written September 22, 1964, to James A. Ford, trust officer at the Colonial American Bank in Roanoke[58] mentioned a hearsay comment from Walton about the coin having belonged to Reynolds:

> As to whether the Mr. Reynolds that Dr. Bolt traded his nickel with for a collection of double eagles still owns the piece I do not know. The list published was that of the last known owners of record. In numismatics these things are taken for granted...altho [sic] for the benefit of beginners such qualifying statement probably should be included, as an individual might be owner of a piece on September 1 and not the owner on September 2.
>
> George told me at about the first convention he exhibited one of the nickels that the piece was ex-Bolt and belonged to Reynolds. That was 12 years ago approximately.

Again, "Reynolds" is only identified by last name, giving no clear proof which Reynolds it might have been.

A letter from Hewitt a week later, on September 28, to Walton's sister Melva Givens was a bit more specific, but still hearsay and not specific enough to be a reliable reference:

> I knew your brother quite well and we were always on the friendliest of terms.
>
> Without doing some research as to the exact dates...off hand I would say that it was at a convention in Washington, D.C. around 1954 that your

---

[58] Letters from Lee Hewitt courtesy of Ryan Givens.

brother <u>George told me</u> [underlining by Hewitt] that the nickel he had with him was the specimen that Dr. Bolt had traded to one of the Reynolds of the tobacco family. It's not uncommon for one collector to show another collectors coins for research or exhibit numerous times.

A handwritten note[59] about Walton's activities found in the estate papers of the executor, Colonial-American Bank of Roanoke, Virginia, said:

> Dr. Bolt Box 358 Marshville, N.C.
> went to Florida with Dr. Bolt in November
> Mr. Walton purchased 1913 nickel from Dr. Bolt

The note doesn't say what year the purchase was made nor whether the purchase was made on the trip to Florida, and it does not specify a 1913 *Liberty Head* nickel. The identity of the writer and the source of the information is unknown. So the note, while tantalizing, sadly must be added to the pile of hearsay testimony.

In any event, there has always been a major problem with the assumption that Reynolds had the coin or even owned it at any time: The Reynolds family could never produce the coin, and no written record can be found that R. J. Reynolds ever owned it and sold or traded it.

Following publicity in 2003 about the discovery of the missing nickel, a member of the Reynolds family, William Neal Reynolds II, told Beth Deisher, editor of *Coin World*, that his father bought the nickel during World War II while his mother, Mrs. Richard J. Reynolds, Jr., was serving on the Assay Commission. He said he saw the nickel in 1950 when he was 10. He claimed that his mother promised him the coin if he graduated from college with decent grades.

He noted that his mother died on December 15, 1961, just three months before Walton's untimely death. He posed the possibility that his mother had loaned the coin on consignment to Walton before she died, implying that it actually belongs to the Reynolds heirs. How that would square with her promise to give him the coin is not made clear. He admitted he had looked extensively and had been unable to find either the coin or any record of it being in the possession of his father or mother.

Noah Reynolds, grandson of the tobacco magnate, has probed into family records for years, as has been reported in numerous published articles since at least 1993, looking for the proof that his grandfather once owned

---

[59] Source: Cheryl Myers and Hugh Wellons.

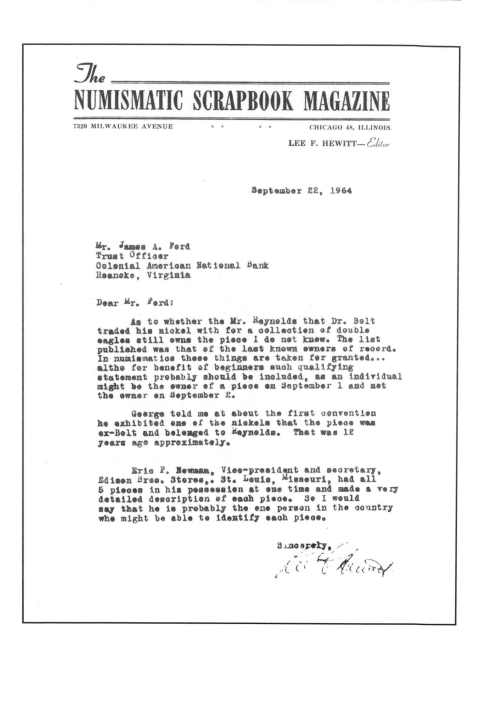

The
NUMISMATIC SCRAPBOOK MAGAZINE

7320 MILWAUKEE AVENUE   « »   « »   CHICAGO 48, ILLINOIS.

LEE F. HEWITT—*Editor*

September 22, 1964

Mr. James A. Ford
Trust Officer
Colonial American National Bank
Roanoke, Virginia

Dear Mr. Ford:

As to whether the Mr. Reynolds that Dr. Bolt
traded his nickel with for a collection of double
eagles still owns the piece I do not know. The list
published was that of the last known owners of record.
In numismatics these things are taken for granted...
altho for benefit of beginners such qualifying
statement probably should be included, as an individual
might be the owner of a piece on September 1 and not
the owner on September 2.

George told me at about the first convention
he exhibited one of the nickels that the piece was
ex-Bolt and belonged to Reynolds. That was 12
years ago approximately.

Eric P. Newman, Vice-president and secretary,
Edison Bros. Stores,. St. Louis, Missouri, had all
5 pieces in his possession at one time and made a very
detailed description of each piece. So I would
say that he is probably the one person in the country
who might be able to identify each piece.

Sincerely,

The
NUMISMATIC SCRAPBOOK MAGAZINE

7320 MILWAUKEE AVENUE « »   « »   CHICAGO 48, ILLINOIS.

LEE F. HEWITT— *Editor*

September 28

Dear Miss Givens:

I knew your brother quite well and we were always on the friendliest of terms.

Without doing some research as to the exact dates...off hand I would say that it was at a convention in Washington, D.C. around 1954 that your brother George told me that the nickel he had with him was the specimen that Dr. Bolt had traded to one of the Reymolds of the tobbaco family. It's not uncommon for one collector to show another collectors specimen. I have borrowed other collectors coins for research or exhibit numerous times.

Eric Newman of St. Louis had all five of the nickels in his possession at one time and made a very detailed study and wrote up the description of each of the coins. We publish the descriptions by Mr. Newman several years ago.

Dr. Bolt obtained the piece from Jim Kelly, who had obtained it from B. G. Johnson of St. Louis. Mr. Johnson sold many of the coins from the Col.Green estate. Mr. Newman being a very good friend of Johnson was given first pick of the set. The original set was five of the liberties and one copper buffalo. At the Cleveland convention last month Mr. Newman told me that he still had the case the coins came in and the copper piece.

Sincerely,

[signature]

Letters from Lee Hewitt, editor of Numismatic Scrapbook Magazine mentioning conversations with George Walton about the mysterious "Reynolds" who supposedly owned the nickel for a time. Courtesy of Eric Newman.

the nickel. To date, the search has turned up nothing evidentiary, not even a mention of it. Reynolds told the authors his search will continue, but the family records are extensive and complex. It's a very big haystack and a very small needle.

An internal memorandum[60] from James A. Ford, trust officer at the Colonial-American National bank, to the Trust Investment Committee noted that *"Numismatic Scrapbook Magazine* has printed an article saying that a Mr. Reynolds of North Carolina owns the 'Bolt Nickel' that George Walton is supposed to have owned at the time of his death." The memo states that the matter had been discussed "with Mr. Garland Stevens, Mr. Bolt, and Ben Stacks. The latter two doubt that Mr. Reynolds does own this Nickel, although he probably did at one time. There is considerable mystery as to the ownership of the fifth Nickel and as to whether or not there might be a sixth Nickel. I feel we have pursued the matter of this as far as can be done and feel there is nothing left for us to do."

The only thing known for certain is that the nickel wound up in the possession of George Walton, who had it with him when he died. Yet even that certainty would not be confirmed for another four decades after his death.

Tragedy In Middlesex

On Friday afternoon, March 9, 1962, George O. Walton paid cash for his hotel bill ($8.47 for two nights) and checked out of the Ponce de Leon Hotel where he often stayed while in Roanoke, Virginia. A bachelor, Walton had no "permanent" address and spent a few weeks at a time in Charlotte, Jacksonville (Florida), and Roanoke. He always lived in hotels. On this stay, he had only been in Roanoke a couple of days before heading out.

He loaded up his Ford station wagon, stopped for 10 gallons of gas and a quart of oil at the By-Pass Gulf Station ($3.10, paid in cash), and headed south for the four-and-a-half-hour, 223-mile trip to Wilson, North Carolina, for a coin show.

With him on this trip, Walton carried a briefcase containing a $250,000 coin collection — quite an impressive array of coins for that time — which Dr. C.A. Bolt described as "about as good a collection as any I know of in this section of the country except for a couple of millionaires who won't let you tell their names."

Charlotte Observer staff writer Victor K. McElheny reported that in addition to the 1913 Liberty Head nickel, Walton's collection included:

---

[60] Courtesy of Cheryl Myers, Hugh Wellons.

— One of less than a dozen complete sets of the coins minted in Charlotte between 1838 and 1861 in the building that once stood on the Post Office property and now is the Mint Museum.

— A complete set of $1, $2.50 and $5 gold pieces minted in Rutherfordton by two German-born metallurgists named Bechtler between 1830 and 1842.

Walton also had five suits and two guns with him in the station wagon. He was a serious gun collector, so it can be assumed that the latter were rare specimens for display or trade rather than for self-defense.

Walton may have intended to put in only a brief appearance at the Wilson show. A handwritten note[61] from coin dealer Kenneth R. Seachman of Ken's Coin Shop in York, Pennsylvania, refers to a meeting to do some coin trading with Walton in Hagerstown, Maryland, the next day, March 10.

Walton had reason to be in high spirits and looking forward to the event in Wilson, billed as that town's first-ever coin show. The show, co-hosted by the Wilson and Goldsboro Coin Clubs (Goldsboro is a town a few miles south of Wilson), was scheduled to open at 9:30 a.m. the following day, Saturday, at the Hotel Cherry. A Wilson collector, Rev. J.L. Bryson, Jr., said Walton had agreed to bring more of his collection than usual as a special favor to the Wilson Coin Club. A feature item in the *Wilson Daily Times*[62] that same Friday touted Walton and his Liberty Head nickel as being the headliners of the show:

Coin Show to Feature
Famous 1913 'V' Nickel

A world-famous 1913 "V" nickel valued at $65,000 will be displayed by George Walton of Charlotte, N.C. Saturday at the Eastern North Carolina Coin Show in Wilson.

The "V" nickel, one of five known in the world today, has won several grand awards at conventions throughout the United States.

Walton, an estate appraiser in Virginia, North Carolina and Florida, has owned the coin since 1946 when he received it in a trade.

The show was reportedly a great success, at least by Wilson standards. The Monday edition of the *Daily Times*[63] proclaimed:

---

[61] Source: Cheryl Myers, Hugh Wellons.

[62] Source: Cheryl Myers.

[63] Courtesy of Cheryl Myers.

More Than 2,000 Visit
Coin Show In Wilson

More than 2,000 persons turned out Saturday for Wilson's first coin show, an event featuring coins and currency ranging from three-dollar bills to cowrie shells.

The report said there were 15 exhibitors from North and South Carolina, along with approximately 25 dealers.

But George Walton was not among them. His impressive coin collection wasn't there, either. He never made it to Wilson.

Darkness fell as Walton drove east toward Wilson on Highway 264 early Friday evening. It was a near-moonless night, with only a thin crescent sliver of a moon and even that was obscured by rain clouds on the showery night. As he neared the city limits of Middlesex in Nash County, only about ten miles away from his destination, Walton steered his Ford station wagon through a slight curve in the rain-slicked highway...and crashed smack into eternity.

At 6:48 p.m. eastern time, Walton's car, heading east, smashed head-on into a car headed west toward the nearby town of Zebulon. The other vehicle involved in the crash was driven by 33-year-old Leona Perry of Rt. 2, Middlesex. She and a passenger in the borrowed 1950 Ford sedan, Mrs. Mae Strickland of Rt. 2, Spring Hope, (Mrs. Perry's sister) were rushed to the Rex Hospital in Raleigh, about 30 miles away. Incredibly, neither was seriously hurt. On Saturday morning, they were both reported to be in satisfactory condition.

Walton was killed instantly. The horrific impact telescoped the front of Walton's station wagon, crushing him. He was 55.

Walton was identified through a newspaper clipping police found in the smashed wagon. Middlesex Police Chief R.E. Gilliam headed the investigation of the crash scene. He was assisted by Middlesex Patrolman Ira E. Boykin and North Carolina Highway Patrolman R.F. Suddarth, along with Nash County Assistant Coroner W.R. Williams. An inquest was scheduled for the following week.

Police found the briefcase with Walton's coin collection in the crumpled station wagon. The coins were not damaged. Chief Gilliam was quoted in *The MANA* Journal as saying, "The 1913 nickel and a quarter-million dollars in coins were retrieved from the wreckage of the Ford station wagon." He added, "We didn't know anything about the value of the coins. But during the investigation, the Charlotte police department knew Walton and told us right away the coins were valuable."

COIN WORLD, Friday, March 23, 1962

George Walton, of Charlotte, N.C., was killed instantly when his 1955 Ford wagon collided head-on with another vehicle on a rain-slicked section of the highway within the city limits of Middlesex, N. C.

Walton Dies . . .
(Continued from Page 1)

Funeral rites were held in Roanoke, Va., on Sunday with committal rites Monday in Greggins-ville Methodist Church, Rocky Mountain.

Bachelor Walton is survived by three sisters, Miss Billie Mae Walton and Mrs. Vesta Roberts of Roanoke, Va., and Mrs. Melb Givens, Salem, Va., near Roanoke, and two brothers, Charley and Frank, Roanoke.

Walton, who headed the Middle Atlantic Numismatic Association in 1956, was highly respected by his fellow collectors, although he had a reputation for being reticent about himself

George Walton

Car Crash Fatal To Nickel Owner

Funeral services were held Sunday, March 11, for George Walton, 55, Charlotte, N. C., nationally known numismatist and owner of one of the five 1913 Liberty head nickels.

Walton met his death in a two-car auto crash near Middlesex, N. C., March 9. The 1913 nickel and a quarter of a million dollars in coins were retrieved from the wreckage of his Ford station wagon.

Middlesex Police Chief R. E.

Gilliam said Walton met his death in a headon crash on U. S. 264, just east of Middlesex, at 6:48 p.m.

The other car involved was driven by Leona Perry, 33. She and a passenger, May Strickland, both of Middlesex, were hospitalized in Raleigh. Their condition was not considered serious.

Chief Gilliam said Walton's collection of valuable coins was placed in the custody of W. R.

Williams, the assistant Nash County coroner.

Walton was enroute to Wilson, N. C., where ne had planned to attend the Wilson-Goldsboro Coin Clubs' show at Hotel Cherry.

Officials were able to identify Walton through a newspaper clipping in the smashea wagon.

Walton, who was traveling alone, was a free lance estate appraiser and worked in Jacksonville, Fla., and Roanoke, Va.

(Continued on Page 2)

Clipping from March 23, 1962, Coin World notice of Walton's fatal accident. Courtesy of Coin World. ©1962 Coin World. Sidney, Ohio, 45365, USA

The first officer on the scene knew of the Wilson coin show and recognized immediately that the coins must be those of an exhibitor and probably very valuable. A police guard was placed at the wreckage site until the collection was impounded in the custody of Nash County assistant coroner Williams and "placed in a bank vault at the Nash County seat, Nashville." Nash County records showed the coins were later released to John W. Stuart, Jr., of Garner, North Carolina, ancillary administrator, according to a 1993 report by Richard Giedroyc in *Coin World*.

Investigators would not say immediately what caused the crash, only that it was being investigated. A memoriam to Walton, signed only with the initials "E.G.J." in the April, May, June 1962 issue of *The MANA Journal* published by the Middle Atlantic Numismatic Association[64] hinted the fault lay with the other driver:

> Life snuffed out in an instant — struck by another car on the wrong side of the road by someone who might not have been in full possession of driving faculties.

Funeral services were held for Walton the following Tuesday, March 13, 2 p.m. at the Gogginsville Methodist Church in Rocky Mount, Virginia, his birthplace. Reverend G.C. Shepherd conducted the service. Pallbearers were Howard Thompson, Garland Miller, Clarence R. Jackson, Howard Patillo, Sonny Economy, and Frank Wright. Interment was in the church cemetery, Franklin County, Virginia, about 12 miles south of Roanoke.[65]

He was survived by three sisters — Miss Billie Mae Walton and Mrs. Vesta Roberts, both of Roanoke, and Mrs. Melva Givens of Salem — and two brothers, Frank and Charles Walton of Roanoke.

According to internal documents[66] kept by the Colonial-American Bank, the coroner held an inquest and found "sufficient evidence of careless and reckless driving "— driving on the wrong side of the highway — was present to hold Mrs. Perry for grand jury. She was charged with manslaughter. Bond was set at $1,000.

Witnesses stated that Mrs. Perry appeared to be alcohol-impaired. Don Creech, an attendant at a Texaco station in Middlesex, said he talked with Mrs. Perry earlier in the afternoon and "observed that she was probably drinking and suggested that she had better stay off the highway, that she could kill someone."

Two other witnesses, Mr. and Mrs. Chester Elks of Washington, North Carolina, testified that the vehicle driven by Mrs. Perry "almost crashed into us" when it barreled onto the highway from a side street in Middlesex. According to the Elks, the vehicle almost hit a telephone pole and sped off down the highway at "a pretty fast rate of speed and was swerving from one side of the highway to the other. We followed and shortly thereafter this car

---

[64] Source provided by Cheryl Myers.

[65] A March 23, 1962, Coin World item on Walton's death reported a slightly different timetable: "Funeral rites were held in Roanoke, Va., on Sunday with committal rites Monday in Grogginsville [sic] Methodist Church, Rocky Mountain.[sic]"

[66] Provided by Cheryl Myers, Hugh Wellons.

crashed with the car driven by Mr. Walton." They were apparently first to arrive on the scene of the accident. Mr. Elks checked the occupants of the vehicles and saw that Walton was dead. He directed traffic at the scene until the police arrived. Mr. Elks clarified that "None of the coins were scattered along the highway as was reported in the paper."

The disposition of the manslaughter charge is not known, except for a notation by Allen W. Staples in the bank's files saying he had been informed that "the trial of the adverse party on a charge of manslaughter was scheduled for August 22, 1962, but that the trial was continued to an unknown date."

The woman's insurance company offered an out of court settlement of $10,000 to release all claims related to Walton's death. The heirs accepted the offer on the recommendation of the estate executor, who indicated to them it was probably the best they could get.

Who Was George Walton?

George O. Walton. Courtesy of Cheryl Meyers.

George Owen Walton was as enigmatic in life as he was in death. Although he was sociable at coin shows and eagerly looked forward to mingling with the collectors and dealers, he was intensely secretive about his private affairs. Perhaps his reticence to reveal personal details resulted from his quiet manner. It's also possible it was a habit learned from his rumored experience in military intelligence.

A headline in the *Charlotte Observer* summed him up succinctly — "George O. Walton Kept To Himself":

> "He doesn't tell his business too much," said Bill Hyatt of Hyatt's Coin Shop in Charlotte. He's the type of fellow who doesn't tell you much," [Dr. C.A.] Bolt said. "He was a nice fella, very quiet. That's why we don't know much about him," said George L. Shaver, a clerk at the Selwyn Hotel [Charlotte]."
>
> His Roanoke family was also in the dark about much of Walton's affairs. His sister, Miss Billie Mae Walton, said he had a room full of guns and swords. But, she said, she didn't know where the rest of his collections were.
>
> His acquaintances "understood" that he was an appraiser of estates for banks' trust departments. His territory, according to his sister, included Charlotte, Roanoke, Jacksonville, Fla., and Tennessee.
>
> Cabell Young, a clerk at the Selwyn Hotel, said Walton was "an employee of the government" when he knew him first 15 years ago.
>
> Bolt said he understood that Walton had worked as some kind of intelligence agent for the government during World War II.

In Roanoke, where Walton lived at the Ponce de Leon Hotel, the local paper said only that he was a "estate appraiser."[67]

The item by Victor McElheny said others interviewed agreed that Walton was a puzzle:

> Gun and ammunition collector Al Cole of Charlotte said that Walton collected large amounts of ammunition. Cole said he often accompanied Walton on collecting trips. "He watched his money on trips just like you and me, and yet he would think nothing of laying out $1,000 for an item he wanted," Cole said.
>
> [Cabell] Young agreed with Cole in calling Walton, "a man I never knew much about. Every now and then," Young said, "we'd chat and he'd show me something he'd bought." Young mentioned a "very fine sword in an ivory scabbard with fine engraving on it." Young said he saw Walton once with "a gold-inlaid blunderbuss type of thing, a funnel-shaped gun. It was way up in the money. Belonged to some ruler."

McElheny related how just a couple of weeks before his death, Walton attended a meeting of the Charlotte Coin Club on February 26. He showed a $50 gold piece minted in honor of the Panama-Pacific Exposition in 1915 in San Francisco. The piece, one of 483 that were struck, was valued at $4,500, a handsome sum for a coin in 1962. As collectors handed the coin around, Walton said, "Don't drop it, you'll chip $1,000 off the price."

A fellow member in MANA, Eldridge G. Jones of Washington, D.C., characterized Walton as "a lone wolf." Quoted in *Coin World* (March 23, 1962), Jones said, "I was associated with him for 10 years, yet I can scarcely sum up two paragraphs about his personal life."

Family members knew little about his affairs, either. Cheryl Myers, Walton's niece (her mother was Melva Givens, one of Walton's sisters), was 11 when Walton died. She recalls little about him except that he called her "Cherry" and he was always dressed up when he came to visit. "We wouldn't see him that often," she said. "He gave us money. Not much, maybe 5 or 10 dollars. We always enjoyed him, and we remember he was always in a suit. He was never at family functions. I don't know how he had a social life."

Cheryl Myers' eldest brother, Ryan Givens, knew little of his uncle. "None of us really knew Uncle George. We would see him every Christmas. He and his girlfriend came by to spend time and bring something for us. We

---

[67] Walton's tax returns list his occupation as "Evaluation Engineer."

never spent too much time talking to him. Uncle George always gave you the impression he was on the go. He came into town just to visit on occasion for business. We rarely saw him. Personally I didn't know him."

Though he was a lifelong bachelor, Walton was occasionally seen in the company of Miss Ellen Harris, who sometimes accompanied him to the many conventions he attended.

Walton was born May 15, 1907, in Rocky Mount, Virginia. It's highly probable that he was descended from his namesake George Walton, one of the signers of the Declaration of Independence in 1776.

George Walton, a signer of the Declaration of Independence in 1776.

The 18th century George Walton, 1740-1804, was born near Farmville, Cumberland County, Virginia. He moved to Savannah, Georgia, to establish a law practice. He was selected as a delegate from Georgia to the Continental Congress, 1776-1777 and 1780-1781. He served Georgia as governor, supreme court justice, and senator. He died in Augusta, Georgia, February 2, 1804. Walton County in Georgia is named after him.

Cheryl Myers has spent some time tracing the genealogical records but has not established a clear ancestral line to the Founding Father George Walton, though there are indications of an indirect connection. The proximity of his birthplace in Virginia to the family's geographic center gives credence to the link.

Myers recalled seeing a document written by the latter-day George Walton, possibly a speech or letter he had written, on which he had scribbled a handwritten note in the margin that said: "by a grand nephew of a signer of the Declaration of Independence, George Walton."

Myers' brother, Ryan Givens, said, "It was about another coin collector and an organization he belonged to…and there was a note on the side in handwriting about it being by a grand or great grand nephew of the George Walton on the Declaration of Independence." Givens said they also found in their uncle's papers an original letter written by the George Walton who signed the Declaration. He said it appeared not to be of great historical importance, but was apparently of interest to his uncle as a keepsake.

Walton began collecting coins in 1919 at age 12 with his father. Thirty years later, he joined the American Numismatic Association as Life Member 229 on February 1, 1949.

He joined the Middle Atlantic Numismatic Association in 1953 as member #323 and became the still-young group's third president in 1956. He was credited with being instrumental in producing "the first successful numismatic convention in the South — Jefferson Hotel, Richmond, Va., 1956," according to *The MANA Journal*. A sister said he belonged to 21 coin collecting organizations.

Typical of many awards Walton accumulated, *The Greenville News* reported in its Sunday edition on October 18, 1960 that he received an award for the best gold collection exhibited at the first convention of the

A young George Walton (seated, far left) with unidentified colleagues, from Walton family archives. Courtesy of Cheryl Meyers.

Blue Ridge Numismatic Association held in Greenville, South Carolina. Dr. C.A. Bolt won an award at the same event for the best display of printing and mint errors. At the first convention of the Appalachian Federation of Coin Clubs in Bristol, Virginia, Walton won the grand award for the show with his 1913 Liberty Head nickel along with other rarities he exhibited.

Walton was fiercely proud of his coin collection and contended that it might even be better than the celebrated collection of Louis Eliasberg, Sr. The *Greensboro Daily News* (October 10, 1959), hopelessly mangling Eliasberg's name, reported:

> Walton said there is an "argument" about who owns the best coin collection in the world, himself or Joseph Eliseburg [sic] of Baltimore. Eliseburg, [sic] he said, values his collection at a quarter of a million dollars. Walton declined to set a value on his.

An Associated Press story datelined Roanoke identified Walton as a "retired government estate appraiser" whose million dollar currency collection included a "priceless" cache of pre-1862 Virginia confederate paper money that he had obtained from a banker. The paper money in question, which Walton aquired in a trade, was apparently found tightly bundled together under a wax seal, stashed away in a secret bank vault where it lay hidden and was ultimately forgotten with the passage of time.

What made the collection so valuable was not the face value of the confederate paper money, reported as $31,272, but the fact that it included 18 of the only extant confederate three-dollar bill specimines.

Roanoke Times writer Milton Garrison, in a follow-up local angle, said the negotiations for the trade involved Walton's 1913 Liberty Head nickel:

> The banker's object, Walton says, was a "swap." He'd had his eye for some time on a 1913 liberty head nickel of Walton's. The coin is worth $12,000. It is one of five in existence.
>
> "He showed me a lot of loose bills and gold," Walton recalls. "He was saving the bundle up. When he did bring it out I almost fell out of my chair."
>
> Some trading talk followed. It ended with Walton "taking off his hands" all the Confederate money. Walton is vague about the price — "plenty," he says — but he still has the nickel.
>
> "It's worth as much as the nickel I think," he said, "but I wouldn't trade the nickel for it."

Walton revealed more of himself than usual to Robert B. McNeil, a reporter for the Richmond (Virginia) *News Leader*, in an October 18, 1956, article[68] on Walton's early life:

> George Walton, who says he has the world's largest collection of $50 gold pieces, won his first gold coin in a "rasslin'" match at "big recess" when he was 12 years old.
>
> Later he underwent another test of physical endurance to get his first $50 gold coin. That time, he recalls, he had to eat "beans that were sour, buttermilk that was so strong I couldn't drink it, and cornbread so hard I couldn't bite it."

McNeil spoke to Walton, whom he described as "a soft-spoken native of Franklin county...president of the Middle Atlantic Numismatic Association," when Walton was in Richmond to make final arrangements for what was dubbed "the first convention of coin and bill collectors south of the Mason-Dixon line." Some 1,500 collectors were expected for the October 26-28 event.

> An enterprising youngster, Walton early turned his various talents to the task of collecting money. By the time he was in his 20's he had accumulated $480 in gold coins. His sources of income were spelling matches, essay contests, baseball games and wrestling.
>
> Four classmates helped him get his first piece of gold. They bet him a $1 in gold, he said, against a coonskin (which he trapped) that he couldn't throw and pin each of them during the hour lunch recess at their school in Franklin's Blackwater section, near Roanoke. He did it and his collection was on its way.
>
> He acquired his first $50 gold coin in 1931 while working in the Civil War battlefield around Fredericksburg as an engineer with the War Department. The men working with him knew he was an avid collector and one of them offered to let him look at some gold coins that were family heirlooms.
>
> Before he got to see the coins, Walton said he first let the man win several games of pool, endured the lunch offered him, waited for the man to finish his after-lunch smoke and bargained over a number of coins of minor value.
>
> "Finally I asked him if he had anything else and he said he had an old medal he wanted me to see," Walton said.

---

68 Courtesy of Cheryl Myers.

The "medal" turned out to be a $50 gold piece made in 1851, which Walton bought for $65. Today, he said, it's worth $1,800.

Walton told McNeil he credited something his father told him as a boy with pointing him in the right direction with his life:

> "When I first started out in life," he said, "all the other boys started smoking." They'd take "rabbit tobacco" down behind the barn, he recalled.
> "One day my father caught us. He told me and my brother that he didn't smoke and if we'd take the money other people spend for cigarets [sic] and put it into something useful, it would be our fortune someday."
> Walton said he has always done just as his father advised. Later, he suggested being a bachelor might have given him a little more money for buying collectors items than he ordinarily would have had.

Walton's enthusiasm for collecting was by no means confined to coins. He amassed impressive collections of guns and ammunition, stamps, watches, ivories, and rare books and documents.

His interest in guns sprouted at an early age when he lived on the family farm in Callaway, Virginia, according to his sister-in-law, Lucille Walton (widow of George's brother, Charles). He was a natural outdoorsman, she said, a competent fur trapper at a young age and a shrewd trader as well. "When he was 6 or 8, he would trap the animals and skin them. Then he'd bring the skins in and shine them up pretty for sale and send them to a furrier place. He would check one local furrier place, and then he'd check another one to get the highest price. He started in coins doing the same thing, and his daddy told him one time, 'One day you'll be a millionaire,' just kidding with him."

Ads for the auction of his weapons collection touted 1,400 hand guns, 350 rifles, 500 swords (including 300 sabers), over 100,000 rounds of collectible ammunition, 30 cartridge boards, 100 canes, large amounts of powder horns, moulds, hunting knives, and other gun equipment. The sale was conducted July 24-27, 1963, by J.G. Sheets & Sons ("Realtors and Auctioneers") at 1705 Franklin Road, S.W., in Roanoke. The sale, conducted on behalf of the estate administrator, Colonial-American National Bank, drew buyers from as far away as Iowa and New Hampshire and realized more than $130,000 (about $750,000 in 2004 dollars).

FAMOUS LAWMAN'S SIX-SHOOTER IN WALTON COLLECTION...

Unbeknown to Walton

One of the items sold in the auction of antique weapons from the estate of George O. Walton carried a special value that not even Walton was aware of. It was only discovered months after the auction, as reported by Bill Cochran of the *Roanoke Times*:

> Local gun collectors let a "Yankee trader" slip a small fortune out from under their noses last summer when the gun collection of the late George Walton was sold at auction in Roanoke.
>
> Paul Selley, a barber and gun collector from Palatine, Ill., a Chicago suburb, purchased several items at the Walton Auction. Included was a nickel-plated single-action revolver, which recently was proven to have been the personal sidearm of W.B. "Bat" Masterson, red-blooded American hero of the Old West.

Selley didn't know the revolver had belonged to Bat Masterson when he bought it. He sold it to a friend, Paul Pasko, Sr., also of Palatine, who wanted an antique gun for target practice. Before he sold it, Selley replaced the hand grips. He noticed an inscription scratched inside one of the old grips that said, "Bat Maston." He mentioned it to Pasko. Pasko bought the old grips and put them back on the Colt six-shooter. Then he wrote to the Colt Company with the serial number asking for more information about it. Colt replied that the weapon had been sold and shipped to W.B. Masterson on July 30, 1885.

Pasko dug further and found the original letter to Colt from Masterson in the Connecticut State Library. The letter was written on stationery from the "Opera House Saloon" in Dodge City, Kansas. Masterson wrote:

> Please send me one of your nickel-plated short .45 caliber revolvers. It is for my own use and for that reason I would like to have a little extra pains. I am willing to pay extra for extra work.

Make it a little easy on the trigger. Have the front sight a little higher and a little thicker than the ordinary pistol of this kind. Put on a gutta percha handle and send it as soon as possible. Have the barrel about the same length as the ejecting rod is. W.B. Masterson.

Cochran added, "Why the name on the grips is Maston instead of Masterson, no one knows. It may be that Bat often shortened his name."

O'Reilly's Plaza Art Galleries, Inc., of New York City, offered "a collection of antique & gold watches from the Estate of George O. Walton" on October 3, 1963, at 11 a.m.

In the afternoon of that same day, at 2 p.m., The Plaza Art Galleries, Inc., conducted the sale of Walton's "Americana books, almanacs, signed documents & manuscripts from the mid-18th Century through the Civil War to the early 20th Century." The sale included half leather bound copies of *Harper's Weekly* from 1861 to 1865 along with Civil War biographies by Sherman, Grant, Lee, Gordon, Davis and other wartime luminaries.

Auctioneers Gordon R. Hammer and Donald D'Amato of Harmer, Rooke & Co., Inc., presided over the September 11-13 sale of Walton's stamp collection. The collection included United States first and second day issues and British Commonwealth of Nations third day issues along with "Air Post stamps of the World. Mongolia, Russia used Abroad" and "Miscellaneous. Collections by Country."

To handle the sale of the redoubtable coin collection in which George Walton took such pride, the estate administrators of Colonial-American National Bank of Roanoke selected the famed Stack's auction house in New York.

What happened then launched tales of a disappearing act that baffled the entire numismatic community for more than 40 years. It appeared that one of the 1913 Liberty Head nickels had simply vanished!

Walton Nickel Declared a Fake...
So Where is the Missing Real One?

A January 1963 consent letter[69] from the "distributees of the Estate of George O. Walton" authorized Colonial-American National Bank of Roanoke, as administrator of the estate, "to sell and liquidate the entire coin and currency collection of the estate at public auction by Stack's of New York."

The letter contained this stipulation:

> 2. Within the aforesaid coin and currency collection is one United States 5¢ piece of the year 1913 which is regarded as extremely rare. This coin is to be turned over to Stack's along with the other coins and currencies, but with the stipulation that such 5¢ piece shall not be offered for auction or sale at a gross price of less than $[blank space], the desire of the undersigned being to obtain the highest possible price in excess of this minimum amount.

The selection of Stack's as the auctioneer for the Walton collection drew less than enthusiastic support from some of Walton's former associates. Eldridge G. Jones of Hyattsville, Maryland, secretary-treasurer of the Middle Atlantic Numismatic Association, had been in touch with the Walton family members since Walton's death and expressed concerns about both the bank and Stack's the previous summer.

On June 12, 1962, he wrote to Charles B. Walton, George's brother:

> It was a pleasure meeting you and Mrs. Walton on Sunday evening....I have enclosed a copy of a letter I wrote to the Bank in answer to a form letter earlier received.
>
> You will note that I have outlined a few points I feel should be brought to their attention as well as letting them know they are "being watched." Although I am not in a position to judge, it appears from your information certain matters to not come up to my thinking on the matter!!
>
> I have offered to assist them, and am at their call in event they wish to contact me = even to the extent of going to the bank for a conference. I shall wait further developments from them.

The "certain matters" Jones was talking about involved some missing personal items, as he spelled out in a June 12, 1962, letter to G.C. Duffy, Trust Officer at the Colonial-American National Bank:

---

[69] This and other letters cited regarding the disposition of Walton's estate provided courtesy of Cheryl Myers and the Walton family.

> Mr. C.B. Walton was in Washington over the week-end; and we had a conference on some of the problems relative to his brother's coin holdings. He was seeking information he felt I might be able to contribute. He appeared to be very much disturbed over the fact that his brother's watch and ring, which I remember seeing him wear many times, had not been located. Having been associated with Mr. George Walton since 1953, when he came into MANA, and being with him at many conventions, I feel certain it was his usual practice to have both his watch and ring with him = if not on himself, certainly in his luggage. I feel sure he had it with him as he was on the way to another convention. It is my opinion that these two items are of considerable value as per earlier conversations with him regarding them. It appears as though a thorough investigation should have located these items long before this date == and if one has not been made, I have suggested to Mr. Walton that to further his interests and those of his brother and sisters that he should retain legal counsel and private investigator at once to pursue the matter.

Jones went on to suggest that sources familiar with Walton's collection would be the appropriate choice for liquidating it:

> In answer to Mr. Walton's request I supplied him a list of the outstanding coin dealers, who are experienced in estate appraisal for administrators, including banks, and who conduct auctions of estates. These are members of The Association, well known to me, and I have no hesitancy in vouching for them. I suggested he share the list with you in the event you may not know the large group as he indicated you were interested in only one firm.
>
> It is possible they may be interested in coming to the Bank to inspect the material, which is frequently done in large estates and holdings such as Mr. Walton's. You may check them out with our President, Dr. Conway A. Bolt, Box 368, Marshville, N.C., who is also one of the outstanding collectors and a friend of Mr. Walton's. Mr. Don Sherer, General Secretary of the American Numismatic Ass'n (the national association) 3520 N. 7th St., Phoenix 14, Arizona will also assist you in further identifying the dealers. May I respectfully suggest you contact all these dealers to evaluate their proposals (all are well acquainted with Mr. Walton and his numismatic interests) relative to the disposition of his extensive holdings.

Later that same month, on June 30, Jones wrote to Walton's sister, Miss Billie Walton of Roanoke expressing impatience with the trust officer at the bank:

To date I have not heard from Mr. Duffy - of the Bank. I wrote to him June 12th; and expected some kind of an answer to my offer to help on the coin end of the estate. Dr. Bolt writes he has also offered his services. He writes: "Stack's would not pay the worth of the collection." I know several dealers I would much rather have the material; and I know all parties would be much more satisfied. May I suggest you ask Charlie [Walton] what he has done with the list I sent him; and if he gave it to the bank, what they have done about it??????????

A week later, July 7, Dr. Conway Bolt wrote to another of George Walton's sisters, Miss Billie Mae Walton of Roanoke (mistakenly addressing her as Miss "Johnie" Mae Walton):

So many people have asked me what has been done about George's Collections and I have not been able to tell them anything definite. I have written to Mr. Duffy, but I am sure that so many have written him that the poor man would need an extra force of secretaries. George had so much knowledge about even this material that is coming up for sale, that the vast majority of the people will never realize its true historical value. George could have written several books, and I think that he was contemplating this right away.

Ignoring the recommendations of Jones and Bolt, the estate administrators at Colonial-American chose Stack's for the coin auction anyway. A bank memo on July 2, 1964 gave the bank's reasoning for the choice:

Inquiry at New York banks indicated that Stack's of New York was perhaps the foremost and most reliable coin and currency dealer and auctioneer in the country. There are various other dealers who wanted to handle the collection and who offered to do so for a less charge than Stack's, but it was the bank's judgment that the collection would bring more and that it would be better handled if Stack's were employed.

The sale of George Walton's collection by Stacks, conducted in two sessions — June 20-22 and October 3-5 — netted $878,101. The *New York Herald Tribune* pointed out that this number shattered a world record of $804,022 previously realized at auction of the collection of Samuel W. Wolfson.

The auction of Walton's collection took place at the Park Sheraton hotel. In a quote to the *Tribune*, Norman Stack suggested that the auction was extremely well attended, with dealers and bidders from all over the country and nearly every state in attendance.

The total sales figure for the collection was an aggregate of $640,101 from a "six-part sale, Wednesday through Saturday night," and the $232,000 realized during the first auction.

The *Herald Tribune* account cited the highest prices realized for the most prized of the pieces in the Walton collection:

On Friday:
- 1849 Mormon $10 gold piece, $14,000
- 1851 Dunbar & Co. $5 gold piece, $11,250
- 1849 Oregon Exchange Co. $10 gold piece, $10,500

On Saturday
- 1930 San Francisco min $10 gold piece, $4,300
- 1642 England oxford triple unite, $3,400
- Total Sale of Foreign Gold, $61,772
- Total Sale of U.S. Gold, $38,694
- Total Sales for Saturday's last two sections $100,466

The Walton Collection auction was a raging success but for one major omission — *the 1913 Liberty Head nickel wasn't in the sale!*

According to bank documents, shortly after the contract with Stack's was signed, Ben Stack went to Roanoke to inspect the collection in person. Something about the 1913 Liberty Head nickel didn't look right to him. The coin was shipped to New York for further examination.

What happened next, as described in a bank memo, resulted in one of the biggest errors in numismatic history:

> JAF [James A. Ford],[70] Charlie Walton and Ben Stack picked it up in New York and took it to the American Numismatic Society which examined it and pronounced it bogus in their presence.
>
> Thereafter it was re-sealed and brought back to the bank by Jas. A. Ford and opened in the presence of all of the heirs who also examined it under a magnifying glass. The alteration was somewhat visible even here

---

[70] In early 2005, Ryan Givens spoke by phone with James A. Ford, who said that he did not accompany the coin to New York as the memo states and did not know who at the ANS made the pronouncement that the Walton nickel was an altered date fake. Ford told Givens he was one of three trust officers assigned by the Colonial American National Bank to handle the very large estate. Ford said he believed it was probably Chapman Duffey, one of the other trust officers, who made the trip. Mr. Duffey is deceased.

and it is believed that a majority of the heirs agreed that it had been altered. The nickel was re-sealed and is now held by the Bank and is expected to be delivered to the heirs.

The nickel that had supposedly been found among the quarter million dollar collection found at the fatal accident scene was returned to the estate as being unacceptable for auction.

The revelation stunned and bewildered family members, who had believed all along that the coin was real. The news sent an electric buzz through the numismatic community, too. If the Walton specimen wasn't real, then where in the world was the real fifth nickel? Everyone knew where four of them were. What happened to the missing coin?

The mystery preoccupied both the Walton family and numismatists for decades. Controversy raged about whether the coin Walton had was real or a fake, as judged by Stack's.

For decades, the numismatic press and popular lore has said that it was Stack's that declared the coin a fake, when all along it was actually the prestigious American Numismatic Society, not Stack's, that made what proved eventually to be monumental mistake. The memo does not specify *who* at the ANS participated in the examination of the Walton nickel, and no other records of the incident in New York have been found. It would take 40 years to discover the ANS' error.

Comments from the numismatic community tended to have an undercurrent of bias against George Walton, either implying or stating flatly that the coin he had shown at so many coin shows over the years was a fake.

The Secret Service very nearly confiscated the Walton nickel because it was deemed an altered coin. They were also interested in several counterfeit pieces Walton owned. A notice[71] from Norwood G. Greene, Secret Service Special Agent in Charge from the Richmond office, said:

> It now appears that all of the coins to which you referred should be surrendered, and if you will mail them to this office, we will mail you a contraband receipt.

Possession of the counterfeit and altered date coins was said to be in violation of Title 18, Section 331 of the U.S. Code, which prohibits the fraudulent alteration of dates or mint marks on genuine coins of the United

---

[71] Courtesy of Cheryl Myers and Hugh Wellons

States for the purpose of enhancing their value as collector's items and thereby defrauding numismatists. Of course, the 1913 Liberty Head nickels were never officially issued by the U.S. Mint, and so they were not "genuine coins of the United States."

A July 27, 1964, letter from the Secret Service to bank trust officer Chapman Duffy warned of seizure, citing Title 18, Section 492 of the U.S. Code, which reads:

> All counterfeits of any coins or obligations or other securities of the United States or any foreign government, or any articles, devices, and other things made, possessed, or used in violation of this chapter, or any material or apparatus used or fitted or intended to be used, in the making of such counterfeits, articles, devices or things, found in the possession of any person without authority from the Secretary of Treasury or other proper officer, shall be forfeit to the United States.

Ten days later, Special Agent Greene followed up with a letter[72] on August 7 saying that after consulting with General Counsel of the Treasury Department, they had decided that "mere possession of coins bearing altered dates or mint marks does not constitute a violation if such coins are not held with intent to defraud and are not, in fact, altered with an intent to defraud anyone." The letter went on to say, "Therefore, it now appears that you may retain the altered 1913 five cent coin under the provisions as heretofore stated by the General Counsel." However, he insisted that certain counterfeit gold and silver coins be surrendered, and they were confiscated by the Secret Service.

Altered date 1913 Liberty Head nickels were fairly common. Since the authentic coins were so treasured by collectors, unscrupulous and clever charlatans would shave and scrape, altering the date of a common nickel to make the date read "1913." Most of them were pretty obvious, especially to a trained eye. But a few forgeries were extraordinarily good and took a numismatic expert to spot them.

Richard Giedroyc of *Coin World*, in a June 21, 1993, front page report, posed the question of whether or not Walton ever owned the real 1913 Liberty Head nickel:

> The Walton connection is the most interesting, and tenuous. No one is certain that Walton ever owned the coin. [Eric] Newman said of Walton:

---

[72] Source: Cheryl Myers, Hugh Wellons

"He's totally unreliable. After he died there was total confusion."[73]

Coin dealer Paul Green of Wisconsin has recently searched for the coin. He said he spoke to Noah Reynolds, grandson of the late R.J. Reynolds, who is commonly thought to have owned the fifth coin. No record of the coin ever belonging to a member of the Reynolds family could be found.

Green said: "Heaven knows where it is. The whole numismatic world is thrown a curve by the R.J. Reynolds front."

He added, "I've always felt the car wreck was a possibility (for the disappearance of the coin)."

Pete Smith, author of *American Numismatic Biographies*, concluded Walton didn't have the coin, as reported by *Coin World*'s Richard Giedroyc:

Smith said: "I now believe the missing piece was never owned by Walton although he may have helped arrange the trade with [Dr. Conway] Bolt. The search should concentrate on Reynolds, whoever that was." There is a fair amount of evidence that Bolt owned the coin and traded it to a North Carolinian named Reynolds.

Numismatic researcher George Fuld of Santa Barbara, California, was one of the few voices disputing the conventional assumptions about Walton, according to Giedroyc:

Fuld differs with those who claim Walton's coin was a fake. He said: "I am morally certain that I saw the Walton specimen about 1960 and that is the lasting impression I have. To the eye it was not an altered date. Again, I didn't make note to this viewing, but if I had to guess it might have been the 1960 ANA at Boston."

Fuld said he believed the stories claiming R.J. Reynolds, of the Reynolds Tobacco Co. fortune, may have owned a specimen and traded it to someone else, possibly Walton.

So pervasive was the assumption that R.J. Reynolds owned the coin (and that it must be kept in hiding by the very secretive family) that it came to be listed in published pedigrees usually as the Reynolds Specimen.

---

[73] Eric Newman said in November 2003 that the quote was given out of context and that what he meant was not that Walton himself was personally unreliable but that the confusion about his ownership of the coin made information about him unreliable.

Giedroyc pointed out that Abe Kosoff, who had owned two of the other 1913 Liberty Head nickels maintained that Walton's coin was a fake all along:

> However, according to dealer Abe Kosoff, the coin Walton frequently exhibited was an altered date coin and not a genuine specimen. Kosoff wrote before his death that Walton's supposed altered coin raises the question of whether Walton ever had access to a genuine coin.

It has not been explained how Kosoff could have known for certain that Walton's coin was an altered date, though there have been unconfirmed rumors that he was one of three people who examined the coin when it was submitted to Stack's and decided it was a fake.

Giedroyc said in his report that one of the owners of the New York auction house indicated that Stack's never received the nickel:

> Harvey Stack of Stack's told *Coin World* in June there was no 1913 Liberty Head 5-cent among the coins his firm received from George Walton's estate. The coins Stack's received were auctioned in June and October 1963.
>
> Stack said of George Walton: "He allegedly had one [1913 Liberty Head 5 cents]. He was supposed to own a lot of great rarities."
>
> Stack said Walton built collections for people including wealthy families in the tobacco industry. It is possible he brokered the coin to a collector in such a family, starting the story that Walton owned it.

In a follow-up story four months later by Giedroyc (October 15, 1993), Stack changed his tune:

> Harvey Stack, owner of Stack's, confirmed that his firm examined the altered coin and returned it to Walton's executor after the 1962 accident.

The front page item was headlined "Attorney confirms tale that 1913 Liberty 5 cents in crash was a fake," and carried the subtitle, "Uncertainty remains: Did Walton own genuine coin?"

The article was prompted, Giedroyc said, by a huge reward that had been posted to lure the coin from hiding:

> Interest in finding the fifth specimen recently led Texas collector Reed Hawn...and the American Numismatic Association to offer a $10,000 reward for the discovery of the missing piece. The coin is believed to have been missing for more than 30 years, possibly as long as 50 years.

Giedroyc said that Arthur Smith, an attorney who had represented George's brother, Charles, in the disbursement of the estate, confirmed that there had been a 1913 Liberty Head nickel specimen in the estate:

> Smith told *Coin World* on Oct. 6 that a 1913 nickel was recovered [from the accident site] and was included in the inventory of coins examined by a representative from an auction house that disposed of George Walton's coins.
>
> Smith said the auction house, Stack's in New York, sent a representative to view the coins. The 1913 Liberty Head 5-cent coins was sent to Stack's in New York for authentication. Smith said Stack's determined that the coin was an altered date specimen and it was returned to the bank trust officer who represented a bank as executor of Walton's estate.
>
> According to Smith, Walton's brother, Charles, obtained the altered date coin. Smith said he understood that Charles Walton stored the coin in a lock box at a bank, possibly later selling it to a person he knew from a local country club.

The report said Lucille Walton, Charles' widow, had no idea where the coin was:

> She spoke to *Coin World* Oct. 5 about the coin. She said she was not aware of either brother ever owning the fifth genuine specimen.
>
> She said her husband collected coins and kept them in both bank lock boxes and in a chest in the basement. The coins kept in the house were stolen during one of two burglaries over the years. Charles Walton died in May 1990.

The 1913 Liberty nickel was not among the coins stolen from Charles and Lucille Walton. Melva Givens, Walton's sister, had bought the coin from the estate as a keepsake of her brother.

Interviewed by the authors in October 2003, Lucille Walton said emphatically that she believed her brother-in-law's nickel to be genuine. "I *knew* it was real. George Walton was not the kind of man to tell someone he had something when he did not. And I knew it had either got lost in the wreck or somewhere along the line. He would never have sold it."

Walton himself was quoted in published reports as saying the nickel "is not for sale at any price. I want to keep it as long as I live," a statement that turned out to be prophetic. He added, "And then, I want it to go to somebody who will appreciate it. Maybe in a museum like the Smithsonian. Then everybody in the country can enjoy it."

George Walton's 1913 Liberty Head nickel in the holder he had specially made.
Courtesy of Coin World..© Coin World

Cheryl Myers stressed that her uncle loved his 1913 Liberty Head nickel. "All the pictures taken before his death in the newspaper, he would always have that coin. He was very proud of the coin. You can see it in the pictures. I don't think he would have ever sold it. He had a chance to own all five and then he didn't but...three weeks later he drove back to St. Louis and he was told that they were sold separately."

Walton had a custom-made holder for his 1913 Liberty Head nickel, engraved with this inscription:

1913 LIBERTY HEAD NICKEL

OWNED BY GEORGE WALTON
M.A.N.A PRESIDENT 1956 A.N.A., L.M. 229
ONLY FIVE OF THESE KNOWN
ORIGINALLY OWNED BY COL. GREEN

It is improbable that Walton would have held such pride in a coin he knew to be an imposter. However, it has been said that Walton possibly had both the real nickel and an altered date. The unconfirmed rumor suggests that he may have sometimes switched them out, possibly for security reasons if he had concerns about being robbed. Besides the coin that was returned by Stack's, no other specimen of 1913 Liberty Head nickel was found in his possessions.

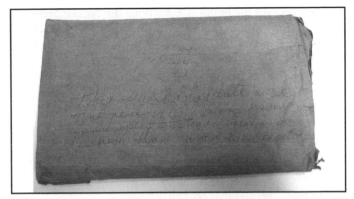

Padded manila envelope in which Melva Givens kept the "altered date" 1913 Liberty Head nickel she acquired from George Walton's estate. Courtesy of Coin World. © Coin World.

Melva Givens acquired the nickel when the heirs divided up the coins rejected by Stack's for auction. "I thought possibly it was because she was born in 1913," said her eldest son, Ryan Givens. "I think she wanted to keep something of Uncle George's, and she got a lot of the counterfeit coins that he had."

Because she was not herself a coin expert, she trusted the Stack's appraisal that the 1913 nickel she had was a fake and not particularly valuable. In fact, the bank inventory listed the coin's value as "NONE." She put it away in a closet in a padded manila envelope with her handwritten inscription:

> This is a changed date and not real 1913. George used it for display instead of real one which has never been located.

Melva Givens was still convinced, though, that her brother had once had a real 1913 Liberty nickel and continued for a time trying to find it.

On March 26, 1969,[74] she wrote to Eric Newman about a letter from Newman to her brother referring to the 1913 Liberty Head nickel. Her letter is both plaintive and hopeful. She hoped maybe he could shed some light on the mystery of the missing coin:

> While looking through some letters, etc. belonging to my late brother, George Walton, I came across a letter from you relative to the 1913 Liberty Head Nickels. Some questions have arisen, and I was wondering if I could prevail upon your time and kindliness to answer them.

---

[74] From Newman's archives.

Did you ever see my brother's collection? the Nickel? Stella gold? Is there a doubt in your mind as to the authenticity of the Nickel; if so, where is the fifth nickel? Did you ever see his material on the history of this nickel?

I am enclosing an envelope for your reply, and any information will be greatly appreciated and rewarded, if profitable.

Newman said in 2003 that he had, indeed, written to Walton — on January 3, 1962, just two months before Walton's death. Prominent numismatist M. Vernon Sheldon had encouraged him to contact Walton a few days before in a short note on American Numismatic Association stationery and dated December 31, 1961:[75]

By all means write to Mr. Walton. I had a most interesting talk with him at Fort Monroe-MANA Convention.

Newman, writing to Walton on behalf of the Eric P. Newman Numismatic Education Society[76] — which he founded to support the development and distribution of information about numismatics — acknowledged Walton's reputation for knowledge of the 1913 Liberty Head nickel and offered to assist him in publishing what he knew:

Vernon Sheldon has told me a little bit about your research with respect to the 1913 Liberty Head nickel. It is very necessary that your material be published, in my opinion, and we want to offer our help in any way we can.

I have the original case in which the five 1913 nickels were kept as well as the regular Indian Head nickel and a copper Indian Head nickel. The copper Indian Head nickel is probably plated but I have not had electric resistance tests made as yet and will do so.

I have examined all of the 1913 Liberty Head nickels and have a file with miscellaneous items in it, most of which, I am sure, you already know.

I will be glad to read over your text when it is written if you wish me to.

I have just completed a book on the 1804 dollar which will be published, the spring, and I am hopeful it will end any doubts about the matter. It is a shame to have to devote so much time to bad coins but I have not neglected my desire to write about genuine ones.

I look forward to hearing from you.

---

[75] Courtesy of Eric P. Newman.
[76] Source: Eric Newman.

Newman never heard back from Walton. The letter obviously arrived, because Melva Givens found it in Walton's papers. It was addressed to Walton's Charlotte address. It's possible he had been spending his time in January and February mostly in Roanoke and Jacksonville and hadn't yet seen the letter from Newman. He would usually spend several weeks in each location.

It seems likely, given the complimentary nature of Newman's letter and the fact that Newman himself was an important part of the 1913 Liberty Head nickel story, that Walton would have responded at the earliest time his busy schedule permitted. If he put it off, it would seem almost certainly because he was so busy at the time. He put it off one day too long.

Newman responded on March 31, 1969,[77] to the inquiry from Melva Givens about his correspondence to Walton:

> We are fully aware of the problem you have on hand and can understand why you are doing a lot of investigating. We presume the 1913 Liberty Head Nickel which George Walton was supposed to have has never shown up.
>
> In answer to your specific questions, I can state that I never saw your brother's collection. I never saw in his possession the 1913 Liberty Head Nickel which he allegedly owned. I know nothing whatsoever of the Stella about which you write.
>
> There was never any doubt in my mind that the nickel which he acquired was one of the five 1913 Liberty Head Nickels and I don't know where that nickel is now. I never had the opportunity of seeing his material on the history of the 1913 Liberty Head Nickel in spite of requesting it.
>
> Originally, all five 1913 Liberty Head Nickels were here in St. Louis, in my possession. We still have the holder in which they were kept. We still have a couple of the coins which were in the holder with them. We also have a large file on the history of the 1913 Liberty Head Nickel.
>
> There certainly is a lot of mystery in your side of the situation and I presume that you are investigating to see whether there is something unsavory in connection with the matter.

Newman did not spell out what he guessed might be "unsavory" about the situation, but the implications were interesting. The courtly tone of the letter and his mentioning that he had never seen Walton's research material

---

[77] From Eric Newman's archives.

"in spite of requesting it," suggested Newman might have still been a bit miffed at Walton for not replying to his original inquiry.

Hearing news of Walton's death, Newman was concerned that whatever research Walton had on the 1913 Liberty Head nickels might be lost in the shuffle of settling the estate. On March 22, 1962,[78] he urged Vernon Sheldon to try his luck at succeeding where Newman had not in getting the material for publication:

> It is very important to have someone obtain the material on the 1913 Liberty Head nickel which George Walton assembled.
>
> You, no doubt, were a good enough friend of his to accomplish this. At an appropriate time perhaps you could ask for it.
>
> You may be interested in knowing that he never answered my letter with respect to it.

What happened to the research material Walton was believed to have was as big a mystery as the disappearance of the 1913 Liberty Head nickel he was supposed to have owned. Both seemed to have vanished.

Melva Givens eventually despaired of finding the real nickel and ended her search. "I think she eventually gave up, and in all this it was never brought up. It sat back in a closet totally forgotten," Cheryl Myers recalled. Melva Givens died March 25, 1992, never knowing the answer to what happened to the real 1913 Liberty Head nickel she was convinced her brother had owned.

The mystery endured for more than 40 years, maddeningly refusing to yield its secrets, perplexing and tantalizing the numismatic world until it was finally solved in 2003.

---

[78] Provided by Eric Newman.

Chapter 8 References

Associated Press. "Secret Vault Yields $3 Bills Of Confederacy." Datelined "Roanoke." Date and publication unknown.

Charlotte Observer. 1959. "$35,000 Nickel Isn't For Sale" (October 15), p. 8-C. Excerpts reprinted with permission of *The Charlotte Observer.* Copyright owned by *The Charlotter Observer.*

Coin World. 1962. "Car Crash Fatal To Nickel Owner" (March 23), p. 1.

Deisher, Beth. 2003. "Liberty Head Legends." *Coin World* (July), p.41-42.
— Deisher. 2005. Interview, May 18th.

Garrison, Milton. "Collector's 'Find' Yields $3 Bills." Roanoke (Virginia) *Times*, p. B-1,2. Date unknown.

Gibbs, William T. 1993. "Mystery surrounds pedigree of coin." *Coin World* (June 28), p.1, 12, 17.

Giedroyc, Richard. 1993. "Where is lost specimen of 1913 Liberty Head 5 cents?" *Coin World* (Vol. 34, No. 1732, June 21), pp. 1, 12.
— Giedroyc. 1993. "Attorney confirms tale that 1913 Liberty 5 cents in crash was fake." *Coin World* (Vol. 34, No. 1750, October 25), pp. 1,26.
— Giedroyc. "Location of 1913 5¢ still unknown." *Coin World.*

Givens, Melva (Mrs. Robert R.). 1969. Letter to Eric Newman (March 26).

Givens, Ryan. 2003. Interview (October 1).

Greensboro, North Carolina, *Daily News.* 1959. "1913 Liberty Head Nickel Is Rare; Only Five Minted" (October 10), p. B-1.

Harmer, Rooke & Co., Inc. 1963. Auction catalog for George Walton's stamp collection (September 11-13).

Herald Tribune News Service, New York. 1963. "Walton Coin Sale Shatters Record" (October 6).

McElheny, Victor K. "George O. Walton Kept To Himself." Charlotte, North Carolina, *Observer.* Date unknown.

McNeil, Robert B. 1956. "$50 Coin Collector Started With Ordeal." Richmond (Virginia) *News Leader* (October 18), p. 6.

The MANA Journal, "E.G.J." 1962. "In Memoriam - George Walton." Middle Atlantic Numismatic Association (April, May, June) p. 8-9.

Myers, Cheryl. 2003. Interview (October 2).

Newman, Eric P. 1962. Letter to George Walton (January 3).
— Newman. 1962. Letter to Vernon Sheldon (March 22).
— Newman. 1969. Letter to Mrs. Robert R. (Melva) Givens (March 31).

— Newman. 2003. Interview by Mark Borckardt and Ray Knight (November 10).

Numismatic Scrapbook Magazine. 1953. "Looks Like There Are Six 1913 Liberty Head Nickels." (December), p. 1169.

O'Reilly's Plaza Art Gallery. 1963. Auction notice of George Walton antique and gold watch collection (October 3).

The Plaza Art Galleries, Inc. 1963. Auction catalog for George Walton books and documents collection (October 3).

Sheets, J.G. & Sons. 1962. Print ads and mailers for George O. Walton Antique Firearms Auction.

Sheldon, Vernon. 1961. Letter to Eric Newman (December 31).

Shelton, Ted. 1960. "N.C. Collectors Win Awards." *The Greenville News*, South Carolina (October 18).

Stack's. 1963. Auction catalog for George Walton coin and paper money collection (June 20-22).

Walker, Laurens. "$50,000 Nickel Is Banked Here." Charlotte, North Carolina, Observer (date unknown).

Walton, Lucille. 2003. Interview by Ray Knight (October 21).

Wilson, North Carolina, *Daily Times*. 1962. "Coin Show to Feature Famous 1913 'V' Nickel" (March 9).
— Wilson *Daily Times*. 1962. "Wreck Kills Coin Expert Bringing $250,000 Exhibit to Wilson Show" (March 10).
— Wilson *Daily Times*. 1962. "More Than 2,000 Visit Coin Show in Wilson" (March 12).

- Chapter Nine -

THE
CLOCKWORK MIRACLE

It took a miraculous series of perfectly-aligned parts to dislodge the missing nickel from its hideaway in obscurity. "What fascinates me about this thing is how it's like a Swiss watch," said Associated Press reporter David Tirell-Wysocki, who was one of the key players in the sequence of events. "So many pieces had to fall in place precisely right for all this to take place." If any link in this story of clockwork precision, ironically unplanned, had been missing, misaligned, or mis-timed, it is virtually certain the much-sought coin would have remained hidden for some years longer.

The extraordinary sequence of circumstances that unveiled the errant coin could not have been planned. The odds of these events lining up in perfect order are so improbable that no rational person would have believed it possible. In fact, the odds were heavily stacked against it happening. It was a classic example of serendipity — a fortunate discovery by accident.

The Beginning: Two Events in January 2003

The first two pieces of the "Swiss watch" fell into place unobtrusively in January 2003. The connection between the two wasn't apparent at the time, but in tandem they set in motion the events that would lead to the discovery of the missing nickel later that year at the end of July.

Legend Numismatics of Lincroft, New Jersey, announced at the FUN show in Orlando that the firm had purchased the Reed Hawn 1913 Liberty Head nickel (the one that appeared in "Hawaii Five-O") from Spectrum Numismatics of Irvine, California. Laura Sperber, one of the partners of Legend Numismatics along with George Huang and Bruce Morelan, told *Coin World* (January 27, 2003) that the deal had actually been struck in August but that paperwork delayed the final transaction until December.

"That's why we chose to announce our purchase here at the FUN show," Sperber was quoted in the *Coin World* report, which included this significant bit of news (though no one then knew the full implications of it):

> She [Sperber] said she and her partners would like to display their
> 1913 Liberty Head 5-cent coin during the ANA convention this summer

in Baltimore and will be contacting ANA officials regarding arrangements for an exhibit.

Meanwhile also in January, Collectors Universe hired Paul Montgomery as president of Bowers and Merena Galleries to replace the departing Q. David Bowers. Bowers had stayed on as president when he sold the Wolfeboro, New Hampshire, company he co-founded (originally as Bowers and Ruddy Galleries) to Collectors Universe in 2002. He reportedly differed with the new owners on the direction they were taking the company, particularly on the dismissal of some key members of Bowers' staff, and had decided to leave.

ANA life member Montgomery, a member of the board of directors of the Professional Numismatists Guild (PNG) and board member and immediate past chairman of ICTA (Industry Council for Tangible Assets), had formerly been a partner and president of Jefferson Coin and Bullion in New Orleans, a coin dealership founded by the late James U. Blanchard III.

Montgomery's entrance to Bowers and Merena Galleries was anything but auspicious. He inherited a tense, unstable situation. He was faced with divided loyalties among employees and the formation of a competitive coin auction company by former employees (also in Wolfeboro). Despite these obstacles, he had a company to run and had to get up to speed quickly on the daily business of the firm and rapidly approaching auction sales. Complicating matters further was the fact that he was commuting on weekends to be with his family still living in Mandeville, Louisiana, a community about 30 miles north of New Orleans across Lake Pontchartrain.

Montgomery had too much on his plate to give much thought to the ANA convention scheduled for the summer. Before his arrival, Bowers and Merena Galleries had been selected to be the official auctioneer for the prestigious event. He knew he would have to turn his attention to it at some point, but at the time, he had to cope with more urgent priorities. When he did get involved, he did it in a huge way — to the tune of a million bucks!

These two unrelated (at the time) events — the chance comment by Laura Sperber at the FUN show about wanting to display her nickel at the ANA convention and Paul Montgomery taking over the reins of the company that would conduct the official auction at the convention — set the stage for an incredibly intricate series of interlinked events that would lead to an epic climax eight months later.

226

Hatching the Reunion Idea

The convention was very much on the minds of executives at the American Numismatic Association. The World's Fair of Money® is one of the ANA's major annual events. Planning was well under way for the 2003 event, scheduled for July 30 - August 3 at the Baltimore Convention Center, 1 West Pratt Street in Baltimore, Maryland. They couldn't know it then, but they would soon have a super promotional idea dropped in their lap, one that would grow to historic, monumental proportions as the event grew near.

"The whole thing started when Laura Sperber announced that she was planning on bringing her 1913 nickel to Baltimore," said Stephen L. Bobbitt, ANA public relations director. Bobbitt and ANA executive director Christopher Cipoletti learned about the proposal from Sperber's announcement in the January *Coin World* article. That was the first they had heard of it.

Bobbitt called the ANA's convention director, Brenda Bishop, to ask if she knew anything about it. She said no. Bishop contacted Sperber to confirm her interest in displaying her famous nickel at the Baltimore convention. Sperber said she initiated the contact with the ANA. Regardless of who made the first move, the parties were in agreement that they wanted to do the display.

Because of their fame and mystique, having even one of the 1913 Liberty Head nickels on display at a coin show draws crowds. The ANA itself owns one of the five celebrated nickels — donated by Aubrey and Adeline Bebee (the one J.V. McDermott loved to show off at the bars he frequented) — and displays it in the ANA Money Museum in Colorado Springs, Colorado.

ANA officials naturally wanted to get a firm commitment from Sperber and Legend Numismatics to show their "TV star" coin. Cipoletti instinctively knew it would be good publicity for the convention. "It is a coin that because of its rarity could draw a lot of attention from the public," he said.

Bobbitt's mind was already abuzz with publicity ideas about it. He called Sperber to find out if she would be attending the ANA's National Money Show in Charlotte, North Carolina, in March. She said she would be. Bobbitt told her he had a display case — the one he usually used to display hundred-thousand dollar bills — that could be adapted to show her nickel. They arranged to meet at the Charlotte show to discuss the details.

Beth Deisher and Donn Pearlman joined the discussion in Charlotte about displaying the Legend Numismatic nickel. Deisher was editor of *Coin World*. Pearlman was president of Minkus & Pearlman Public Relations, Inc.

Pearlman, a former member of the ANA's board of governors, was a consultant assisting the ANA with general news media publicity and promotion for their annual conventions — the National Money Show™ in the early Spring, and the World's Fair of Money® each summer. He also worked on public relations assignments for Bowers and Merena Galleries, the official convention auctioneers.

During the conversation, Beth Deisher had a brilliant inspiration: "Why don't we try to get them *all* together?" Bobbitt and Pearlman looked at each other and said, "Why didn't we think of that?"

They all agreed it would be a major promotional coup for the convention. "We'll make it a reunion," they said. If having one 1913 Liberty Head nickel at a show was always a big draw, just think what a sensation it would be to have *four* of them! It would be a fitting event to mark the 90th anniversary of the nickels.

They immediately set their minds to how to make it happen. They wanted to work quietly, so word didn't get out prematurely. They had some delicate negotiation work ahead of them to get the nickels lined up for a reunion.

"We knew we had Laura's, and we knew we could get the ANA's nickel," Bobbitt said. "And Donn was sure we could get Dwight Manley's coin."

Pearlman called Manley on his cell phone to ask him about it. Without hesitation, Manley said, "Sure." Manley was always supportive of any educational offerings by the ANA. Pearlman cornered Chris Cipoletti at the show, who quickly agreed to bring the ANA nickel. "Almost instantly, we had three of the five coins and were 60% there," Pearlman recalled.

They were feeling pretty good about their progress, but there was a hitch. Two hitches, in fact. There was, of course, the missing nickel that no one had been able to find for more than forty years. And there was the Smithsonian to deal with. The Smithsonian owns the 1913 Liberty Head nickel donated by the Norweb family.

Smithsonian Nickel Almost a No-Show

The Smithsonian Institution doesn't loan out its exhibits to just anyone. There are very specific and exacting criteria to be met before a request will even be considered. Then there's the formidable approval process to overcome. The request must successfully navigate several levels of review to be approved. It's a daunting undertaking.

Beth Deisher said she had friends at the Smithsonian who might help. She agreed to make some calls to see what could be done about getting the fourth known coin for the reunion. Chris Cipoletti also had some high-level contacts within the Smithsonian.

Deisher called Douglas Mudd, collection manager of the National Numismatic Collection, part of the Smithsonian's Museum of American History. The museum's 1913 Liberty Head nickel was his responsibility (along with 1.6 million other objects).

Mudd was receptive to the idea of lending the Smithsonian coin to be part of an historic reunion of the 1913 Liberty Head nickels. "I thought it would be a very interesting idea. Certainly collector interest would be way up there," Mudd said. "It's one of those classic stories that gets people excited because of the rich history attached to it. From that standpoint, it would be a worthwhile project."

First, Mudd wanted to know more about the event to determine if it qualified under the strict guidelines established by the Smithsonian for loaning out its artifacts. "We are responsible for these items, and we have a set of procedures on who and how we can allow items to get out of the building," Mudd said.

He had to be assured that the host who would be responsible for the coin was legitimate, capable of keeping the coin secure, was not profiting from the event, and would not use the coin to promote a product. Since the coin would be appearing in Baltimore under the auspices of the ANA's Money Museum, the request met the qualifications (even though coins and other merchandise are bought and sold at the show, the ANA itself is not involved in these transactions and is chartered as a non-profit corporation).

Mudd agreed to shepherd the proposal through the Smithsonian approval process. He could not himself make the decision, but could work the system on behalf of the project. He consulted with curator Richard Doty about it and contacted the Smithsonian's loan office, which must issue the necessary paperwork. The loan office can decide whether or not a particular borrower is appropriate and has the power to kill a loan application without ever issuing the paperwork.

He told his supervisor he thought it sounded like a good idea that would generate a lot of favorable publicity for the Smithsonian's numismatic collection. The fact that the show would be in Baltimore, just a 40-mile drive from Washington, D.C., helped the case; transporting the coin would be relatively easy. Mudd also pointed out that if the Smithsonian's nickel were not included in the reunion, its absence would be conspicuous and could create a backlash against the Smithsonian. "People would know that the Smithsonian coin was not there, and negative publicity would be easy to get by not going," Mudd said. Doty agreed.

The proposal worked its way through committees to the director, Dr. Brent Glass, and seemed to be making favorable progress. Then it ran into what almost proved to be a fatal stumbling block.

While the project labored its way through the time-consuming approval process at the Smithsonian, new developments on the 1913 Liberty nickel reunion were crackling elsewhere. Laura Sperber saw an opportunity to capitalize on the anticipated hubbub the reunion would cause. She and one of her partners, George Huang, collaborated with Stephen Geppi and John Snyder of Diamond International Galleries to stage a gala pre-opening reception to display the four nickels in Timonium, Maryland, just a short drive from Baltimore. High-profile dignitaries and invited guests would get a preview first look at the reunited nickels.

Sperber had more than a sociable interest in underwriting the toney soiree. Though she had been quoted as saying about the Legend Numismatics nickel in January, "It's not for sale, it's part of a collection we're building," she wanted to impress some potential buyers for the nickel at the Timonium party.

That threw a monkey wrench into the works at the Smithsonian and very nearly killed the chances of getting their coin for the reunion. The loan committee and collection committee, which had first recommended that the nickel go to the convention, balked when they learned of the Diamond International Galleries reception involving display of the coins.

The Smithsonian considered the ANA show and the Timonium reception to be two separate events. They approved the ANA convention display, but considered the gala reception appearance in Timonium to be out of bounds. The objection was based on two reasons: 1) The reception was for VIPs by invitation only. Smithsonian rules dictate that displays of its articles are free and open to the public; 2) Diamond International is a for-profit company. Smithsonian guidelines forbid displaying the museum's objects in conjunction with events held by any commercial enterprise.

"We do not lend objects to profit events for institutions," Mudd said. "It is written in stone." The committee reported the proposal to Dr. Glass with a negative recommendation. He could accept or override their recommendation. Barring evidence of any extenuating factors, he would in all likelihood accept their recommendation. For the time being, it seemed the Smithsonian nickel would be missing from the reunion display after all.

But the art of compromise came to the rescue. Diamond International Galleries president John Snyder hadn't given up on getting the Smithsonian coin. "At the last minute, we had an agreement that if they loaned us the coin we would show it from 9-12 in the morning" at a free exhibit open to the public, Snyder said. "That eliminated the stumbling block for Glass" and opened an avenue for him to approve the request.

The fact that the public exhibit proposed by Snyder would be designed for education, particularly for children, and because the VIP gala was strictly a non-commercial event mitigated the objections. Douglas Mudd said, "Dr. Glass was able to look at the larger picture and see that the event is for education; nobody is making any untoward profit out of it. They aren't making any money off of the Smithsonian object. They were not getting any direct benefit other than good will."

Dr. Brent D. Glass, director of the Smithsonian's National Museum of American History. Courtesy of Diamond International Galleries.

All during the process, Beth Deisher and Chris Cipoletti kept up their determined lobbying efforts and undoubtedly had a favorable influence on Dr. Glass' final decision.

In the end, Glass approved the loan of the Smithsonian's 1913 Liberty Head nickel for both the ANA convention and the Timonium gala. The extraordinary events that followed and the massive worldwide publicity for the event proved his decision to be a wise one.

Dreaming Up a "Hook"

While the Smithsonian drama ground on at a glacial pace, Donn Pearlman's fertile imagination churned with ideas to grab headlines for the convention. The adrenaline rush he got from the nickel reunion prospect cranked his creative machinery into overdrive.

He knew he had three 1913 Liberty Head nickels to talk about in his press blitz. That's good, he thought. There was a good chance he would have four nickels. Even better. But what if…just imagine…what if the mysterious fifth nickel could be uncovered in time for the show? It would be the historic moment of a lifetime for numismatists!

In early May, Pearlman sat in his office wondering what it would take to bring the missing nickel out of hiding. Previous reward offers up to $10,000 hadn't done the trick. What about a million dollars?

"I thought that a generous reward for the missing coin would be a wonderful 'hook' to get publicity for the show — and, who knows!, perhaps actually find the coin," Pearlman said. "I reasoned that since the Walton coin was unseen for 41 years, if it still existed it might not be in nice condition anymore. Surely, though, the fifth known 1913 Liberty nickel would be worth at least $1 million just for its rarity — and whatever story accompanied it for being out of sight for so long. Odds were, though, that no reward money would be paid because the coin would not be found; however, the ANA and its Baltimore convention would get a million dollars worth of 'free' publicity."

So it would be a win-win situation whether or not anybody showed up with the missing nickel to claim the reward. Pearlman couldn't wait to float the idea to the ANA. "I called Steve Bobbitt, the ANA Public Relations Director, and offered ANA 'first refusal' on the reward idea," Pearlman explained. "I suggested that the ANA offer a minimum $1 million reward, or, I asked, would it be better if we presented the idea to their official auctioneer for the Baltimore convention? The ANA decided it would be better to see if the auctioneer, Bowers and Merena, would like to do it."

As negotiations to assemble the four nickels unfolded, Pearlman kept Paul Montgomery at Bowers and Merena in the loop with periodic emails along the lines of "You can't tell anybody, Paul, but we're trying to unite the nickels together."

Montgomery, preoccupied with more immediate priorities, had little time to think about something still eight months away. It was still very much back-burner stuff to him.

In addition, he was skeptical. His first response was, "It'll never happen. You'll never get the Smithsonian coin." Still, he acknowledged that having three of the nickels was pretty impressive and better than having none. "So go get 'em," he instructed.

Pearlman needed to get some publicity going for the show, by then only about three months off. He wanted to use the reward story for his big hook. Time to make another call.

Pearlman arranged a conference call with himself and Paul Montgomery, president of Bowers and Merena Galleries; David Hall, president and board member of Collectors Universe (parent company of Bowers and Merena Galleries); and Michael Haynes, chief executive officer and board member of Collectors Universe. He asked them, "Would you pay a million bucks for the fifth nickel?" He explained his reasoning: maximum publicity impact, minimum cost, no downside risk.

The executives were taken aback by the startling proposal, but only for a few seconds. Montgomery answered with a nonchalant "Sure." David Hall added offhandedly, "I'd pay $10,000 just to be the first one to see it." Montgomery said he would, too.

Pearlman hung up the phone and wrote a press release announcing the million-dollar reward offer. He ran it by Montgomery.

"I read through it. It's hilarious. It's really a pretty cool story," Montgomery recalled. "But we tabled it for several weeks." He wanted to give more thought to it for two reasons: 1) Should we do it? and 2) What will the industry perception be? He was sensitive to how the numismatic community would react to such a flamboyant splash from the usually traditionalist Bowers and Merena Galleries. "How was it going to fit in a Bowers-less Bowers and Merena dynamic?" he wondered. They were also still awaiting word from the Smithsonian so they would know whether they had four or only three of the nickels for a reunion display. A story about that was planned to follow about two weeks after the reward story broke.

Montgomery put the reward idea on hold for the time being. He hadn't mentioned the possibility of the reward offer to his staff, not even to his executive vice president, Mark Borckardt. He had other, more pressing matters on his mind.

Recent fractures within the company over the departure of David Bowers (who was well-known in the small, close-knit community of Wolfeboro, New Hampshire; he still lived there) got more complicated when some former B&M employees set up another auction company virtually across the street; Wolfeboro is not a big place. That was too big a distraction. Montgomery decided to move the company headquarters out of Wolfeboro.

He talked it over with the board at Collectors Universe. They decided to move the company to Mandeville, Louisiana. His family lived there, and he was well familiar with business resources available in the area.

The process of setting up a new office in Louisiana and transferring operations was soon well underway. Only a handful of employees from Wolfeboro would be transferring to Louisiana. All the others accepted a generous severance package and were serving out the time until the New Hampshire office closed down. At the same time, new employees had to be hired in Louisiana and brought up to speed on their new jobs. The circumstances made a normally challenging work routine even more difficult.

Pearlman kept the subject of the reward release in front of Montgomery. Finally, Montgomery gave the green light, in part to get Pearlman off his back about it. Pearlman knocked out the final draft of the press release:

New Hampshire Coin Dealer Offers
$1+ Million Reward For Missing Nickel

(Wolfeboro, New Hampshire) — Who says a nickel won't even buy a cup of coffee anymore? A reward of at least $1 million is being offered by a New Hampshire coin dealer for the discovery of a missing 1913 Liberty Head nickel, a rare coin last seen by collectors 40 years ago.

"Only five Liberty Head nickels with the date, 1913, were made under mysterious circumstances. One of them has not been seen since the early 1960s," explained Paul Montgomery, President of Bowers and Merena Galleries of Wolfeboro, New Hampshire (www.BowersandMerena.com), a division of Collectors Universe, Inc. (NASDAQ: CLCT).

"To coax it out of hiding, we'll pay at least $1 million to purchase the fifth known 1913 Liberty nickel. In fact, we'll pay $10,000 just to be the first to see it," he said.

The nationwide bounty hunt is being launched in conjunction with the American Numismatic Association (www.money.org) World's Fair of Money convention to be held in Baltimore, July 30 to August 3.

"This year is the 90th anniversary of these legendary rare coins. It would be wonderful if we could display the missing coin at our convention this summer. It would be the first time in about 40 years anyone has seen it in public," said Lawrence Lee, curator of the American Numismatic Association Money Museum which owns one of the famous nickels.

The missing 1913 Liberty Head nickel portrays "Miss Liberty" on the front and a large Roman numeral, "V," on the back to indicate a value of five cents. Millions of nickels with that common design were produced from 1883 through 1912, and today most are worth less than a dollar, according to Montgomery.

"Only five Liberty Head nickels were made with the 1913 date, apparently late in 1912 as a test of coin-making equipment, explained American Numismatic Association spokesman Steve Bobbitt. "But then the Mint eliminated the Liberty Head design, and all the other United States nickels dated 1913 depict a Native American Indian on one side and a buffalo on the back."

"One of the five 1913 Liberty Head nickels has been unaccounted for since the early 1960s when it may have been owned by North Carolina coin dealer, George O. Walton, who was killed in a car crash in 1962," said Montgomery.

"Two of the five coins now are in museums, including The Smithsonian Institution; two others are in private collections. The fifth one could be anywhere."

"After vanishing from the hobby more than 40 years ago, we're not sure what condition the missing coin is in today. Of course, we'll pay significantly more than a million dollars if it's still well preserved," said Montgomery.

At a 1996 auction, Bowers and Merena sold a pristine condition 1913 Liberty Head nickel owned by the estate of Baltimore banker, Louis E. Eliasberg, Sr., for $1,485,000. It was the first rare coin to ever break the million dollar mark.

Here are the locations of the four other 1913 Liberty Head nickels: The Smithsonian Institution, Washington, D.C.; the American Numismatic Association Money Museum, Colorado Springs, Colorado; private collection of sports agent Dwight Manley of Newport Beach, California; and private collection of Legend Numismatics of Lincroft, New Jersey.

Pearlman dated the story for release on May 23, 2003, the Friday before the long Memorial Day weekend. Holidays are usually slow news times, so he reasoned the story would have a better chance for good placement.

He sent an advance copy exclusively to David Tirell-Wysocki at the Concord, New Hampshire Bureau of the Associated Press, with an offer to set up an interview with Paul Montgomery. Pearlman had connected with Tirell-Wysocki on previous occasions when the AP reporter covered stories about Bowers and Merena, located not far away in Wolfeboro. Pearlman, a former radio newsman (25 years with CBS at WBBM in Chicago), had known Tirell-Wsyocki for years, from a time when the latter worked at a radio station in Boston.

Pearlman figured that coverage by the Associated Press would be the most efficient way to get the story on the wires and get the widest coverage the fastest way possible. Tirell-Wysocki liked the story and indicated interest in an interview.

Pearlman set up a phone session with Montgomery. He cautioned Montgomery about mentioning the move to Louisiana. He worried that New Hampshire-based Tirell-Wysocki might lose interest if Bowers and Merena wasn't going to be a local company anymore.

Then he waited and watched the news wires to see what would happen. What happened was beyond his wildest PR man dreams. He launched a story that captured the public imagination and took off on its own, running on a growing supply of media energy for months and leading to a stunning surprise ending!

Setting the Hook

A seasoned newsman with more than 30 years experience, David Tirell-Wysocki served on the general assignment desk at the Concord, New Hampshire, Bureau of the Associated Press. He had previously done stories on Bowers and Merena, including items on their being auctioneers for a couple of famous ship wrecks, the *S.S. Central America* and the *S.S. Brother Jonathan*.

Tirell-Wysocki called Montgomery on Tuesday, May 20. Montgomery was reluctant to do the interview at that moment because he had people waiting outside his office to see him and was up to his eyeballs in work. Still, he didn't want to lose the free publicity, so he took the call.

Tirell-Wysocki asked Montgomery, "Is this a search for a coin, a business promotion, or publicity for the ANA show coming up in Baltimore?"

"All three," Montgomery replied. "There's a little bit of a gimmick to it," Montgomery confessed, "But it's all about finding the coin. Everybody in the industry would love to see it."

Montgomery explained that, while the expressed purpose was to find the missing nickel, the underlying goal was to get the general public talking about the coin and entice new people to become interested in coin collecting.

"I don't know if they really thought they would find it," Tirell-Wysocki said. "I think they were shocked when it showed up."

Tirell-Wysocki wanted corroborating sources. "I don't like to go with one perspective on something like this," he said. He contacted Larry Lee, curator of the American Numismatic Association's Money Museum, and *Coin World* editor Beth Deisher.

He asked them, "Is this as big of a deal as Bowers and Merena thinks it is? They said 'Absolutely!' Then I realized that this was a good story. That added credibility to it."

Donn Pearlman kept in touch with Tirell-Wysocki on the progress of the story. Just before Montgomery left the office on Thursday for his weekend commute to Mandeville, Pearlman called him with an update. "He wrote the story and he's going to put it on the wire, so you may get some calls," he told Montgomery. He was alerting Montgomery to the possibility that other news media might contact him for interviews when the story broke on the AP wire.

Because he wouldn't be in the office on Friday, Montgomery called his second-in-command, Mark Borckardt, into his office late Thursday. He told him very briefly about the million-dollar reward offer and the press release.

It was an offhand, oh-by-the-way briefing. Montgomery also mentioned it in passing to the receptionist, Katrina Harrington: "If you get a couple of phone calls from the press, just refer them to Mark, or take a message and I'll return them when I get back."

As Montgomery was leaving, Borckardt said, "It'll never work."

"What'll never work?" Montgomery asked.

"That coin's gone," Borckardt said. He assumed that the failure of so many efforts before to find the coin meant it was forever lost. He reasoned that if it existed, its sheer value would have brought it to the market long before then.

Montgomery recalled later about that exchange, "It never occurred to us that we were going to find it. It never occurred to us."

All during the holiday weekend, Donn Pearlman kept an eager, and sometimes anxious, eye on the news wires, watching for the story to break. It finally hit on Monday, May 26 — Memorial Day. There amid the usual tributes to America's war casualties, Tirell-Wysocki's story broke the news on Associated Press wires about the million dollar reward for the first time:

Coin Experts Hope Reward Will Uncover Mystery Nickel

By DAVID TIRRELL-WYSOCKI
Associated Press Writer

A nationwide bounty hunt is underway — with a $1 million reward. The target: a 90-year-old nickel.

After being born of questionable, some say clandestine, circumstances, five 1913 Liberty Head nickels surfaced in the 1920s. Four are accounted for, but the fifth has been missing for at least 40 years.

"There's a little bit of gimmick to it," concedes Paul Montgomery, president of Bowers and Merena Galleries of Wolfeboro, N.H., which is offering the reward. "But it's all about trying to find the coin."

The Liberty Head Nickel was minted from 1883 to 1912. It was replaced the following year by the Indian or Buffalo Nickel.

However, five Liberty Nickels were minted illegally, possibly by a mint official. They were never placed into circulation and even were considered illegal to own for many years because they were not a regular issue.

Two are in private collections, two are in museums, but the fifth has confounded collectors for decades.

"Everybody in the industry would love to see it," said Montgomery.

As one story goes, the coin may have been owned by a North Carolina dealer killed in a car crash in 1962. Part of the mystery is a theory that the dealer was carrying the coin to a buyer named Reynolds.

People have searched the roadside, said Lawrence Lee, curator of the American Numismatic Association Money Museum, which owns one of the nickels.

"He was killed on his way there," Lee said. "Did the Reynolds' family actually get it? Was it in the car wreck?"

A larger question might be: Was it an authentic coin?

Beth Deisher, editor of *Coin World* magazine in Sidney, Ohio, has researched the missing coin for several years.

Its whereabouts are "a great mystery," she said.

Deisher said a nickel was among the coins recovered from the car wreckage, but it was not one of the original five. Someone had altered the date to make it look like a 1913 specimen, she said.

The dealer, George Walton, "claimed to have access to the genuine, through a client named Reynolds," she said. "We believe he had an altered date coin he often carried with him and put on display."

She said she has found no evidence that Walton was taking coins to a Mr. Reynolds. "He was killed at an intersection in Enfield, N.C., not far from where he lived," she said. "He was probably on his way home from a coin show."

She said the last confirmed owner wrote in the 1940s that he had traded the coin to a Mr. Reynolds. She said no one even knows who Mr. Reynolds is.

Lee said many have claimed to have the missing coin.

"There are lots of counterfeits," he said. "We have maybe 50 examples in the museum."

Often, he said, someone will scratch a 1910 nickel to make the date read 1913. But the genuine coins have other identifying features, he said.

In 1996, Bowers and Merena auctioned one of the 1913 nickels for $1.4 million. It was the first coin to sell for more than $1 million. That's why the company is offering at least $1 million for the missing one.

The renewed hunt coincides with the American Numismatic Association's convention in Baltimore this summer. Bowers and Merena is the convention's official auctioneer.

Montgomery said it's possible someone has the coin and doesn't know its significance, but not likely.

Lee believes publicity will get people to start looking for it again, and maybe it will show up in an estate or a grandmother's attic. He figures if the owner knows about the coin, "they couldn't resist, sooner or later, bragging to somebody or selling it to somebody."

Deisher said the coin's whereabouts are anyone's guess and she has an important tip for the bounty hunters.

"If anybody thinks they have the coin, don't try to shine it or clean it," she said. "Treat it very, very gingerly because cleaning it would harm it."

©Copyright. Associated Press. All Rights Reserved. Distributed by Valeo IP.

Larry Lee's comment about the missing nickel showing up in "a grandmother's attic" proved to be very nearly prophetic. It was found in a grandmother's closet.

Million Dollar Reward Mania

The response to the million dollar reward story was instant, massive, and overwhelming.

The first hint of what was to come hit early. Memorial Day was no holiday for Debbie McDonald, direct sales manager for Bowers and Merena Galleries. She was alone in the office rushing to make last minute preparations for the Long Beach Coin and Collectibles show, which would be opening three days later in California (May 29-June 1). She was to meet Paul Montgomery at the Long Beach Convention Center the next day. The phones were quiet because the switchboard was on night service, meaning that only calls to a personal night line number could get through.

She was startled when her phone rang. She wasn't expecting anyone to call, certainly not a network television producer.

"I was the only one in the office when 'Good Morning America' called asking for me. That was the first I knew anything about the reward," McDonald said. "They called May 26th, Memorial Day. They got my night line by going on the Internet and finding the name of another employee, Mary Tocci. They called her at home, and she gave them our personal night line number at work."

"The caller said, 'Hi, this is Good Morning America. We're looking for Debbie McDonald.' I told them that was me and asked what I could do for them. They wanted a comment on the million dollar nickel."

McDonald had not the slightest idea what they were talking about. Experience told her not to admit it, though. "I knew enough about this business never to say, 'I don't know.' They didn't know I was in the office alone, so I put them on hold and called Paul's cell phone. I knew he was in Louisiana. I was a little sharp with him. 'Do you think you should have told me?' I snapped out. I could have killed him for leaving me in the dark about it."

Paul Montgomery instructed her to get the number and he would return the call. He told her briefly about the reward offer and tried to calm her down.

McDonald was even more animated when she heard the company had put a million dollars on the line to find the coin. " 'Are you *kidding*?' I screamed. My first thought was, OH MY GOSH! This will be explosive. The thought of a huge amount of phone calls and letters when we were in the middle of moving to Louisiana…well, I started to panic. I was excited first, then panicked. Paul said not to worry, it's great publicity and we can handle it. He said, 'Just go with the flow, and I will call you later.' That was reassuring. He sounded like it was all under control. Then I calmed down and thought it was an absolutely great idea, and everything would be okay." Little did she know…

Montgomery was working in the yard at his house in Mandeville. It was late afternoon on Memorial Day when his wife, Amy, brought the phone out to him. She was annoyed that he was working on what was supposed to be a day off. She thought he needed to relax, since he had been putting in 20-hour days for four months straight and away from home to boot.

On the other end of the line was a producer from the ABC News show "Good Morning America." They wanted him to come to New York to do an interview the next morning, Tuesday. He was caught off guard, and stammered that he couldn't do the interview because he had to catch a plane the next morning to attend a coin show in California. The producer, not to be put off so easily, said they could do the interview by remote from the studio of ABC's New Orleans affiliate, WGNO-TV.

The interview would be very early, and his flight wasn't until 9 a.m. So he agreed, saying he would drive to the station in New Orleans. "They said, 'No-no-no, we'll send a limousine for you.' Because they didn't want me to get lost or not be able to find a parking space," Montgomery said.

The limo arrived at 4:30 a.m. as planned and drove him to the WGNO-TV studio at the foot of Canal Street on the east bank of the Mississippi River. Montgomery searched about for a bit in the basically empty television station until he found a crew person, who directed him to a small studio and wired him with a microphone in front of a remotely-operated camera.

Then he was left alone in the studio, with occasional messages over the intercom speaker from the control room. He had no idea who would be interviewing him or what they would ask. He wouldn't even see the person, just hear the questions through an earpiece.

He was nervous, not from being camera-shy, but with the realization that many important people would be watching him. "It's not just about the nickel deal," he recalled thinking. "It's about the new Bowers and Merena. It's about the new president. It's about industry perception."

Even though it was cold in the studio, he was sweating under the bank of bright lights trained on him. The interview was moved back several times because of a breaking story about two soldiers being killed in Iraq. He began to realize he was running out of time. He had a plane to catch. "So you can imagine my anxiety going up exponentially by the moment."

A number of times, ABC flashed pictures of the 1913 Liberty Head nickel as a teaser for the upcoming interview, but eventually one of the local TV crew told him they would re-schedule his interview for the next morning's show. They could either tape it or arrange to do it at the Long Beach affiliate. "But I guess it would be old news by then. They never did call back," said Montgomery.

He didn't get on national TV that morning, but he did get on his plane. Even though the interview itself didn't take place, the frequent teaser promos about the million dollar reward on "Good Morning America" reached millions of viewers and added media power to the AP story, spreading the word rapidly.

Montgomery still didn't think the reward story was a big deal. He figured that the "Good Morning America" interview-that-didn't-happen was just because a million dollar reward for nickel was an ear-catching novelty story to the TV news people. The fact that the interview kept getting bumped up by other things confirmed in his mind that it wasn't a big deal to the newshounds, either.

He called in to the office to tell them he wasn't going to be on TV and for everybody to get to work. He was running late for his flight to California, so he cut the call short and ran for the plane. What he didn't know is that all hell broke loose on the phone lines in Wolfeboro.

"When we got into the office on Tuesday morning," recalled Mark Borckardt, "The switchboard was lit up like a Christmas tree. We had twelve incoming phone lines. Every one of those lines was lit."

There were 500 voice mails on the recorder. The receptionist was dumbfounded with what to do about them. Borckardt told her just to delete them. There was no way the meager staff could answer all or even a part of them with the incoming calls still jamming the phone lines.

Many of the calls were from media people trying to contact Montgomery, who at that time was somewhere in the sky on the $3\frac{1}{2}$-hour flight to Los Angeles. "Paul had no clue," Borckardt said. "I started getting interview requests - from a radio station in Boston, one in Seattle, a newspaper in Houston…"

"They couldn't reach me because I was in the air," Montgomery said. "My phone at home was ringing off the wall."

TV station WBZ in Boston sent a news crew to the Bowers and Merena office to interview Mark Borckardt. New England Cable News also sent a crew. In the midst of talking with them, Borckardt paused to do a news clip with a crew from WMUR-TV sent over from Manchester, New Hampshire.

Along with the clamor of calls from the news media wanting interviews, the staff was bewildered by a deluge of calls from people who were absolutely positive they had the missing coin, or from people who had an old coin and wondered how much it was worth.

"I HAVE AN OLD COIN…"
SOME THINGS NEVER CHANGE.

To create any interest on the part of the general public, newspaper articles on numismatics naturally have to deal with the great rarities which command large prices - in other words, it is merely an appeal to cupidity, and practically the only result is a flood of inquiries to the newspaper offices from people who possess a few old, badly worn coins and desire to know the value of these old keepsakes. And the strange part of it is that not one inquiry in a thousand will have any bearing on the coins of which the article treated.

So great has become the nuisance in this respect that many of the larger papers have put a taboo on anything of a numismatic nature unless the matter is so prepared that letters of inquiry in relation thereto seem an impossibility. Nor can they be greatly blamed in the matter, as any dealer or writer who has spent hours in answering a mass of foolish interrogatories readily will concede.

Theodore J. Venn - "The Best Way to Create an Interest in Coins" *Numismatist*, January 1921

For the staff at Bowers and Merena, the flood of calls was disconcerting not only by its magnitude but because they had no idea what it was all about or what they were supposed to do about it. The employees were understandably ruffled. They hadn't been told of the million dollar reward offer and learned about it on the news like everybody else.

Pam Roberts, who had been with the company a couple of years and was one of the few employees making the move to Louisiana, heard something about the reward for a coin but didn't connect it to Bowers and Merena. As she was getting ready for work, her husband, Brett, saw the picture of the nickel on "Good Morning America" and called out to her about it as she was walking upstairs to take a shower. She was annoyed and ignored it. She took a call as soon as she walked into the office at 8:30. "I got to work and get a call from someone asking me if we were the company looking for the coin. I told them no."

Most of the employees weren't in the best spirits to begin the day, considering that they were soon to be laid off and out of work. The Wolfeboro office would be closed very shortly.

Carol Travers was one of the employees who was losing her job. She had been offered a transfer but declined for family reasons. Initially she was upset that they hadn't been prepped for this, adding to the frustrations she and others felt about losing people (about half the staff had already departed), being understaffed, and the closing down of the office, on top of the fact that they were working on an important auction.

Even with her own frustrations, she empathized with the callers. "I felt sorry for them," she said of hearing the letdown in their voices when they learned they weren't going to be millionaires after all." Some of the personal stories of the callers touched her, and it was stressful having to burst their dreams. Still and all, Travers said later, looking at the incident in retrospect, "It was exciting…just not at the best time."

It didn't help matters that the office was in an advanced state of moving. "The office was a mess — boxes everywhere," said Pam Roberts. "We were in the middle of packing." A technician from the home office of Collectors Universe was scheduled to come in that day and shut down all the computers and phone systems. It was an absolute madhouse.

Normal business halted in its tracks. "We were paralyzed," Borckardt said. "We had to use our cell phones to call out," he said, "because the office lines were constantly all tied up."

Meanwhile, Paul Montgomery, having arrived in Los Angeles and rented a car, tried to call in to the office as he drove to Long Beach. "I couldn't get through," he said. He was miffed that the president of the company couldn't contact his own staff. "I'm wondering what in the world is going on — the phone system is screwed up, nobody is answering the phone, and when I did get through, it just rang and rang and nobody answered, so I was really getting torqued."

He persisted and finally connected with Jamie Ashby. She recognized his voice immediately and snapped, "Oh, it's *YOU*." Her voice dripped with resentment. Montgomery was startled and baffled by the reaction. "It sounded like, 'You are not the person I want to talk to, because you caused all this mess.'" He had no idea at the time why she should be hostile to him, and he took offense that a subordinate would speak to him in that tone of voice, even one that was being laid off. "I was thinking, 'Man, that was rude. I'm supposed to be the one that's teed off here because you're not answering the telephone.' But Mark was short with me on the phone, too. He said, 'Paul, it's going crazy, the phone is ringing off the hook, and I'm gonna have to go.' I said, 'Okay' and left it at that." Montgomery still didn't fully appreciate the pandemonium his staff back home was suffering through.

Debbie McDonald tried through the day's journey to Long Beach to call in to the office, too, with only occasional success. "Every time I stopped, I would make a quick call, and the only way to describe the office was complete chaos," she said. "There were 12 incoming lines, and the operators couldn't keep up with them. They told me it was a continual stream of calls with every light on the switchboard lit up all day. Every time I called, it just complicated matters more. They just could not talk to me."

In all the bedlam, Mark Borckardt called the employees together around 10:00 a.m. for a briefing on the situation. He actually knew little more than they did, but he had to restore some semblance of order and tell them how to handle the calls. He gave them a short information spiel to tell the callers. They were to instruct the callers to take their coin to a coin dealer in their area and have it authenticated.

"Everyone had to take calls," Borckardt said. "Jamie Ashby, Cheryl Perry, Carol Travers, Mary Tocci, Pam Roberts, Sue Mitchell, Andy Pollock…everybody had to get involved" with the phones along with receptionist Katrina Harrington.

"We were already stressed out about the ANA," said Sue Mitchell, Pam Robert's sister and a relative newcomer to the staff. She would also be moving with the company to Louisiana. "It was the worst timing for something like that," she said, referring to the chaos of the phone calls adding to all the other pressures. They were just a few days from the deadline for consignments to be finalized for the ANA auction.

"We spent at least 10 minutes on each call," Mitchell said. "They would say, 'I don't have a 1913 nickel but I have one from 1912. What is that worth?'" Most people assumed that if a 1913 nickel was worth a million dollars, then one that was older than that must be worth even more. "We would tell them we weren't looking for a 1912 coin, and they would be upset like they lost megabucks. I mean, you would get people who would not let you hang up. After three hours, we thought, 'This is crazy.' Then Mark changed the rules and said if they think they have the real one, they need to send us a photo of it. The point was that we didn't want to scare anyone away by not helping them, but we couldn't help them. I wanted to hang up on people. I was pissed. There were times when we hated this 1913 nickel."

Pam Roberts was in a foul mood about it, too. "I was pissed at Paul Montgomery for not calling me at home and telling me this was going to happen, at Mark Borckardt for not giving us much information to go by, Collectors Universe in general for doing this at a bad time, and Sue because she was near me." Roberts broke down crying.

The situation was not much better at the Mandeville office. When the phones were switched over, the skeleton staff there had to cope with the frequent calls about the coin. The volume of calls had dropped somewhat but was still considerable and posed a problem for the staff trying to unpack and connect computers, receive and arrange office equipment and furniture, install safes, get files set up, and the myriad of other nitpicking details of getting an office up and running. In the meantime, they still had to try to take care of business, with the all-important ANA auction looming over everything.

The first receptionist hired at the new office left after a week. Judith Wyman came on board at the Mandeville office on June 11. Duty assignments were still in flux, so she was assigned to help the *new* new receptionist answer the phones. Soon she was asked to be the point person in handling the inquiries on the coin reward, answering the calls and responding to letters, voice mails, and emails.

By then, the technical staff had installed a recorded answering machine message instructing those calling about the nickel reward to contact a coin dealer for authentication and call back if they had the real thing. That took care of a lot of the calls, but many callers were persistent enough to leave a message on the recorder. The company's website also carried a photo of a real 1913 Liberty Head nickel for people to compare to and instructions on how to get their coin authenticated if they believed they had the missing one.

When the flood of inquiries slowed to a trickle after a few weeks, Wyman tallied them up and totaled nearly 10,000 phone calls, voice mails, emails, and letters. That didn't count all the ones that were lost from people who couldn't get through because the lines were busy, or whose calls to the voice mail were deleted. "I'm sure many fell through the cracks," she said.

Bowers and Merena Galleries wasn't the only one being swamped by calls about the million dollar reward. Coin dealers around the country were being bombarded with calls about the reward and with inquiries about old coins people were digging up out of their old trunks and drawers and other long forgotten places.

Many of them were congratulatory, crediting Bowers and Merena for stirring up huge interest among the general public in rare coins. Others weren't so complimentary. "I got a fax from a dealer in New Hampshire," Borckardt said, "A one-man operation who was angry at us because he was getting all these 1913 nickel calls on his toll-free number, meaning *he* couldn't get any other business done. He was going to charge us, send us a bill for his 800 telephone line charges."

Fortunately, the congratulations far outweighed the complaints. "There were a lot of dealers who said this was the best thing that had happened for their business," Borckardt said, "Because it was bringing people into their stores."

Hopeful callers overwhelmed the Concord, New Hampshire, Associated Press bureau switchboard. "We got so many calls at the bureau that we all had Bowers and Merena phone numbers taped to our phones so we could refer the calls to them," said David Tirell-Wysocki.

He explained that an historic first at the bureau resulted from the onslaught of calls about the nickel. "We leave 'carry-over' notes for the next shift about incoming calls. The person who works overnight carries over all assignments from the night before to the next morning. One of my colleagues wrote in a carry-over note, 'I think I spoke with every American with a nickel in his or her possession.' We did a feature on it. This is the first time we ever made a carry-over note into a story."

The affair didn't exactly endear Tirell-Wysocki to his fellow newshounds. "I walked in and everybody looked at me like, 'THANKS....you turned the place upside down!'" he said. "When I would walk in the door, everyone would shake their heads and say, 'Glad you're here because now we can hand all the calls to *you*.'" They weren't really angry with him. It was their gruff news clan kind of back-handed admiration for hitting a home run with a blockbuster story. He posted several follow-up features on the reactions to the reward.

Even competitors grudgingly acknowledged the coup Bowers and Merena had pulled off. "I got a call from Steve Ivy of Heritage," Borckardt said. Ivy was co-chairman of Heritage Numismatic Auctions in Dallas, Texas, Bowers and Merena's biggest competitor. "I think he was jealous. He said something to the effect of, 'Why didn't I think of this first?' I had the feeling he was impressed with the whole idea."

Meanwhile, Paul Montgomery, who had been buffered from the chaos by being at the Long Beach coin show, began to feel the effects of the news. "I got inundated with dealer questions and comments," Montgomery said. "It was mostly complimentary, with comments like, 'Good idea!' and, 'It's gotten a lot of publicity for the hobby.' I was getting the lion's share of credit for it even though it collectively involved a lot of people to come up with the idea."

He ran into Laura Sperber of Legend Numismatics, owner of the Hawn specimen 1913 Liberty Head nickel. "You're really pretty close to owning my coin," she joked.

Montgomery encountered Steve Ivy, who was manning the Heritage table right next to Bowers and Merena's on the bourse floor. They bantered along basically the same lines of Ivy's earlier conversation with Mark Borckardt about the reward story.

"We were joking and laughing about it," Montgomery said, noting wryly to Ivy that it couldn't have come at a better time, what with all the sale pressures his company already had on it. "'Yeah, great idea, bad time,' he says to me.' Then he revealed that they actually had a meeting over at Heritage to think over their response to our offer. They even considered coming back over the top of us with a two million dollar offer. I told him, 'Well, if you had done that, I would have just bought Laura Sperber's coin, cracked it out [of the sealed certification case], and sold it to you. I could have made an easy million bucks.' He laughed."

Montgomery had been shielded from media calls for interviews because he could only be reached on his cell phone. He had threatened his employees with dire consequences if anybody let that number out. Ivy teased him about it. "So…Paul…how much is it worth to you not to give out your cell phone number?" Ivy asked. "Thousands of dollars," Montgomery replied.

Debbie McDonald was manning the Bowers and Merena booth at the Long Beach show, and it was difficult to get any business done. "Everyone was coming to the booth, both dealers and the public. We were inundated with questions and people who thought they had the nickel. They would ask, 'If I don't have the 1913, is a 1912 or 1910 worth something?' We did buy some coins and do some business, as much as we could with filtering through all the questions," McDonald said.

McDonald returned to New England only briefly, just long enough to tidy up some personal affairs before leaving for Louisiana. By then, the phones were shut off at the Wolfeboro office and switched over to the Mandeville office. "When I got there, it was exactly the same thing. I think I had over twelve hundred emails waiting for me," she said.

The fury of inquiries continued for days, then gradually tapered off in the following weeks with periodic surges when someone in the media ran a follow-up story. Montgomery figured it would die down and be forgotten. He was happy with the result of a great publicity promotion.

What he didn't know was that an eager reporter at a Roanoke, Virginia, newspaper had an angle on the story that would eventually turn it into an even bigger media sensation than the million dollar reward!

Media Frenzy Lures a Nibble

Mason Adams, not long out of college (where he wrote for the school newspaper), had joined the *Roanoke Times* a couple of months earlier, in 2003. Adams had done a few minor assignments, but was ambitious to hit a big story that would make his editors sit up and take notice of the cub reporter. He got his chance with the million dollar reward story. Not only did he come up with a story that won feature status in the Sunday centerspread section of his newspaper, but he himself became a crucial link in this history-making series of events.

The *Roanoke Times* ran the story about the Bowers and Merena reward offer. The story prompted a call from a reader. "Apparently a gentleman named Harold Bowman called one of my editors, Dwayne Yancey, and said he had known George Walton," Adams said. "Dwayne came to me and said, 'Mason, I have a story for you. It may be a wild goose chase, or it might be good.' He gave me Mr. Bowman's statement and a copy of the Associated Press story and told me to find out what I could about Mr. Walton and his life. He wanted a local angle on the story." Walton had lived in Roanoke, and it was believed he had relatives still in the area.

Adams started by looking through the phone book, without any luck. "Most of the people who were related to Mr. Walton or had even known him were dead. I went to our librarian and asked her to do a search on any of George Walton's family, anything we could find," he said. He went to the paper's morgue and dug through old archives. "I found the mug shot [of Walton] that we had used in an article and found some articles about him when he lived in this area." There were a few items about Walton and his coin and an obituary story.

The main piece of interest was the obituary, which contained names of relatives. Adams collected names from the articles and gave them to the paper's librarian, Belinda Harris, to run a search on them. "She came back with a list of names and numbers and said most of the people were dead."

Adams spoke with Harold Bowman, whose call had started the assignment. Bowman, a Roanoke county resident, said George Walton had dated his best friend's sister. Bowman remembered Walton as "a bit of a braggart."

In his feature that ran June 15, 2003, (three weeks after the news broke on the million-dollar reward story) in the *Roanoke Times* Sunday centerspread, Adams related Bowman's comments about Walton:

> "I never saw him without a real nice double-breasted suit," Bowman said. "He was a coin collector, a gun collector and other antiques. And a gem collector. He had a lot of everything. He showed me a double handful of gold coins one time, and a handful of cut polished gemstones, unmounted. I never saw the coin [the Liberty nickel], but he told me he had it." Walton had thin hair, which he combed straight back, Bowman said. He was stout but always looked trim in his suit. "He always looked just as sharp as could be," Bowman said. "I never did see him in casual dress."

Adams found a few other people who knew a little something about Walton, but not much. One remembered the name of Arthur Smith, an attorney involved with the Waltons. "I followed that for awhile," Adams said, "And it turned out he was in a nursing home and his memory was not too good."

From some information Belinda Harris turned up, Adams pursued the professional angle and checked into numismatic sources. "I talked to Lawrence Lee from ANA, and he said I should talk to Beth Deisher," at *Coin World*, Adams said. Deisher filled him in on some of the theories that had been published about Walton and the disappearance of the nickel. He was a little surprised to learn how well Walton was known in the numismatic world — "a person living in Roanoke and not necessarily known, but in the world of coin collectors he was a bit of a legend."

Then he got his first real break in the story, though it was not an easy one. The librarian had come up with something: "I have a number for Lucille Walton," Harris told Adams. Lucille Walton was George Walton's sister-in-law, widow of his brother Charles.

Adams called the number. Lucille Walton was suspicious when he told her he wanted to know about George Walton and his coin. Her home had been burglarized twice and coins that had belonged to Walton stolen.

"I didn't know who he was," Lucille Walton said. "He wanted to send his cameraman here to take pictures of the clippings that I had. I had to find out about him before I would let him come." After satisfying herself that Adams was a legitimate reporter and not a robber, she agreed to an interview.

He found Lucille Walton, then in her 70s, spry and alert. But he also saw that she was somewhat defensive at first. "She was a little sensitive about what people said about him. People doubted he had the coin, and she was upset about that. That and the fact that she inherited some of his coins and had her house broken into twice," Adams said.

In his story, Adams detailed what he learned from Mrs. Walton:

> Lucille Walton said she did not know [George] Walton well. She remembers his charisma and showmanship, largely from several newspaper articles written about him during his life. "I have one clipping where George Walton was flipping the [Liberty] nickel in the air and catching it. He said it wasn't the real nickel, but he had the real one put away in the bank down in Charlotte." Lucille Walton said. "It's in one of those clippings he goes on and says he saw all five of them, and he could have bought all of them. 'Famous George.' He was famous. There are pictures of him with his rare coins and all these famous big shots. These...people would put him down. You know how tales go," Lucille Walton said. "Some people say he would tip very little, but that was because George didn't want people to think he had much money."

Adams dug into the disappearance of the Walton coin, exploring the published reports of the 1962 crash that killed Walton and rumors that the missing nickel was still somewhere at the crash site:

> For years, collectors were seen walking with metal detectors along North Carolina 264, looking for a gleam in the grass. "There's a real myth about that car wreck that's grown up," said [Lawrence] Lee. "We don't really know [what happened], but it sure makes a good story. I've also heard that half the people don't know the real site of the wreck and are looking in the wrong place."
>
> Most coin experts now agree that the 1913 Liberty nickel found at the wreck was a fake, a 1910 Liberty nickel, which is fairly common but can be made to look like a 1913 nickel by scratching out part of the date. Walton apparently kept the fake for everyday use at shows, while the real nickel was in a safe-deposit box in Charlotte.[79]
>
> After the wreck, the fake nickel was acquired by one of Walton's siblings, now deceased. That coin now resides with one of Walton's other

---

[79] Only one 1913 Liberty Head nickel was found in George Walton's collection, the one that was labeled a fake by appraisers at Stack's. It remains a mystery whether Walton actually had both a fake nickel as well as the real one.

relatives in the Roanoke Valley, who does not want to be identified because of the coin's notoriety.

Other parts of the Walton collection were acquired by Charles Walton, George's brother and Lucille's husband. Lucille Walton said her husband kept the coins in their basement. Their coin collection, however, was stolen in the early 1990s. "When it hit the papers that my husband inherited the money, we were robbed twice," Lucille said. "Our coin collection is gone. We had it in the basement. It was silly for us to have it there."

So where is the real 1913 Liberty nickel? Lucille Walton doesn't think her brother-in-law would have sold it. "He wouldn't have sold that nickel. He was going to build a museum in Myrtle Beach [S.C.] and put that coin there, and all his stuff," Lucille said. "He wouldn't have sold that nickel under any circumstance."

But [Beth] Deisher thinks that Walton sold the nickel shortly after he acquired it. She said it is unlikely a dealer such as Walton would have held onto such a valuable piece for 15 or more years. "He often said he 'had access' to it," Deisher said. "He probably had sold or traded the genuine coin to a client and knew where it was."

There are many people who believe it was perhaps a wealthy collector in the Southeast, because that seems to be where most of his clients were. But his reach of clients could literally be anywhere. That's where the trail really just goes cold. "It is very likely that the coin resides in an old-time collection. Either it's still sitting in a collection somewhere, or sometimes collections are stolen," Deisher said. "If something like that happened, it's not worth melting, and it could have been casually spent. That just opens up, literally...this coin could be anywhere."

Lucille Walton suggested that Adams speak to her nephew Ryan Givens. He was the Roanoke Valley relative in Adams' story who didn't want to be identified. Givens lived in Salem, on the outskirts of Roanoke in western Virginia.

Adams tried for days without success to contact Givens, calling repeatedly and leaving voice mail messages. Finally he used a reverse directory to look up Givens' address. He drove to the house and, getting no response at the door, left a note. Givens called him back that day.

Ryan Givens was not aware of the million dollar reward until Adams told him about it. Givens was guarded in his answers. "I don't remember that Ryan said a whole lot," Adams said. "I used him as a source reference in the story, though. One thing he did say is, 'We have the fake coin that George had.'"

That got Adams' attention. He was aware that his editor, Dwayne Yancey, was considering running his story as a feature in the Sunday edition centerpiece, the *Roanoke Times'* biggest circulation edition. He needed some photo support to go with his text to liven up the presentation. Pictures of the actual coin at the center of the controversy would be powerful.

"I was ecstatic," Adams said. He asked Givens if he would bring the coin in to the newspaper so their staff photographer could shoot it. "He didn't want to be in the story. I told him, 'We can work with you.' The session was set up, and Givens brought the coin with him, still in its original plastic holder that Walton had made up for it, along with stacks of auction books and other Walton memorabilia.

Roanoke Times staff photographer Kelly Hahn-Johnson had set up lights in the studio for the shoot. "One idea we had was to shoot the nickel with Ryan's face out of focus in the background where he wasn't really recognizable. He didn't want to be named." That was one of the shots used with the article.

The shoot produced pictures to illustrate the story, but triggered a more significant sequence of developments that would ultimately lead to the re-discovery of the missing nickel!

The photo session stirred a buzz among the newspaper staff on duty that day. Maybe it was just a break in the daily routine or maybe they sensed this might be a really neat story. A growing number of the usually blasé staffers drifted in to see what the commotion was about.

"Some 20 or 30 people came back to the photo department to look at it. It was to be a pretty good story," Adams said. Another photographer, Eric Brady, came in. He and Givens were discussing the coin and speculating that it might be real, not a fake. "I thought, 'Wouldn't that be crazy if it turned out to be *the* nickel, the real one?'"

Givens said he had harbored suspicions for some time that Stack's had made an error in identifying the coin as fake. He had taken the coin out numerous times and compared it to photos he saw in print and on the Internet of the other real 1913 Liberty Head nickels. He couldn't see how it was any different. He had assumed that, because he wasn't a numismatist, he just didn't have the knowledge to pick out the fine points that an expert might see.

He had considered getting second opinion on the authenticity of the coin, but since neither he nor any of the living Walton family members personally knew any expert numismatists, the notion always got shuffled aside. He planned to get around to it someday.

Photographer Brady, himself a coin collector, volunteered to take some high-quality close-up diagnostic pictures of the coin that Givens could send to some numismatic experts for another opinion. Givens didn't want to send the coin itself to anybody he didn't personally know.

After Adams' story ran, he got a call from Beth Deisher. "Can you put me in contact with the man who has the altered date coin? We would like to have him at the Baltimore show," Deisher told Adams.

Adams said, "I had agreed with Mr. Givens that I would not give out his name or number." So he told Deisher he would relay her request and let the man respond if he chose to.

"I called Mr. Givens' number and, of course, I could never get him. So I left a message on his answering machine saying that Beth Deisher from *Coin World* wanted to talk to him. I left her number, and I guess it went from there."

Ryan Givens called Beth Deisher. "She asked if I had it [the altered date nickel] and told me about the convention in Baltimore," Givens said. "She said they would be displaying the 1913 Liberty Head nickels and, because the legend of the Walton coin was well-known, they wanted to include it in the display with the others. She suggested I contact Mr. Lee of the ANA."

Ironically, though the million-dollar reward story stirred up a connection, that wasn't what coaxed the coin out of hiding. "The million dollars had nothing to do with our bringing it forward, except that if hadn't been for the reward, the *Roanoke Times* would not have picked up on it and called me," Givens said.

It was toward the end of June 2003 when Givens called Larry Lee, curator of the Money Museum at the American Numismatic Association in Colorado Springs. The convention in Baltimore was only a few weeks away.

After learning more from Lee about plans for the 1913 Liberty Head nickel reunion display, Givens responded favorably but said he would first have to check it out with the rest of the family. He had inherited the coin in partnership with a brother, Richard Givens, and two sisters, Bette Givens and Cheryl Givens Myers, after the death of their mother, Melva Givens (one of George Walton's sisters), in 1992.

Cheryl Myers lived near Washington, D.C., 240 miles away from her brother Ryan in Salem, Virginia. When the story came out in the Roanoke newspaper about the nickel and George Walton, Myers spoke with Lucille Walton about it.

"She said 'Your mother had the altered date coin,'" Myers recalled. "I called Ryan and asked him if he had the altered date coin and he said yes. He came up a couple of weeks later and brought a picture the *Roanoke Times* had taken of it."

The photo was one from the original photo shoot. It was not a close-up, so Myers, who was skilled with computer imaging, scanned the picture and enlarged it digitally to get a bigger image of the coin. "It wasn't a clear picture, and you could not see a lot of detail," she said.

She worked at computer enhancing the image to get a clearer view. She also tried overlaying the image of their coin with a photo of the ANA's 1913 Liberty Head nickel posted on their web site. They appeared very similar to Myers' eyes, though she was not a trained numismatist.

"Ryan told me he had talked with Larry Lee at the ANA, and he asked if I would correspond with Mr. Lee because he wanted to see the coin." Rather than letting the coin out of their grasp just yet, they decided to send the digital image instead.

"He was not discouraging, but he sounded disappointed" with the quality of the picture, Myers said. "I told him we could get better pictures of it."

Lee remembered trying to let her down easy. "I was trying to prepare her for the worst news. But she was sharp and knew what she was doing. She would not be easily put off."

Ryan Givens took *Roanoke Times* photographer Eric Brady up on his offer to shoot some high-quality digital close-ups of the coin. Cheryl Myers again overlaid the image on the ANA coin image. It looked like a match. She sent the new photos to Lee.

The sharper image of the coin gave Lee a more accurate tool to work with. What he saw stirred his interest. There were a couple of diagnostic points on the reverse that looked promising. "The one that caught my eye on the Walton coin was the ear of corn," Lee said.

He knew it was believed the reverse die used to make the nickels had apparently been slightly loose and got looser with each strike. So the detail of the kernels in the ear of corn got progressively less distinct. He began to sense that maybe, just maybe, this coin was actually the real one, after all!

Lee did some overlay comparisons of his own, checking the alignment of surface features of the Walton coin to photos of the ANA and Eliasberg specimens.

The evidence, though provocative, was inconclusive, so he didn't let on his rising hopes to Myers. "I didn't always tell her what I was thinking, so she told me that I was leading her on. It was late in the game before I told her" there was a better than average possibility the coin was authentic, Lee said.

Lee emailed the photos to Paul Montgomery and Mark Borckardt. Their first reaction was that it was not real. They had numismatist David Hall look at it. He had the same reaction. Still, there was just enough look-alike with the known real coins to warrant at least an examination of the Walton coin if it was made available.

By then, Myers was more convinced than ever that Stack's had made a mistake and that the nickel handed down through the Walton family was, in fact, genuine. "I think Ryan and I were 90 to 95 percent sure." The only thing keeping them from being totally certain was the fact that Stack's was a reputable company, so it was always assumed by the family that they couldn't be wrong.

Baltimore was not too far from either of them, so Myers and Givens told Lee they would bring their nickel for the exhibit. Lee said he would arrange for some experts to examine their coin to determine if it was the real thing.

Lee had a strong hunch it was real. He wanted to have it looked at before the convention opened on Wednesday, July 30. He would be arriving at the last minute, so he enlisted Donn Pearlman to set it up.

Pearlman made arrangements with Paul Montgomery, Mark Borckardt, and John Dannreuther (Montgomery's numismatic mentor from Memphis) to meet with the Walton family members at the Baltimore Convention Center on Tuesday morning, July 29.

The final pieces of the story were falling into place like clockwork.

Chapter 9 References

Adams, Mason. 2003. "Million-dollar mystery persists years after Roanoker's death." Roanoke (Virginia) *Times* (June 16).
— Adams. 2003. Interview (October 3).

Bobbitt, Stephen L. 2003. Interview (October 14).

Borckardt, Mark. 2003. Interviews (September 2, 3, 9).

Cipoletti, Christopher. 2003. Interview (October 2).

Deisher, Beth. 2003. Interview (October 8).

Givens, Ryan. 2003. Interview (October 1).

Montgomery, Paul. 2003. Interviews (September 2, 3, 9).

Mudd, Douglas. 2003. Interview (October 10).

Pearlman, Donn. 2003. Interview (September 23).
— Pearlman. 2003. "New Hampshire Coin Dealer Offers $1+ Million Reward for Missing Nickel" (Press release, May 23).

Tirell-Wysocki, David. 2003. Interview (October 14).

— Tirell-Wysocki. 2003. "Coin Experts Hope Reward Will Uncover Mystery Nickel" (AP Wire, May 26).

Venn, Theodore J. 1921. "The Best Way to Create an Interest in Coins," *The Numismatist* (Vol. XXXIV, No. 1, January), p. 3.

- Chapter Ten -
SECRET MIDNIGHT MEETING

"It was like a James Bond thing," Paul Montgomery said, speaking about the clandestine midnight meeting when he and a panel of other coin experts made a final decision on the Walton coin's authenticity. "I half expected to see secret agents from my competitors lurking in the shadows," he joked. But the meeting was no joking matter.

The Walton Nickel: First Contact

News about the million-dollar reward for the missing nickel continued to pop up here and there, mainly in print and on the Internet. But no mention was made about the Walton coin appearing at the ANA show in Baltimore. The small group that had been involved in correspondence about the possibility the Walton coin could be real kept it tightly under wraps. They didn't want to leak even a hint of it, to avoid embarrassment if it wasn't real and to preserve the impact of the story if it was.

Donn Pearlman checked into the Sheraton Inner Harbor Hotel near the Baltimore Convention Center on Monday, July 28. He went into action as soon as he arrived. "My dance card was full," he said. He had a busy schedule of activities handling media contacts about the ANA show. Also on his agenda: Set up a time and place for Paul Montgomery and Mark Borckardt to meet with the Walton family members and look at their coin.

At Montgomery's suggestion, Pearlman had called Memphis coin dealer John Dannreuther on the preceding Friday to invite him to the meeting, too. Montgomery had once worked with Dannreuther and considered him his mentor. Dannreuther had not seen any of the photos of the Walton coin and hadn't been in on the conversations about it. He would bring a completely unbiased perspective to the examination.

Pearlman made arrangements to use a small VIP room just off the main convention floor near the registration center, a room being used by the ANA for temporary storage of supplies for the show. Boxes were piled on the tables. There was no place to sit. But it was private, and he didn't expect it to be a long meeting.

The seven examples of altered date 1913 Liberty Head nickels that John Dannreuther had with him at the July 30 session with the Walton heirs in Baltimore. Courtesy of Coin World. © Coin World

Montgomery and Borckardt figured it would be a brief courtesy meeting to go through the motions of looking at a fake coin, let the owners down gently, and go on with the pressing business of getting set up for the show and all-important auction. Dannreuther brought along seven altered date 1913 Liberty nickels he had. He anticipated it would only take a couple of minutes to determine the Walton coin was a fake, then he would produce the altered date coins from his pocket to show the owners how common such fakes were.

Ryan Givens had driven to Washington, D.C., to spend Monday night with his sister, Cheryl Myers, and her husband, Gary. The three of them drove up to Baltimore Tuesday morning. They were confident but apprehensive at the same time. By then, Givens and Myers were convinced they had the real thing.

"We were 95 percent sure it was real," Givens said. "I knew the million dollar reward was out there. I also knew that Paul [Montgomery] said he would pay $10,000 to be the first to see it. That is what really interested me, not the million dollar reward." Givens had done enough homework to know the coin would probably be worth much more than a million dollars if it was authentic.

Still, these were experts they would be meeting with, and there was a possibility they knew something the Walton family members didn't. There was the possibility the experts might say no, it was not real.

They had been instructed to look up Donn Pearlman, whom they had not met before, at the convention center when they arrived. He spotted them easily when they walked in. "They didn't have the driven, harried look" of coin dealers preparing for one of the biggest and most important coin shows of the season, Pearlman said.

Speaking in code because other people were in earshot, Pearlman alerted Beth Deisher from *Coin World* by phone that "The package has arrived." He called the convention office to page Montgomery, Borckardt, and Dannreuther on the public address system to meet him in the lobby. He summoned a security guard from Positive Protection to accompany them. It was 11 a.m., Tuesday, July 29.

"When I heard the page," Montgomery recalled, "I knew where the meeting was. It's funny...even though I was completely prepared to tell them no, I did grab my checkbook out of my briefcase, just in case. I had it in my coat pocket when I went to the meeting."

He became a little anxious when he couldn't find Borckardt. Borckardt was the senior numismatist for Bowers and Merena, and Montgomery felt he needed a better expert than himself to rely on. "I located Debbie McDonald and told her to find Mark and have him meet me in the lobby."

Borckardt was already in the lobby, waiting in line to get a cup of coffee. Montgomery caught up with him there, and they were joined by Donn Pearlman.

"Then J.D. [John Dannreuther] walked up," Borckardt said, "And he pulled seven altered date nickels from his pocket. Casually he said 'Here's mine' and held them out." These were the coins he planned to show the Walton family members when it was confirmed the coin was a fake.

They went to the meeting room. Beth Deisher was there along with the three Walton family members (Ryan Givens and Cheryl and Gary Myers) and the security guard from Positive Protection.

There being no seats available, the group stood in a small circle. Pearlman presided over the introductory courtesies, saving Montgomery for last. He ceremoniously turned to Givens and said, "Well, Mr. Givens, this is Paul Montgomery. He's the one who offered $10,000 to see the coin first. So I think it would be appropriate that you should hand it to him first."

The three coin experts huddled apart from the rest. Borckardt and Dannreuther chomped at the bit to see the coin, but Montgomery had first crack at it.

Initially, what he saw wasn't promising. "On first glance, there was a halo around the 1 and scratches around the 3" in the date on the coin, he said. A halo would indicate something had been changed on the coin, and the scratches suggested some tooling on the date. "I didn't have a loupe with me, so I handed it to Mark."

Though he had doubts, he said as he passed the coin to Borckardt, "You know what? It's real easy to call it fake, *but*..." He didn't finish the sentence.

Borckardt produced a loupe (a small magnifying glass used by numismatists to study fine detail in coins) from his coat pocket and examined the coin. Beth Deisher said she got her first clue about the outcome of the examination from Borckardt's reaction. "The color drained from his face."

Dannreuther took the coin and instantly recognized it was real. "When they handed me the coin and I first looked at it, I had this rush. I was expecting an altered date, and when I held it a foot away, I knew it was real. I had seen the other ones [authentic 1913 Liberty Head nickels], and I knew what they looked like. I knew it was real and was shocked. I almost dropped it," Dannreuther said.

"I could tell by the fabric of the coin. 'Fabric' is hard to describe to a layman. Fabric is like looking at a painting and knowing that it is done by a particular artist. You know his style. The fabric of a coin is like looking at a silver dollar and knowing that it is a Philadelphia silver dollar as opposed to one from the Carson City or San Francisco mints. The 1913 Liberty nickels have this off-color look that can't be described. The striking characteristics [from the press strike], the feel, the look — it just had to be real. A lot of things went through my mind, and the main thing was, how did this mistake happen?"

His excitement was quickly dimmed, however. "When I put a glass to it, I saw the porosity around the date," Dannreuther said. Porosity shows up as minute gas bubbles in the metal that indicate heating of the coin, implying alteration. "In about three seconds, I swung from 90 percent sure it was real to 60 percent sure it was fake," Dannreuther said.

That could have ended the session in the first five minutes. Then Donn Pearlman produced a photo enlargement of the Eliasberg specimen, the finest known 1913 Liberty Head nickel. The numismatists started comparing the coin in their hands with the photograph. The emotional pendulum started to swing back the other way in favor of the Walton coin being real.

The main thing they were looking at was the alignment of the date on the coin face. If the coins were struck using the same die, the date should be in precisely the same position on the face of both coins. It was. Dannreuther looked at the alignment of the date with the denticles, the beads around the perimeter of the coin. These also should be identical on both coins. They were.

As the coin experts huddled and murmured, the Walton family stood aside patiently, quietly, trying to read some kind of clue from their body language. The message was inconclusive.

"I was kind of worried. I was nervous," Givens said. "When I saw how they were talking, I thought they might have found something that was not right about it. I could not tell."

Myers said that she didn't quite know what to look for to guess what their opinion was. "Maybe if I had seen somebody else authenticate a coin, I could have gotten more out of their body language," she said.

The numismatists continued to check specific points in comparing the Walton coin to the Eliasberg photo. Gradually it started to dawn on them that there was no question about the authenticity of the Walton nickel. However, each of them was hesitant to make a definitive statement.

"Nobody wanted to be the one to stick his neck out, because we had too many people in the room to hear it...and this was a million-dollar deal we're talking about," said Montgomery.

Finally Borckardt broke the silence. "I said, 'In my opinion — and I tend to be conservative — I'm 98 percent certain this is real.'" Dannreuther and Montgomery quickly agreed.

"But wait," Montgomery said. "I'm not willing to put a hundred percent seal of approval on this yet, because it's too big of a deal. I told the Walton family that all three of us were reasonably sure. 'But before you get your hopes up,' I said, 'I want to make sure. I want to be positively sure. We're looking at a photograph and looking at a coin under lights that are not the best for this,'" Montgomery said.

Their reaction wasn't what Montgomery expected. Meeting them for the first time, he found them to be Southern courteous, calm spoken, unpretentious people. However, he thought a discovery like this would be a big enough jolt for them to "bust loose" a little. "I thought it was worth at least a 'Hot-diggity!'" he said.

They took it in stride. "They didn't jump up and down and scream like they'd just won the lottery," Montgomery said. "They accepted the news with kind of a reserved dignity."

It wasn't that they were obscenely wealthy people to whom a million dollars was peanuts. They were and are quintessentially middle-income America, everyday folk of moderate means, and a million dollars meant a lot of money to them. However, it wasn't the money they had come for.

"We were just relieved," Givens said. The family was aware of unflattering stories about their uncle George Walton, about how he presented a fake nickel as being real. They weren't impressed so much by the fact that they owned a coin worth a fortune as they were that their uncle's name was at last being vindicated. "We came in thinking it was real, and this was the last chance to get it straight and have it known that Uncle George did have the real one all along. It felt good," Givens said. It was exoneration, at last, for their uncle George that most pleased them. Soon, very soon, they believed, the world would know about it.

Thinking of practical matters, Borckardt said to the others, "We have a golden opportunity. We have the other four real coins right here in Baltimore. So if we can sit down and look at it alongside the other four, we will know with 100 percent certainty."

About then, Chris Cipoletti, executive director of the ANA, strolled in, accompanied by his assistant, Kim Kiick. Cipoletti's appearance was accidental. It hadn't been planned for him to be involved. He had come in regarding the ANA's equipment and supplies stored in the room.

The timing was perfect. The group apprised him of what they had found. They discussed how they could look at all five coins and come to a final decision in time to announce it at the opening ceremonies the next day. If what they believed to be true was confirmed, Cipoletti would get the honor of making the public announcement of the historic find.

Montgomery wanted to bring in a few more expert eyes to double-check their findings. He would invite David Hall, a well-known numismatist who founded PCGS (Professional Coin Grading Service) and, not coincidentally, was the majority stockholder of Collectors Universe, parent company of Bowers and Merena. "After all, it was *his* million bucks we were putting up," Montgomery chuckled.

He asked Dannreuther's advice on who else they should get. Dannreuther suggested Fred Weinberg and Jeff Garrett. "Fred is an expert on error coins and mint processes," Dannreuther said. "Jeff has a great set of eyes for coins, and he's good with counterfeits. Whenever I have a doubt, I take it to these two people."

Montgomery and Borckardt concurred without further deliberation. "They were the obvious choices for this purpose," Montgomery said.

Jeff Garrett headed up Mid American Rare Coin Galleries Lexington, Kentucky. He was co-author with Ron Guth of the popular book *100 Greatest U.S. Coins* (Whitman Publishing, Atlanta), for which the authors won the Robert Friedberg Literary Award. Garrett also won the Abe Kosoff Award from the Professional Numismatists Guild (PNG).

Fred Weinberg was president of Pacific Rim Numismatics, doing business as Fred Weinberg & Co. in Encino, California (which he touts with the tongue-twisting slogan "The Rarer Error Dealer"). He served as a consultant on numismatics to the Federal Deposit Insurance Corporation (FDIC), Federal Trade Commission (FTC), and the Secret Service. He worked frequently with government and law enforcement agencies on court cases involving the authenticity of coins.

The group in the room turned their attention to next steps. "Immediately Pearlman's wheels are turning," Montgomery said, "And he's saying, 'Okay, we need to keep this quiet. We can't talk about this until you've assembled your team and you can sit down with all of the coins.'" Pearlman's assignment was to handle the logistics of the meeting.

There was a stumbling block, though. Cipoletti told them the other four coins were being transported to Timonium, Maryland, ten miles north of Baltimore, to be displayed at a gala reception for dignitaries being held that night at Diamond International Galleries. The coins would not be available until after they could be released from the reception. That meant they wouldn't be arriving back in Baltimore until nearly midnight.

The group would just have to wait. They had no choice.

It would be an agonizing wait. They were all about to burst with the monumental news they were hiding. But it was agreed that until they were absolutely certain, they had to keep a lid on it, just in case it might be possible they were wrong. Experts had been wrong before about this coin. They didn't want to repeat the mistake.

Montgomery said he would contact the other numismatists to invite them to the session. He tried all day to reach David Hall but couldn't find him. Hall was somewhere in the air on the way from Los Angeles and not available by phone. To minimize the risk of a leak, he waited until the afternoon to approach Fred Weinberg and Jeff Garrett about participating in the midnight authentication session.

Handmade receipt issued by Paul Montgomery to Ryan Givens. Montgomery quietly kept the Walton coin in the Bowers and Merena safe during a long day's wait to have it authenticated in a secret midnight meeting of coin experts. Courtesy of Bowers and Merena Galleries.

Montgomery didn't think it was wise for Ryan Givens to be walking around all day with a million-dollar coin in his pocket. He recommended to Givens that he keep the coin in the Bowers and Merena safe. Givens agreed. Montgomery didn't have a receipt pad with him, so he grabbed a blank purchase invoice and handwrote in "Merchandise Receipt." Both he and Givens signed it.

Montgomery asked an armed security guard to accompany him with the Walton nickel to the Bowers and Merena booth, where he placed it into a safe. Debbie McDonald was hard at work in the booth handling details for the show and paid no heed to what Montgomery was doing. He was always in and out, so it wasn't unusual. He didn't tell her what he had put in the safe.

"It wasn't because I didn't trust her," Montgomery said. "If she knew the coin was there and was asked about it, she could give it away by her manner if not her words. Debbie is one of the most honest people I've ever met. It's not in her to lie, even for a good purpose." Besides guarding against an unintentional leak, he also didn't want to distract her or put any more pressure on her than she already had preparing for the opening of the coin show. "She would have been a nervous wreck about security," he said.

Keeping a Lid on the Secret

Keeping a lid on the secret took superhuman restraint.

"Three or four times during the day," Borckardt remembered, "I ran into John Dannreuther and he would simply smile and say, 'I've got a secret.'"

The group couldn't help exchanging knowing glances when they encountered each other during the long day. "It was part of the fun of it, knowing something huge that no one else knew," Borckardt said, "But I wanted to shout it out."

Dannreuther admitted he couldn't hold it in entirely. "I told my two daughters and told them they couldn't say a word."

Pearlman called David Tirell-Wysocki of the Associated Press to give him a heads-up that something big might be breaking. He wanted to have press coverage at the ready the instant the story could be released. He asked whether Tirell-Wysocki wanted to handle the story out of the Concord, New Hampshire, bureau or let the Baltimore press bureau cover it. Tirell-Wysocki said he should call Baltimore. Pearlman did. They wanted to break the story immediately. He offered to let them send a reporter and photographer to cover the authentication session if they would wait. He persuaded them to hold off.

Despite the secrecy, word of what was going on almost slipped out. Some employees of the ANA had learned about the morning meeting and heard that the coin had been authenticated. They came by the Bowers and Merena booth and asked Debbie McDonald if it was true. She had no clue what they were talking about, didn't even know that her bosses were meeting with the Walton heirs, and had no knowledge of the coin being in the safe beside her. She could answer with complete innocence that she didn't know anything about it.

(In fact, McDonald didn't learn about the celebrated nickel being in the safe right next to her until two months later when she was told about it during an interview. She was stunned. "I can't believe it was right there! This was such an important coin, if I would have known it was at our booth, I

Just after 11:00 a.m., July 29, 2003, in a small room being used for storage off the main exhibit area of the Baltimore Convention Center, Paul Montgomery gets his $10,000 first look at the Walton nickel, missing from public view for more than 40 years. Anxiously awaiting their turn to examine the coin are John Dannreuther (center) and Mark Borckardt. Courtesy of Minkus & Pearlman Public Relations, Inc. ©

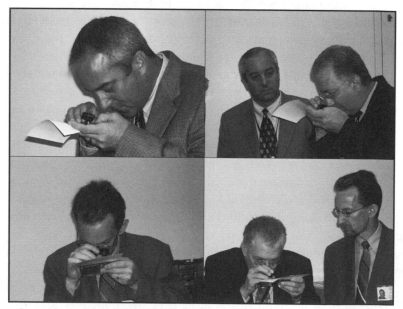

Stunned by what they see, Paul Montgomery, Mark Borckardt, and John Dannreuther study the coin with extra care. It's almost too good to be true...They want to be sure. Courtesy of Minkus & Pearlman Public Relations, Inc. ©

Comparing the Walton specimen with a close-up photo of the famous Eliasberg 1913 Liberty Head nickel, the experts — Paul Montgomery (left), John Dannreuther, and Mark Borckardt — agree: The Walton nickel is likely genuine! Courtesy of Minkus & Pearlman Public Relations, Inc. ©

With 98% certainty that the nickel is real, the coin experts pose with the Walton family members for a celebratory photo to mark the occasion. From left: Gary Myers, Paul Montgomery, Cheryl Myers, Ryan Givens, John Dannreuther, and Mark Borckardt holding the long-lost Walton nickel. Courtesy of Minkus & Pearlman Public Relations, Inc. ©

would have worried about every person who walked on that side of the booth. I had no idea!")

As it happened, a cryptic three-sentence conversation that would have meant nothing to an eavesdropper came *that* close to breaking the story wide open.

ANA education director, Gail Baker, getting no satisfaction from McDonald, intercepted Mark Borckardt and asked him straight out, "So, what happened?"

"I really can't talk about it," Borckardt replied.

"Okay, thanks. That's all I need to know," Baker said and walked away smiling.

Borckardt can keep a secret but his honest face can't. Baker told Borckardt later, "Mark, if the coin wasn't real, you would have just said so and that would be the end of it. But when you said you can't talk about it, that's all I needed to know." The perceptive Baker had guessed the secret.

Borckardt was alarmed and alerted Montgomery about the conversation with Baker. Montgomery quickly got in touch with Chris Cipoletti. "Chris, you've got a leak. You've got to stop this right now, because this is bad," he said. Cipoletti found Baker and instructed her to keep mum about what she had accurately figured out.

As the afternoon wore on, Montgomery decided it was time to approach Jeff Garrett and Fred Weinberg about joining the midnight session. "It was fun to tell Jeff. It was fun to tell Fred," he said.

Montgomery paged Garrett to drop by the Bowers and Merena booth. When Garrett showed up, Montgomery tried to be nonchalant. "Jeff, I have something I want you to help me with."

The obliging Garrett responded, "Sure, what is it?"

"I think we have a winner."

"What are you talking about?"

"I think we found the 1913 nickel. I need you to help me authenticate it," Montgomery said.

Garrett gasped. "You've gotta be kidding me!"

Montgomery told him the developments to that point. "I said, 'Mark and J.D. and I have already looked at it, and we just need somebody else, a few other guys to help us authenticate it. I'm setting up a meeting for midnight tonight to look at it alongside the other four coins. Would you want to participate with us?'"

"Absolutely!" Garrett exclaimed. "I would consider it a great honor."

At first, Fred Weinberg was standoffish about it. He had a lot of work to do and was mildly annoyed by the intrusion...until he learned what was up.

Montgomery was trying to keep the secret close to the vest and not reveal any more than he had to. He went to Weinberg's table in late afternoon.

He leaned over and asked, "What are you doing at midnight?"

Weinberg responded, "What did you have in mind?"

"Do you have a cell phone?" Montgomery asked.

Weinberg said yes. Montgomery asked for the number. Weinberg gave it to him but wanted to know what it was all about. "It wasn't as simple as saying to him, trust me, you're going to want to do this," Montgomery remembered.

Weinberg complained that he was tired and had already been there a week getting ready "and now you want me to meet on some deal in the middle of the night that I don't even know what it is." Montgomery realized he would have to be more direct.

"Fred, we found the coin," he said.

"Oh. Then I accept!" Weinberg replied. No further explanation was needed. He knew what Montgomery meant.

So the authentication team was set. There would be six numismatists on the panel, with collectively more than 200 years of experience among them: John Dannreuther, Jeff Garrett, David Hall, Fred Weinberg, and, of course, Paul Montgomery and Mark Borckardt.

Ryan Givens and Cheryl and Gary Myers had time to kill after they talked briefly with *Coin World*'s Beth Deisher about what transpired that morning. They were calm, relaxed. They considered the midnight authentication a formality. They were absolutely certain their uncle's nickel was the genuine article. Any nagging doubts had been eliminated in their minds. "It wasn't a done deal," Givens said, "But we were pretty confident by then."

They wanted to relax. "We had lunch and took in the aquarium," Givens said. ANA's Larry Lee had invited them to an exhibition of the four known 1913 Liberty Head nickels in Timonium, Maryland, that night. They decided they would go. It would be the first time in their lives to see their nickel's siblings.

Timonium: First Public Showing in 80 Years

It was billed as "The Ninety Years of Liberty Gala" in a review by Stacia Brown in *Comic Book Marketplace*, a publication of Steve Geppi's Gemstone Publishing:

> From the lobby's Trevi Fountain replica, strategically placed by the door, inviting guests to cast coins and wishes into its beautiful base, to the

lavish, silver-frosted chocolate cake molded into a three-dimensional 1913 Liberty Head dessert and surrounded by a moat of milk chocolates wrapped in 1913 Liberty Head nickel-imprinted foils, the coin reception, hosted by Legend Numismatics and Diamond International Galleries, in cooperation with American Numismatic Association and the Smithsonian's National Museum of History, and held Tuesday night (July 29), was heralded by all in attendance as the gala of the summer. The reception marked the first reuniting of the four 1913 Liberty Head nickels in 60 years and their first public showing in 80 years. Together, the four coins are valued at more than $10.5 million.

Baltimore magazine, also published by Geppi, carried a write-up on the event filed by Christianna McCausland in its August 2003 issue:

> More than 200 VIPs and luminaries of the collectibles world mingled at an invitation-only Timonium exhibit and party that featured millions of dollars in rare stamps, comic-book art, and gold, but even the impressive guest list couldn't outshine the main event, which led to the sale of a historic nickel for a record $3 million.

The Timonium event grew out of a collaboration between Legend Numismatics partners Laura Sperber and George Huang and Diamond International Galleries executives Stephen A. Geppi and John K. Snyder. Geppi was owner and chief executive officer of Diamond. He was also owner of its sister company, Diamond Comic Distributors and publisher of *Baltimore* magazine. Snyder was president of Diamond International Galleries.

Diamond was co-sponsor with the ANA of the 1913 Liberty Head nickel display at the World's Fair of Money, which was accompanied by a showing of oil paintings by legendary Disney artist Carl Barks. Among his many distinctions, Barks created the irascible money-hungry Scrooge McDuck character while he was at Disney. After retiring from the company, he created a series of dazzling oil paintings featuring McDuck and his nephews, always themed around McDuck's love of money.

Laura Sperber invited 40 of her top clients to the party, "People that really collected coins on a big level," John Snyder said. She had reason to believe one or two of them had an interest in buying the 1913 Liberty nickel owned by Legend Numismatics.

The guest list included luminaries from the Smithsonian, two Maryland congressman, representatives from the governor's and mayor's offices, prominent Baltimore businessmen, the state superintendent of schools, TV and news personalities, publishers and editors, and a number of famous lights from the numismatic world, among them Dwight Manley, Edward Lee, and Q. David Bowers.

Dr. Brent Glass and several of his staff from the Smithsonian National Museum of American History were on hand, including Bill Withuhn, curator; Valeska Hilbig, senior public affairs associate; and Douglas Mudd, collection manager.

The centerpiece of the gala was, of course, the display of the four 1913 Liberty Head nickels, which had been transported from Baltimore for the event. It was the first public showing of the four nickels since the early 20s.

The coins were presented in a hand-built display case provided by Diamond, which had originally been built to display comic books. "It worked perfectly," Snyder said. "We donated the use of it at the convention."

Snyder had been alerted a couple of days earlier that there was a possibility the missing 5th nickel might come out of hiding at the convention. "Donn [Pearlman] told me a number of people had called in, and there were a few that looked promising." Just in case, provision was made in the display for the fifth coin. "If anybody was paying close attention," Snyder said, "They could see there was another hole for the fifth coin," if it showed up.

The known owners (from right to left: Edward Lee, Dwight Manley, Chris Cipoletti of the ANA, and Laura Sperber of Legend Numismatics) offer the media a unique opportunity to photograph all four of them at once. Imagine the surprise when this journalist discovered that her picture captured not four nickel owners, but FIVE. Ryan Givens, a completely anonymous owner at the time this picture was taken, leans over the display case, hand on chin (far left). Courtesy of Coin World. © Coin World.

Enjoying The Ninety Years of Liberty Gala at Diamond International Galleries are Smithsonian National Museum of American History curator, Bill Withuhn (l.); director, Dr. Brent Glass; and senior public affairs associate Valeska Hilbig. Present but not shown, collection manager, Douglas Mudd. Courtesy of Diamond International Galleries. ©

Elegant display of the four 1913 Liberty Head nickels at the Diamond International gala. Courtesy of Diamond International Galleries. ©

Adding spice to the festive event, Carl Barks' Scrooge McDuck paintings were on display, along with four extremely rare 1918 "Inverted Jenny" stamps courtesy of collector and former broadcast personality Kelly Confer and two gold bars from the famed shipwreck *S.S. Central America* provided by Dwight Manley. Security was tight. Two police cruisers stood guard outside.

Guests began arriving about 7:00 p.m. Along with tasty refreshments and a once-in-a-lifetime chance to view the famous nickels, each of the guests that night received a commemorative "goody bag" of gala favors that included a plastic piggy bank safe with chocolate 1913 Liberty Head nickel coins, Uncle Scrooge cards, ANA World's Fair of Money brochures, certified copies of Gemstone's Free Comic Book Day offering, copies of *Numismatist* magazine, and Lucite replicas of the 1913 Liberty Head nickel coins, among other items.

At 8:00, the formalities got underway, with welcoming comments by emcee Stephen Geppi. He introduced Aris Melissaratos, Secretary of the Department of Business and Economic Development, representing Maryland Governor Robert Ehrlich. Melissaratos read a proclamation from the governor declaring July 27-August 3 "World Money Week in Maryland."

Smithsonian's Dr. Brent Glass emphasized the educational significance of the 1913 Liberty Head nickel reunion. He pointed out that this was the reason the Smithsonian had consented to participate in the event by loaning its 1913 Liberty nickel specimen for the display.

Then Geppi introduced Q. David Bowers, who had written a small booklet on the nickels for the occasion. After some opening niceties, Bowers dropped a bombshell on the proceedings when he unexpectedly called Dwight Manley and Ed Lee to the podium. He announced to the crowd that Manley had sold the famous Eliasberg nickel to coin dealer Edward C. Lee for "approximately three million dollars." Lee handed Manley a check for the undisclosed amount as cameras flashed.

The actual deal had been in the works for a month or so and was finalized the night before. This was the first public announcement of it, an ideal high-impact photo-op.

John Snyder's heart skipped a beat. "That was a shock, because we had told the Smithsonian we were not going to sell anything." In fact, it was a strict condition imposed by the Smithsonian before they would consent to allowing their coin to be shown at the Timonium event. "I am sitting there thinking, oh, help me, Lord," Snyder said. He was in a terribly awkward spot. He expected a fuss from the Smithsonian contingent.

To his great relief, the Smithsonian staff was forgiving. "They seemed to dismiss it as a public relations thing, not something we at Diamond did by design, and we didn't get any monetary benefit from it," Snyder said. "We had no clue it was going to happen."

The Smithsonian people saw no real harm done. The sale, they learned, didn't actually take place at the gala; it had already been agreed the night before. "There was some concern," Smithsonian's Douglas Mudd said, "But not major concern. It didn't make a big splash" with the Smithsonian dignitaries.

Laura Sperber wasn't as forgiving. She was upset. She and her partners had invested a lot of time and effort to pull together this major event first and foremost for their customers to show appreciation for their business. Not coincidentally, they also harbored the underlying purpose of persuading a collector to buy *their* 1913 nickel. Bowers' unexpected and unscheduled announcement trumped their efforts and chilled their hopes to find a buyer for the Hawn specimen.

"We had actually had two very substantial offers on our coin at that time. That announcement spooked them off," Sperber said. She was still fuming about it when interviewed nearly 2½ months later. "It was not supposed to be announced there. We knew it was sold; they (Manley and Lee) extended the courtesy of telling us. But they were not supposed to announce it until after the party."

Steve Geppi soothed things a bit when he introduced Sperber last from the podium. He gave her all the credit for making the gala possible. "She didn't say anything," Snyder said. "Laura doesn't like to speak in public," he noted. It probably didn't help that she was still seething from Bowers' surprise announcement.

Even months later, Bowers, Manley, and Lee seemed unaware that the apparently spontaneous announcement had stirred consternation for anyone or was in any way considered a faux pas. Asked about the controversy later, Manley said, "Actually, I don't know what you're talking about. Dave thought it would be nice because I don't like to speak publicly, and Dave did a nice job." Bowers replied to the question by saying, "For information about the party in Timonium, you would best contact Laura Sperber as she planned the party and it was hers, not mine." Lee, who indicated he had not met Bowers before that night, said the announcement was unplanned. He gave no indication that he had been previously aware of any controversy about it.

After the speechmaking, the guests milled about admiring the fabulous exhibits. The 1913 Liberty Head nickels attracted the most attention, naturally.

Larry Lee introduced the Walton family heirs to the other nickel owners present. At one point in course of the evening, Ryan Givens bumped into Dwight Manley and they chatted briefly. Manley did not know about the authentication session scheduled to take place in just a few hours.

At 10:00 p.m. the guests of honor — the four 1913 Liberty Head nickels — were removed from the display case for the trek back to the convention center in Baltimore. They were transported in a police car, carried in the pockets of their escorts. "Chris Cipoletti had the ANA's coin, Douglas Mudd had the Smithsonian's, and I had the other two," Snyder said.

Ironic Awards Ceremony at the PNG Dinner

The members of the authentication team didn't put in an appearance at the party in Timonium. They instead attended a dinner in Baltimore hosted by the Professional Numismatists Guild, climaxing PNG Day at the convention.

By coincidence, Paul Montgomery was scheduled to present a special award to Jeff Garrett, one of the numismatists selected for the authentication team.

As a member of the board of directors of PNG, Montgomery had the honor of presenting the organization's member of the year award, the Abe Kosoff Award, named for the founder of PNG, to Garrett for his outstanding contributions to the hobby. Long before the Walton coin appeared on the scene, Montgomery was on the PNG's selection committee for the award and was instrumental in picking Garrett.

The presentation itself had special irony for both men, each knowing they were about to participate in something that would absolutely blow away this jaded audience of some 300 veteran been-there-done-that numismatists. "Even as I was singing his praises," Montgomery recalled, "All I could think about was the '13 nickel. I wanted to scream it out."

It was less of a stress for Garrett, who hadn't yet seen the Walton coin and wasn't as affected by the excitement over what he was about to be involved in. Not yet having any basis for it, he was not certain, as was Montgomery, that the Walton coin was real.

Besides, he was basking in the glow of winning back-to-back honors. In addition to the Abe Kosoff Award, he and Ron Guth were presented with the Robert Friedberg Literary Award for *100 Greatest U.S. Coins*.

Afterward, as they were leaving the dinner, Montgomery sidled next to Garrett and quietly said, "Call you later. I'll call you as soon as I hear from them." He was referring to the anxiously-awaited arrival of the four nickels from Timonium.

The Moment of Truth

After the PNG dinner, each of the authentication team members retired to his hotel room, except for David Hall. Hall was still in transit and hadn't yet been heard from.

Donn Pearlman had secured the use of a VIP conference suite at the convention center for the authentication session. It was no easy task because the place was shut down tight for the night.

The security people weren't thrilled about admitting people inside in the middle of the night with millions of dollars in rare coins and other valuable merchandise to guard. The threat of theft and robbery has always ranked high priority at coin shows, but the added danger of terrorist attacks ratcheted the worry quotient several notches higher. All those precious coins could buy a lot of explosives on the black market if the terrorists got hold of them. The security people insisted on having armed guards present in the room at all times while the meeting was taking place.

The police car with Chris Cipoletti, Doug Mudd, and John Snyder — the valuable nickels inconspicuously tucked in their pockets — arrived shortly after 11:30 p.m. Pearlman called Montgomery. "The eagle has landed," was all he said, and he hung up. He was really getting into the James Bond thing and having fun with it. He had some other calls to make.

Montgomery was in his room at the Hyatt Regency, across the street from the convention center. He buzzed the other members of the authentication team and told them to meet him in the hotel lobby in ten minutes. He still hadn't found David Hall. They would just have to do it without him.

Mark Borckardt fairly raced to the lobby. He was the first one there. John Dannreuther arrived not far behind him.

As they awaited the others, in walked David Hall, luggage in tow. He had just arrived from the airport. Dana Samuelson, another coin dealer, was with him. They had shared a ride from the airport.

As Hall was checking in at the registration desk, Borckardt walked over to him and asked, "David, have you talked with Paul?" He couldn't say much more because Samuelson was standing there with them.

Hall replied that he had not spoken with Montgomery. Borckardt said, "Well, he's coming down to the lobby here in a few minutes, and you might want to wait."

Hall sensed that something unusual was up. What could be so important that Montgomery needed to see him in the middle of the night? Even though it was late, he'd been traveling the better part of a long day, and he was tired, he waited.

Montgomery, Jeff Garrett, and Fred Weinberg arrived very shortly. Montgomery was surprised and relieved to see David Hall at the check-in counter. "Cool," he thought.

While Hall was filling out the registration form, Montgomery bent close to his ear and whispered, "I think we found it."

"What are you talking about?" Hall responded, not looking up from his writing.

"The 1913 nickel. I think we've got a winner." Hall stopped writing in mid-stroke.

Montgomery quickly explained that he, Borckardt, and Dannreuther had seen the so-called fake Walton coin, and they were sure it was real. "I've been looking for you all day. We need you...now. It's appropriate that you be part of this deal. We're going over to authenticate it right now. That's why all these guys are here."

Tired as he was, Hall's mind was suddenly racing, catching up with the huge implications of what he was hearing. "I was not skeptical," he recalled. "If Paul said it was real, he thought it was real. I was overwhelmed by the impact and importance of the event that could unfold. And I'm pretty jaded."

Hall didn't even wait to go to his room and freshen up. He grabbed his luggage and headed for the door. "Bring it on," he said.

The six numismatists walked out into the clear, muggy July night on their way to what would be a career highlight none of them would ever forget.

As they crossed the street to the convention center, Montgomery called Donn Pearlman on his cell phone to let him know they were on the way. Pearlman directed him to come around to a back entrance.

"It was all very cloak-and-dagger," Montgomery said. "We couldn't help looking around to see if we were being followed." Of course, the street was basically empty at that hour of the night. Even so, their imaginations were over-revving with the excitement of their clandestine mission. "It was tempting to fantasize a Humphrey Bogart type in a trench coat and pulled-down hat lurking in the shadows, watching us," Montgomery admitted.

Jeff Garrett wrestled with conflicting emotions as they walked. "I was excited about being asked to help authenticate a mega-coin like this, but then you think about the responsibility of what you're about to do. There was a very strong desire, I could feel, to be able to declare that the coin had been found. However, we had to be sure we didn't get a big egg on our face and find out this is a big scam."

Garrett had not met the Walton heirs. He wondered if anyone had checked them out. "Has anybody done a background check on these people to see if they are the real Walton family?" he asked, only half in jest. For a million dollars, con artists will go to great lengths to put on a convincing pose. Montgomery dismissed the concern.

They were admitted through a back service entrance by a stern-faced gun-toting guard and led through an indoor parking garage. It reminded Borckardt of the setting for one of those spy movie rendezvous scenes where secret agents hand off a package to a contact.

When they entered the room where the session was to take place, Montgomery was shocked. "There were thirty people in the room!" The exact body count is uncertain, but in any event, there were a lot more people than Montgomery had anticipated.

He hadn't expected there to be anyone except the authentication team and Donn Pearlman present for the "secret" meeting, which was obviously not all that secret by then. "I was expecting *nobody* but the six of us to be there," Montgomery said.

The gathering included the three Walton family members; Chris Cipoletti, Larry Lee, and Stephen Bobbitt from the ANA; Douglas Mudd from the Smithsonian with his security guards; John Snyder from Diamond International Galleries; Baltimore bureau Associated Press reporter Sarah Brumfield with a photographer, Steve Ruark; and security guards from Positive Protection.

Noting all the beefy security guards with their heavy artillery, John Dannreuther quipped, "This is the safest place in Baltimore." The guards didn't laugh. "They had no sense of humor, that we know of," he said later. Fred Weinberg couldn't even remember if they *had* guns. "They were all so big they could have been carrying half the Army's weapons under their coats and you couldn't have seen them."

Robert Evans was there, too. He had nothing to do with the session. The conference room was being used for storage of valuables for the show. Evans gained fame as the discoverer of the *S.S. Central America* shipwreck treasure. He had come in to check on his stash of gold ingots from the shipwreck that would be on display during the show. He overheard some mention of the 1913 Liberty nickel. He was curious why so many people were there at that time of night. He hung around to see what was going on.

Borckardt said when they were asked later what Evans' connection to the event was, he made up a rationale. "It's simple. He was representing Dwight Manley." Technically speaking, of course, Manley himself had no direct connection to the event anymore, since he had sold his 1913 Liberty nickel to Ed Lee. However, Borckardt hadn't been at the Timonium gala to hear the announcement and was unaware of the sale until later.

Montgomery was upset about the presence of so many people. Before going any further, he called Donn Pearlman aside.

"Donn, if this coin is not genuine, then this is the worst thing that could ever possibly happen to us, having all these people see it flop," Montgomery told him. He was also concerned that the pressure of so many eyes watching could compromise the objectivity of the examination and prejudice the outcome. "We can't talk candidly with all these people in this room."

Pearlman understood and concurred, reluctantly. He asked everyone not essential to the authentication to wait outside the room.

There was some negotiation about who was "essential." Doug Mudd insisted that he and his security guards must remain. They were obligated to keep their eye on the Smithsonian coin at all times. Larry Lee from the ANA museum also stayed. A couple of burly armed guards from Positive Protection representing the show weren't about to budge, because they were responsible for all the show valuables stored in the room.

Finally, the Big Moment was upon them. Paul Montgomery, Mark Borckardt, David Hall, John Dannreuther, Jeff Garrett, and Fred Weinberg were about to perform a task so monumental that few numismatists ever in a lifetime have such an opportunity and honor.

A very large conference table stretched before them, covered with a white cloth. The authenticators took their seats, lined up along the same side of the table. The 1913 Liberty Head nickels were set out on the table before them. Two of the coins — the Smithsonian and ANA specimens - were "raw," that is, not encased in holders. The Eliasberg and Hawn specimens were in "slabs," the tamper-proof plastic cases used by grading companies to seal a coin they have certified. The Walton coin was in the plastic holder that George Walton had made up for it. It was secured with screws and the coin could easily be taken out for three-dimensional inspection.

Being able to see three of the coins in three dimensions was important. The edges of the slabbed coins couldn't be seen. The "loose" coins could be examined in total. The edges of a coin tell volumes about its identity from the distinctive markings made on the coin in the press by a given set of dies.

There were no specific ground rules laid down about how to conduct the authentication process. None were needed. These were professionals. Every one of them knew how the process worked. "Everybody in the room knew that we were either going to talk each into it or we would talk each other out of it," Montgomery explained. "You bring in enough people whose opinions are respected, and a consensus eventually emerges."

Montgomery had no illusions about his rank among the group of experts. "I came in sixth. I mean, I've been in this business a lot of years, but I'm a trader. I pay attention to market action. I don't have the kind of intricate knowledge about the coins themselves that the rest of the guys had. That's why they were there. That's why I called them in."

Each of the experts approached the process in his own individual way, focusing on details he was most familiar with and knowledgeable about.

"Jeff Garrett and David Hall both wanted to see the Walton coin right away," Borckardt remembered. "Fred Weinberg didn't."

Weinberg wanted to be certain of what he was comparing to first. "He wanted to scrutinize every one of the other four coins close-up in person to understand what a real one was supposed to look like," Borckardt said. "He refused to look at the Walton piece until he was satisfied he had a clear vision of a real one."

One by one, they handed the coins down the row. In the beginning, they didn't talk much, absorbed in the task of searching for minute tell-tale details.

- Paul Montgomery was looking for die nuances, the signature markings left on coins that are unique to each set of dies. If the Walton coin had the same kind of unique markings the others had, it would be proof positive to him that it was struck with the same set of dies. There were minor differences, but on crucial checkpoints, all five coins looked basically alike to him. The exercise corroborated his instinct from the morning session that the coin was real. He took a back seat to allow more time for the other experts to spend looking at the coins.

During the proceedings, an odd and disturbing thought struck Montgomery: *What if we discover that the Walton coin is real but that one of the other coins is a fake?* Even though he had no reason to suspect the authenticity of the other four nickels, the enormity of the moment and the potentially negative implications of such a find stood every nerve edge on end, alert to any possible flaw in the scene. The thought was fleeting, though, and after an anxious heart-pounding couple of seconds, he blew it off, saying nothing of the uneasy notion to the others.

At one point, someone on the team asked if they could take the Walton coin out of its holder so they could examine its edge. Montgomery went outside to the waiting group to ask permission of the Walton heirs. "Naturally, everyone jumped up expecting an answer. They were disappointed when I couldn't tell them anything yet," Montgomery said.

- Mark Borckardt looked closely at date placement. The year dates were hand-stamped into the dies, so that each die was actually slightly different from any other years. If the alignment of the dates on all five coins relative to other surface features precisely matched, there could be no question they all came from the same die. The dates on all five coins aligned almost exactly the same. "I was absolutely 100% satisfied that they were struck from the same die," he said.

- David Hall also zeroed in on the character of the date on the Walton coin, for a different reason. When a date has been altered on a coin, there are always clues left at the scene of the crime. A sharp-eyed coin detective who spots these characteristics can tell that the coin has been doctored — changes in coloration of the metal, porosity from microscopic bubbles caused by heating the coin, miniscule scratch or file marks, the shape of a numeral in the date. On close examination, he found that all the coins had essentially the same kind of porosity in the same place. His gut feeling almost instantly was that the Walton coin was authentic.

- John Dannreuther noted there were vertical pin scratches between the digits and below the date. They looked like scratches caused by someone testing the 3 digit to see if it could be pried off. It's a little like pulling on Santa's beard to see if it's fake or real. Shaving a numeral from legitimate coin and gluing it onto another is a common method of counterfeiting rare coin dates. It was obvious the test failed, meaning the numeral 3 was stamped onto the coin, not glued.

He also noted a dark area in the metal below the 9, not a sign of tampering but a common trait caused by the way the blank planchets for the coins are prepared before being stamped into coins.

He noted the detail in a kernel of corn on the reverse side. The amount of detail varied from coin to coin. He realized that the reverse die must not have been tightened down securely and was a bit tilted in the press, probably because the maker was in a hurry. The force of each strike caused it to slip alignment slightly. It dawned on him that he could decipher, with a strong degree of confidence, the order in which the coins were struck:

1. Smithsonian specimen.
2. Hawn specimen.
3. Eliasberg specimen.
4. Walton specimen.
5. ANA specimen.

"I can't be 100 percent sure my theory is correct. But I'm 99 percent sure," Dannreuther said. His theory would account for the slight variations in feature placement among the five coins.

- Jeff Garrett had seen all four of the known real nickels at one time or another. "I had done research on the Smithsonian coin and had held it in my hand. I had seen the ANA coin on exhibit, and I was present at privates trades of the other two nickels," he said. His first interest was whether or not the Walton coin was a proof specimen and not a worn or circulated example. None of the 1913 Liberty nickels were proofs in the strictly technical sense of the term. The planchets had not been polished before stamping, and it was apparent they had only been struck once (probably in haste) instead of the customary two strikes required for the sharpest detail in a proof coin.[80]

"They are proofs. Imperfect proofs. They were made with proof dies but business strike[81] planchets," Garrett said. Garrett was also interested in the fabric, the overall look of the coin. "Does it have all the characteristics that a proof Liberty nickel would look like?" was the question on Garrett's mind. He is known for having a keen intuitive eye for rare coin qualities.

He looked closely at the 3 in the date. "The 3 on the Walton coin looked exactly like the 3 on the other coins," Garrett said.

---

[80] Eric Newman said in an interview that his impression of the coins was that they were struck on different quality planchets, probably whatever the perpetrator could put his hands on in a hurry.

[81] "Business strike" means everyday, ordinary, run-of-the-press quality — nothing special.

- Weinberg was arguably the most knowledgeable of the group in mint processes and how they affect the appearance of a coin. He declined to look at the Walton coin until he had inspected all the other four nickels.

Unlike the others on the panel, he had not personally seen any of the nickels before, only photographs of them. "Coins have a visual 'smell' that tells an experienced eye whether the coin is good or bad. It speaks to you visually," he said. "I didn't want to be tainted by looking at the fifth coin when I had never seen the other four." Mixed metaphors aside, Weinberg's almost Zen-like sensitivity to the nickels prepared him mentally for a more technical forensic examination.

He noticed immediately how crude the 3 was on all of the coins. "Obviously, it was hand-stamped into the die used to make the coins," he said. The 3's on all of the coins was of a typeface unlike any commonly used by any U.S. mint on American 20th century coins, he said. "There was never another hand-cut 3 like that in the 20th century" on American coins, Weinberg asserted.

The critical test was the edges of the nickels. The way the press, the dies, and the impressed metal reacts when struck leaves distinctive markings on the edges of a coin. "It's just like you can tell a bullet was fired from a particular gun. A coin is the same thing," Weinberg claimed. "When the coin is ejected, it pops up from the collar [the press flange holding the coin disk in place] coming up just like a bullet leaving the barrel of a gun. I reasoned that if all these coins were struck on the same night from one press, the collar marks should match."

He held the three unslabbed coins on edge and compared them side by side with a magnifying glass. The markings lined up perfectly. "They all had the same collar marks."
Weinberg said as far as he knew, this was the first time that the forensic test of comparing collar marks had been used to authenticate a coin.

The evidence before them was so powerfully convincing that after only about ten minutes, the consensus was plainly evident: The Walton coin was authentic.

The realization so overwhelmed the team that they could scarcely grasp the magnitude of what they had discovered. It was too big a concept to get their minds around in one reach. They had to stretch their imaginations and work up to it gradually.

"I kept looking at J.D. and saying are you really sure? Asking Fred, are you really sure?" Hall said.

The session turned into a kind of game among them, with first one then another coming up with some point of comparison for the others to look at. They didn't want to let go of the moment. They wanted to savor it. Even with all their extraordinary individual professional experience and accomplishments, none of them had ever been party to something this big. All of them believed they would never have another experience in their lifetimes to top or even match this moment.

The six coin experts began to realize that they were fused in a unique fraternity that no one else could ever join, because there's no second time to be first. That night they had become the first professional numismatists to see all five genuine 1913 Liberty Head nickels together since 1943, more than 60 years. They would also be the first numismatists to declare officially that the Walton coin, considered a fake altered date coin for over 40 years, is an authentic specimen.

Finally, David Hall took charge of the session. "Okay, I want to take a poll," he told the group. He asked the panel one at a time what their percent of confidence was that the Walton coin was authentic. The answers ranged from 98 to 100 percent certainty.

It had taken them less than thirty minutes to confirm one of the greatest discoveries in modern numismatic history. The time was 12:15 a.m., Wednesday, July 30, 2003.

It was time to let the world in on their fabulous secret.

Exhausted but exhilarated, members of the authentication team pause for a portrait to mark the historic moment at 12:30 a.m., July 30, 2003, in the Baltimore Convention Center. Seated, from left: John Dannreuther, Paul Montgomery, Mark Borckardt. Standing, from left: David Hall, Fred Weinberg, Jeff Garrett. The real stars of the moment — the five genuine 1913 Liberty Head nickels — are on the table in front of them. Courtesy of Minkus & Pearlman Public Relations, Inc. ©

It's real! Snapped only moments after the final decision of the panel had been rendered, the photo captures a happy mood. Seated, from left: David Hall, John Dannreuther, Jeff Garrett. Standing, from left: Paul Montgomery, Lawrence J. Lee, Mark Borckardt. Only barely in the shot on the right: Fred Weinberg. Courtesy of Minkus & Pearlman Public Relations, Inc. ©

They can hardly believe what they have just experienced. John Dannreuther (left), Paul Montgomery, and David Hall are all smiles with the five 1913 Liberty Head nickels on the table before them, the first time they have been seen in the same place at the same time for more than 60 years. Courtesy of Minkus & Pearlman Public Relations, Inc. ©

Paul Montgomery (right) calls the Walton family — Gary Myers (left), Ryan Givens, and Cheryl Myers — aside to break the news to them in private: Their 1913 Liberty Head nickel believed since the early 1960s to be fake, is actually the real thing! Courtesy of Minkus & Pearlman Public Relations, Inc. ©

Listening to the official announcement from the authentication team are Sarah Brumfield, correspondent for the Baltimore bureau of the Associated Press (left), and Walton family members Cheryl Myers, Ryan Givens, and Gary Myers. Courtesy of Minkus & Pearlman Public Relations, Inc. ©

Overwhelmed by the news that their uncle George Walton's name has at last been cleared, the Walton family heirs savor the triumphant moment. From left, Gary Myers, Ryan Givens, Cheryl Myers. Associated Press reporter Sarah Brumfield interviews Paul Montgomery (back to camera) and John Dannreuther in the background. Courtesy of Minkus & Pearlman Public Relations, Inc. ©

Chapter 10 References

Bobbitt, Stephen L. 2003. Interview (October 14).

Borckardt, Mark. 2003. Interviews (September 2, 3, 9).

Bowers, Q. David. 2003. Letter response to email interview (October 24).

Brown, Stacia. 2003. "The Ninety Years of Liberty Gala: A Night in Pictures." *Comic Book Marketplace* (Vol. 3, No. 105, August), pp. 37-40.

Cipoletti, Christopher. 2003. Interview (October 2).

Dannreuther, John. 2003. Interviews (October 2,4).

Deisher, Beth. 2003. Interview (October 8).

Garrett, Jeff. 2003. Interview (October 2).

Givens, Ryan. 2003. Interview (October 1).

Hall, David. 2003. Interview (October 10).

Lee, Edward C. 2003. Interview (October 23).

McCausland, Christianna. 2003. "A dream party for collectors and a record sale." *Baltimore* magazine (Vol. 96, No. 10, October), pp. 58-59.

McDonald, Debbie. 2003. Interview (September 30).

Manley, Dwight. 2003. Faxed response to emailed interview (October 16).

Montgomery, Paul. 2003. Interviews (September 2, 3, 9).

Mudd, Douglas. 2003. Interview (October 10).

Myers, Cheryl. 2003. Interview (October 2).

Pearlman, Donn. 2003. Interview (September 23).

Snyder, John K. 2003. Interview (October 9).

Weinberg. Fred. 2003. Interview (October 3).

- Chapter Eleven -

FOUND!
NUMISMATIC SHOCK OF THE CENTURY

The Secret Revealed

Outside the room where the authenticators were making history, the small crowd that had been evicted before the session began to grow restless. They had been kept waiting in the dimly-lit meeting hall for the better part of a half-hour.

The initial excitement that had lured them away from a good night's sleep to be witnesses to an extraordinary event dribbled away as they sat, stood, leaned on something to pass the time in the empty convention hall. The minimal night lighting in the hall further muted their spirits. They had used up their supply of chatty small talk.

Some of them, who had reason to believe the Walton coin was authentic, had expected the session to be a formality of validation. What was taking so long for the "jury" to reach a verdict? Had they found something wrong with the coin after all?

The fact that Paul Montgomery at one point came out to ask the Walton family if it would be okay to take their coin out of its holder made Ryan Givens anxious. "I got worried there. They may have seen something that was not right. I was getting worried again because it was taking a long time."

AP reporter Sarah Brumfield chatted with the Walton family. Donn Pearlman paced and kept glancing at the door, hoping for a break in the tension…and good news he could release to the press.

When the door to the security room opened, all eyes and ears leapt to full alert. Paul Montgomery emerged and approached the Walton family members. Everyone scrutinized his face and body language for a clue to the outcome. He put on his best poker face, trying not to let the cat out of the bag until the Walton heirs heard it first.

He escorted Cheryl and Gary Myers and Ryan Givens into the room as Donn Pearlman herded the rest of the gathering in behind them. Montgomery took the Walton family to one side of the room apart from the others to break the news to them in semi-private. Mark Borckardt joined the huddle.

Montgomery told them three things: "It is genuine. Congratulations. God bless you."

"IT IS GENUINE. CONGRATULATIONS. GOD BLESS YOU."

For a moment, they were speechless. "They were in shock," Montgomery said. "There were tears in Cheryl's eyes. Gary was just kind of stunned. When I told them, I reached out and grabbed Ryan's hand. He was shaking."

Ryan Givens said that, although he had thought the coin was real, he did not fully realize the significance of it until that moment. "It never really hit me until then what this nickel really was. To me it was just a rare coin. They [the numismatists] seemed to be overwhelmed by it. It overwhelmed me that *they* were overwhelmed."

Cheryl Myers felt a swell of joy mingled with regret "that Uncle George was not there. I wish he could have seen it."

Their reaction affected Montgomery profoundly. "That will always be the greatest moment in my career. That is the pinnacle of my career. Nothing can top that."

"Too often in our business we're put in the unfortunate and unavoidable position of disappointing people," he explained. "Everybody and his brother, it seems, has a coin he thinks is worth a million bucks. Something they've dug up in a closet or a coin their grandma gave them. Every coin office or store in America gets maybe twenty calls like this every day, and we have to tell them, 'Sorry, sir, but your hundred-and-fifty-year-old silver dollar is only worth about seven or eight bucks.' They don't understand that it's about how rare it is, not how old it is. So we tell them the real value, and they're let down. We spend a good part of our professional lives disappointing people, though none of us likes doing that. I've said all my career, just once I'd would like to tell somebody that they've actually got more than they think they do."

The "just once" had finally come, and it was a whopper. "Finally, I got to tell somebody, 'Your coin is not only genuine, but it's worth more than a million bucks!'" Montgomery said.

Being the bearer of good news for a change was all the more satisfying to Montgomery and Borckardt because they truly liked the family. "Unassuming, quiet, pleasant, salt of the earth people," was the way Borckardt characterized them. Montgomery thought to himself, I'm so happy this happened to such nice people.

While Montgomery and Borckardt briefed the Walton family off to one side, the rest of the assembly milled about scanning faces and straining to hear snippets of several conversations to find out the panel's decision.

David Hall got the group's attention for the official announcement: "Ladies and gentlemen, PCGS has declared this coin to be a genuine 1913 Liberty nickel."

A round of applause and delighted exclamations erupted. Donn Pearlman and Steve Ruark, the Associated Press photographer, began snapping pictures. AP correspondent Sarah Brumfield interviewed the Walton family and members of the authentication team.

The atmosphere was festive as everyone shared with each other bits of the experience from their perspective.

Though it was the wee hour of a new day, nobody was sleepy, and nobody wanted to leave right away. Montgomery and Givens huddled with the ANA's Larry Lee, and they agreed that the Walton coin should be displayed with the other four nickels for the duration of the show and that Chris Cipoletti would make the formal public announcement of the discovery at the opening ceremonies coming just hours from then at 9:00 a.m.

The security guards from Positive Protection were getting antsy about having so many strangers milling around the store of valuables they were charged with protecting. Except for one or two in the crowd, they didn't know these people from Adam and kept their eyes alert to where everybody's hands were. If anything were missing in the morning, it would be their behinds in a sling. They strongly hinted it was time for everybody to go and set about ushering the group outside. Nobody was inclined to protest; they were big guys with big guns.

"It was 12:45 when we left the convention center. Mark and I were the last ones out the door," Montgomery recalled. "Mark said, 'Boy, I could use a drink.'"

"But everything was closed," Borckardt said.

So they reluctantly shook hands goodnight and went to their hotel rooms.

Sleepless in Baltimore

Montgomery's wife, Amy, was already asleep in bed. When he came in, she stirred briefly and mumbled, "Well, is it real?" "Yeah! Its real!" Montgomery replied, bubbling over with excitement and ready to tell her all about it. "That's nice," she said, and rolled over to go back to sleep. With nobody to talk to, Montgomery paced, too keyed up to rest.

Borckardt called his wife, Mary, in Mandeville, Louisiana. "Do you know what time it is?" she asked in a sleepy voice. "Yes, I do," Borckardt said, "And if I had just shot a 300 game of bowling I'd call you - this news is *bigger*!" That got her attention. Borckardt is a bowling fanatic who has registered several officially sanctioned perfect games. She knew this must be something really important if it was bigger than that. "Oh." she said. "Well, what happened?" He filled her in on the news about the nickel. She muttered congratulations. In five minutes, she was asleep again.

Meanwhile, the press folks were working through the night. Beth Deisher didn't go to the midnight session, staying in her hotel room instead to work on her front-page story about the nickels scheduled to be posted on *Coin World*'s web site at 10:00 a.m. after the announcement at the opening ceremonies of the show. Donn Pearlman called her about 1:00 a.m. "The eagle has landed. It's genuine," he told her.

Pearlman's fingers were flying on the keyboard, too, as he typed press releases on the startling discovery. He would hold them until he got word from the Associated Press that the story was on the news wire. He had promised Sarah Brumfield an exclusive. He asked her to call him as soon as the story cleared the AP wire.

Brumfield called a little before 2:00 to say the story was out. Associated Press computer logs show Brumfield's story hit the newspaper wire at 01:28:37 a.m. and the broadcast wire a few minutes later at 1:40:00 a.m.:

Missing 1913 Liberty Head Nickel Appears

By SARAH BRUMFIELD, Associated Press Writer.

BALTIMORE - A million-dollar mystery was solved early Wednesday with experts certifying that a nickel that had been missing for decades is the fifth 1913 Liberty Head nickel.

Relatives of the late George Walton, a North Carolina coin dealer, took the coin to the experts at the American Numismatic Association convention that opened Wednesday. The relatives did not want to be identified.

The family had put the coin away after Walton's death because they didn't believe it was genuine, said Paul Montgomery, president of Bowers and Merena Galleries, a Louisiana-based coin dealer and auction house.

They decided to bring it out for inspection after learning that Montgomery had offered a $1 million reward for the coin and $10,000 just to be the first to see it.

The association brought the six experts together late Tuesday. After comparing the coin to four documented coins, they declared the coin authentic early Wednesday.

The family had no immediate plans to take Montgomery up on his offer of $1 million for the coin. However, Montgomery said he would write the relatives a check for $10,000 for letting him be the first to see it on Tuesday.

The Liberty Head nickel was replaced by the Indian or Buffalo nickel after 1912, Montgomery said. But five Liberty nickels with 1913 dates were minted illegally by Mint official Samuel K. Brown.

Two of the coins are now in private collections and the other two are in museums.

The reward amount was based on the auction of a 1913 nickel for $1.4 million in 1996. It was the first coin to sell for more than $1 million.

©Copyright. Associated Press. All Rights Reserved. Distributed by Valeo IP.

Pearlman immediately launched his mobilization plan, rushing down to the hotel business center to send notices to all the major media outlets on his list of contacts to call or fax. "I faxed Good Morning America, Early News, Today, CBS - all major media in Baltimore and Washington."

The media advisory he sent out was brief:

Missing Million-Dollar Nickel Confirmed,
Now In Baltimore at World's Fair of Money®

The missing $1 million 1913 Liberty Head nickel, the subject of recent, prominent reward stories and a nationwide search, now is in Baltimore and goes on public display for five days beginning Wednesday, July 30. Unaccounted for since 1962, it was quietly brought to town Tuesday for authentication at the American Numismatic Association's World's Fair of Money.

It is being publicly reunited for the first time since 1920 with the four other known specimens (including one from The Smithsonian) in a once-in-a-lifetime, $12 million exhibit at the World's Fair of Money in the Baltimore Convention Center. The event is open to the public and admission is free.

Pearlman said he got only a couple hours sleep before arising at 5:00 a.m. to go back on duty.

Montgomery couldn't get to sleep right away, so he turned on the TV around two o'clock. In a few minutes, though, he nodded off, exhausted by the tense day and night.

He came to, vaguely aware that a phone was ringing somewhere. Only partly awake, he wondered, "Is that the phone ringing?" By the time he was fully awake, the ringing had stopped. He wasn't even sure he had heard anything.

In truth, the phone *was* ringing...in the adjoining room (also in his name) where his children slept. Myra Lee, 14, Katy, 12, and David, 8, dozed through it, or if they heard the phone ringing, they ignored it on the assumption one of their parents would answer it.

Borckardt had managed to settle down enough to drift into a restless sleep when his bedside phone rang at about 2:30. Awakened but still in a fog, he thought: Boy, that wakeup call sure came fast. But it wasn't the hotel operator.

A female voice asked if he were Mark Borckardt. He affirmed his identity. She said, "I'm terribly sorry to bother you. I'm calling from Good Morning America." He couldn't believe it. It had only been a little more than an hour since they left the convention center.

"I've been trying to reach Paul Montgomery, but he's not answering in his room," she said.

Borckardt told her he had just left him. "I know he's in his room," he said.

"We'd really like to have him on the show this morning. We know how much he enjoyed being on the show the last time," she cooed.

Borckardt hesitated and said, "Uh...ma'am, he wasn't on your show. He was at the newsroom in New Orleans, but he never got on because he was bumped."

Unfazed, the caller pressed on with scarcely a pause. "Well, we'd like to get him on the show this time and correct that." Borckardt gave her Montgomery's cell phone number.

Montgomery's cell phone was turned off. That didn't stop her. The hotel phone rang. Apparently she had badgered the hotel desk clerk to see if there was another room number besides the one they'd tried earlier.

"She wanted to send a limo for me right away to take me to New York," Montgomery said. It would take about a four hour drive from Baltimore to get there for a 6:30 a.m. taping. Montgomery declined. "I told her I had an auction to put on."

The producer from "Good Morning America" was not to be denied and called back a few more times with alternate propositions, eventually getting Montgomery to agree to do an interview in Baltimore with their affiliate.

Her last call came at 5:30 in the morning. "Uh, can we have an exclusive on that?" she asked. Montgomery's fuse was growing short at that point. He told her, "I need to talk to my publicity guy and find out what commitments he has made. Call me at 10 o'clock. Now, is there anything else you'd like to ask me? There is no other good reason for you to call me tonight, right?" Except for a couple of short catnaps, he got no sleep that night.

The story did appear on "Good Morning America," using footage supplied by the Baltimore affiliate station.

A Smash Hit at the Show

Montgomery hit the deck running that morning. He arrived at the convention center about 6:30 a.m. Borckardt followed shortly. The excitement during the night notwithstanding, they had a very important auction to put on. Bowers and Merena was the official auctioneer for the convention. They still had a lot of preparations to finalize.

The preparations got put on hold while they went to observe the opening ceremonies for the show at nine o'clock.

Chris Cipoletti, executive director of the American Numismatic Association took the podium before a crowd of about 300 people waiting for the official opening of the show. After some brief announcements and speeches, Cipoletti shocked the audience when he said: "I am sorry to say that you are not going to see four authentic 1913 Liberty Head nickels..." A murmur rippled through the crowd. "...You are going to see five."
It took a minute for the implication to soak in.

Montgomery was observing the crowd reaction. "About half the room had a blank stare because they didn't know what he meant. The ones who understood gasped; I heard comments like 'No way!', 'This is just incredible,' 'I can't believe it.' They were very vocal," he said.

From the time the doors opened Wednesday morning until the show closed at 2:30 Sunday afternoon, a constant stream of visitors lined up to view the astonishing display of the most famous American coin quintet in history. Most of the time it was a 45 minute wait in line to view the display. It was a fitting triumph honoring the 90th anniversary of the 1913 Liberty Head nickels.

At intervals during the show, Borckardt could not resist being drawn to the exhibit area "to make sure the coins were still there," he rationalized. It was really to soak up the crowd's enthusiasm. He found it exhilarating, and relived for a few minutes the thrill of having been involved in making it all happen.

Invariably, someone would recognize him and say, "So, Mark, what was it like being one of the authenticators for the nickel?" When he started to describe the experience, people nearby would stop what they were doing and

The overwhelming crowd response to the exhibit brought smiles to some of the executives responsible for making it possible. From left, John K. Snyder, president of Diamond International Galleries; Donn Pearlman, president of Minkus & Pearlman Public Relations, Inc.; and Christopher Cipoletti, executive director of the American Numismatic Association. Courtesy of Minkus & Pearlman Public Relations, Inc. ©

Donn Pearlman and Coin World editor Beth Deisher share with the Walton heirs a rare moment around the display of the famous nickels sans crowds. From left, Pearlman, Ryan Givens, Gary Myers, Deisher, and Cheryl Myers. Courtesy of Minkus & Pearlman Public Relations, Inc. ©

gather around. "I ended up giving a talk to 30 or 40 people" each time it happened, he said.

Montgomery got caught up in some impromptu seminars on the floor, too. During one of them, the Walton family was in the group. Since they had insisted on remaining anonymous, nobody else knew they were the owners of the mystery Walton coin. Ironically, many of the questions from the audience were about the family. People wanted to know more about them and why they had kept the coin a secret all that time. Montgomery didn't uncover their identity, but the knowing glances between them were irresistible.

The lure of the five 1913 Liberty Head nickels drew huge crowds to the ANA World of Money show. Borckardt said he was told it was the second highest attended ANA convention ever.

Press Frenzy

Television crews, radio sound crews, newspaper reporters and photographers buzzed around the convention center, nabbing anybody they thought might be important. The story was reported worldwide. The national TV networks picked up the story. Even media halfway around the world picked it up; *The Hindu*, India's national newspaper, carried the story in both its print and Internet versions. Beth Deisher's front page item in *Coin World* proclaimed in large letters: **Found!**

Donn Pearlman was busy doing interviews himself, including one with NPR (National Public Radio) and setting up interviews with Paul Montgomery.

Around ten o'clock on the first day of the show, Montgomery found Borckardt and told him, "Mark, I'm scared to death. I haven't worked on this auction at all in the last two days, and we've got a lot going on." He was besieged with press requests for news interviews.

Mark calmly answered, "Okay, I've got it. Let me take care of it. You take care of the press."

Montgomery pitched in on the auction when he could, but he was relieved to have Borckardt take charge of it. He had his hands full with the media.

"I did L.A. radio drive time, I did CNN, I even did an interview for London morning drive time," Montgomery said. He got a call from a BBC radio producer asking him if he would standby for an interview with the on-air host of a morning radio show (Montgomery didn't remember the deejay's name). He could hear the radio program in the earpiece of his phone. In his English accent, the incredulous deejay said, "This bloody yank paid ten thousand dollars just to see a coin, a nickel!"

Montgomery sensed that the amused radio personality was setting him up to make fun of him. After about a 10-minute interview, the radio host asked him, "Why would you pay ten thousand dollars just to be the first one to see it."

"So I could be on the BBC," Montgomery shot back.

Silence. "Oh...I get it," the deejay laughed.

Doubting Thomases

Every miracle has its Doubting Thomases. The miraculous clockwork of events that led to the discovery of the missing nickel and reunion of the five 1913 Liberty nickels was too much for some skeptics to swallow. The story had hardly hit the news wires before rumblings started circulating that it was all a carefully contrived publicity stunt by the ANA and Bowers and Merena to promote the Baltimore show. The hullabaloo about the million-dollar reward, the melodramatic midnight discovery just hours before the show opening of a coin nobody had been able to find in 40 years — it was all too perfect, they said. It just could not have happened by accident, they argued.

Without knowing all the facts, their doubts were understandable, considering the If factor. The odds against the perfect alignment of crucial events to allow it all to happen were astronomical.

If...

- Stacks hadn't declared the Walton nickel a fake in 1963 ...
- The Walton family hadn't held onto a supposedly worthless nickel...
- Laura Sperber hadn't mentioned she would like to show her 1913 Liberty nickel at the ANA show...
- Beth Deisher hadn't had the idea to hold a reunion of the nickels at the show...
- Any of the nickel owners had declined to loan their specimens for the exhibit...
- Donn Pearlman hadn't had the inspiration to post a million dollar reward to find the missing nickel...
- Bowers and Merena and Collectors Universe hadn't agreed to put up the reward money...
- David Tirell-Wysocki hadn't been interested in putting the million-dollar reward story on the Associated Press wire...

- Mason Adams' editor, DwayneYancey at the *Roanoke Times*, hadn't assigned him to do a local angle on the reward story...
- *Times* librarian Belinda Harris hadn't found a phone number for Lucille Walton...
- The Walton family had refused to be interviewed by Adams...
- Adams hadn't connected the Walton family with Larry Lee at the ANA...
- Cheryl Myers hadn't persisted in getting Larry Lee to take another look at photos of the Walton nickel...
- Larry Lee hadn't seen some reason in the photos of the coin sent by the family to think the Walton nickel might possibly be the real thing...
- Paul Montgomery, Mark Borckardt, and John Dannreuther hadn't agreed to a courtesy meeting with the Walton family to look at their coin...
- The authentication team of Montgomery, Borckardt, Dannreuther, David Hall, Jeff Garrett, and Fred Weinberg hadn't been totally in agreement that the Walton nickel was real...

...*If* any one of these conditions had not occurred *exactly* as it did *when* it did, then the whole thing almost certainly would not have happened. The very fact that the sequence of events was so fantastically, improbably complex, bordering on impossible, should be the most convincing clue that it was no invention. Even the most gifted off-the-wall creative screenwriter would be hard-pressed to come up with such a scenario.

To the charges that the whole thing was a put-up publicity deal, Paul Montgomery laughed and said, "I'm just not that smart." He took it as a left-handed compliment that anyone would think he was clever enough to have been part of dreaming up such a harebrained scheme. "We couldn't have planned it this well. Even if we were that creative, my thought would have been, 'Naw, it'll never fly. Nobody would ever believe it,'" he said.

"Just think about how absurd the entire concept is," said Mark Borckardt. "It's that simple." He responded to the skeptics with a gentlemanly rebuke in a guest editorial appearing in the August 18 edition of *Coin World*:

> A few skeptical people attending the convention suggested that this reunion was a masterfully choreographed publicity stunt, our firm knowing the whereabouts of this nickel prior to the reward first being offered. Of course, nothing could be further from the truth. Perhaps Paul

Montgomery or I approached Stack's in 1962, when I was 5 years old, and Paul was at the ripe age of 1, suggesting to them that they declare this an altered coin, because we would need to plan a promotion 40 years later to offer an award and "rediscover" the missing coin. Then, we would schedule a midnight authentication meeting to examine the coin. To those who have suggested such a scenario, I would respectfully ask that you think a little more about this!

Donn Pearlman was less charitable. "To those who liked the way the promotion was handled, I say 'Thank you.' But those who say we knew where the real coin was before the publicity started are clueless nincompoops." Pearlman took well-founded professional pride in his role in handling public relations for the event. It was a masterful campaign that captured worldwide headlines. He rankled at the suggestion, though, that anyone involved had known beforehand that the real nickel would miraculously appear the day before the convention. The truth is that nobody seriously believed it would ever be seen again. They only hoped it might.

Pearlman titled his monthly column in *Numismatist* magazine (October 2003) "Coin-spiracy" in a satirical barb aimed at the detractors. The subhead said, "A 1913 Liberty Head nickel came out of the closet, but apparently left a few people clueless." The article related the chain of actual events that led up to the discovery and rebutted the allegation that "It was a scam, a stunt."

Of course, everyone involved in the search hoped the missing coin would be found, but no one in the hobby knew the truth until the day before the convention opened. The allegation of a "fix" suggests that since 1962 everyone knew the coin was genuine, but waited 41 years to reveal it so we could all have a big party in Baltimore in 2003. If that were true, the authenticators surely would have scheduled a more convenient time than midnight to get together, and the folks at Bowers and Merena certainly would have found a way to avoid the more than 10,000 phone calls, faxes and e-mails from the public, all claiming to have the missing nickel.

Jeff Garrett said, "If anybody knew about it ahead of time, they should get an Oscar for their reaction when they found out it was real."

The Case of Mistaken Identity

The obvious question that arose after the Walton nickel had been authenticated by an expert panel of numismatists was: How could the coin have been called fake by experts 40 years before?

Beth Deisher reported in *Coin World*:

> Harvey Stack, president of Stack's, told *Coin World* July 29 that he does not personally recall having seen the coin in 1962. He said his cousin, Ben Stack, worked with an attorney, Arthur Smith, who served as executor of Walton's estate. Stack said he is not aware of who from Stack's determined the coin to be an altered date nor does his firm today, more than 40 years later, have any records that may reveal such information. "I remember being involved with helping to prepare the catalog for the sale of Mr. Walton's coins. Beyond that, I just don't remember," he said.

The numismatists involved in the 2003 authentication that reversed the "altered date" label for the Walton nickel were unanimous in defending the original Stack's decision. (It was not known until later examination of the Walton estate executor's files that, although Ben Stack first raised the red flag about the coin's authenticity, it was actually an unidentified member or members of the American Numismatic Society who made the deciding confirmation that it was a fake.)

"I hate that Stack's got a bad rap for the deal," Paul Montgomery said. "When they did it, it was 1962. They didn't have technology available to us, like the digital photo comparisons. And not as much was known about the 1913 Liberties then. Besides, there were six of us, and we had all five coins to look at. They only had the one. With all five of the coins to look at, even an average numismatist could determine if it was authentic. But I would never have been able to authenticate the coin without all the resources we had."

In his August 18 *Coin World* guest editorial, Mark Borckardt addressed the issue:

> I would also like to share my personal respect of the Stack's firm, including present and past individuals associated with the firm. Perhaps a representative of their firm did state that this coin was an altered date 40 years ago as has been reported. As I examined the coin, I realized that any numismatist, myself included, could have easily made such a pronouncement at that time. Numismatic knowledge was not what it is today and they absolutely did not have access to the other four coins for a side-by-side comparison at that time, a once-in-a-lifetime opportunity we were given in Baltimore during the authentication process. Further, this coin has some very light and totally random scratches, porosity and discoloration in the date area, which would lead any of us to make an altered date determination lacking any other evidence.

"I really felt it was going to be an altered coin," said John Dannreuther. "I could not see how Stack's could have missed on that. I did not know about the porosity in the 3 of the date. I think if I had been in that position, I would have done the same thing [as Stack's]."

Dannreuther pointed out that as a member of PNG, the Professional Numismatists Guild, Stack's would have been obligated to guarantee that the coin was real. If it were proven to be otherwise, they would have had to make good on the purchase price. That would probably have been around $35,000 — big money in 1963 when the Walton auction was held. They would have been risking a $35,000 liability to make a $3,500 commission. "Not many people want to do that unless they are really confident in what they are guaranteeing," Dannreuther said.

Fred Weinberg said, "If somebody had showed me that coin by itself and I had not seen another 1913 nickel, I might have assumed it was altered from a regular coin."

The Walton family harbors no ill will toward Stack's for the mistaken identity of the coin 40 years ago. They credit Stack's with conducting a highly successful auction of Walton's other coins, which set a record at the time. And they recognize that, had the 1913 Liberty nickel been sold as genuine, they would not be in possession of a coin now worth between two and three million dollars. They are philosophical about the long years that their uncle George Walton's reputation suffered. In the context of the 2003 revelation, they consider Walton's name to have come out better for it in the long run. "If the coin had been sold, he would probably have just been forgotten," Ryan Givens said. "As it turns out, he has become famous."

The $10,000 "Finder's Fee"

The Waltons left the convention center around two in the afternoon on Wednesday and drove back to Virginia. Ryan Givens and Cheryl and Gary Myers returned on Saturday.

They chatted with Donn Pearlman and several members of the authentication team, and observed reactions from the long lines of people viewing the exhibit of the five 1913 Liberty nickels. Eventually, they made their way to the Bowers and Merena booth.

Paul Montgomery brought up the $10,000 he had promised to pay for the first peek at the famous missing coin. "Why don't we get together so I can give you a check?" he told them. They met about 3:30 in the afternoon in the same conference room where the authentication session took place, sitting at the same table where Montgomery broke the news to them that

The $10,000 "finder's fee" check. Courtesy of Bowers and Merena Galleries.

Paul Montgomery writes check for $10,000 to Walton heirs for allowing him to be the first numismatist in more than 40 years to see the missing 1913 Liberty Head nickel. Courtesy of Minkus & Pearlman Public Relations, Inc. ©

their nickel was officially real. They spent a half-hour or so reliving the experience, relating little details so they could lock them in memory. Donn Pearlman was there with his camera at the ready to record the occasion.

Finally, Montgomery pulled out his checkbook and said, "Let's do this thing." Pearlman snapped photos. Montgomery had had no hesitation in making what may have seemed to the uninitiated to be an extravagant offer. From a business standpoint, it made perfect sense. The publicity value it earned was incalculable, the kind of public awareness and credibility that no amount of paid advertising could buy. It was worth every penny of the $10,000 and much more.

Montgomery paused while writing the check. "When I got to the remarks part, I signed the check and asked Mark, 'What should I put in here?'"

"Finder's fee," Borckardt replied. So Montgomery wrote: "Finder's fee for # 5."

Givens and Myers told Montgomery they would forgo his million dollar reward offer, at least for the time being. Montgomery had told them earlier that their coin was worth considerably more than that. More important, though, was the fact that they just didn't want to let it go.

"We decided we were not going to get rid of it anytime soon," Givens said. "We wanted it to stay in the family. Paul used the word 'heirloom.' It has been in our family for sixty years. It's not something you can just put up for sale. It will not be a great day when it is sold. We told this to Paul. I think he understood."

Montgomery told them, "This story alone is going to add a million dollars to the price tag of your coin. So you have no downside by keeping it."

They had the immediate concern, however, of what to do with their prized coin when the show closed the following day. They had no armed guards or armored trucks for protection. "My sister commented that we couldn't just walk of there with it in our pocket," Givens said. "We were afraid."

They spoke with Chris Cipoletti and Larry Lee about loaning the Walton nickel to the American Numismatic Association. The ANA execs were delighted to have the coin for displays.

The arrangement solved the Walton family's security problem. "Larry had said 'If you want, we'll stick it in the Brinks truck with the rest and send it back," Givens recalled.

It also meant that more people would get to see the long-lost nickel and learn the true story of George Walton. "Uncle George was a member of the ANA, and I think he would have wanted it this way. It would be out there for the public to see," Givens said.

They discussed the ANA arrangement with Montgomery and Borckardt, who readily endorsed the idea. "Uncle George's nickel" was going on tour.

"Uncle George's Nickel" on the Show Tour

The lead item for *Coin World*'s September 8, 2003, issue announced:

Walton 1913 5¢ on loan to ANA
Coin set for display at September Long Beach Expo

Collectors will get additional opportunities to view the "lost" Walton specimen of the 1913 Liberty Head 5-cent coin that was "found" in July...

The coin will make its West Coast debut Sept. 18 to 21 at the Long Beach Coin, Stamp & Collectibles Expo, in Long Beach, Calif.

"All of us no the Long Beach Expo staff are absolutely thrilled the [relatives] of George O. Walton want collectors to have the opportunity to personally see this important coin. This will be the first time the Walton specimen has ever been displayed in California," said Ronald J. Gillio, expo general chairman.

Numismatic Guaranty Corporation of America (NGC) announced its confirmation of the Walton specimen's authenticity in the September 29, 2003, *Coin World*. ANA director Chris Cipoletti said, "As the association's official grading service, NGC was asked to inspect it and verify the legitimacy of this great numismatic rarity."

News camera crew from KCBS-TV, Los Angeles, videotapes Walton coin exhibit at Long Beach Expo in September 2003, the first public appearance of the coin on the West Coast. Courtesy of Minkus & Pearlman Public Relations, Inc. ©

Bowers and Merena Galleries staffers Sue Mitchell (left) and Debbie McDonald share the spotlight with the famous Walton nickel at the Long Beach, California, expo.

NGC vice president Rick Montgomery (no relation to Paul Montgomery) compared the Walton coin to the specimen owned by the ANA. "I have had the opportunity to analyze other examples of this rarity," he said, "And there is no question in my mind that this piece is genuine. If I were to grade it as part of the NGC grading team, I would say this coin would likely grade Proof 62."

The Walton coin has not been encapsulated as a certified coin but continues to be displayed in the engraved plastic case which George O. Walton had made for it.

The new-found celebrity of the Walton specimen earned it a trip to the prestigious FUN show at the beginning of 2004. The famous "missing" nickel made its first-ever appearance at the Florida United Numismatists Convention at the Orange County Convention Center in Orlando January 8-11.

Paul Montgomery said in a December 11, 2003, Bowers and Merena press release announcing the special appearance: "FUN officials say there is no record of Mr. Walton bringing his famous nickel to any FUN convention prior to his death in 1962. I am absolutely thrilled we are able to bring this coin to Orlando so that collectors in the Southeastern United States will have a chance to see it in person."

FUN board member and historian, Gene Hynds, could not recall the Walton nickel appearing at any previous convention, beginning with the first one in 1955.

FUN president, Mark Lighterman, had a personal reason to look forward to the exhibit. "I remember being a young numismatist, new to the hobby in the early 1970s, when I attended a coin show in South Florida where one of the other five known 1913 Liberty Head nickels was displayed. I do not remember anything else about that show except the excitement of viewing this great rarity. Now 30 years later, I am president of FUN, and just as excited in being able to help display the long-lost George Walton coin. I hope this exhibit will excite another new collector to continue in our great hobby."

The colorful, illustrated exhibit was produced by the ANA. After the FUN show, the next major stop on the tour was the ANA National Money show in Portland, Oregon, March 26-28. The Walton specimen was scheduled to continue touring with historic appearances at other major shows.

Reflections on the "Thill of a Lifetime"

Being involved with the reunion of the storied 1913 Liberty Head nickels and the discovery of the missing member of the quintet had a profound effect on those closest to it. For a numismatist, this was the kind of thing one only dreams about happening, let along being actually a part of the story. Even months after the historic events of July and August in Baltimore, the main players in the saga - veteran experts who have notched an impressive array of honors and professional credits ? still found it hard to believe they had played a starring role in one of numismatic history's most dramatic tales.

Paul Montgomery called it "the pinnacle of my career. Nothing can ever top this." Besides the extraordinary personal gratification he got from the experience, he noted that all the publicity about the million dollar reward and the discovery of the missing nickel gave a huge boost to the hobby of coin collecting. "I think we sent two very clear messages to America," he said. "One is, Look in your closet. You might have a coin worth a fortune in there. The second is, Rare coins are valuable - you can make money with them."

He remembered a biblical verse a friend of his pointed out to him after the story was reported in the New Orleans area news media. Devoutly religious, Montgomery said one day Christian Lloyd Marsh, a coin collector and professor at the New Orleans Baptist Theological Seminary, sent him a note attached to an article referring to a verse of scripture in the Book of Luke. "When I looked it up," Montgomery said, "I smiled when I recognized a familiar verse, 'The Parable of the Lost Coin.'"

Or suppose a woman has ten coins and loses one. Does she not light a lamp, sweep the house, and search carefully until she finds it? And when she finds it, she calls her friends and neighbors together and says, "Rejoice with me; I have found my lost coin."

— Luke 15: 8,9 NIV

Mark Borckardt, an ardent bowler, said, "This far exceeded anything I ever felt when I bowled a 300 game. In fact, it topped anything I've ever experienced except getting married and the birth of my children."

David Hall commented, "We were on Cloud 9 for the whole show. It was a biggie. I was overwhelmed with the impact and importance of what happened. And I'm pretty jaded. It was really a once-in-a-lifetime numismatic event…so amazing how all the stars were lined up perfectly. It was a miracle, a monumental event."

John Dannreuther said he will never forget the thrill that rushed through him when he first held the Walton coin the morning before the formal authentication. "Immediately I knew it was real. I was shocked. I almost dropped it."

Jeff Garrett called it the high mark of his career. "Even the most jaded coin dealers that have been around for years were interested in seeing all four [nickels] together. But to see all five was a fantasy ending to the story."

Fred Weinberg said, "My head was spinning. I realized I was part of an incredible historic event that had never taken place before. I was very excited and proud…it was amazing. Everything was absolutely thrilling, one of the crowning capstones of my numismatic career. It was the highlight of my career both as a dealer and a collector."

Donn Pearlman told several people at the show: "I probably should retire…because there is nothing that could ever top this."

Ryan Givens was pleased that his uncle George Walton's name had been restored to a place of honor. "That experience will stick in my mind forever," he said. "Finally, something had been done to set it all straight. It [Walton's nickel] was authenticated. It was real. That was it."

Cheryl Myers was awed by the experience. "I couldn't have been more proud, humbled, and honored to see our nickel among the other four," she said, concluding with a happy flourish: "WHAT A WEEK!"

For the throngs who viewed the five 1913 Liberty Head nickels close-up on those memorable summer days in Baltimore, 2003, most will no doubt long remember the moment as the singular lifetime highlight of their coin collecting experience.

Considering the history of extraordinary "nothing can ever top this" events that enrich and enliven the captivating history of the 1913 Liberty

Head nickels, it's hard to imagine that the next 90 years in the story of these maverick coins could more eventful than the last 90. What story will they tell?

Chapter 11 References

Bobbitt, Stephen L. 2003. Interview (October 14).

Borckardt, Mark. 2003. Interviews (September 2, 3, 9).
— Borckardt. 2003. "Once-in-a-lifetime opportunity thrilling." *Coin World* (August 18), p. 10.

Bowers and Merena Galleries. 2003. "Bowers and Merena Displays Famous 1913 Liberty Nickel at FUN Convention." Press release (December 11).

Brumfield, Sarah. 2003. "Missing 1913 Liberty Head Nickel Appears." Associated Press wire story (July 30).

Cipoletti, Christopher. 2003. Interview (October 2).

Coin World. 2003. "Walton 1913 5¢ on loan to ANA" (September 8), pp. 1, 95, 98.
— *Coin World.* 2003. "NGC confirms authenticity of Walton 1913 Liberty nickel" (September 29), p. 76.

Dannreuther, John. 2003. Interviews (October 2,4).

Deisher, Beth. 2003. Interview (October 8).
— Deisher. 2003. "Found!" *Coin World* (August 18), p. 1.

Garrett, Jeff. Interview (October 2).

Givens, Ryan. 2003. Interview (October 1).

Hall, David. 2003. Interview (October 10).

The Hindu. 2003. "Missing nickel appears" (August 9). Web site accessed February 27, 2003 at http://www.hindu.com/thehindu/yw/2003/08/09/stories/2003080901470400.htm.

Montgomery, Paul. 2003. Interviews (September 2, 3, 9).

Myers, Cheryl. 2003. Interview (October 2).
— Myers. 2003. Personal diary notes (June 22-August 3).

Pearlman, Donn. 2003. Interview (September 23).

Snyder, John K. 2003. Interview (October 9).

Weinberg. Fred. 2003. Interview (October 3).

- Chapter Twelve -

AN
UNFINISHED TALE

This telling of the 1913 Liberty Head nickel epic nears its end. But it will not be the end of the story. As the legend of these historic coins continues to grow, new mysteries and controversies inevitably will tease and taunt the coin sleuths of tomorrow.

New episodes in this fascinating tale have been developing even as this book was being written.

Bowers and Merena Galleries, which posted the million dollar reward that prompted the discovery of the long-missing Walton coin, was sold by Collectors Universe to Spectrum Numismatics, a division of Greg Manning Auctions, Inc., in February 2004. Paul Montgomery, who had been president of Bowers and Merena Galleries, left the company to become president of U.S. Coin in Houston, where he had begun his career in numismatics. Mark Borckardt moved to Dallas to assume the dual duties of senior cataloger and senior numismatist at Heritage Galleries.

Other players in the story were on the move, too. Larry Lee and Stephen Bobbitt left the American Numismatic Association to pursue other business interests. Douglas Mudd departed the Smithsonian Institution to become curator of the ANA Money Museum in Colorado Springs.

Rumors began circulating in early 2004 that the two privately-held 1913 Liberty Head nickels had again changed hands.

Edward C. Lee, whose purchase of the Eliasberg specimen from Dwight Manley was publicly announced the very night the Walton coin was authenticated in Baltimore, denied the rumor. "It is not true," he said in March 2004, regarding change of ownership of his nickel.. He said he had heard it rumored that someone might be interested in buying his nickel, but that he had not been contacted with an offer. The coin was displayed jointly by Lee and the Professional Coin Grading Service (PCGS) at the FUN Show in Orlando in January 2005.

The Hawn specimen changed hands in early 2004 when Legend Numismatics sold the nickel to an anonymous buyer in a private treaty transaction brokered by Blanchard and Company, reportedly for about $3 million (another mystery to keep the numismatic world curious!).

Then in June 2005, Legend Numismatics purchased Ed Lee's Eliasberg nickel for $4.15 million, setting another new record price for the 1913 Liberty Head nickels. The Eliasberg nickel gained about one million dollars of value in less than two years!

The life story of a rare coin is seldom static, and the biography of the 1913 Liberty Head nickels is more rambunctious than most. If the next 90 years of the story prove as colorful and event-filled as the last, the saga will entertain coin buffs for decades, perhaps centuries to come.

The confounding nature of the 1913 Liberty Head nickel history is that finding answers often spawns new questions. The most perplexing of all is that the body of evidence suffers from gaps obscured by darkness. The shadows hide crucial facts essential to completing our knowledge of these nickels. Even Sherlock Holmes was, on rare occasions, stumped by the absence of information critical to a solving a case.

We know more about the 1913 Liberty Head nickels than we did when we began this journey of discovery. Yet we still do not know who made the coins or when or why. Unless and until some new evidence reveals the solution to the seminal mystery of their origin, the Case of the 1913 Liberty Head nickels remains open.

It may forever remain unknown who slipped into the Philadelphia Mint pressroom and hurriedly stamped out the now-famous nickels. The destruction of Mint records that may have yielded some clues to the dies used to make the nickels rendered those facts unknowable save in the memories of those who may have seen the contents, and they are dead or not willing to talk. The reason for the destruction continues to be an enigma, too.

The true identity of "Reynolds," the "wealthy North Carolina businessman" said to have owned the Walton specimen at one time eludes us still. We may never know for sure, but the search goes on.

Given the penchant of these nickels to be magnets for mysteries, it will be no surprise that still newer enigmas will evolve. These and other new chapters will no doubt be chronicled by future scribes.

To be continued...someday.

Chapter 12 References

Borckardt, Mark. 2004. Interview (March 8).

Lee, Edward C. 2004. Interview (March 4).

Lee, Lawrence. 2003. Interview (December 11).

Montgomery, Paul. 2004. Interview (March 8).

Sperber, Laura. 2004. Interview (March 15).

THE LIBERTY NICKEL TIMELINE

1792

April 2: George Washington signs a bill authorizing a national coinage for the United States of America, using a decimal system of denominations rather than the British pound system.

1837

Dr. Lewis Feuchtwanger proposes to Congress the use of nickel in American coinage.

1857

May 25: U.S. produces first American coin with nickel content — the mainly copper one-cent coin contained 1/8 nickel.

1861

December: American citizens begin hoarding gold coins as Civil War looms.

1862

June: Silver coins begin disappearing from circulation in U.S.

1863

Tycoon Joseph Wharton corners market on nickel supply by buying the Gap Nickel Mine in Lancaster, Pennsylvania.

1865

March 3: Congress authorizes the issue of three-cent pieces made of nickel to replace three-cent paper notes.

1866

May 16: Act of Congress establishes the "nickel" five-cent piece to replace paper five-cent "shinplasters." Influenced by Joseph Wharton, nickel mining tycoon. James Barton Longacre developed shield design, used until Liberty Head introduced in 1883. Shield nickel was first base-metal five-cent piece in U.S. history; previously had the silver half-dime.

1881

Mint Director A. Loudon Snowden orders Charles E. Barber, Engraver of the Mint, to prepare pattern dies for cent, three-cent, and five-cent coins.

1882

Modifications to design - No CENTS nickels prototype.

1883

January 30: Snowden unveils the Liberty Head nickel design at a special ceremony. Production of No CENTS nickels begins - 5.5 million struck. Coins were modified and passed as counterfeit $5 gold pieces, called "Racketeer" nickels. Snowden orders Barber to add CENTS.

1887

U.S. Mint issues regulation making emission of coins from experimental dies unlawful unless they are patterns for coins to be issued for circulation in the same year. (This makes 1913 Liberty Head nickels illegal if struck in 1912, among other reasons).

1903

December 18: Samuel Brown goes to work for Philadelphia Mint. Assistant Curator of the Mint Cabinet Collections.

1906

April: Samuel Brown proposed for membership in the American Numismatic Association in *The Numismatist*, vouched by Stephen K. Nagy and a Dr. Heath.
June: Samuel Brown listed in *The Numismatist* as member # 808.

1911

May 4: Eames MacVeagh writes to his father, Secretary of Treasury Franklin MacVeagh, suggesting a new nickel design. Secretary MacVeagh initiates design process.

1912

June: Secretary of the Treasury Franklin aMacVeagh approves new coin design for buffalo-Indian head nickel by James Earle Fraser.

December 13: US Mint officially stops making Liberty nickel; last Liberty nickel struck. Director of the Mint, George E. Roberts, instructs the Superintendent of the United States Mint at Philadelphia: "Do nothing about five cent coinage for 1913 until the new designs are ready for use." Samuel Brown is Clerk or Storekeeper of the Philadelphia Mint.

December 1912-January 1913: Presumed time when five Liberty Head coins are produced by unknown person at the Philadelphia Mint.

December 26: Chief engraver Charles Barber receives Buffalo/Indian Head nickel models from James Earle Fraser.

1913

January 7: First experimental Buffalo/Indian nickels struck.

February 21: Production begins of Buffalo/Indian nickel.

November 14: Samuel Brown leaves employment of the Philadelphia Mint "To enter business for self."

1919

December: Ad by Samuel Brown in *The Numismatist* offering to pay $500 apiece for any 1913 Liberty Head nickels. First public awareness of their existence.

1920

January: Second ad by Samuel Brown in *The Numismatist* offering to buy 1913 Liberty Head nickels, raising ante to $600 per coin.

February: Third ad by Brown offering the Liberty Head nickels in *The Numismatist.*

August: Samuel Brown exhibits a Liberty Head nickel at ANA convention in Chicago, first public display of one of the coins.

Samuel Brown exhibits all five Liberty Head nickels at Rochester (New York) Numismatic Association meeting - possibly the first time the coins had all been seen displayed publicly together. Date unknown.

1924

January: Samuel W. Brown retires from Pierce Brown, Co., in North Tonawanda, New York.

August Wagner offers five 1913 Liberty Head nickels in *The Numismatist*. Bought by Stephen K. Nagy.

Samuel Brown serves on Assay Commission 1924-25.

1926

Stephen Nagy sells 1913 Liberty Head nickels to Wayte Raymond who in turn sells them to Col. E.H.R. Green.

Col. Edward Howland Robinson Green buys all five 1913 Liberty Head nickels from Wayte Raymond.

1932-33

Samuel W. Brown serves as mayor of North Tonawanda, New York.

1936

June 8: Col. E.H.R. Green dies in Lake Placid, New York.

1937

Col. Green coin collection appraised by F.C.C. Boyd, New York.

1941

Burdette G. Johnson, in collaboration with Eric P. Newman, acquires the five-coin set in a coin case with three other coins (eight in all).

1943

Eric P. Newman keeps finest of the five 1913 Liberty Head nickels for his collection. B.G. Johnson sells one of the nickels to F.C.C. Boyd and the remaining three to James Kelly.

Kelly sells one nickel each to Fred Olsen, Dr. Conway A. Bolt, and J.V. McDermott.

1944

F.C.C. Boyd sells nickel to dealers Abe Kosoff and Abner Kreisberg. They sell it to King Farouk of Egypt.

Fred Olsen sells 1913 Liberty Head nickel to King Farouk of Egypt via B. Max Mehl.

1945?

Dr. Conway Bolt trades Specimen 2 to someone named "Reynolds"?

1945 or 1946

George O. Walton trades for Specimen 2 from an unspecified "North Carolina businessman," often believed to be tobacco tycoon R.J. Reynolds.

1946

King Farouk attempts unsuccessfully to sell 1913 Liberty Head nickel at auction by Numismatic Fine Arts in New York.

1948

Eric Newman sells Specimen 1, the finest known of the five nickels, to Abe Kosoff for $2,000.

1949

Abe Kosoff sells finest known 1913 Liberty nickel to Baltimore collector Louis Eliasberg for $2,350.

1952

King Farouk is overthrown by military government in Egypt, exiled, and his personal possessions confiscated, including the coin collection.

1954

Egyptian government sells Specimen 3 to dealer Sol Kaplan for $3,750.

1955

Sol Kaplan sells Specimen 3 to the Norweb Family - Ambassador R(almond) Henry, Sr., and Emery May Holden Norweb (Mrs. Norweb was the actual owner, not her husband).

1961-1969

Eva Adams serves as Mint Director, during which time valuable records are destroyed for reasons still unexplained.

1962

March 9: George Walton dies in car crash.

March 23: Coin World item mentions that Dr. Bolt traded Specimen 2 to "a Winston-Salem Millionaire. In 1945 Walton got the nickel in a trade for about $3,750."

1963

Stack's appraises Walton coin collection, conducts auction; 1913 Liberty Head nickel specimen returned to Walton estate as "altered date" fake.

1967

J.V. McDermott sells Specimen 5 to Aubrey & Adeline Bebee for record $46,000.

1972

Edwin Hydeman sells Specimen 4 to World Wide Coin Investments for $100,000.

1973

December. Specimen 4 featured in episode of TV series "Hawaii Five-O." Episode "The $100,000 Nickel." (World Wide Coin owned it).

1977-1981

Stella Hackel Sims serves as Director of U.S. Mint, during which time important Mint records for the period 1912-1913 are destroyed, apparently illegally.

1978

Norweb Family donated Specimen 3 to Smithsonian Institution. World Wide Coin Investments sold Specimen 4 to Dr. Jerry Buss ($200,000).

1993

Attorney Arthur Smith, representing Charles Walton, brother of George O. Walton, confirms in *Coin World* that a 1913 Liberty Head nickel was recovered at car crash site where George Walton was killed, and that Stack's had declared the coin an altered date.

Reed Hawn sells Specimen 4 to Dwight Manley for Spectrum Numismatics ($875,000).

American Numismatic Association and Texas collector Reed Hawn offer $5K each (total $10K) for missing coin — unclaimed.

1996

Jay Parrino pays record $1.485 million for Specimen 1 from Eliasberg estate.

2001
Dwight Manley pays record $1.84 million for Specimen 1 from Jay Parrino.

2002
Dwight Manley sells Specimen 4 to Legend Numismatics —
Huang/Moran/Sperber ($1.84 million)

2003
March: Beth Deisher and ANA pursues idea for an historic reunion of the
four known 1913 Liberty Head nickels.
May 23: Bowers and Merena offers $1 million reward for missing nickel,
$10K to be first to see it.
July 29: Q. David Bowers announces at pre-opening gala in Timonium,
MD, that Edward Lee buys Eliasberg coin from Dwight Manley for
record $3 million (est.).
July 30: In a secret midnight session, the missing coin - the Walton
specimen - is authenticated at Baltimore ANA show, all 5 coins reunited
for the first time in 40 years.
September 18-21: Walton coin goes on display solo at Long Beach Coin,
Stamp & Collectibles Expo, Long Beach, CA.

2004
January: Legend Numismatics sells Hawn specimen to an anonymous buyer
reportedly for about $3 million, said to be a new record for the 1913
Liberty Head nickel.
January 8-11: Walton specimen displayed for first time ever at FUN show
in Florida.

- Appendix B -
PEDIGREE NOTES

Tracking the provenance[82] of the 1913 Liberty Head nickels can be an exercise in frustration. So many hands have passed the coins around this way and that, it sometimes seems like trying to keep up with the flashing sleight of hand in a street magician's cups-and-balls trick.

With rare coins, there's no deed registered with the county registrar as in real estate, no title or license document required by the state as with a vehicle, no record of sales and background checks as required by the federal government for firearms transactions. There's not even an official pedigree registry as with horses and other prize animals. Records of coins sold in public auctions provide some measure of authenticity, but many rare coins change hands in "private treaty" transactions between individuals that become known to the public only if the parties to transaction choose to let it be known. If they prefer to keep the transfer private and anonymous, as is their right, the trail of provenance develops gaps of ambiguity.

Numismatic researchers attempt to fill these gaps of knowledge with best guesses and hearsay folkloric evidence. The provenance of the 1913 Liberty Head nickels is fraught with such gaps, some so foggy that they may never be deciphered with dependable accuracy.

Researching and documenting the chain of ownership of celebrated rare coins gets complicated further by the haphazard method, if method it can be called, of nomenclature for the coins. The quandary is: What do you call a particular coin to identify which one you're talking about?

A Coin By Any Other Name...

There's no problem identifying a one-of-a-kind rare coin, such as the 1870-S three dollar gold piece. There's only one, so everybody knows which coin you mean.

When there are more than one of the same typedate and mintmark issue of a coin, however, as with the five 1913 Liberty nickels, it becomes

---

[82] The provenance of a coin is its proof of origin, the record of the chain of ownership that comprises its pedigree.

more difficult to keep them sorted out. The problem is that what they are called in the numismatic literature keeps changing.

Coins that are submitted to coin grading services for certification get an assigned identity number that is unique to them. However, the identity is only good for as long as the sealed coin holder is intact. It is not uncommon for collectors to "crack" a holder (or "slab," as they are commonly called) to resubmit a coin to a grading service again, or to a different one, in hopes of getting a better opinion of grading. Coin grading is an art, not a science, reliant on subjective opinions of the graders. Studies on inconsistencies between grading services and the problem of "grade inflation" continue to stir emotional controversy in the industry/hobby. A coin submitted anew for grading thus acquires a new number identity, different from the one it previously had, with no documentation linking the two as being the same coin.

Furthermore, grading and certification of rare coins is a relatively new procedure, introduced in 1980s. References to coins prior to that lacked the benefit of any systematic designation like a certification number from a recognized grading service. Coins were not encapsulated in tamper-proof holders until 1986 when PCGS was founded. Prior to that, no one "guaranteed" the grade.

Auction catalog lot numbers and descriptions are useful to a limited degree in tracking a coin's pedigree. However, the lot number for a coin is different in each catalog. So it takes a numismatic detective with access to an extensive, up-to-date library of auction catalogs and the accounting nose of an IRS auditor to track a particular coin's path through the auctions. Even at that, a given coin may change hands privately several times between its appearances in public auctions, with no record of the interim transactions.

Identifying coins by photos published in auction catalogs is also unreliable, at least with regard to the older ones. Auction catalogs prior to the 1970s often used "stock" photos for coins. So what was shown was not always the actual coin being sold.

In the absence of any systematic industry standard for identifying rare coins, an informal tradition evolved from the linguistic imperative of needing some kind of conversational handle to hang on a given object in order to talk about it. Collectors started nicknaming coins for some famous person who once owned them — usually after they're dead and gone. One of the 1913 Liberty Head nickels is widely known as the Eliasberg specimen, for example, because the most famous collector to have owned it was Louis E. Eliasberg, Sr., one of the most celebrated coin collectors in history.

Challenges in Identifying Individual Rare Coins

This "system" of referring to specific coins suffers from major flaws that in many instances further aggravate the confusion rather than diminishing it. Famous coins tend to attract famous owners. The coins change hands from one famous owner to another equally, or maybe even more, famous owner. As a practical matter, an owner who plunks down several million dollars for a coin has paid for the right to call it whatever he or she pleases! People gradually begin to refer to the coin by the next name and the next, as the procession of owners grows.

For researchers, the moving target of continually evolving rare coin nicknames can often prove to be challenging. The lack of consistency forces the chronicler to be intimately familiar with the name of every owner in a coin's pedigree in order to know which coin a particular document may be referring to. A document in one particular year or period will speak of the "so-and-so nickel" and another document from a different time may refer to exactly the same coin by an entirely different nickname. If you don't happen to know the name of every owner who possessed the coin, you might be led to believe they are two separate coins. (An example of this phenomenon figures in the theory that there are actually six 1913 Liberty Head nickels, as previously mentioned!)

Collectors and the coin industry rely on published pedigrees to keep track of a given coin's provenance. The trouble is, they often don't agree. The discrepancies occur from different interpretations of the folklore regarding those undocumented gaps mentioned earlier, as well as from different outlooks on who should be included in the pedigree.

Some numismatic writers attempt to name every single person or organization that ever had custody of a coin, even for the briefest of times. Others find this approach cumbersome and try to streamline the pedigree by leaving out the interim handlers (dealers, for example, who take temporary possession of the coins while seeking a new owner) and concentrating only on those who retain possession for a reasonable length of time. The definition of a reasonable length of time depends on the subjective opinion of the writer. What is a reasonable length of time...a month, a year, two years, five?

Putting three, four, or five pedigree listings for a given coin side by side will often not match up on the same lines. When they do agree, it may very well be that one was simply derived from another on the assumption that it is correct. The consequence of this replication is that an error in the original pedigree becomes multiplied by as many times as it gets repeated in other publications.

Naming Conventions for the 1913 Liberty Head Nickels

Published pedigrees for the 1913 Liberty Head nickels exhibit the kind of inconsistent confusion described in the foregoing discussion. To clarify matters for the purpose of this narrative, the coins have been identified throughout as follows:

#1 Smithsonian Specimen
#2 Hawn Specimen
#3 Eliasberg Specimen
#4 Walton Specimen
#5 ANA Specimen

The number given for each coin is the order in which they are believed to have been struck in the press. Expert coin technician John Dannreuther determined the probable order of strike by examining the clarity of detail in the finer elements of the design, such as the kernels on the ears of corn. The detail is greatest in the first ones struck and degrades with each subsequent strike. "On the Smithsonian coin, I noticed…that you could see each kernel of corn," Dannreuther recalled of the night in 2003 when he and a panel including five other expert numismatists examined all five Liberty Head nickels.

On the last coin, "The corn is as flat as can be," Dannreuther said. He also noted: "The length of the wire rim was also considered as I believe the die 'tilted' in striking, as in the haste with which they were struck, one of the set screws on the die was not sufficiently tightened. This would lead to both weak corn and a 'shifting' of the wire rim."

Numbering the 1913 Liberty Head nickels in the order they were produced makes more sense and is a far more reliable designation than attempting to order them by quality or condition, as most pedigrees have historically done. Except for the finest known specimen (Eliasberg), there is considerable disagreement among numismatists as to the relative quality of the remaining coins, resulting in a confusing array of pedigree listing orders. Using the believed order struck, as confirmed by six experts viewing the five coins side by side, should eliminate the discrepancies.

Quality/Condition of the 1913 Liberty Nickels

It's important to emphasize that the above numberings assigned to the nickels are not the rank of quality/condition as they exist today. Mark Borckardt, senior numismatist for Bowers and Merena Galleries (he did some of the cataloging for the famous Eliasberg Collection Sale in 1996), identified the nickels by quality in this order:

1. Eliasberg Specimen: Finest Known. Proof-66 (PCGS).
2. Hawn Specimen: Second Finest Known. Proof-64 (PCGS).
3. Walton Specimen: Third Finest Known. (Not certified).
4. ANA Specimen: Fourth Finest Known. (Not certified).
5. Smithsonian Specimen: Fifth Finest Known. (Not certified).

NICKEL NICKNAME CROSS-REFERENCE

To help alleviate confusion when comparing notes with mentions of the coins in the numismatic lore, these notes may be useful in correlating the references:

Smithsonian Specimen: Even though King Farouk of Egypt owned the coin and the Smithsonian has held it longer than anyone else - 26 years - the Norweb Family name is frequently attached to it. This coin is often referred to in the lore as the Norweb Family Specimen or Norweb-Smithsonian Specimen.

Hawn Specimen: A parade of famous collectors have been drawn to this coin - Fred Olsen, King Farouk, Edwin Hydeman, Dr. Jerry Buss, Reed Hawn, and Dwight Manley among them. In recent times, the Hawn moniker has been the most commonly used designation. Other references to it in various articles are the Olsen Specimen, the Hydeman Specimen, or the Legend Specimen.

Eliasberg Specimen: Most widely known as the Eliasberg specimen. Sometimes described as the Eliasberg-Manley Specimen and more recently as the Eliasberg-Manley-Lee Specimen (Curious note: Edward Lee's last name and the initials of Louis E. Eliasberg are the same ? LEE.)

Walton Specimen: Until July 2003, erroneously known generally as the Reynolds Specimen. In at least one instance, listed as the Missing Specimen.

ANA Specimen: Variously called the McDermott Specimen, the McDermott-

ANA Specimen: the Bebee Specimen, and the McDermott-Bebee Specimen.

There may be other variants of the nicknames, but these are the ones most frequently encountered in researching the 1913 Liberty Head nickels.

Appendix B References

Bowers and Merena. 1996. "The Louis E. Eliasberg, Sr., Collection," Bowers and Merena Galleries auction catalog (May 20-22), pp. 221-228.

Breen, Walter. 1988. *Complete Encyclopedia of US and Colonial Coins* (New York: Doubleday), pp. 246-254.

Dannreuther, John 2003. Interview (October 4).

Deisher, Beth. 2003. "Liberty Head Legends," *Numismatist* (July), pp. 37-43.

Newman, Eric. 2004. Email (January 2004).

Peters, Gloria, and Cynthia Mohon. 1995. *The Complete Guide to Shield & Liberty Head Nickels* (Virginia Beach, Virginia: DLRC Press), pp. 164-172.

- Appendix C -
ADDITIONAL OWNER BIOGRAPHY NOTES

F.C.C. Boyd

Frederick Cogswell C. Boyd was a collector and part-time coin dealer in New York City. He was the owner of "The World's Greatest Collection" of coins sold at auction by Numismatic Gallery (1945-1946).

A New York City native, Boyd quit school at 13 to become apprenticed as a printer. By age 17, he was a traveling salesman. He became advertising manager of the American Tobacco Company in New York, worked for H.B. Claffin & Co., and eventually became manager of Union News Company, where he retired in 1946 as vice president of the company. He served on the board of the National Recovery Administration during the 30s and on the board of the Office of Price Administration during World War II.

Boyd started collecting coins around 1899 and became associate curator of modern coins for Yale University. He became life member #5 of the American Numismatic Association and a life member of the American Numismatic Society. He was president of the New York Numismatic Club in 1916-1917 and 1923. He was elected posthumously to the ANA Numismatic Hall of Fame in 1978.

Government of Egypt

In an online feature for Gold Rush Gallery's Writers Corner, "Numismatic Gumshoe: On the Trail of King Farouk," Carl N. Lester described the problems of cataloging the mammoth Farouk collection under the watchful eye of the Nasser military regime of Egypt:

> Because Fred Baldwin had to catalog the coins in Cairo, under military guard, and in a short period of time, it was not possible to do the great collection justice. Due to its sheer size, most of the coins were sold in large lots (often with fifteen or twenty coins per lot), sorted by denomination, with a variety of dates and mintmarks. Thus, most lots had a combination of rare and common coins.

The collection originally included a 1933 Saint-Gaudens double eagle, but the coin was withdrawn from the sale at the request of the American government. The U.S. Treasury claimed that the coin had been stolen from the Mint after an order to melt down all the 1933 $20 gold coins followed President Roosevelt's edict making it illegal for Americans to own gold. The fate of the coin remained in doubt until 2002 when it was monetized by the Treasury in a ceremonial exchange. It is the only surviving 1933 double eagle in private hands.

Naturally, a number of high-profile American coin dealers and collectors were interested in the collection, among them Abe Kosoff, Sol Kaplan, Bob Schermerhorn, James Randall, Paul Wittlin, and Hans Schulman. Prominent collectors included John J. Pittman, Gaston DiBello, and Ambassador & Mrs. R. Henry Norweb.

The 1954 auction at Koubbeh Palace, Cairo, proved to be bonanza for dealers and collectors, as Carl Lester noted:

> A number of factors prevented the coins from reaching their optimum value at the auction. These included the remote location, the uncertain financial arrangements, the political instability, the large lots, and the awkward manner in which the coins were presented for lot viewing. Collectors such as John J. Pittman realized the true opportunity to acquire important pieces at "fire sale" prices and made the most of it. Mr. Pittman reportedly took out a second mortgage on his residence to finance the trip and his purchases, which turned out to be among the most significant of his numismatic career.
>
> The sale was complicated by the fact that King Farouk had outstanding bills in excess of $300,000 from dealer Hans Schulman. After much uncertainty and following negotiations with the Egyptian government, an arrangement was made whereby Mr. Schulman was issued a credit in the amount of the due bills, against which auction purchases could be made. In order to recover his financial interest, Mr. Schulman became a major buyer at the auction, often allowing other dealers to obtain coins from his repurchased lots.

Louis E. Eliasberg, Sr.

Louis E. Eliasberg, Sr., was life member 169 in the American Numismatic Association. He was also a member of the Baltimore Coin Club.

He became interested in coins in the 1920s, according to a biographical sketch by his son, Richard A. Eliasberg, and started collecting them:

> When Franklin Roosevelt campaigned in 1932 on a platform of remaining on the gold standard and then immediately after his inauguration

had legislation passed removing the United States from the gold standard, my father never forgot that action and correctly believed it was the end of stable money and the beginning of the devaluation of the dollar.

Numismatists were one of the few classes of individuals who could legally own gold, which further sparked my father's interest in collecting coins, and his enthusiasm grew by leaps and bounds. He rapidly purchased coins during the 1930s, and in 1942 he was presented with the opportunity to acquire the John H. Clapp Collection in its entirety.

Eliasberg set the numismatic community abuzz with the purchase of the famed collection of John H. Clapp. Eliasberg bought the entire collection for $105,000, at that time an all-time record high for a single numismatic transaction. Stack's earned a $5,000 commission, according to John Dannreuther, and also sold the duplicates in 1947.

Eliasberg Estate

Bowers and Ruddy Galleries auctioned Eliasberg's gold coin collection October 27-29, 1982, as "The United States Gold Collection."

May 20-22, 1996, Bowers and Merena Galleries sold off the smaller denomination copper, copper-nickel, and silver coins in the collection along with pattern and colonial coins. This was the auction that Eliasberg's 1913 Liberty Head nickel brought a record $1,485,000.

Bowers and Merena Galleries conducted the final Eliasberg auction on April 6-8, 1997, disposing of the larger denomination silver coins and miscellaneous exonumia.[83] The Eliasberg 1804 Draped Bust dollar brought a record $1,815,000 in this sale.

In total, the sale of the Eliasberg collection brought in $44 million to the estate.

King Farouk

When King Faud I of Egypt died in April 1936, the crown passed to his son, Farouk I (also spelled Faruk). He married Queen Farida in January 1938, a marriage that produced two daughters but no male heirs. So he divorced Farida to marry Narrima Sadak in 1951, yielding a son, Ahmed Faud Narrima Sadak in 1951.

Coin dealers learned that dealing with Farouk could be a difficult

---

[83] Exonumia includes numismatic items that are not coins or paper money, such as tokens, medals, or scrip.

undertaking. He was reputed to be notorious for buying a coin, substituting one like it of a lesser quality that he already had, and trying to return it for a refund, saying he didn't want it after all. He was also known to return coins he bought if he soon after found another of the same kind he liked better. Dealers found it took a long time to get paid for their sales to Farouk, particularly if the invoice were for more than $10,000. Farouk could personally okay payments smaller than that amount, but larger invoices had to be routed to the Egyptian treasury for approval. Dealers wised up and began to limit his purchases to less than $10,000 per invoice.

Farouk also collected stamps, watches, books, comic books, and binoculars. His "toys" included three yachts, five airplanes, and 98 automobiles. Like Colonel E.H.R. Green, he also had a taste for exotic pornography, paid for by the Egyptian treasury.

King Farouk seemed to love the pleasures of life more than he cared for running a country (in a time when monarchies were increasingly considered an anachronism). It's ironic that the meaning of his name is Arabic in "one who knows right from wrong." His reign over Egypt was

King Farouk, deposed monarch of Egypt and prolific collector. Courtesy of ANA.

noted primarily for incompetence. Unrest stirred in the country.

The 1948-49 Arab-Israeli War hastened the demise of Farouk's regime. Israel won the war, trapping an Egyptian major, Gamel Abdel Nasser, and his men for several months. Nasser was eventually allowed to return to Egypt, a bad omen for Farouk.

Nasser led a military coup to oust Farouk on July 26, 1952. Farouk was exiled to Rome, and his lavish collections were seized by the military junta. Farouk died in exile in Rome, Italy.

Colonel E.H.R. Green

London-born Edward Howland Robinson Green was the son of Edward Henry Green and Henrietta ("Hetty") Howland Robinson. His mother was a shrewd (many would say shrewish) financial predator who became notorious as "The Witch of Wall Street." She amassed a great fortune with her investment acumen and held onto it tightly with a

Postcard photo of Hetty Green's residence in Bellows Falls, Vermont. The caption calls it HOME OF RICHEST WOMAN IN THE WORLD.

miserliness that became legendary. By reputation, she would have been a good match for Scrooge and Marley.

Eric Newman related two anecdotes from his extensive files of clippings that illustrate the extent of her picayunish bent. "She would send Colonel Green out to buy a newspaper in the morning, read it, and send him out to sell it again. Once when he was to have his picture taken, someone wanted to have his suit pressed so he would look his best. She said, 'Just press the front half. That's all that will show in the picture.'"

Hetty Green's stinginess had a dark side. When her son "Ned" was 14, he suffered a dislocated knee in a sledding accident. Hetty Green refused to hire a doctor to treat it, attempting to treat the injury at home and at free clinics. Because it was not attended properly, the leg had to be amputated seven inches above the knee.

Henrietta Howland Robinson Green, known as Hetty Green and "The Witch of Wall Street." Courtesy of Coin World.

Perhaps to make up for her maternal failings, Hetty gave her son a set of trains to play with. Actually, it was a whole railroad. She gave him the Texas Midland Railroad. Green was said to be "never happier than when he rode in the cab of a steam engine on the TMRR. His palatial Pullman car was variously called 999, Mabel, the Lone Star, and again, 999."

Because of his amputated leg, Colonel Green's title did not arise from military service. Rather, Mr. Green was appointed 'Colonel' in a letter from the Governor of Texas on November 10th, 1910.

According to Arthur H. Lewis in his book *The Day They Shook the Plum Tree*, the letter from the Governor to Mr. Green was prompted by an election day toast.

On November 8th, 1910, Mr. Green returned home to Terrell, Texas in his Pullman car, presumably to cast his vote. According to Mr. Lewis, Governor O.B. Colquitt proposed the following toast to a gathering of friends that included Mr. Green: "To 'Colonel' E.H.R. Green, the newest and finest member of my staff." Two days later, Mr. Green's formal appointment as 'lieutenant colonel' arrived in the form of a letter from the Governor.

The item does not say lieutenant colonel of what outfit, but presumably it would have been the state militia or a national guard unit. Neither does it say whether the appointment included any functional duties or was purely honorary. In any case, Green liked the sound of it and carried the title for the rest of his life.

Green had a proclivity for the racier side of life. He was the ultimate high-roller, carrying around bundles of $10,000 bills and lavishly spending "$3,000,000 a year on yachts, coins, stamps, diamond-studded chastity belts, female teenage 'wards,' pornography, orchid cultures and Texas politics," according to *Numismatic Scrapbook Magazine* (July 1968). Arthur Lewis reported that at Green's Biscayne Bay, Florida, estate, "To the rear of the projector was a vault containing the colonel's library of pornographic films, which experts considered the world's choicest."

Not long after Green's 22nd birthday, he and some friends visited the red light district in Chicago. There Green fell head over heels for a redhead named Mabel Harlow, so said Mary Cammack of Dallas, Texas. Mabel was also known by the names Mrs. M.E. Staunton, Mrs. Wilson, Mrs. Kitterage, deVries, or Campbell. According to Lewis, Cammack said, "Mabel was beautiful and had long, wavy, red hair which she would let down to her hips. She used to allow my older sister to comb it out for her. She used lots of make-up, but on her it looked good." Green courted Mabel for 26 years and married her on July 10, 1916, just nine days after his mother died.

Green was active in Republican politics and served as chairman of the Texas Republican State Committee. He was also a director of the St. Louis Exposition of 1904.

Q. David Bowers said of Green in *American Coin Treasures and Hoards*, that in "the annals of American coin hoarders Green's name is in the first chapter."

Reed Hawn

"I started out as a collector, but after buying coins realized it was a good investment medium," Reed Hawn told *Coin World*'s Paul Gilkes in June 1993. The Austin, Texas, collector continued, "It didn't take a rocket scientist to figure that out. Besides the enjoyment I got from the coins, I also learned I could make money. But I also realized it was a long-term investment."

Then 43, Hawn had been collecting coins for 30 years. He started as a teenager filling "penny boards" with date and Mint mark coins that he cherry-picked from pocket change. Hawn said his father, although not himself a coin collector, encouraged young Reed in his hobby. In the early 1960s, his father gave him a goloid metric dollar pattern. Hawn sent the piece to noted coin dealer Abe Kosoff to get information about it. Kosoff responded with a detailed letter that further engrossed Hawn in numismatics. Hawn said he became hooked by the "roll mania" of the early 60s and bought rolls of uncirculated U.S. coins.

Hawn became a career investor, with diverse interests in venture capital, investments, independent oil and gas production, real estate, and breeding and selling Arabian horses.

He helped finance the ANA library catalog and has written for *Coin World* on occasion. He is a fellow of the American Numismatic Society.

James Kelly

James F. Kelly was born in Dayton, Ohio, in 1907 and worked in his father's grocery store. He launched his career as a coin dealer in 1936, working with Burdette.G. Johnson in St. Louis until 1946.

Kelly opened a coin store in Dayton under his own name. Business must have been good, because on February 1, 1959, he moved to a larger facility and called the company World Numismatiques. He conducted the ANA convention auctions for 1950, 1951, 1961, and 1962. "Always in front," read Kelly's ads that appeared regularly on the inside front cover of *The Numismatist*.

Kelly was named president of Paramount International Coin Corporation, which he formed June 30, 1964, along with Michael DiSalle, Max Humbert, and James Ruddy (who later joined with Q. David Bowers to form Bowers and Ruddy Galleries). Paramount absorbed World Numismatiques in 1966.

James Kelly wrote the U.S. *Trends* column in *Coin World* from 1960 to 1968 and published *Coins and Chatter* from 1948 to 1962. He was awarded the Medal of Merit from Central States Numismatic Society in 1953.

Abe Kosoff/Abner Kriesberg (Numismatic Gallery)

It's an interesting fact that Abe Kosoff was born the very same month and at almost the same time that the 1913 Liberty Head nickels are thought by many to have been made — in late December 1912. He also got married in December, on Christmas Eve, 1933.

New York City-bred Kosoff graduated from New York University. He also attended New York City College and Columbia University.

Kosoff opened his first coin shop in 1937 and later established Numismatic Gallery in New York City in 1940. Eight years later, in 1948, he opened a branch of the company in Beverly Hills, California. He was partners with Abner Kriesberg until July 1, 1954.

From 1940 to 1971, Kosoff conducted 85 auction sales involving 106,590 lots. The sales included eight ANA convention sales. In 1982, he was named to the Board of Overseers for Adelphi University's Institute of Numismatic and Philatelic Studies

He wrote *Early U.S. Dimes* in 1945 and was co-editor with Kenneth Bressett on the *Official American Numismatic Association Grading Standards for United States Coins* published in 1977. He also compiled the 7th edition of *United States Pattern, Experimental and Trial Pieces* written by J. Hewett Judd. He wrote a column for *Coin World* called "Kosoff Commentary," which was published as a book titled Abe Kosoff Remembers in 1981. He was also a contributor to *Numismatic Scrapbook Magazine*. He won the ANA Farran Zerbe Memorial Award in 1972 and was elected to the ANA Numismatic Hall of Fame in 1982, just one year before he died in Palm Springs, California.

Dwight Manley/Spectrum Numismatics

Beth Deisher, editor of *Coin World*, once compared Dwight Manley to B. Max Mehl, calling them "The ultimate numismatic showmen." In a June 18, 2001, editorial, Deisher wrote:

> "Whatever he does, he does with a flair and a touch of class. It is always the biggest and best or some other superlative."
> Describe anyone you know?
> Had you been at the Long Beach Coin & Collectibles Expo…you might have heard such comments describing Dwight Manley, the collector-dealer-sports agent who dazzled more than 14,600 people with a spectacular new exhibit featuring the finest known of the legendary 1913 Liberty Head nickels.

Of course, it could have been said anytime in the past 18 months because Manley is also the driving force behind the traveling "Ship of Gold" exhibit that has provided a close-up and personal view for an estimated 1.3 million people of some $20 million worth of gold treasure salvaged from the SS Central America.

Actually, the comments were written some 23 years ago by Abe Kosoff, describing the legendary B. Max Mehl of Fort Worth, Texas.

Manley and Mehl both won renown for their intuitions for spectacular promotion. In his day, Mehl's contemporaries affectionately called him the "P.T. Barnum of numismatics." Manley might bear the same title today. As Deisher said of Manley:

> At heart Manley is a showman who considers displays such as the "1913 Liberty Head Nickel" [a display of the Eliasberg Specimen, which Manley owned after selling the Hawn Specimen] and the "Ship of Gold" to be rare educational and promotional opportunities for the hobby and the business of coin collecting.

Stephen K. Nagy

Viewed as a composite sketch from the descriptions of him in the numismatic lore, Stephen K. Nagy gives the appearance of a man always "up to something" of questionable intent, though nobody can quite figure out what it is or catch him at it. His connections at the Mint and with other players in the 1913 Liberty nickel saga insinuate a deeper involvement than has ever surfaced.

Nagy became interested in coins as a teenager in the late 1890s. In 1907, when he was 21, he teamed up with his father-in-law, John W. Haseltine, in the coin trade. Nagy may have learned some of the borderline (or sometimes over the line?) tricks of the trade from Haseltine. Haseltine was said to have close connections within the Philadelphia Mint, enabling him to gain access to duplicates and other objects not generally available to anyone else.

Haseltine and Nagy, partners for a number of years, strategically leaked a rumor in 1907 about the existence of trade dollars dated 1884. It was widely believed that none existed. The following year, they displayed for the first time an 1885 trade dollar, the first time anybody had heard of such a coin with that date.

Their knack for producing coins for sale which had never been known to exist bears a striking and eerily familiar resemblance to the 1913 Liberty

Head nickel scenario with Brown. The coincidences don't end there. Subsequent to the 1907 revelation of the existence of 1884 trade dollars, Nagy and Haseltine, in collaboration with Philadelphia coin dealer Henry Chapman, handled several MCMVII Ultra High Relief $20 gold coins that had miraculously come into their hands, with the help of mint engraver George T. Morgan.

Henry Chapman reportedly claimed in a conversation with Edwin Marshall to have owned the 1913 Liberty Head nickels at one point. George T. Morgan was chief engraver at the Philadelphia Mint during the time Samuel Brown worked there. Stephen Nagy co-sponsored Brown for membership in the ANA. The coincidences could be innocent enough, but they are provocative nonetheless.

On at least one occasion, Haseltine and Nagy clearly stepped too far over the line, even for the permissive practices of their day. The partners, along with Edgar H. Adams, sold two $50 gold pattern coins[84], each dated 1877 and each of a different variety. Haseltine had acquired the coins from R.A. McClure, curator of the Mint Cabinet in the 1890s. The buyer, who paid $10,000 each for the rarities, was none other than Adams' pal, William H. Woodin, a wealthy industrialist who later became the U.S. Secretary of the Treasury. When coin collectors heard about it, they raised a huge stink, crying out that the coins should have stayed at the Mint. The Treasury Department demanded the return of the coins. As compensation for giving up the coins, Woodin got "several crates" of old patterns from earlier dates, said to be many thousands of pieces.

Eric P. Newman/B.G. Johnson

Eric Newman, who got started collecting coins when his grandfather gave him an 1859 one-cent piece, looked upon Burdette Johnson as his mentor. The longtime relationship between them began when Newman was just a young boy visiting Johnson's coin shop, St. Louis Stamp and Coin. Still spry of mind at 92 when interviewed in November 2003, Newman recalled how the close bond between the two began.

"As a boy of 10 years old, my allowance was about five cents a week, and the carfare downtown was, I think, three cents. I couldn't go down to the coin dealer, Mr. Burdette G. Johnson, more than once every three weeks. I would want to spend my nickel, or dime if I had accumulated that much,"

---

[84] A pattern coin is one struck as a design test to see how it is going to look in actual practice and to ascertain if it will strike up properly. A pattern is a design type never accepted for regular use.

Newman said. Johnson pointed Newman toward a discipline of learning that would lead the young boy eventually to become one of the world's premier numismatic researchers and historians.

"I saved my money and accumulated my assets. I began collecting them in a small, very nice way. One day I wanted to buy a coin for a dime, and Johnson wouldn't sell it to me because he said I didn't know anything about the coin. He handed me a book and said, 'If you read this book and the next time you come back - bring me back my book - if you can recite the book to me, I will sell you the coin.' That changed my life.

"Each time I would go downtown, he would give me a book, and then I could buy coins. We did that for several years. That was my beginning with Johnson, and we became sort of real interesting friends. I was just a pup, and he was a mature dealer, a wholesale dealer."

Burdette G. Johnson, St. Louis coin wholesaler, the last person, along with Eric Newman, to own the entire set of five 1913 Liberty Head nickels. Johnson avoided the camera, and this image of him was extracted from a group photo by the staff of Numismatic Scrapbook Magazine. *© Amos Press.*

Johnson's determination to instill in the young Newman a passion for reading about the coins he bought probably grew from his own learning experiences. Johnson was self-educated, according to Pete Smith's biography of him, and read a book the day after he learned to read. Johnson was partners with David A. Sutherland in St. Louis Stamp and Coin until he bought out Sutherland on September 21, 1908. Johnson handled large consignments of coins from the Virgil Brand estate, which he sold for Armin Brand. He died on a streetcar while enroute to work on February 24, 1947.

Newman proved to be an apt pupil and took his mentor's lessons to heart. After graduating from the Massachusetts Institute of Technology and Washington University School of Law, Newman pursued the practice of law. All the while, his prodigious passion for numismatics continued undiminished.

Newman's list of accomplishments, honors, and accolades could fill several columns of a book. To highlight a few: Served on the Council of the

American Numismatic Society, perennial teacher at ANA summer seminars in Colorado Springs, chairman of the U.S. Assay Commission, and frequent lecturer at prestigious forums such as the International Numismatic Congresses of 1967 and 1973, the American Philosophical Society, and American Numismatic Association Educational Forums. He is winner of the ANA's Farran Zerbe Award (1969), nine Heath literary awards (for the numerous books and articles he has published), and the Burnett Anderson Memorial Award for Excellence in Numismatic Writing (2001). He won the Huntington Medal, highest award by the American Numismatic Society in New York, in 1978, and the Medal of the Royal Numismatic Society of England. Newman was inducted into the Numismatic Hall of Fame in 1986 and was named Numismatist of the Year for 1996.

He founded the Eric P. Newman Numismatic Education Society to assist others in writing and research, helping with writing book introductions, editing manuscripts, and furnishing materials for publication. (Newman contributed a substantial amount of information and resources for this book.)

He was also responsible for establishing the Eric P. Newman Education Center at Washington University Medical Center, only blocks from his home. He and his wife, Evelyn, have been tireless activists for civic projects in St. Louis.

The December 29, 2003, *Coin World* announced plans for the $3 million Newman Money Museum to be constructed on the campus of Washington University in St. Louis, where Newman earned his law degree. "The museum will house exhibitions, some of them on a rotating basis, from Newman's extensive collection, which is known as particularly strong in Colonial and Early American coins and paper money," reported Eric von Klinger.

Eric P. Newman met Colonel E.H.R. Green while a student at MIT and later inquired about buying pieces in Green's collection from his estate. Courtesy of Eric Newman.

Norweb Family

Raymond Henry Norweb, Sr., was born in Nottingham, England (home of the legendary Robin Hood) and moved to America in the early 1900s. He graduated from Harvard in 1916. He married Emery May Holden. They had two sons and a daughter.

After passing a civil service exam, Norweb entered the foreign service, with postings in Paris, the Netherlands, Chile, Mexico City, the Dominican Republic, Portugal, Panama, and Cuba. He retired from the diplomatic service in 1948.

Henry Norweb served on the Assay Commission in 1966 and on the council for the American Numismatic Society from 1960 to 1978.

Emery May Holden was born in Salt Lake City, Utah. She was the granddaughter of Liberty Emery Holden, who founded the Cleveland *Plain Dealer* newspaper. She and Henry Norweb were married in 1917 in Paris when he was stationed there with the U.S. diplomatic corps. She drove an ambulance and worked in French hospitals during The Great War. Their first son was born in a cellar during an air raid.

Emery Norweb served on the Assay Commission in 1955. She joined the American Numismatic Association in 1914, earning a 50-year membership medal in 1964. At the time of her death, she had been an ANA member nearly 70 years. She served on the American Numismatic Society council from 1969 to 1978.

Both Henry and Emery May Norweb died in hospitals in Cleveland.

The Norwebs donated a 1913 Liberty Head nickel to the Smithsonian Institution in 1978 to commemorate their wedding anniversary. Peters and Mohon cite an August 17, 1977, letter to Dr. V. Clain-Steffaneli, Curator of the Smithsonian's Division of Numismatics, in which Emery May Norweb (who was suffering from failing eyesight and wished to retire from coin collecting) wrote:

> The Norweb Collection would like to give the Smithsonian our Liberty head 1913 nickel on the celebration of our 60th wedding anniversary. It seems fitting that it should come to rest in Washington as my husband served over thirty years in the United States Diplomatic Service and retired with the permanent title of Ambassador. I, too, am glad to see it there as one of the great issues of the mint whether by mistake or design.

We will be valuing the piece at $225,000, since this is an asking price which has been published by a dealer in the June *Numismatist* 1977.

Our son, Henry Norweb, Jr., will bring the coin to you when he finds out which date you will be there to receive it. Our anniversary is October 18th so I hope you will not put the coin on display before that date.

Numismatic News News Editor Bob Lemke headlined his August 26, 1978 announcement of the donation "Smithsonian Institution Receives American Rarity":

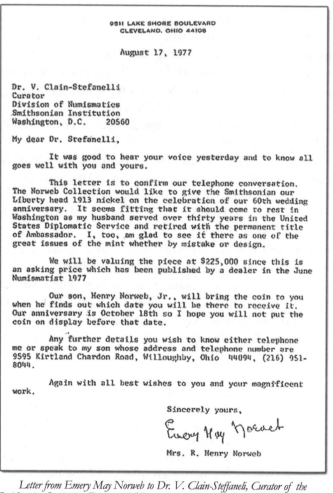

9511 LAKE SHORE BOULEVARD
CLEVELAND, OHIO 44108

August 17, 1977

Dr. V. Clain-Stefanelli
Curator
Division of Numismatics
Smithsonian Institution
Washington, D.C.   20560

My dear Dr. Stefanelli,

It was good to hear your voice yesterday and to know all goes well with you and yours.

This letter is to confirm our telephone conversation. The Norweb Collection would like to give the Smithsonian our Liberty head 1913 nickel on the celebration of our 60th wedding anniversary. It seems fitting that it should come to rest in Washington as my husband served over thirty years in the United States Diplomatic Service and retired with the permanent title of Ambassador. I, too, am glad to see it there as one of the great issues of the mint whether by mistake or design.

We will be valuing the piece at $225,000 since this is an asking price which has been published by a dealer in the June Numismatist 1977

Our son, Henry Norweb, Jr., will bring the coin to you when he finds out which date you will be there to receive it. Our anniversary is October 18th so I hope you will not put the coin on display before that date.

Any further details you wish to know either telephone me or speak to my son whose address and telephone number are 9595 Kirtland Chardon Road, Willoughby, Ohio 44094, (216) 951-8044.

Again with all best wishes to you and your magnificent work.

Sincerely yours,

Emery May Norweb

Mrs. R. Henry Norweb

Letter from Emery May Norweb to Dr. V. Clain-Steffaneli, Curator of the Smithsonian Institution Division of Numismatics, offering to donate the Norweb's 1913 Liberty Head nickel. "Courtesy of DLRC Press.

What is in effect the United States' national coin collection, at the Smithsonian Institution in Washington, D.C., has been enhanced through the donation of one of the five known specimens of the 1913 Liberty nickel.

Mrs. Emery-May Norweb, Cleveland, Ohio, donated the coin she bought at the King Farouk auction in 1954 for $3,750. Mrs. Norweb told the News she began the process of transferring the coin last year, in honor of the 60th anniversary of her wedding to R. Henry Norweb.

Lemke reported there had been a long, unexplained delay by the Smithsonian in publicly announcing acceptance of the gift:

> Mrs. Norweb could shed no light on why it has taken so long for the Smithsonian to release news of the donation. "I don't quite know all the machinations," she said, in reference to the Smithsonian's method of accession though a complex committee and departmental system. She added, "It's (the 1913 nickel) not something you'd want to put in an envelope with a two-cent stamp on it."

Radio news broadcaster Paul Harvey reported on August 16, 1978, that the donor had turned down a $300,000 offer for the coin. Lemke described her reaction:

> Mrs. Norweb laughed and said, "They (the press) can say what they want, but that's my private business."

Wayte Raymond

The page facing Samuel Brown's want ad for a 1913 Liberty Head nickel in the December 1919 issue of *The Numismatist* displayed a half-page ad for New York coin dealer Wayte Raymond, doing business under the auspices of Anderson Galleries at 489 Park Avenue. Raymond described himself as a "Dealer in rare coins of all countries."

Pete Smith's *American Numismatic Biographies* identifies Raymond simply as "Dealer and Publisher." Smith lists 43 books and monographs authored by Raymond and 20 titles by other authors that he published, including works by Eric Newman and Walter Breen. From 1934 to 1957, Raymond edited and published *The Standard Catalogue of United States Coins*, with later editions crediting John J. Ford as associate editor and Walter Breen as researcher.

By virtue of five ancestors who served in the Revolutionary War, Raymond was a member of the Sons of the Revolution. He was also a Mason (as was Samuel Brown).

Raymond joined the ANA at the age of 16 and later tried unsuccessfully to form a partnership with Fort Worth coin dealer B. Max Mehl. Instead, he pursued other partnerships and associations, during which time he employed such noted numismatists as John J. Ford, Walter Breen, Stuart Mosher, and Richard Kenney. Among his clients was the celebrated collector Colonel E.H.R. Green.

Smithsonian Institution

The Smithsonian Institution's National Museum of American History houses the National Numismatic Collection. It is the largest numismatic collection in North America and one of the largest in the world. The collection includes 1.6 million historical objects - more than 450,000 coins and 1.1 million pieces of paper currency.

The collection grew from a core of 18,000 pieces given to the Smithsonian in 1923 by the U.S. Mint. Though the collection includes specimens of history's earliest coins from 2,700 years ago, the emphasis is on the development of United States coins and medals.

The collection includes many priceless rarities, among them the Brasher half doubloon, 1849 double eagle, and two 1877 fifty dollar patterns. Among the most popular rarities in the collection are the 1913 Liberty Head nickel donated by Henry and Emery May Norweb), all three types of the 1804 dollar, and two of the three known 1933 double eagles.

Appendix C References

Allenbaugh, Carl H. 1972. "A Pair of Brash Contender Coins Challenge for the $100,000 Pinnacle - A History of Intrigue Surrounds The King of American Coins and Its Heir Presumptive." *Coin Prices* (May) pp. 1-5.

Bowers, Q. David. 1975. "The Legendary 1913 Liberty Head Nickel," Bowers and Ruddy Galleries *Rare Coin Review* 22 (Spring), p. 32-38.
— Bowers. 1991. *American Numismatic Association Centennial History Volume II* (Wolfeboro, New Hampshire: Bowers and Merena Galleries for American Numismatic Association), p. 460.
— Bowers. 1996. "The Louis E. Eliasberg, Sr., Collection," Bowers and Merena Galleries auction catalog (May 20-22), pp. 221-228.

— Bowers. 1997. *American Coin Treasures and Hoards.*

Certified Coins web site. 2003. Accessed October 21, 2003, at certifiedcoins.com/credentials.asp.

Coin World Almanac, Millennium Edition. 2000. (Sidney, Ohio: Amos Press) p. 560.

CoinWorld.com. 2003. "Legend Numismatics buys legend." Posted January 20, 2003. Web site accessed September 25, 2003, at http://www.coinworld.com/news/012703/news-5.asp.

Davis, M.D., Chief of Reference Service Branch, General Services Administration. 1962. Reply to Eric Newman regarding employment of August Wagner (July 6, 1962).

Deisher, Beth. 2001. "How'd you like to sell a 1913 five-cent for $2,000?" *Coin World* (June 11), p. 1.
— Deisher. 2003. "Liberty Head Legends," *Numismatist* (July), p. 37.
— Deisher. 2003. "Finest-known 1913 5¢ sets new price record." *Coin World* (August 18), pp. 2, 30.

Eliasberg, Richard A. 1996. "The Collector, My Father - A Biographical Sketch." From *Louis E. Eliasberg, Sr. King of Coins* by Q. David Bowers (Wolfeboro, New Hampshire: Bowers and Merena Galleries), pp. 1-7.

Gans, Edward, and Henry Grunthal. 1946. Mail Bid Sale and List of Prices Realized.

Gelbert, Doug. 2003. "Who Was Hetty Green?" Web site, accessed January 15, 2003, at http://coco.essortment.com/whowashettygr_ricf.htm.

Gibbs, William T. 1993. "Mystery surrounds pedigree of coin." *Coin World* (June 28), p. 1.

Gilkes, Paul. 1993. "Reed Hawn says time has come to pass along 'joy of ownership.'" *Coin World* (June 21), p. 1.

Hughes, C.W. & Co., Inc., Mechanicville, New York. Hetty Green residence picture postcard (1916).

Kagin, Art. 2003. Interview (October 17).

Kelly, James. 1967. Auction catalog, Annual ANA Convention, Miami, Florida (August 11).

Lemke, Bob. 1978. "Smithsonian Institution Receives American Rarity." *Numismatic News* (August 26), p. 3.

Lester, Carl N. 2003. Gold Rush Gallery web site - "Writers Corner - Numismatic Gumshoe: On the Trail of King Farouk." Accessed September 18, 2003, at www.goldrushgallery.com/gumshoe.html.

Lewis, Arthur H. 1963. *The Day They Shook the Plum Tree* (New York: Bantam Books/Harcourt, Brace & World), pp. 126-127.

McKenna, Alexander A. 1941. Letters to Eric Newman (December 16, 18, and 29).

Nationmaster.com Encyclopedia. 2003. "Gamel Abdel Nasser." Web site accessed January 7, 2004, at www.nationmaster.com/encyclopedia/Gamel-Abdel-Nasser.

Mervis, Clyde D. 1968. "World's Most Valuable Coin," *Numismatic Scrapbook Magazine.*

Newman, Eric P. "1913 Nickels," handwritten coin descriptions (undated).
— Newman, 1941. Letters to Alexander McKenna, (December 13 and 27).
— Newman, 1941. B.G. Johnson's inventory of 1913 Liberty nickels.
— Newman, 1943. B.G. Johnson's invoices for sales of 1913 Liberty Head nickels.
— Newman. 1976. *The Early Paper Money of America* (Iola, Wisconsin: Krause Publications, Inc.), jacket notes.
— Newman. 1996. Letter to Q. David Bowers (January 15).
— Newman. 2003. Interview (November 17).
— Newman. 2003. Email response to query about B.G. Johnson selling nickels to Col. E.H.R. Green (December 17).
— Newman. 2003. Email response to query about date notations on B.G. Johnson's inventory sheet (December 20).
— Newman. 2004. Email response to query about date and price of sale to Abe Kosoff (January 17).

New York State Historical Association web site. "The 1930s." Accessed December 21, 2003, at http://www.yorkers.org/leaflets/pdfs/1930s.S.pdf.

Numismatic Scrapbook Magazine. 1968. "World's Most Valuable Coin" (Vol. 34, No. 389, July), pp. 1064-1073.
— *Numismatic Scrapbook Magazine.* 1971. "Liberty 1913 Nickel Offers Mystic Aura" (Vol. 37, No. 430, December 24), p. 1158.
— *Numismatic Scrapbook Magazine.* 1973. "Liberty 1913 Nickel Story Footnotes" (April), p. 368-372.
— *Numismatic Scrapbook Magazine.* 1958. "Proof That Advertising Pays - The Story of the 1913 Liberty Head Nickel" (Vol. XXIV, No. 3, March), p. 457-459.

Numismatic News. 1974. "2½ Cents Worth of Famous Nickel Costs Bowers & Ruddy $100,000" (November 23), p. 51.
— *Numismatic News.* 1978. "Rare Liberty Nickel Fetches Record Price In Private Sale to Unnamed Show Biz Star" (July 22), p. 1.

The Numismatist. 1919. Wayte Raymond classified ad (Vol. XXXII, No. 12, December), p.512-513.
— *The Numismatist.* 1921. "The Rare 1913 Nickel" (January).
— *The Numismatist.* 1923. August Wagner classified ad (Vol. XXXVI, No. 12, December), p. 612.

— *The Numismatist*. 1924. August Wagner classified ad (Vol. XXXVII, No. 1, January), p. 51.

— *The Numismatist*. 1924. August Wagner classified ad (Vol. XXXVII, No. 2, February), p. 208

Ogilvie, Jack W. 1963. Letter to Don Taxay (October 14). Letter provided by Eric P. Newman.

Peters, Gloria, and Cynthia Mohon. 1995. *The Complete Guide to Shield & Liberty Head Nickels* (Virginia Beach, Virginia: DLRC Press), pp. 164-172.

Smith, Pete. *American Numismatic Biographies*, (Minneapolis, Minnesota: Remy Bourne-Ramm Communications, Inc.), pp. 43, 105, 129, 190-191.

Smithsonian Institution. 2004. "The National Numismatic Collection." Smithsonian National Museum of American History web site, accessed January 8, 2004, at americanhistory.si.edu/csr/cadnnc.htm.

Zerbe, Farran. 1937. Letter to Eric Newman responding to his inquiry about Missouri money in Colonel Green's collection (June 2).

BIBLIOGRAPHY

Adams, Mason. 2003. "Million-dollar mystery persists years after Roanoker's death." Roanoke (Virginia) *Times* (June 16). Reprinted with Permission. Copyright 2003, *The Roankoke Times*.

Allenbaugh, Carl H. 1972. "A Pair of Brash Contender Coins Challenge for the $100,000 Pinnacle - A History of Intrigue Surrounds The King of American Coins and Its Heir Presumptive." *Coin Prices* (May) pp. 1-5. Reprinted with permission of Krause Publications, Inc. © Krause Publications.

American Numismatic Association web site. Accessed November 2003 at www.money.org/h tml/edu nick.html.

Associated Press. "Secret Vault Yields $3 Bills Of Confederacy." Datelined "Roanoke." Date and publication unknown.

Borckardt, Mark. 2003. "Once-in-a-lifetime opportunity thrilling." *Coin World* (August 18), p. 10. Excerpts reprinted with permission of Coin World © *Coin World*.

Bowers, Q. David. 1975. "The Legendary 1913 Liberty Head Nickel," Bowers and Ruddy Galleries *Rare Coin Review* 22 (Spring), p. 32-38.
— Bowers. 1980. *Adventures with Rare Coins* (Los Angeles: Bowers and Ruddy Galleries, Inc.), pp. 6-15.
— Bowers. 1983. *United States Gold Coins, An Illustrated History* (Wolfeboro, New Hampshire: Bowers and Merena Galleries), p. 84.
— Bowers. 1991. *American Numismatic Association Centennial History Volume II* (Wolfeboro, New Hampshire: Bowers and Merena Galleries for American Numismatic Association), p. 460.
— Bowers. 1996. "The Louis E. Eliasberg, Sr., Collection," Bowers and Merena Galleries auction catalog (May 20-22), pp. 221-228.
— Bowers. 1997. *American Coin Treasures and Hoards.*
— Bowers. 2002. *More Adventures with Rare Coins* (Bowers and Merena Galleries), p. 316-317.
Excerpts reprinted with permission of Bowers & Merena Galleries, Inc. © Bowers & Merena Galleries.

Breen, Walter. 1988. *Complete Encyclopedia of US and Colonial Coins* (New York: Doubleday), pp. 246-254.

Brown, Samuel W. 1919. Classified ad, *The Numismatist* (Vol. XXXII, No. 12, December), p. 513.
— Brown. 1920. Classified ad, *The Numismatist* (Vol. XXXIII, No. 1, January), p. 44.

Brown, Stacia. 2003. "The Ninety Years of Liberty Gala: A Night in Pictures." *Comic Book Marketplace* (Vol. 3, No. 105, August), pp. 37-40. Excerpts reprinted with permission of Diamond International, Inc. © Diamond International.

Brumfield, Sarah. 2003. "Missing 1913 Liberty Head Nickel Appears." Associated Press wire story (July 30). ©Associated Press. All rights reserved. Distributed by Valeo IP.

Cassel, David. 2003. "Glossary of Numismatic Terms." Accessed November 2003 at www.uspatterns.com/uspatterns/glossary1.html.

Certified Coins web site. 2003. Accessed October 21, 2003 at certifiedcoins.com/credentials.asp.

Charlotte Observer. 1959. "$35,000 Nickel Isn't For Sale" (October 15), p. 8-C. Excerpts reprinted with permission of *The Charlotte Observer.* © *The Charlotte Observer.*

Coe, William D. 2003. Letters: "Rochester Club Viewed American Legends in 1920" (Vol. 116, No. 10, October), p. 14.

CoinPeople.com's Virtual Coin Museum web site. Accessed November 2003 at www.coinpeople.com/forums/viewtopic.php?t=74.

Coin World. 1962. "Car Crash Fatal To Nickel Owner" (March 23), p. 1.
— *Coin World.* 1963. "Three Numismatic Scholars Share Comments On Controversial Nickel" (December 27), p. 26.
— *Coin World.* 2003. "Walton 1913 5¢ on loan to ANA" (September 8), pp. 1, 95, 98.
— *Coin World.* 2003. "NGC confirms authenticity of Walton 1913 Liberty nickel" (September 29), p. 76.
Excerpts reprinted with permission of Coin World © *Coin World.*

CoinWorld.com. 2003. "Legend Numismatics buys legend." Posted January 20, 2003. Web site accessed September 25, 2003, at http://www.coinworld.com/news/012703/news-5.asp.

Coin World Almanac, Millennium Edition. 2000. (Sidney, Ohio: Amos Press) p. 560.

DC Superman National Comics. "Superman's Girl Friend Lois Lane" JAN No. 54 (1965). © 1965 DC Comics. All Rights Reserved. Used with permission.

Davis, M.D., Chief of Reference Service Branch, General Services Administration. 1962. Official transcript of employment of Samuel W. Brown (July 6, 1962).

Deisher, Beth. 2001. "How'd you like to sell a 1913 five-cent for $2,000?" *Coin World* (June 11), p. 1.
— Deisher. 2003. "Liberty Head Legends," *Numismatist* (July), p. 37.
— Deisher. 2003. "Found!" *Coin World* (August 18), p. 1.
— Deisher. 2003. "Finest-known 1913 5¢ sets new price record." *Coin World* (August 18), pp. 2, 30.
Excerpts reprinted with permission of Coin World © *Coin World.*

Dickerson, Bill. 1999. "The Man Who Could Stop the Mint," PCGS, Professional Coin Grading Service web site. Dated June 1999. Accessed November 2003.

Eliasberg, Richard A. 1996. "The Collector, My Father - A Biographical Sketch."

From *Louis E. Eliasberg, Sr. King of Coins* by Q. David Bowers (Wolfeboro, New Hampshire: Bowers and Merena Galleries), pp. 1-7.

Etymology Online web site. Accessed December 2003 at www.etymonline.com/j2etym.htm.

Evans, George G. 1885. "Coining Press" illustration by F.B. Schell, *Illustrated History of the United States Mint* (Philadelphia: Dunlap & Clark), p. 38.

Evans, Torence. 2003. "Freemasonry - The 1913 Liberty Head Nickel & Its Masonic Link", The Masonic Forum on AOL web site. Accessed December 2003 at members.aol.com/forumlead/History/Freemasonry-1913.htm.

Gans, Edward, and Henry Grunthal. 1946. Mail Bid Sale and List of Prices Realized.

Ganz, David L. 1993. "Officials claim some famous rarities illegal," *Coin World* (October 4). Excerpts reprinted with permission of David Ganz and Coin World

Garrett, Jeff, and Ron Guth. 2003. *100 Greatest U.S. Coins* (Atlanta: Whitman Publishing), p. 10-11.

Garrison, Milton. "Collector's 'Find' Yields $3 Bills." Roanoke (Virginia) *Times*, p. B-1,2. Date unknown.

Gelbert, Doug. 2003. "Who Was Hetty Green?" Web site, accessed January 15, 2003, at http://coco.essortment.com/whowashettygr_ricf.htm.

Gibbs, William T. 1993. "Mystery surrounds pedigree of coin." *Coin World* (June 28), p. 1, 12, 17. Excerpts reprinted with permission of Coin World © *Coin World.*

Giedroyc, Richard. 1993. "Where is lost specimen of 1913 Liberty Head 5 cents?" *Coin World* (Vol. 34, No. 1732, June 21), pp. 1, 12.
— Giedroyc. 1993. "Attorney confirms tale that 1913 Liberty 5 cents in crash was fake." *Coin World* (Vol. 34, No. 1750, October 25), pp. 1,26.
— Giedroyc. "Location of 1913 5¢ still unknown." *Coin World.*
Excerpts reprinted with permission of Coin World © *Coin World.*

Gilkes, Paul. 1993. "Reed Hawn says time has come to pass along 'joy of ownership.'" *Coin World* (June 21), p. 1.
— Gilkes. 2002. "1933 double eagle brings $7.59 million!" (posted July 30, 2002), CoinWorld.com web site. Accessed December 5, 2003, at www.coinworld.com/news/081202/News_bulletin1.asp.
— Gilkes. 2003. "Secret Service assumes control of investigation," *Coin World* (August 25), pp. 1, 18.
Excerpts reprinted with permission of Coin World © *Coin World.*

Greensboro (N.C.) *Daily News.* 1959. "1913 Liberty Head Nickel Is Rare; Only Five Minted" (October 10). p. B-1. Excerpts reprinted with permission of the *News & Record.*

Harmer, Rooke & Co., Inc. 1963. Auction catalog for George Walton's stamp collection (September 11-13).

Hight, Mitch. 2003. Coin-Gallery Online web site. Accessed November 2003 at www.coin-gallery.com/cguscoinage.htm.

The Hindu. 2003. "Missing nickel appears" (August 9). Web site accessed February 27, 2003 at http://www.hindu.com/thehindu/yw/2003/08/09/stories/2003080901470400.htm.

Herald Tribune News Service, New York. 1963. "Walton Coin Sale Shatters Record" (October 6).

Hughes, Brent H. 1971. "The 1913 Liberty Head Nickel," Slide presentation.

Kelly, James. 1967. Auction catalog, Annual ANA Convention, Miami, Florida (August 11).

Legal Information Institute. 2004. United States Code. Web site accessed February 11, 2004, at www4.law.cornell.edu/uscode/.

Lemke, Bob. 1978. "Smithsonian Institution Receives American Rarity." *Numismatic News* (August 26), p. 3. Excerpts reprinted with permission of Krause Publications, Inc. © Krause Publications, Inc.

Lester, Carl N. 2003. Gold Rush Gallery web site - "Writers Corner - Numismatic Gumshoe: On the Trail of King Farouk." Accessed September 18, 2003, at www.goldrushgallery.com/gumshoe.html. Excerpts reprinted with permission of Carl Lester. Courtesy of www.goldrushgallery.com. © Carl Lester.

Lewis, Arthur H. 1963. *The Day They Shook the Plum Tree* (New York: Bantam Books/Harcourt, Brace & World), pp. 126-127.

Jordan, Louis. University of Notre Dame web site. Accessed November 2003 at www.coins.nd.edu/ColCoin/ColCoinIntros/HalfDisme.intro.html.

Julian, R.W. 1987. *Coin World* (April).
— Julian. 2001. "Hackel's Mint Record Destruction." Numismatic Bibliomania Society E-Sylum web site (Vol. 4, No. 22, May 27), accessed November 10, 2003 at www.coinbooks.org/club_nbs_esylum_v04n22.html.
— Julian. 2003. "Five-cent coins remain staple of circulating coinage in U.S.," *Coin World* (November 24), p. 16.
Excerpts reprinted with permission of R.W. Julian. © R.W. Julian.

McCausland, Christianna. 2003. "A dream party for collectors and a record sale." *Baltimore* magazine (Vol. 96, No. 10, October), pp. 58-59. Reprinted with permission by Diamond International Galleries.

McElheny, Victor K. "George O. Walton Kept To Himself." Charlotte, North Carolina, *Observer.* Date unknown. Excerpts reprinted with permission of *The Charlotte Observer.* © *The Charlotte Observer.*

McNeil, Robert B. 1956. "$50 Coin Collector Started With Ordeal." Richmond (Virginia) *News Leader* (October 18), p. 6. Excerpts reprinted with permission of *News Leader* © *The Times-Dispatch.*

The MANA Journal, "E.G.J." 1962. "In Memoriam - George Walton." Middle Atlantic Numismatic Association (April, May, June) p. 8-9.

Mervis, Clyde D. 1968. "World's Most Valuable Coin," *Numismatic Scrapbook Magazine*, pp. 1064-1073. Excerpts reprinted with permission of *Numismatic Scrapbook Magazine*. © Amos Press, Inc.

Morris County Library. 2003. "How much did it cost in Morris County, New Jersey?" Web site accessed September 2003 at www.gti.net/mocolib1/prices/1912.html.

Morris, Evan. 2003. The Word Detective web site. Accessed December 2003 at www.word-detective.com/070698.html.

Murdock, Dan. 2003. "Unethical behavior," Letters to the editor, *Coin World* (August 25), p. 11. Excerpts reprinted with Permission of *Coin World* © Coin World.

National Archives and Records Administration. 2004. Web site accessed February 11, 2004, at www.archives.gov/welcome.

Nationmaster.com Encyclopedia. 2003. "Gamel Abdel Nasser." Web site accessed January 7, 2004, at www.nationmaster.com/encyclopedia/Gamel-Abdel-Nasser.

Newman, Eric P. 1978. Letter to the editor "A few corrections." Coin World (August 13), p. 4. Excerpts reprinted with Permission of Eric Newman.

New York State Historical Association web site. "The 1930s." Accessed December 21, 2003, at http://www.yorkers.org/leaflets/pdfs/1930s.S.pdf.

Numismatic News. 1973. "Mint Would Confiscate '64 Dollars," (Vol. XXI, No. 9, February 27, 1973), p. 1, 8.
— *Numismatic News*. 1973. "Mint Ready to Seize 1964 Dollars, Maybe 1913 'V' Nickels, Too," (Vol. XXI, No. 25, June 19, 1973), p. 1, 48.
— *Numismatic News*. 1974. "2½ Cents Worth of Famous Nickel Costs Bowers & Ruddy $100,000" (November 23), p. 51.
— *Numismatic News*. 1978. "Rare Liberty Nickel Fetches Record Price In Private Sale to Unnamed Show Biz Star" (July 22), p. 1.
— *Numismatic News*. 1978. "Smithsonian Institution Receives American Rarity" (August 26), p. 3.
Excerpts reprinted with permission of Krause Publications, Inc. © Krause Publications, Inc.

Numismatic Scrapbook Magazine. 1953. "Looks Like There Are Six 1913 Liberty Head Nickels." (December), p. 1169.
— *Numismatic Scrapbook Magazine*. 1958. "Proof That Advertising Pays - The Story of the 1913 Liberty Head Nickel" (Vol. XXIV, No. 3, March), p. 457-459.
— *Numismatic Scrapbook Magazine*. 1968. "World's Most Valuable Coin" (Vol. 34, No. 389, July), pp. 1064-1073.
— *Numismatic Scrapbook Magazine*. 1971. "Liberty 1913 Nickel Offers Mystic Aura" (Vol. 37, No. 430, December 24), pp. 1158-1178.
— *Numismatic Scrapbook Magazine*. 1973. "Liberty 1913 Nickel Story Footnotes"

(April), p. 368, 370, 372.

Excerpts reprinted with permission of *Numismatic Scrapbook Magazine.* © Amos Press, Inc.

The Numismatist. 1913. "Proceedings of the Annual Convention" (Vol. XXVI, No. 10, October), pp. 487-503.

— *The Numismatist.* 1919. Wayte Raymond, Samuel W. Brown classified ads (Vol. XXXII, No. 12, December), p. 512-513.

— *The Numismatist.* 1920. Samuel W. Brown classified (Vol. XXXIII, No. 1, January), p. 44.

— *The Numismatist.* 1920. Samuel W. Brown classified (Vol. XXXIII, No. 2, February), p. 90.

— *The Numismatist.* 1920. Samuel W. Brown classified (Vol. XXXIII, No. 3, March), p. 131.

— *The Numismatist.* 1920. "Notes of the Convention," (October), p.466.

— *The Numismatist.* 1921. "The Rare 1913 Nickel" (January), p. 17.

— *The Numismatist.* 1923. August Wagner classified ad (Vol. XXXVI, No. 12, December), p. 612.

— *The Numismatist.* 1924. August Wagner classified ad (Vol. XXXVII, No. 1, January), p. 51.

— *The Numismatist.* 1924. August Wagner classified ad (Vol. XXXVII, No. 2, February), p. 208.

— *The Numismatist.* 1928. "Two Extreme Rarities in Recent U.S. Coinage" (Vol. XLI, No. 4, April), p. 236.

— *The Numismatist.* 1944. Samuel W. Brown obituary notice (August), p. 707.

Excerpts reprinted with permission of *The Numistmatist.* © *American Numismatic Association*

Numismaticworld. 2003. "1933 Saint-Gaudens Auction Ignites Red Hot Coin Market at New York ANA," (Blanchard and Company , Inc. web site Numismaticworld, Vol. 4, No. 1), accessed December 5, 2003, at http://numismaticworld.net/vol4-1/article1.html.

Numismedia. 2003. Series Spotlight: Liberty Head Nickels. Web site accessed August 19, 2003, at www.numismedia.com/series/liberty5.shtml.

Ogilvie, Jack W. 1963. Letter to Don Taxay (October 14). Letter provided by Eric P. Newman.

O'Reilly's Plaza Art Gallery. 1963. Auction notice of George Walton antique and gold watch collection (October 3).

Parrino, Jay. 2003. The Mint (Kansas City, Missouri) web site, accessed January 11, 2003, at http://www.jp-themint.com/about.cfm.

Pearlman, Donn. 2003. "New Hampshire Coin Dealer Offers $1+ Million Reward for Missing Nickel" (Press release, May 23). Reprinted with permission. © Minkus & Pearlman Public Relations, Inc.

Peters, Gloria, and Cynthia Mohon. 1995. *The Complete Guide to Shield & Liberty*

Head Nickels (Virginia Beach, Virginia: DLRC Press), pp. 2-7; 46-47, 164-172. Reprinted with Permission.© DLRC Press.

The Plaza Art Galleries, Inc. 1963. Auction catalog for George Walton books and documents collection (October 3).

Ratzman, Leonard J. 1964. "The Buffalo Nickel, A 50-Year-Old Mystery," *Whitman Numismatic Journal* (Vol. 1, No. 5, May), p. 21.

Reiter, Ed. 1994. "Flirting with a Million," *COINage* (Vol. 9), p. 109. Excerpt reprinted with Permission.© COINage, Inc.

Ruddy, James F. 2003. *Photograde* (Irvine: Zyrus Press, Inc. by license from Bowers and Merena Galleries, Irvine, California), p. 14.

Sheets, J.G. & Sons. 1962. Print ads and mailers for George O. Walton Antique Firearms Auction.

Shelton, Ted. 1960. "N.C. Collectors Win Awards." *The Greenville News*, South Carolina (October 18).

Smith, Pete. 1992. *American Numismatic Biographies* (Minneapolis, Minnesota: Remy Bourne-Ramm Communications, Inc.), pp. 37, 43, 105, 129, 190-191.

Smithsonian Institution. 2004. "The National Numismatic Collection." Smithsonian National Museum of American History web site accessed January 8, 2004, at americanhistory.si.edu/csr/cadnnc.htm.

Snyder, John K. 2003. "90 Years of Liberty" poster (Baltimore: American Numismatic Association, Diamond International Galleries.)

Stack's. 1993. "Records Are Made To Be Broken!" Post-sale full-page ad in *Coin World* (November 8), p. 29.

Superior Stamp & Coin Co., Inc. 1978. Press release: "1913 Liberty Nickel Sold by Superior for $200,000.00 to Anonymous Collector." Reprinted with permission of Superior Galleries © Superior Galleries

Taxay, Don. 1963. *Counterfeit, Mis-Struck, and Unofficial U.S. Coins* (New York: Arco Publishing Company, Inc.), p. 15.
— Taxay. 1963. Personal correspondence to Eric P. Newman (October 22, November 17, December 18).
— Taxay. 1966-69. *The U.S. Mint and Coinage* (New York: Arco Publishing Company, Inc.), pp. 340-346.

Tirell-Wysocki, David. 2003. "Coin Experts Hope Reward Will Uncover Mystery Nickel" (AP Wire, May 26). ©Associated Press. All rights reserved. Distributed by Valeo IP.

United States Department of the Treasury. 2003. "Important Events in Treasury History in November." Web site, accessed November 10, 2003, at www.ustreas.gov/education/history/events/11-nov.html.

Van Ryzin, Robert R. 1993. "Tale of 1913 Liberty Head nickel fit for Hollywood."

Numismatic News (October 15), p. 16. Excerpts reprinted with permission of Krause Publications, Inc. © Krause Publications, Inc.

Venn, Theodore J. 1921. "The Best Way to Create an Interest in Coins," *The Numismatist* (Vol. XXXIV, No. 1, January), p. 3. Excerpts reprinted with permission of *The Numistmatist*. © American Numismatic Association

Walker, Laurens. "$50,000 Nickel Is Banked Here." Charlotte, North Carolina, *Observer* (date unknown). Excerpts reprinted with permission of *The Charlotte Observer*. © *The Charlotte Observer*.

Weekly Reader. 2003. "A Million-Dollar Nickel" (Vol. 82 No. 4, September 19), p. 6.

Wilson, North Carolina, *Daily Times*. 1962. "Coin Show to Feature Famous 1913 'V' Nickel" (March 9).

— Wilson *Daily Times*. 1962. "Wreck Kills Coin Expert Bringing $250,000 Exhibit to Wilson Show" (March 10).

— Wilson *Daily Times*. 1962. "More Than 2,000 Visit Coin Show in Wilson" (March 12).

Excerpts reprinted with permission of the *Wilson Daily Times*. © *Wilson Daily Times*

Woodin, William H., Secretary of the Treasury. 1933. "Under Executive Order of the President," Publication 2-16064, U.S. Government Printing Office.

The Word Detective web site. Accessed December 2003 at www.word-detective.com/070698.html.

Zerbe, Farran. 1937. Letter to Eric Newman responding to his inquiry about Missouri money (June 2).

Index

"V" Nickel: 27, 30, 193.
100 Greatest U.S. Coins: 16, 19, 265, 277, 357.
1804 Draped Bust dollar: 158, 337.
1913 Liberty Head nickel: 2, 15-17, 19, 21, 39, 53-54, 56, 60, 62-63, 66-67, 69, 71-72, 74-75, 80, 84-85, 88, 91, 98-100, 103-104, 112, 121-125, 138-139, 145-148, 150, 152-154, 157-158, 160-164, 166-174, 178-180, 183, 185, 189, 192, 202, 210, 212, 215-221, 225, 228-229, 231, 234-235, 241, 245, 247, 250, 253-254, 263, 269, 272, 275, 288, 296-297, 304, 307, 313, 315-316, 322-325, 337, 343-344, 347-350, 352, 355, 357-359, 362.
1933 Saint-Gaudens: 80-82, 86-87, 89, 160, 335, 360.
Act of March 3, 1865: 23.
Adams, Eva: 47, 49-50, 65, 323.
Adams, Mason: 9, 248, 303.
Allenbaugh, Carl H: 179, 350, 355.
altered date: 153, 172, 210-217, 238, 253, 260-262, 286, 305, 324.
Alton, Illinois: 150.
A-Mark Precious Metals: 155.
American Numismatic Association: 5-6, 16, 19, 30, 73, 80, 84, 91, 97, 100, 107-110, 113, 139, 151, 158, 160, 167, 173-174, 179, 201, 214, 218, 227, 234-236, 238, 253, 272, 296-297, 299-300, 308, 315, 320, 324, 335-336, 342, 346-347, 350, 355, 361.
ANA: 60, 66, 70, 80, 85, 89, 93-94, 96, 98, 101, 110, 113, 118, 123, 134, 139, 144, 150, 152, 158, 168, 173, 175-179, 213, 225-232, 236, 244-245, 249, 253-254, 259, 264, 267, 270-272, 275, 277, 280-281, 284, 295, 301-303, 308-311, 313, 315, 321, 325, 330-331, 335, 338, 341-342, 344, 346-347,

350-351, 356, 358, 360.
American Numismatic Biographies: 104, 140, 169, 176, 180, 213, 349, 353, 361.
Anderson Galleries: 121, 349.
Appalachian Federation of Coin Clubs: 202.
Archivist: 49-50.
Ashby, Jamie: 244.
Assay Commission: 68, 97, 189, 322, 346-347.
Associated Press: 202, 221, 225, 235-237, 246, 248, 267, 280, 289, 295-296, 302, 313, 355.
Atlanta: 19, 101, 153, 158, 265, 357.
Auction: 16, 56, 62, 71, 81, 89, 113, 120-121, 139, 146, 149-151, 155, 157-161, 166-167, 171, 177, 179, 204-207, 209-211, 214-215, 217, 221-222, 226, 233, 235, 243-245, 252, 260, 296-299, 301, 306, 323-324, 328, 332, 335-337, 342, 349-351, 355, 357-358, 360-361.
Augusta, Georgia: 200.
Baker, Gail: 270.
Baldwin & Co: 145.
Baltimore: 14, 19, 66, 85, 167, 202, 226-227, 229-230, 232, 234-236, 238, 253, 255, 259-260, 264-265, 267-268, 272-273, 277, 280, 287, 289-290, 295-299, 302, 304-305, 311-312, 315, 323, 325, 336, 358, 361.
Baltimore Convention Center: 227, 255, 259, 268, 287, 297.
Barber, Charles E.: 28, 57, 320.
Barber, Charles Edward: 27, 58.
Barks, Carl: 272, 275.
Barnum, P.T.: 123, 343.
BBC: 301-302.
Bebee, Adeline: 84, 113, 173, 227, 324.
Bebee, Aubrey: 84-85, 170, 177-178, 183.
Bernard vs. the United States: 85.
Blanchard, James U.: 226.
Blue Ridge Numismatic Association: 202.
Bobbitt, Stephen: 9, 280, 315.

Bolt, Dr. Conway A.: 169-170, 208, 322.
Booth, Professor James: 24.
Borckardt, Mark: 1-2, 6, 13, 134, 222, 233, 236, 241-242, 244-245, 247, 254-255, 259, 268-271, 278, 281, 283, 287, 293, 298, 303, 305, 312, 315, 330.
Borgos, Henry: 47.
Boston: 122, 213, 235, 242.
BOWERS AND MERENA GALLERIES: 2, 6-7, 14, 37, 62-63, 88, 139, 179, 226, 228, 232-234, 237, 239, 246, 266, 296, 307, 310, 313, 315, 330, 332, 337, 350-351, 355, 357, 361.
Bowers and Ruddy Galleries: 19, 33, 62, 88, 139, 149, 152, 155, 226, 337, 341, 350, 355.
Bowers, Q. David: 6, 9, 16, 33, 67, 121, 161-162, 179-180, 226, 273, 275, 325, 340-341, 351-352, 356.
Bowman, Harold: 248-249.
Boyd, F.C.C.: 113, 122, 137-138, 143-144, 151, 185, 322, 335.
Boyer, Alden Scott: 54.
Boykin, Ira E.: 194.
Brady, Eric: 252, 254.
Breen, Walter: 40, 121, 349-350.
Brillinger, Mrs. George: 70-71, 88, 97.
Bristol, Virginia: 202.
Brooks, Mary: 49.
Brown, Carry B.: 97.
Brown, Samuel W.: 14, 33, 39, 54, 60, 68, 70, 74, 87, 91, 93, 95-98, 103-104, 112, 115, 321-322, 356, 360.
Brown, Stacia: 271.
Brumfield, Sarah: 280, 289, 293, 295-296.
Buffalo nickel: 30, 34-37, 39, 54, 56, 63, 72-73, 122, 237, 297, 361.
Buono, Victor: 153.
Bureau of the Mint: 65, 79.
Buss, Dr. Jerry: 113, 149, 156-157, 324, 331.
Calhoun, John C.: 26.
California Gold Marketing Group: 161, 167.
Callaway, Virginia: 204.

caprice: 39, 71, 128.
Carey, Mike: 70, 96.
Carlson, Sam: 175.
Carson City: 262.
Chapman, Henry: 40, 120, 344.
Charlotte Coin Club: 199.
Charlotte, North Carolina: 184, 187, 221-222, 227, 358, 362.
Chicago: 54, 70, 96, 98-102, 174-175, 205, 235, 321, 340.
Chicago Coin Club: 96, 100.
Chinese auction: 155.
Christmas: 36, 40-41, 61-62, 132, 199, 241, 342.
Cipoletti, Christopher: 227, 300.
Civil War: 22, 203, 206, 319.
Clark, Spencer M.: 23.
Clark, William: 23.
Cleveland: 40, 70-71, 88, 97, 347, 349.
CNN: 301.
cobalt: 24.
Cochran, Bill: 205.
Coe, William D.: 9, 102-103.
Cohen, Brian: 73.
Coin Prices: 174, 179, 350, 355.
Coin World: 13, 15-16, 57, 63, 69, 71-72, 74-76, 78, 82, 85, 87-88, 91, 124-125, 133, 139, 144, 146, 151-152, 154, 158, 163, 167-168, 170, 179-180, 184, 189, 195-196, 199, 212-215, 217, 221, 225, 227, 236, 238, 249, 253, 260-261, 271, 296, 300-301, 303, 305, 309, 313, 323-324, 339, 341-342, 345-346, 351, 355-359, 361.
Coinage: 21-22, 24, 30, 34, 37-38, 46, 56-61, 63, 65, 68-69, 79-80, 89, 98, 319, 321, 358, 360-361.
Cole, Al: 199.
Collectors Universe: 9, 226, 232-234, 243, 245, 264, 302, 315.
Colorado Springs: 80, 158, 179, 227, 235, 253, 315, 346.
Complete Guide to Shield and Liberty Head Nickels, The: 21, 30, 60, 63, 89, 104, 140, 169, 180, 332, 353, 361.
Concord, New Hampshire: 235-236, 246, 267.
Confederacy: 22, 221, 355.
Confer, Kelly: 275.

confiscation: 71, 74, 83, 85-86.
Congress: 23-24, 175, 200, 319.
Connecticut State Library: 205.
Continental Congress: 200.
Copper: 15, 22-26, 28, 55, 78-79, 116, 133-134, 145, 161, 163, 218, 319, 337.
Cornely, Robert: 154.
counterfeit: 36, 39, 63, 211-212, 217, 320, 361.
Counterfeit, Mis-Struck, and Unofficial U.S. Coins: 39, 63, 361.
Cullum, S.A.: 175.
Daily News: 40, 63, 186-187, 202, 221, 357.
Dallas: 6, 175, 246, 315, 340.
D'Amato, Donald: 206.
Dannreuther, John: 9, 13, 46, 66, 74, 255, 259-261, 267-269, 271, 278, 280-281, 283, 287-289, 303, 306, 312, 330, 337.
Dannreuther, John ("J.D."): 18.
Dayton, Ohio: 56, 138, 149, 341.
de Silva, Buddy: 156.
Declaration of Independence: 200-201.
Deisher, Beth: 15, 124, 133, 160, 163, 168-169, 189, 227-228, 231, 236, 238, 249, 253, 261-262, 271, 296, 300-302, 305, 325, 342.
Denver: 28, 57, 65, 84.
Denver Mint: 84.
Detroit: 59, 98.
Diamond International Galleries: 19, 168, 230-231, 265, 272, 274, 280, 300, 361.
Dickerson, Bill: 27.
die: 39-41, 45-46, 49-50, 58, 69, 71-74, 79, 98, 134, 248, 254, 263, 282-285, 330.
Disney: 16, 272.
Dodge City, Kansas: 205.
Doty, Richard: 229.
double eagle: 34, 71, 74, 80-82, 84, 86-88, 101, 160, 335-336, 350, 357.
Drew, Nancy: 16, 149.
Duffield, Frank G.: 59, 125.
Duffy, G.C.: 207.
Eastern North Carolina: 193.
Economy, Sonny: 196.
Edwin M. Hydeman Collection

of United States Coins: 152.
Egypt: 81, 85, 113, 143-145, 150, 322-323, 331, 335, 337-338.
Ehrlich, Governor Robert: 275.
Eliasberg, Louis: 15, 39, 113, 161, 164-166, 202, 323.
Eliasberg, Louis E , Sr: 62, 163, 166, 179, 235, 328, 332, 336, 350-351, 355-356.
Emmy: 154.
Encino, California: 265.
engraver: 26-27, 36, 38, 40, 45-46, 57-58, 60, 72, 74, 153, 320-321, 344.
E-Sylum: 47-48, 63, 358.
Evans, George G.: 53.
Evans, Robert: 280.
Executive Order: 80-81, 89, 362.
fabric: 116, 262, 284.
Fahnestock, Wayne: 96-97.
Fairchild, C.S.: 79.
fake: 153, 161-162, 172, 207, 210-211, 213-214, 217, 221, 250-252, 260-262, 264, 279, 282-283, 286, 288, 302, 304-305, 324, 357.
Federal Deposit Insurance Corporation: 265.
Federal Record Act of 1950: 49.
Federal Register: 49.
Federal Trade Commission: 265.
Feuchtwanger, Dr. Lewis: 23, 319.
five-cent: 16, 21, 23, 25, 29, 34-35, 55, 57-59, 75, 115, 122, 124, 133, 139, 179, 319-320, 351, 356, 358.
flans: 26.
Florida United Numismatists: 167, 310.
Ford, James A.: 188, 192, 210.
Ford, John J. Jr.: 75.
Fort Worth, Texas: 53, 123-124, 343.
fractional currency: 23.
Franklin Institute: 24.
Fraser, James Earle: 34-35, 37, 62, 321.
Fred Olsen: 113, 149 150, 322, 331.
Friedberg, Robert: 265, 277.
Frontier Chocolate Company: 96.
Fuld, George: 213.

FUN show: 225-226, 310-311, 315, 325.
Gans, Edward: 151.
Ganz, David L.: 85.
Gap Nickel Mine: 25, 319.
Garner, North Carolina: 195.
Garrett, Jeff: 16, 264-265, 270-271, 277, 279, 281-282, 284, 287, 303-304, 312.
Garrison, Milton: 202.
General Services Administration: 95, 103, 118-119, 139, 351, 356.
Geppi, Stephen A.: 272.
German silver: 23-24.
Gibbs, William T.: 16, 151, 184.
Giedroyc, Richard: 195, 212-213.
Gilkes, Paul: 82, 85, 87, 158, 341.
Gilliam, R.E.: 194.
Gillio, Ronald J.: 309.
Givens, Bette: 172, 253.
Givens, Melva: 172, 188, 196, 199, 215, 217, 219-220, 253.
Givens, Melva W.: 113, 172.
Givens, Richard: 172, 253.
Givens, Ryan: 172, 188, 199, 201, 210, 217, 251, 253-254, 260-261, 266, 269, 271, 277, 288-289, 293-294, 300, 306, 312.
Glass, Dr. Brent D.: 231.
Gobrecht, Christian: 26.
Gogginsville Methodist Church: 196.
gold: 15, 22-23, 27-29, 34, 55, 62, 80-82, 85, 113, 145, 148, 159, 161, 167, 180, 186, 188, 193, 199, 201-204, 206, 212, 218, 222, 249, 272, 275, 280, 319-320, 327, 335-337, 343-344, 351, 355, 358, 360.
Goldberg, Ira: 156-157.
Good Morning America: 239-241, 243, 297-299.
Green, Col. E.H.R.: 54, 112, 117, 120, 139, 163, 322, 352.
Green, Hetty: 40, 139, 179, 339, 351, 357.
Greensboro: 40, 63, 185-187, 202, 221, 357.
Greensboro, North Carolina: 221.
Greenville, South Carolina: 202.
Greg Manning Auctions, Inc: 315.

Grunthal, Henry: 151, 179, 351, 357.
Guinness Book of World Records: 149, 152.
guns: 23, 171, 193, 198, 204, 280, 295.
Guth, Ron: 16, 19, 265, 277, 357.
Hahn-Johnson, Kelly: 252.
half dime: 22.
Hall, David: 9, 232, 254, 264-265, 271, 278-279, 281-283, 286-288, 295, 303, 312.
Hammer, Gordon R.: 206.
Hamrick, John: 9.
Hardy Boys: 16, 149.
Harmer, Rooke & Co., Inc: 206, 221, 357.
Harrington, Katrina: 237, 244.
Harris, Belinda: 249, 303.
Harris, Ellen: 200.
Hawaii Five-O: 16, 149, 153-154, 225, 324.
Hawn, Reed: 113, 149, 157-158, 179, 214, 225, 324, 331, 341, 351, 357.
Hayden, Eleonora: 48.
Haynes, Michael: 9, 232.
Heath, Dr. George F. : 93.
Hewitt, Lee: 38, 67, 69, 71, 78, 188, 191.
Hickory Museum of Art: 184.
Hickory, North Carolina: 184.
Highway 264: 194.
Hilbig, Valeska : 273-274.
Hobbs Manufacturing Company: 36.
Holsman, Henrietta: 82.
Hotel Cherry: 193.
Huang, George: 160, 225, 230, 272.
hub: 39, 72.
Hughes, Brent: 66, 117.
Hughes, Robert L.: 113, 155.
Hyatt Regency: 278.
Hyattsville, Maryland: 207.
Hydeman, Edwin: 149, 151, 324, 331.
Hynds, Gene: 310.
Illustrated History of the United States Mint: 53, 62, 357.
In God We Trust: 26.
Industry Council for Tangible Assets: 226.
Iowa: 176, 204.

Irvine, California: 159, 225.
Ivy, Steve: 246-247.
J.G. Sheets & Sons: 204.
Jack W. Ogilvie: 70, 73, 96.
Jackson, Clarence R.: 196.
Jacksonville, Florida: 184, 192, 198, 219.
James Smithson Society: 148.
Jefferson Coin and Bullion: 226.
Jefferson Hotel: 201.
Johnson, B.G.: 54-56, 112, 116-117, 120, 133, 135, 137-140, 143, 149-150, 161, 164, 169, 173, 185-186, 322, 344, 352.
Jones, Eldridge G.: 199, 207.
Julian, R.W.: 22, 45, 48, 57, 65.
Kagin, Art: 9, 135.
Kansas City: 167, 180, 360.
Kaplan, Sol: 113, 146, 177, 323, 336.
Kelly, James: 54, 113, 120, 137-138, 149-150, 169, 173, 176-177, 183, 185, 322, 341.
Kiick, Kim: 264.
King Farouk: 15, 81, 85, 113, 125, 143-145, 149-152, 180, 322-323, 331, 335-338, 349, 351, 358.
Kosoff, Abe: 15, 113, 123, 138, 140, 143-146, 149, 151-152, 154, 161-165, 170, 177-178, 183, 214, 265, 277, 322-323, 336, 341-343, 352.
Kreisberg, Abner: 113, 143, 322.
Lake Placid, New York: 121, 322.
Lancaster, Pennsylvania: 25, 319.
Lane, Lois: 16, 19, 356.
leather case: 54-55, 69, 117, 128, 133-134, 161.
Lee, Edward: 9, 167, 273, 325, 331.
Lee, Lawrence: 9, 234, 238, 249.
Legend Numismatics: 113, 149, 159-160, 179, 225, 227, 230, 235, 247, 272, 315, 325, 351, 356.
Lemke, Bob: 147, 348.
Lewis and Clark: 23.
Lexington, Kentucky: 265.
Liberty Head nickel: 2, 15-17, 19, 21, 27, 30, 34, 39, 41, 53-54, 56, 60, 62-63, 66-67, 69, 71-72, 74-75, 80, 84-85, 88, 91, 98-

100, 103-104, 112, 121-125, 138-139, 145-148, 150, 152-154, 157-158, 160-164, 166-175, 178-180, 183, 185, 189, 192-193, 202, 210, 212, 215-221, 225, 228-229, 231, 234-235, 237, 241, 245, 247, 250, 253-254, 263, 269, 272, 275, 288, 296-297, 304, 307, 313, 315-316, 320-325, 337, 343, 347-350, 352, 355, 357-359, 362.
Lighterman, Mark: 311.
Lincoln: 27, 35.
Lincroft, New Jersey: 159, 225, 235.
Lloyd, Harold: 156.
Longacre, James Barton: 26, 319.
Lord, Jack: 153.
Los Angeles: 62, 152, 154, 157, 242-243, 265, 309, 355.
Lubbock, Texas: 177.
Macallister, James: 56.
MacNickel: 174.
MacVeagh: 34-37, 73, 320.
Manchester, New Hampshire: 242.
Mandeville, Louisiana: 226, 233, 236, 240, 245, 248, 296.
Manley, Dwight: 9, 113, 149, 159-161, 167-168, 228, 235, 273, 275, 277, 281, 315, 324-325, 331, 342.
Marsh, Christian Lloyd: 311.
Marshall, Edwin: 120, 344.
Marshville, North Carolina: 170, 189.
Maryland: 168, 193, 207, 227, 230, 265, 271-272, 275.
Masonic: 55, 63, 100, 103, 357.
Masonic Forum: 55, 63, 103, 357.
McCausland, Christianna: 272, 290, 358.
McCulloch, Hugh: 27.
McDermott, Betts: 176-177.
McDermott, J.V.: 85, 113, 150, 173-174, 178, 187, 227, 322, 324.
McDuck, Scrooge: 16, 272, 275.
McElheny, Victor K.: 192.
McNeil, Robert B.: 203.
Mehl, B. Max: 53, 74, 91, 113, 122-124, 149, 322, 342-343,

350.
Melissaratos, Aris: 275.
Memorial Day: 235, 237, 239-240.
Memphis, Tennessee: 18, 175, 255, 259.
Merrimack, New Hampshire: 168.
Mervis, Clyde D.: 39, 120, 150, 169.
Mid-American Rare Coin Galleries: 265.
Middle Atlantic Numismatic Association: 184, 201, 203, 207, 221, 359.
MANA: 184, 187, 194, 196, 199, 201, 208, 218, 221, 359.
Middlesex, North Carolina: 192, 194, 196.
Miller, Garland: 196.
Minkus & Pearlman Public Relations, Inc.: 159, 227, 268-269, 287-289, 300, 307, 309.
Mint Director: 14, 23-25, 34-37, 41, 48, 50, 82, 87, 320, 323.
Miss Liberty: 174, 176, 234.
Mister X: 14, 156-157.
Mitchell, Sue: 9, 244, 310.
Mohon, Cynthia: 21, 30, 60, 63, 89, 104, 140, 176, 180, 332, 353, 361.
Money Museum: 80, 158, 179, 227, 229, 234-236, 238, 253, 315, 346.
Money Museum (ANA): 227, 315.
Montgomery, Paul: 1-2, 5-7, 13, 226, 232, 234-235, 237, 239-240, 243, 245, 247, 254-255, 259, 262, 266, 268-269, 271, 277, 281-282, 287-289, 293, 296, 298, 301, 303, 305-307, 310-311, 315.
Montgomery, Rick: 310.
Morgan silver dollar: 40.
Morgan, George T.: 40, 58, 344.
Morgenthau, J.C.: 121.
Mudd, Douglas: 9, 229, 231, 273-274, 276-277, 280, 315.
Mulvaney, Tom: 9.
Murdock, Dan: 82.
Myers, Cheryl: 172, 184-185, 187, 189, 192-193, 196, 199-200, 203, 207, 211-212, 216,

220, 253-254, 260, 269, 288-289, 294, 300, 303, 312.
Nagy, Stephen K.: 93, 112, 121, 320, 322, 343.
Nash County, North Carolina: 194-195.
Nasser, Gamel Abdel: 145, 180, 335, 338, 352, 359.
National Archives and Records Administration: 49, 63, 359.
NARA: 49.
National Money Show: 227-228, 311.
National Museum of History and Technology: 148.
Nebraska: 178.
Neill, Will N.: 149, 151.
New Hampshire: 62, 139, 167-168, 179, 204, 226, 233-236, 242, 246, 255, 267, 350-351, 355-356, 360.
New Netherlands: 74.
New Orleans: 226, 240, 298, 311.
New York: 30, 35, 53, 62-63, 67, 81-82, 89, 96-97, 100, 121, 127-129, 138-140, 151, 158, 168, 206-207, 209-211, 214-215, 221, 240, 298, 321-323, 332, 335, 342, 346, 349, 351-352, 355, 358-361.
Newman, Eric P.: 15, 24, 39, 55, 63, 65-67, 69-71, 75-76, 78, 83, 85, 88-89, 95, 97, 101-102, 104, 112-113, 116-120, 126-135, 137-140, 143-144, 149, 156, 161-165, 169, 173, 180, 185, 187, 191, 212-213, 217-222, 284, 322-323, 332, 339, 344-346, 349, 351-353, 359-362.
Newport Beach, California: 235.
nicks: 22, 25.
Ninety Years of Liberty Gala: 271, 274, 290, 355.
NO CENTS (nickel): 29, 320.
North Carolina: 40, 53-54, 169-171, 183-185, 187, 192-196, 221-222, 227, 234, 238, 250, 296, 316, 323, 358, 362.
North Carolina Coin Clubs: 185.
North Tonawanda, New York: 54, 56, 67-68, 91, 96-98, 103, 321-322.

Norweb Family: 113, 143, 147, 228, 323-324, 331, 347.
Norweb, Emery May: 146-147, 323, 347-350.
NPR: 301.
Numismatic Bibliomania Society: 47, 63, 358.
Numismatic Fine Arts: 113, 149, 151, 169, 323.
Numismatic Guaranty Corporation: 309.
NGC: 309-310, 313, 356.
Numismatic News: 83-84, 88, 102, 104, 147, 155, 157, 167, 180, 348, 351-352, 358-359, 362.
Numismatic Scrapbook Magazine: 24, 38-39, 53-54, 63, 71, 78, 89, 97, 104, 120, 135, 139-140, 150, 168-169, 171, 174-178, 180, 184-185, 188, 191-192, 222, 340, 342, 345, 352, 359-360.
Numismatist, The: 55, 59, 63, 70, 73, 91, 93, 97-100, 103-104, 115-116, 121, 125, 127, 140, 152, 155, 256, 320-322, 341, 349, 352-353, 355, 360, 362.
Oklahoma: 175.
Omaha, Nebraska: 177-178.
Orange County Convention Center: 310.
Orlando, Florida: 225, 310, 315.
Palatine, Illinois: 205.
Parable of the Lost Coin: 3, 311.
Parrino, Jay: 113, 161, 166-167, 324-325.
Pasko, Paul Sr.: 205.
Patillo, Howard: 196.
Patterson, Robert M.: 23.
Peace dollar: 84-85.
Pearlman, Donn: 227, 231, 236-237, 255, 259, 261, 263, 278-281, 293, 295-296, 300-302, 304, 306-307, 312.
pedigree: 11, 17, 85, 115, 117, 121, 123, 125, 127, 129, 131, 133, 135, 139, 143, 149, 161, 169, 173, 179, 183, 221, 327-331, 351, 357.
Pennsylvania, University of: 25.
Perry, Cheryl: 244.
Peters, Gloria: 21, 30, 60, 63, 89,

104, 140, 176, 180, 332, 353, 361.
Philadelphia: 14, 24-25, 27-28, 33, 37, 40, 42-43, 45, 48, 52-53, 57, 59, 62, 65, 68, 70, 73, 84-87, 94-98, 115-116, 118, 120-121, 176, 262, 316, 320-321, 343-344, 357.
Philadelphia Mint: 24-25, 27, 33, 37, 40, 45, 48, 52-53, 57, 65, 68, 70, 73, 84, 87, 94, 316, 320-321, 343-344.
Phoenix: 208.
Photograde: 58, 63, 361.
Pine Tree: 170.
Pollock, Andy: 244.
Pollock, James: 25.
Portland, Oregon: 311.
Positive Protection: 261, 280-281, 295.
Powills, Mike A.: 175.
private scrip: 23.
private treaty: 92, 150, 159, 315, 327.
Professional Coin Grading Service: 27, 30, 264, 315, 356.
PCGS: 27, 30, 264, 295, 315, 328, 331, 356.
Professional Numismatists Guild: 5, 16, 226, 265, 277, 306.
PNG: 226, 265, 277-278, 306.
provenance: 17, 327, 329.
Racketeer Nickels: 29.
Raleigh, North Carolina: 194.
Ranta, Hugo: 84-85, 87.
Rare Coin Review: 6, 19, 33, 62, 88, 139, 350, 355.
Raymond, Wayte: 91, 112, 120-121, 140, 322, 349, 352, 360.
Reed, Ira: 56, 101.
Reiter, Ed: 69.
Revised Statutes: 79.
reward: 14, 122, 124, 214, 231-234, 236-237, 239-241, 243, 245-249, 251, 253, 255-256, 259, 261, 296-297, 302-303, 308, 311, 315, 325, 360-361.
Rex Hospital: 194.
Reynolds family: 189, 213.
Reynolds, Noah: 9, 189, 213.
Reynolds, R.J.: 170, 183-184, 213, 323.
Reynolds, William Neal, II: 189.

Richmond, Virginia: 187, 201, 203, 211, 221, 358.
Roanoke, Virginia: 184, 189, 192, 196, 198-199, 202-210, 219, 221, 248-249, 251-255, 303, 355, 357.
Roberts, George E.: 34-35, 65, 87, 321.
Roberts, Pam: 9, 243-245.
Roberts, Vesta W.: 172.
Rochester Numismatic Association: 103.
Rocky Mount, Virginia: 196, 200.
Roosevelt, Franklin: 80, 336.
rouleaux: 24.
Ruark, Steve: 280, 295.
Ruddy, James: 138, 341.
Russell, Margo: 75-76, 78.
Saint-Gaudens, Augustus: 34.
Saint-Gaudens: 34, 80-82, 86-87, 89, 160, 335, 360.
Salem, Virginia: 253.
Samuelson, Dana: 278.
San Francisco Mint: 28, 57, 59, 61, 65, 199, 262.
Savannah, Georgia: 200.
Schell, F.B.: 53, 62, 357.
Scrooge McDuck: 16, 272, 275, 339.
Secret Service: 80-81, 85, 87-88, 101, 211-212, 265, 357.
Secretary of the Treasury: 34, 73, 79-80, 86, 89, 321, 344, 362.
Selley, Paul: 205.
Shaver, Daniel: 9.
Sheldon, Vernon: 101-102, 218, 220-221.
Shepherd, Reverend G.C.: 196.
Sheraton Inner Harbor Hotel: 259.
Sherer, Don: 208.
Shield With Rays nickel: 26-27.
shinplasters: 23, 319.
Shuford, Alex A.: 184.
Sims, Stella Hackel: 14, 47, 49-50, 324.
Smith, Arthur: 215, 249, 305, 324.
Smith, Pete: 169, 176, 213, 345, 349.
Smithsonian Institution: 113, 143, 148, 180, 228, 234-235, 315, 324, 347-351, 353, 358-

359, 361.

Snowden, A. Loudon: 24, 27, 320.

Snyder, John: 9, 230, 272, 275, 278, 280.

Snyder, Willard: 121.

Spectrum Numismatics: 9, 113, 149, 159, 225, 315, 324, 342.

Sperber, Laura: 9, 160, 168, 180, 225-227, 230, 247, 272, 276, 302, 317, 325.

Spring Hope, North Carolina: 194.

St. Louis: 78, 117, 126, 128, 150, 161, 164, 185, 187, 216, 219, 340-341, 344-346.

Stack, Harvey: 214, 305.

Star Rare Coin Encyclopedia and Premium Catalog: 124.

Stern, Alvin: 9, 151.

Stevens, Morton: 154.

Strickland, Mae: 194.

Stuart, John W. Jr: 195.

Suddarth, R.F.: 194.

superintendent: 27, 37, 40-41, 57, 65, 272, 321.

Superior Stamp & Coin: 19, 113, 149, 156-157, 180, 361.

Superman: 16, 19, 356.

Swasey, Ambrose: 40.

Tatum, Josh: 27, 29.

Taxay, Don: 21, 24, 30, 39, 63, 65, 69-76, 89, 96, 104, 118, 140, 353, 360.

Texas: 6, 16, 53, 123-124, 157-158, 175, 177, 214, 246, 324, 339-341, 343.

The Mint in Kansas City: 167.

The Palace Collections of Egypt: 145.

The Plaza Art Galleries, Inc: 206, 222, 361.

The U.S. Mint and Coinage: 21, 30, 63, 361.

Thompson, Howard: 196.

three-cent: 23, 25, 27, 319-320.

Timonium, Maryland: 168, 230-231, 265, 271-272, 275-277, 281, 325.

Tirell-Wysocki, David: 9, 225, 235-236, 246, 267, 302.

Tocci, Mary: 239, 244.

Travers, Carol: 9, 243-244.

Treasury Department: 74, 79,

81-82, 85-86, 92, 212, 344.

Trotter, Powell B.: 175.

Tucker, Warren: 152, 155.

Tucson, Arizona: 174.

U.S. Mint: 14, 21, 26, 30, 42-43, 45, 48-49, 63, 65-66, 68, 82-83, 85-87, 92, 94-95, 119, 212, 285, 320, 324, 350, 361.

U.S. Treasury Department: 81.

union: 22-23, 163, 169, 335.

United States Code: 49, 63, 358.

United States Mint: 47, 49, 53, 58, 62, 65, 78, 83, 86, 118, 321, 357.

Van Ryzin, Robert R.: 102.

Venn, Theodore J.: 242.

Virginia: 30, 55, 63, 89, 104, 140, 180, 184, 189, 192-193, 196, 200, 202-204, 221, 248, 251, 253, 255, 306, 332, 353, 355, 357-358, 361.

Wacks, Mel: 156.

Wagner, August: 55, 103, 112, 115-116, 118-121, 139-140, 322, 351-353, 360.

Walker, Laurens: 187.

Walton County, Georgia: 200.

Walton, Billie Mae: 172, 196, 198, 209.

Walton, Charles: 196, 215, 251, 324.

Walton, Charles B.: 172, 207.

Walton, Frank: 172.

Walton, George O.: 40, 53-54, 113, 169-172, 183-184, 191-194, 198, 200-201, 203, 205-209, 211, 214-217, 219-222, 234, 309-310, 323-324, 358, 361.

Walton, Lucille: 9, 204, 215, 249-251, 253, 303.

Washington, George: 21, 319.

Washington, Martha: 21.

Weekly Reader: 16, 19, 362.

Weinberg, Fred: 9, 41, 61, 69, 74, 264-265, 270-271, 279-282, 287, 303, 306, 312.

Weinman, Greg: 9, 86.

Weinman, Greg M.: 49, 66.

Wellons, Hugh: 189, 192-193, 196, 211-212.

Wharton School of Business: 25.

Wharton, Joseph: 25, 27, 319.

white cents: 22.

Williams, W.R.: 194.

Wilson, Ed: 101.

Winston-Salem, , North Carolina: 113, 169, 171, 185-188, 323.

Wisconsin: 139, 176, 213, 352.

Withuhn, Bill: 273-274.

Wolfeboro, New Hampshire: 62-63, 139, 179, 226, 233-234, 350-351, 355-356, 361.

women: 51-53.

Woodin, William H.: 80, 344.

World of Money: 167, 301.

World Wide Coin Investments: 113, 149, 152, 154, 324.

Wright, Frank: 196.

Wyman, Judith: 9, 245.

Yancey, Dwayne: 248, 251.

Young, Cabell: 198.

Zebulon, North Carolina: 194.

Zerbe, Farran: 101, 127-128, 140, 342, 346, 353, 362.